Back Bay Books / Little, Brown and Company
Hachette Book Group USA
237 Park Avenue, New York, NY 10017
Visit our Web site at www.HachetteBookGroupUSA.com

Originally published in hardcover by Little, Brown and Company, November 2006
First Back Bay paperback edition, October 2007

Library of Congress Cataloging-in-Publication Data
Miller, Chris.
   The real animal house : the awesomely depraved saga of the fraternity that inspired the movie / Chris Miller. — 1st ed.
      p.   cm.
ISBN 978-0-316-05701-1 (hc) / 978-0-316-06717-1 (pb)
   1. Alpha Delta Phi. Dartmouth Chapter — Anecdotes.   2. Animal house (Motion picture)   I. Title.
   LJ85.A465M55 2006
371.8'55 — dc22   2006024928

10 9 8 7 6 5 4 3 2 1

Q-FF

Printed in the United States of America

THE REAL
ANIMAL HOUSE

The Awesomely Depraved Saga of the
Fraternity That Inspired the Movie

CHRIS MILLER

BACK BAY BOOKS
Little, Brown and Company
NEW YORK · BOSTON · LONDON

To family,
wherever you find it

THE *REAL* ANIMAL HOUSE: A *REAL* FOREWORD

CHRIS MILLER GOT TO DARTMOUTH in 1959, joined the Alpha Delta Phi fraternity, and I guess we could say that the rest is apocryphal. By the time Chris and I met in 1975, his "Tales of the Adelphian Lodge" were among the most popular stories published in *National Lampoon,* and Chris was frequently out of New York reading those and other stories of his to college audiences all around the country. How I came to be at the *Lampoon* in those days is a long chapter for the book I'm currently too lazy to write, but this is the relevant part.

In early '75, I was performing in *The National Lampoon Show* in a New York cabaret with John Belushi, Gilda Radner, Bill Murray, Brian Doyle-Murray, and Joe Flaherty. Our producers were Matty Simmons, publisher of the *Lampoon,* and Ivan Reitman, at that time a successful young Canadian producer with great entrepreneurial instincts who had made considerable money producing and distributing exploitation films like *Cannibal Girls* ("They eat men!"). But Ivan was looking beyond another off-Broadway *Lampoon* cabaret show; what Ivan imagined, and what he proposed to Matty Simmons, was the first *Lampoon* feature film.

Our show had opened to mixed reviews and so-so business, but the run extended through the summer of that year, when Lorne

Michaels came talent-scouting for his new NBC venture, *Saturday Night* (the *Live* would be added later). Lorne took John Belushi and Gilda, then the ill-fated Howard Cosell variety show came and took Bill and Brian Murray, along with the brilliant Christopher Guest, a veteran of the *Lampoon's* hit off-Broadway show *Lemmings,* and a standout on *NatLamp's Radio Hour.* I had left the *Lampoon* show a couple of months earlier to direct a PBS series in L.A. for my good friend Michael Shamberg — which is not to say I would have been cast on *SNL* had I been there — but this sets the stage for the genesis of *Animal House,* the movie.

BEFORE THEY ALL WENT their separate ways, Ivan asked Brian, Bill, and John to write a treatment for the first *Lampoon* movie using material from our show and some appropriate articles from the magazine. He offered to pay them $2,500, but astute businessmen that they were, they demanded $2,500 *each!* "Forget it," Ivan must have said. "I can get Ramis to do it alone for $2,500." And so he did. Faced with the assigned material, I looked for a unifying setting and theme, and it was at that point that Anne, my wife at the time, said, "Why don't you write a college movie?" In fact, I had had some extraordinary experiences at Washington University in St. Louis; I joined a fraternity and lived for two years in the Zeta Beta Tau house and then another two years in an off-campus apartment.

What characterized my college years, 1962 to 1967, was the dramatic shift in mood and focus that began with the Kennedy assassination and continued through the onslaught of the free speech movement, the civil rights struggle, and the anti-war movement, all fueled and somewhat intensified by what I call a "national voluntary drug-testing program." In that period, fraternities were becoming increasingly marginalized as students converted their anarchic energy to legitimate political protest and activism, and the free-form social experiments of countercultural lifestyles like communes and collectives. In that new context, the old Greek system made less and less sense, and the film treatment I wrote attempted to describe that shift. I called it "Freshman Year," but when I submitted it to Matty and Ivan, it was clear that nobody liked it enough to move forward. What we all recognized was that it lacked the spirit and hard comic edge of the *Lampoon*, so at that point I suggested working with a *Lampoon* editor, Doug Kenney, *Harvard Lampoon* alum and one of the founding partners of *National Lampoon*.

Doug was a Harvard graduate from Chagrin Falls, Ohio, and the *Lampoon*'s leading comic authority on puberty and adolescence. He had edited and compiled *Lampoon*'s highly successful high school yearbook parody and had authored two classic *Lampoon* pieces, *First Lay Comics* and *First High Comics,* elements of which later found their way into the screenplay for *Animal House.* Given Doug's particular bent (he'd also written a novel called *Teenage Commies from Outer Space*), we set aside the notion of doing a college movie and instead laid out a high school film. Our story concerned Charles Manson in high school, a strangely seductive, demented loner living in the white-bread world of a typical midwestern suburb, corrupting the local youth and forming a depraved cult of flying-saucer-worshipping teenage zombies. We called it *Laser Orgy Girls.* The marketing slogan for the popular *American Graffiti* had been "Where were you in '62?" Ours was "Where was he in '63?" To Matty and Ivan's credit, they actually liked it, but after a moment's reflection suggested we go back to the idea of doing a college movie.

ENTER CHRIS MILLER, the lanky, good-natured Connecticut-looking gentile whose boundless enthusiasm for the golden age of fraternity life instantly put us back on the right track. Doug and Chris were *Lampoon* colleagues, and the three of us bonded quickly. What followed was an initial three-month period of forty-hour weeks on the eleventh floor of the Lampoon building at Fifty-ninth and Madison, bankers' hours spent totally debriefing each other on the American college experience. Working with Chris's treasure trove of published Adelphian Lodge stories, Doug's Harvard experiences, and my own fraternity days at Washington University, we compiled a virtual database of every funny thing that ever happened to any of us; every distinctive character we'd known; all the extraordinary and outlandish things we'd heard about fraternity life from our fathers, uncles, brothers, and cousins; and, finally, every single college myth we could remember hearing. Furthermore we looked back and discussed classic gang comedy, from Our Gang to Archie comics, identifying relevant archetypes for our emerging narrative. But what galvanized all our thinking right from the start was the term *animal house,* not just as a title but as the organizing thematic element from which everything else flowed.

In the pages of Chris's stories you will, of course, find characters and incidents depicted in the film. What didn't make it into the film were some of the really hard-core events, true stories that the producers and executives at Universal found too shocking or disgusting to include in a film intended for general release, even with its R rating. In fact, we were told that when Ned Tannen, the president of Universal, read the script for the first time, he appeared disturbed and said, "I don't get it. These are the heroes?" Reassured by the studio's younger executives, principally Thom Mount and Sean Daniels, the studio proceeded, and the movie went on to become, in 1978, the highest-grossing comedy of all time.

THOSE TOO-DISGUSTING STORIES? They're right here. Because finally the real Pinto is telling all, his unique experiences in one of the truly legendary animal houses, expressed in his own distinctive voice. "Sickness is health, blackness is truth, drinking is strength," the perverse and subversive motto of both the Deltas and the ADs, colors these pages as Chris lovingly, ironically, and sometimes ruefully recalls a time when Eisenhower was in the White House, Ozzie and Harriet were on TV, and Holden Caulfield was in all our heads. Go nuts.

Harold Ramis
June 16, 2006

HEY, MAN! WHAT IT is? I've been languishing in the fleshpots of Tasmania for many years, but now I'm back to let *you* know I can really shake 'em down!

If you're wondering what "A Mostly Lucid Memoir" means, so am I. No, seriously. Readers, I've made every effort to portray my sophomore year accurately, but since I was totally hammered most of the time, you can't hold me to any of this, okay? In return, assuming we meet someday, I won't hold you to anything, either. As Otter states in *Animal House,* "The whole point is to have a good time."

Okay. Next, I did something a little unusual with the writing.

In a memoir, the voice is customarily in the first person. And so it is here — until I join the fraternity and become Pinto. Thenceforth, it was necessary to write in the third person. I had become part of a group of guys so interconnected that their experiences were my experiences and vice versa. To tell my story — Pinto's story — I have to tell the other guys' stories simultaneously. We shared lives.

One other thing: Please preserve the anonymity of my dear friends by not asking which stories are real. Pretty much all of them are, but don't ask. This way my brothers, should anyone go to the trouble of tracking them down, will be left with plausbile deniability. Can you imagine, say, Nosehole, who today is mayor of Philadelphia, being specifically identified as the AD who thrust his head up the Skidmore dorm mother's skirt? No way!

Now go turn on Hank Ballard and the Midnighters and let everyone say *ow!*

Chris Miller
June 2006

THE REAL
ANIMAL HOUSE

CHAPTER ONE

Ye Nob Hill Inn

"THE MOST IMPORTANT THING when you go to college," Ace Kendall declared, "the single most important thing"— he paused for effect —"is never, ever to join a fraternity."

I shifted in my seat. Ace's assertions were making me uncomfortable. They tended to do that. "Yeah, well, easy for you to say. They don't *have* fraternities where you go. At Dartmouth, that's all there is."

"Hey, man, go hiking. Write a poem. Plant a tree. There're all kinds of things to do without wasting your time drunk in some smelly frat-house basement." When Ace smiled, he looked like a devil, only a blond one.

"Ace, what are you talking about? You're drunk *now.* You *like* being drunk."

"True, but this isn't a fraternity. This is Ye Nob Hill Inn."

Indeed it was. The jukebox, with its great forties jazz sides, was blasting away. Jan the bartendress was shaking up drinks. The electric Ballantine beer sign was making its bouncy arcs of color on the wall. Having all recently turned eighteen, my three best high school friends and I were ensconced in a booth, drinking beer and smoking cigarettes.

"And," Ace went on, "I'm with friends I *chose*. Guys I came to know naturally, over four years at Roslyn High. Unlike in a fraternity, where you have to like whoever they pledge, whether you really do or not."

"Ace, what is this animus toward fraternities?" said Josh. "Can't you ever live and let live?" Josh, up at Rochester, was already in a house, one of the Jewish ones. He was a weight lifter who made fun of weight lifting. Still, he enjoyed it when his highly developed pecs, abs, biceps, triceps, lats, and what-have-you drew attention on the street.

"Oh, he's just trying to be boho." Froggie, in his Ivy League clothes and Ivy League haircut, looked like a model in a J. Press catalog. He was quoting what some dopey girl at a party one night had said when Ace attempted to recite Beat poetry. He hadn't gotten far.

Now, as then, Ace chose to ignore the comment. "I'll tell you. But first . . ." He signaled to Jan, who came right over. She was large and hearty. She and her husband, Eddie, ran the joint. Eddie looked like Jack Teagarden. Jan was Rocky Graziano with breasts.

"Hey, check it out." She nodded at the elevated TV, where Douglas Edwards was delivering the late news. "Man's got a bad-breath face."

I considered it. Yes, by God, Douglas Edwards *did* have a bad-breath face. It was something about his lips. Jan was often perceptive this way.

Ace ordered another round and Jan went off to get it. "Okay, fraternities. You have to be a conformist, man."

"You're right," said Josh. "Every last guy in my house is a Yid."

"You know what I mean." Ace touched his soul patch reflexively with an index finger. "Plus, they discriminate. They're breeding grounds for prejudice and elitism. Bet you don't have any Negroes. Bet you don't have any guys with beards."

"We took a quadruple amputee last month, though," Josh said. "And there's this ax murderer we have our eye on."

"At Amherst," Froggie put in self-righteously, "there's at least one dwarf in every house."

"I stand by my point," said Ace. "If you're black, or weird, or, you know, a homo or something, you don't get into a house."

"A *homo?*" the rest of us cried.

"Sure," Ace said. "They can't help being homos. Black guys can't help being black guys. Why shouldn't they get in fraternities too?"

I myself would soon have to decide about joining one. It was not an easy choice, and Ace's assertions were making it harder. But — "Ace, Dartmouth is this little island in the middle of nowhere. I don't need to plant trees — there's millions of them. Plus, the closest girls' school is an hour away. Half the time we're buried under blizzards. How am I supposed to live as an independent up there? If I joined a house, I might have some fun. You know, friends? Parties? Rock 'n' roll?"

"But those things are the bait, man. It's how they lure you in . . . and then, *whomp,* the jaws close and you're lost! First thing you know you're a corporate robot in a gray flannel suit who does what he's told, has two and a half kids, and lives in the suburbs. In a house made out of ticky-tacky!"

I shook my head. "That's bullshit. I'm never going to do that. I just — Ace, listen. My freshman year was horrible. They put me in a dorm room with these two guys — one never talked about anything but sports and the other didn't talk at all. They didn't know anything about what's cool. I'd mention the Five Satins, and Brad thought I was talking about a basketball team and Isaac just looked at me. I want to have some *fun* up there, you know?"

Jan arrived with the beer and Ace took a drink. "Look, you're not going to find many Five Satins fans at Dartmouth anyway. It's totally Republican up there. They probably listen to Dixieland or Glenn Miller or something. Now at Grinnell we have these hoots —"

"'Hoots'?" said Josh.

"Owl music," said Froggie. "It's very now."

"Hootenannies, you shitheads. Folk music! And we visit Negro churches and get to know the, uh, Negroes who, you know, sing spirituals and stuff there. I met great Negroes last semester."

I sighed. Meeting great Negroes was fine by me, especially if the Negro in question happened to be Bo Diddley or one of my other musical heroes, almost all of whom were black. For rock 'n' roll was the very defining influence of my being. *Nothing* was more important than this musical gift from the gods that had arrived in New York, along with redoubtable disc jockey Alan Freed, back in late '54. But I wasn't sure there *were* any Negroes in New Hampshire, much less ones with electric guitars. The life Ace was talking about would be fine if you were going to school in Alabama or Los Angeles or even here on Long Island, but at Dartmouth? It was different up there.

And now, somehow, summer vacation was all but over. I'd finished my swell job with the Roslyn school system — cleaning desks and toilets with the school janitors — a week ago. The day after tomorrow I'd be returning for my sophomore year, which began with this horrible thing called rush, the process that sorted the majority of Dartmouth guys into one or another of the school's twenty-four fraternities and left the rest high and dry, condemned to three years of unaffiliated assholehood. This latter category would include guys with grave zit problems; or breath that was like poison gas; or glasses so thick they magnified their eyes, making them resemble Mr. Toad; and, well, yeah, Negroes, although there were only three of them allowed per class, which meant a grand total of twelve in the whole school at any given time, and some of those were African. And homos? At Dartmouth? As far as I knew, I'd never actually met a homo. They were really rare, as I understood it, maybe only one guy in a thousand. So of which group would I be a part — the conformist, square, yet fun-loving fraternity guys? Or the wretched social outcasts? It wasn't much of a choice.

"You know," Ace said to me, "Kerouac and Ginsberg and Cassady never joined fraternities. Look at the fun *they* had."

It was true — being on the road and smoking gage and digging starry dynamos sounded extremely cool. But there again, gage at Dartmouth was probably rarer than homos. What would work for Ace at Grinnell seemed impossible at the Big Green.

"Maybe so," said Josh to Ace. "Maybe I should be like you and sing folk music and integrate Negroes. But you know what? *I* got laid last spring. Did you?"

Ace flapped his mouth once or twice. "Well, uh, I got a hand job from this chick behind the kiln . . ."

"I rest my case." Josh returned to his beer, his biceps flexing prodigiously as he brought it to his mouth.

And there, it seemed to me, was the crux of the matter. Even if it took becoming a corporate robot, getting laid was number one. I gazed at girls as a man obsessed. If fraternities were the road to that, I'd join in a minute. The key thing to be striven for in life, I felt, almost as important as listening to rock 'n' roll, was continuous sexual activity with every beautiful woman I could find.

"Ace, I don't know. Folk music doesn't exist at Dartmouth. If you read poetry, they think you're weird. What if I did join a house?"

"You might be sorry," Ace said quietly.

"Or he might have a ball," said Froggie.

"And get laid and blown," put in Josh.

On the TV was that senator, Kennedy, who was running for president. They watched awhile. Actually a pretty cool-looking guy, I thought. Sharp dresser. The fraternity subject slipped away now and we united in laughter and the verbal play, punctuated by expressions of sexual yearning, that had gotten us through high school. Eventually, Jan threw us out so she could close. With many slurred assertions of undying friendship in the parking lot, we bade each other farewell until Thanksgiving and drove in our separate directions. I made it home without mishap, hit the sack, and dreamed I was a corporate robot, marching with thousands of other corporate robots off a cliff and into a sea of beer.

CHAPTER TWO

The Last Dinner

CLANG CLANG CLANG!

With a groan, I woke up.

Good morning, said my hangover cheerily. *Aaaargghhhhh!*

I tried to hide from it under the covers. This tactic didn't work. *Aw, man, do we have to do this? It's my last day of vacation!*

Your fault, schmuck, my hangover pointed out.

I got myself vertical and put my feet on the floor. My head-throbbing became worse. I got real daring and opened my eyes. There were my jeans, the underpants nestling in them like an egg in a rumpled nest, my shoes and socks directly beneath both. Quick undress last night, it seemed.

Clang clang clang!

That was my mother, signaling me from downstairs. There was a heat pipe my room shared with the kitchen, and she would bang it with the back of a knife when she wanted me. Glancing at the clock, I found it to be noon. *Shit.*

Pulling on my clothes rapidly, I found the aspirin in the bathroom cabinet and availed myself of several. Splashing water in my eyes, I dried off and looked in the mirror. Regular features, normal face. Stupid crew cut! In high school, I had had a DA — long all over and combed back on the sides to make a vertical ridge down the back.

DA — duck's ass. I'd actually managed to look cool for a while. Now, because my father insisted, I had this dorky flattop. It was what you had to wear at an esteemed institution like Dartmouth, according to my all-knowing dad. The guy in the mirror no longer resembled Mr. Rock 'n' Roll, as I liked to think of myself. I looked like Mr. Dick Face.

In the kitchen, my mother greeted me with an expression of concern. "Do you know what time it is? My God, how are you going to get everything done?"

"Mom, I just have to pack a few things. Don't get nervous, okay?"

She halved an orange, put one of the domes in the squeezer, and splashed juice into a little glass. I sat at the kitchen table, accepted my OJ, and downed it.

"I could fry some eggs. Or how about oatmeal? Or —"

"How about a Swiss cheese sandwich?"

"But you haven't had your breakfast yet!"

"Mom, it's lunchtime."

"Well, okay."

Reluctantly, she made me the sandwich. As usual, I had to add mayonnaise.

"How can you use so much of it?"

"I *like* mayonnaise."

She shook her head sorrowfully. "You're going to make yourself sick."

"Never have." I crammed the last of the sandwich into my mouth. "Mm, be'r go pack, 'kay?"

Off I went, up the stairs with my half-assed suitcase — a hand-me-down that might have been used by hobos in the thirties — and tossed it on my bed. It smelled of mildew from the cellar. Unused to packing, I paused. What would I need?

I ransacked the drawers of my dresser. Underwear, socks, jeans, chinos, T-shirts. Hanging in the closet was a faded blue denim work shirt I'd bought for going with Ace Kendall to the Village Gate to hear Nina Simone and, on another occasion, to dig the folksingers in Washington Square. While I could have told you the singers and label of any rock 'n' roll group you cared to name, I knew shit about folk music. Well, there were those guys, the Kingston Trio. Up at school, I'd made out with a girl to their song "Scotch and Soda." I decided to bring it. Who knew, I might make a road trip to Bennington this year, and they loved their blue denim work shirts at Bennington.

Like an astronaut realizing he's forgotten to turn on his oxygen, I became aware there was no music playing! Slapping some 45s on my little fat-spindled record player, I felt relief wash over me as Little Richard came on. Did I ever love Little Richard! Here is what that esteemed musical madman had done during a show at the Brooklyn Paramount in 1957:

They'd saved him for last, of course. He came out and started singing, and within a minute and a half sweat was rolling down his face and streaming from his chin as if there were an endlessly full invisible bucket tilted over his head. He sang all his great songs — "Tutti Frutti," "Long Tall Sally," "Keep a Knockin'"— and finally climbed *on top of his piano* and screamed, "Yeaaaaahhhh!"

"*Yeaaaahhhhh!*" we screamed back.

"*Yeaaaahhhhh!!*" Little Richard cried.

"*Yeaaaahhhhh!!*" we cried.

"*Yeaaaahhhhh!!!*"

"*Yeaaaahhhhh!!!*"

"Yuh — !" Little Richard's voice choked off and a terrible look came over his face. He clutched his heart . . . *and fell off the piano, into the orchestra pit!*

The audience converted at once from hedonistic frenzy to state of shock, looking at one another in horror. Sam "the Man" Taylor, who led the band, got an incredibly worried look on his face and began swinging his arms, triggering Alan Freed's closing theme, "Right Now, Right Now." And then — Little Richard catapulted out of the orchestra pit, landed on the stage, and screamed, "*YEAAAAAHHHHHHH!!!!*"

The audience, a thousand strong, experienced simultaneous rock 'n' roll orgasms and fell back, spent. Little Richard finished his song and the show ended, but what he had done resonated for me forever. It was the greatest act of showmanship I'd ever seen. Yes, I definitely wanted my Little Richard records.

Last year, as a "pea green freshman," I'd actually been afraid to bring my music with me. Guys at Dartmouth, I'd decided, would look askance at my greasy teenage rock 'n' roll, probably preferring Mozart or something. Well, that hadn't proved to be the case; what they *did* listen to was lots of jazz: Ahmad Jamal, Miles, like that. Good stuff — my musical knowledge continued to expand. And Johnny Mathis, but only for make-out purposes. And, yes, even a little rock 'n' roll, though leaning toward the squarer, more Caucasian variety.

So, this year, I'd bring my records. Probably need two of those 45 carriers — that would supply me with a hundred singles. And wouldn't Brad go batshit! Brad, my unsophisticated midwestern roommate, enjoyed Bobby Rydell and Freddy "Boom Boom" Cannon but turned pale when the Flamingos hit one of their high, shimmering harmonies. *Ignorant white man.* I began carefully choosing records to piss him off, lots of harmony groups with falsetto obbligatos and love lyrics, the sort of songs my pal Billy called New York creamers. For instance, the Harptones and the Heartbeats, and songs like "Florence" by the Paragons and "The Wind" by the Jesters. And some of those crazed rockabilly cats, I'd want them, too — Carl Perkins, Jerry Lee Lewis, Billy Riley, and Gene Vincent. And Elvis, but only his stuff on the Sun label. The man had gone horribly downhill since he'd moved to RCA Victor, recording icky ballads for pubescent girls. Since his army tour, he'd basically done shit, or so my rock 'n' roll friends and I felt. It was one of my earliest experiences of decay.

What else? A little science fiction? I inspected my brick-and-board bookcase. There were my main men: Robert Sheckley, Philip K. Dick, Cordwainer Smith, Theodore Sturgeon, and Jack Vance. And, ahem, my complete run of *Galaxy* magazine, from issue number one, in October 1950, to the present. The best of all SF magazines. I loved science fiction; it gave me comfort during teenage alienation attacks. The ability the writers displayed in imagining other realities seemed the mental equivalent of bench-pressing four hundred pounds. They should be national heroes but were ignored. Who could explain? Still, bring my books to school? Where would I put them? And the suitcase was getting full. Maybe a *couple* of them would fit, I decided, and tossed in a Frederik Pohl novel and a William Tenn short-story collection. Okay, what else?

My eyes fell on my safe. It was an old iron safe I'd found abandoned somewhere, and Froggie had helped me lug it up to my room when no one was looking. It was about the size of an orange crate and had two wooden drawers lined with green felt. Though it lacked a lock, which probably disqualified it as a true safe, it was where I kept my special stuff: Superman and Captain Marvel comics from the forties; a switchblade knife I'd gotten from a hood — Vinnie Abbondandelo — whom I'd tutored in social studies; Korean War soldiers made of painted lead, with bazookas and howitzers; and other detritus from the initial eighteen years of my life. But what I was thinking about, specifically, was a certain shoe box I kept in there. . . .

Pulling it out, I looked inside. There they were, my girls. I hated leaving them here. My picture collection had been culled from many magazines: *Titter, Beauty Parade,* and *Sizzle,* with their sluts in bras, stockings, and garter belts; *Rogue, Topper,* and *Cavalier,* featuring girls who were slightly less skanky; and the most recent addition to the field, *Playboy,* which actually showed nipples. These were kept on the highest shelf at Mr. Kanufsky's candy store, behind a barricade of wood, so that only the titles could be seen. When I worked up the guts to purchase one, I'd get it home, take it to my room, tear out the three or four pages with the best pictures, and drop 'em in the shoe box. The girl on top was a good example: a pretty brunette wearing only a man's shirt. She stood there, smiling invitingly, her legs wide apart, the shirt covering all her illegal parts. But in my *imagination* I could see everything. Well, maybe not see, exactly. More like *feel.* I could imagine running my hand right up to where *it* was located. It would be soft, fuzzy, and slightly moist. I knew this from instinct, not experience. Touching *it* was still in my future. God, was I looking forward to that!

There was a special way I thought about my paper ladies. Each, I felt, was an individual whom I almost knew, and when I took matters into my own hands, it was like having a date with them. Dating two-dimensional women had advantages, too — they never said no and I always respected them in the morning. In a way, I was actually in love with all of them. I began leafing through them now, my eyes caressing remembered breasts and buns, and —

— looked down to discover a hard-on attempting to push its way out of my pants and fuck my own navel. Ah, what a mighty, throbbing boner it was! But this was no time for beating off. The afternoon had fled and someone might knock on my door at any moment to announce the imminence of dinner. I gave it a slug with my fist, attempting to discourage it. This did not work. Well, I'd just have to outwait it. As for the pictures, it would not be wise to bring them to school. It was hard enough finding a time and place to beat off there without dragging a box of pictures along. Usually, you had to lock the bathroom door and work fast. Nor was the bedroom secure, with roommates wandering in and out. And if Brad or Isaac ever caught me, I'd never live it down. So I put the pictures back in my safe and sealed it with masking tape, hoping my family would take the hint and respect my privacy. Yeah, sure.

It seemed time to call Suzette. Suzette was my sort-of girlfriend. She didn't believe in going steady and had never been willing to hang my ring on a chain around her neck, as was the custom at Roslyn High. She did, however, make out with me a lot. Which in her case meant great amounts of hugging and kissing — and little else. Well, that was the way it went, I told myself. My day would come. At least she wasn't an idiot, like most Roslyn girls.

"Hello?"

"Hi. It's me."

"Well, hi, you."

"Are we on for eight?"

"Mm-hm. And Daddy said we can use the living room tonight."

What great news! The living room was where our chief action would occur, but usually Mr. Kornfeld occupied it, watching TV. He was not a passive viewer, either; he would tune in Bishop Sheen and shout cheerfully rude remarks as the insipidly smiling cleric delivered his uplifting homilies. I had joined him in this sport once or twice, and we'd vied in hurling insults at the screen. It had been fun. But this wouldn't do tonight. I was off to New Hampshire and Suzette to Chicago, as in "University of." Shit, I might not get to make out with anyone until we were both back for Thanksgiving!

"Cool. So what are you doing?"

"Reading *Finnegan's Wake*."

"Sounds cheerful."

"It's *wonderful*."

"What's the plot?"

"It doesn't really have a plot."

"Okay. Is it serious or funny?"

"It's, I don't know, it's everything."

"Anyone get laid?"

"Don't be silly. You think I'm reading *Battle Cry*? This is James Joyce!"

I'd heard the name but was vague on the man's oeuvre. Perhaps I should return to the agenda.

"Well, I'm sure looking forward to seeing you. I'm really going to miss you, Suzette."

"I know. I can't wait to feel your arms around me."

She couldn't? Whoa. It was unusual for her to speak this way. Was What's-his-name's *Wake* getting her hot? Maybe tonight would be a scene from *my* book, the aforementioned *Battle Cry*. After all, here I was, driving off to this faraway island of academia, so maybe she'd consent to go "all the way" with me, as Kathy had with Danny before he left for Guadalcanal. My hard-on returned at the thought, and though I boinked it with a copy of *The Rise and Fall of the Third Reich*, it wouldn't go away.

"Hey! Get down here! It's dinnertime!"

My father's bellow, however, worked a mighty anti-erectile mojo that caused it to vanish like a Popsicle in a blast furnace. "Uh, see you later, Suzette." I hung up and got down there.

Mom had dolled up the table for my good-bye dinner: lace tablecloth, the good plates, lots of silver. The table itself was mahogany and old. The crystal vase was filled with violets — Mom was quite the gardener, surrounding the house each year with beautiful chrysanthemums, zinnias, and rhododendrons. Being eighteen, I didn't give a shit, but a neutral observer would have thought things rather pretty out there. On the sideboard stood silver serving bowls, napkin rings, and a pair of antique Tiffany tea sets from different eras. There had once been money in my family but my maternal grandfather was a drunk and pissed it away. What was left were these handed-down pieces of furniture and jewelry. Which was great for my parents, who dug decorous dining. Everything had to be just so.

"Where's your goddamned brother?" my father asked, draining his martini on the rocks.

"I don't know. He wasn't upstairs."

Dad went to the back door. Wilson had a laboratory in the garage, having combined three different Gilbert chemistry sets on a workbench there. "Wilson!" he bellowed.

"Coming, Mother!" It was a catchphrase from the radio show *Henry Aldrich.*

They came to the dining room and sat down. My brother, Wilson, was somehow allowed to have more hair than I was — a big, blond drop of it across his forehead — which I found grossly unjust. I'd tried various ways to inch my hair longer without my father noticing, but JC Senior, as Wilson and I called him, had been vigilant as a hawk. I was going to Dartmouth; I had to look *clean cut.*

Wilson took a seat and accepted a plate from Mom. It was heaped with carrots, peas, and potatoes. He regarded them as if they were cat vomit.

JC Senior had begun to carve. Roast beef was an event meat, saved for Thanksgiving and other occasions. My father considered carving to be a manly art. The ritual began with the stroking of knife against sharpening steel, which made a cool *shwoop-shwoop* sound. Then he would plunge the special two-tined carving fork into the meat, which would squish down and emit juices and produce a steady stream of pink-red beef slices. They would stack up on the carving board like the meat at the delicatessen, except Dad was doing this by hand, not with some machine. He was an artist with the knife.

At length, everyone's plate was full and we fell to ingestion.

"Did you wash your hands?" Mom asked Wilson.

"Sure." He immediately put them below the table.

"You did not," said Dad. "Get in there and wash your fucking hands."

"John!" cried Mom.

Wilson reluctantly left the table. I, who hadn't washed my own hands, hummed a little tune and took a bite of beef.

"Christ," muttered Dad. He poured himself another glass of Gallo Hearty Burgundy. Making an indefinite gesture with his hand, he turned to me. "Are you ready for school?"

"Yeah, I guess."

"Car gassed up? Bags packed?"

"Oh, yeah."

"Now you'll be rushing soon, right?"

Wilson wandered back in. "Rush, rush, rush. Doesn't anyone relax anymore?"

The remark was not dignified with an answer.

"Yeah, I guess." I still felt indecisive about joining a house. As for rushing, it scared the shit out of me. "How do you handle it, Dad? All those people judging you."

"Just let 'em see you're a real Dartmouth man." He drained his glass and poured another. "You'll do fine."

"Hey, how 'bout giving me some of that?" Wilson suggested.

"Ha-ha," said Dad.

"Just drink your milk," said Mom.

"I hate milk. It tastes like calcium."

I regarded him curiously. "What does calcium taste like?"

"I don't know. I just made it up. I know what salt tastes like."

"Everyone knows what salt tastes like."

"Yeah, but I know it better."

"Eat your vegetables," Mom directed him.

"I hate —"

"Never mind," roared Dad. *"Eat them!"*

Making elaborate expressions of disgust, Wilson placed extremely small spoonfuls of the pea/carrot mixture in his mouth.

Dad turned back to me. "As I said, you'll do fine. Now that we got you that haircut. . . ."

"Yeah, thanks a lot."

"I don't know why you want all that long hair anyway. You look like a fag."

"John!"

"A lot of guys have longer hair these days." This meant hair that came a little over the collar and could be combed back on the sides. "What, I should be like Froggie, wear that nice little part and Ivy League pants with a belt in the back?"

"Yeah!" said Wilson.

"You're going to an Ivy League school," Mom pointed out.

"That doesn't mean I have to wear pants with a belt in the back. What's the point of having a belt in the back?"

"Never mind the goddamned belt in the back! Just look clean cut." Those words again. "Is your sport coat pressed?"

Who knew? It was buried amongst the stuff I'd thrown in the trunk of my proud and mighty motorcar. JC Senior had come through with a green '54 Ford, now that I was a sophomore and could have wheels at school. It took seven or eight hours to drive from Roslyn to Hanover, New Hampshire.

"Sure."

"Okay. So just make a good impression."

"Hey, you hear that song by the Impressions?" Wilson held his spoon before his mouth and sang, "'Your precious love-uv-uv, means more to me —'"

"Goddamn it, don't sing that nigger music at the dinner table!"

I leaned over and spoke sotto voce to Wilson. "I heard it. It's great!"

We slapped palms like black jazz musicians pleased to see each other.

"More peas?" asked Mom.

"I'll have some, France," said Dad, holding out his plate. To me he said, "I hope you met some SAEs last year."

SAE, or Sigma Alpha Epsilon, had been my father's house at Dartmouth, back in the twenties. He'd played sax in the Barbary Coast, the college jazz band, and drunk bathtub gin. Some guy had gone blind from it once, but JC Senior had avoided that affliction.

"Oh, sure, lots of SAEs." Yeah, like none. I vaguely knew where their house was, but hadn't, in fact, met *any* fraternity guys, except for the Pi Lams in the next room — Pi Lambda Phi was another Jewish house — and Al Heller, down the hall, who was an Alpha Delta Phi.

"Good. Well, you don't *have* to pledge SAE, but it sure was good when I was there." He downed his wine. "We had a party one night. This girl took her panties off, climbed on the dining table, and —"

"*John!*"

"Aw, well, Christ."

"Hey, I want to hear this!" cried Wilson.

I did, too, but Mom's embarrassment would be too much to deal with. Ever the diplomat, I changed the subject.

"So, Mom, great dinner."

"Thank you, dear."

"I wanted to hear that," grumbled Wilson. He used his spoon to catapult a pea at my forehead.

"Hey!" I said.

"Goddamn it, you stop that! Eat your dinner! Why don't you listen and learn? In two more years, *you'll* be going to college."

"Not me! I'm going to live in the Village with Negroes and drug addicts! I'm going to sing in a band." Leaping from his seat, Wilson went to his knees on the floor, reciting into his spoon: "'You know, it so hard to love someone! Yes, it so hard to love someone that don' love you! And it carry a heavy burden on yo' heart to know that the someone they love is yo' verra bes' friend!'"

"Christ on a crutch! Stop that! Get back in your chair!"

Wilson was doing the recitation from the Bobby Marchan song "There's Something on Your Mind." For a pain in the ass, he sure was cool.

He continued: "'I tell you, when someone is rockin' yo' cradle better than you can rock yo' cradle yo'seff, there's —'"

Dad, with a horrified expression, stole a look at Mom to see if she got the implications of *rockin'*, and turned on Wilson in fury. "You shut up this minute! For Christ's fucking sake!"

"John!"

I couldn't hold back anymore — I burst out laughing. Unfortunately, I was in the middle of a sip, and Pepsi flew from my mouth to decorate the tablecloth with an aerosol of amber.

"Jesus!" roared Dad. "Can't you two eat dinner decently? I'm never doing this again! Goddamn it, France, I'm eating alone from now on!"

The two-tiered dinner system had been a fact of life around here for some time: the kids at six, JC Senior and France at seven thirty. Except on special occasions, like tonight, when an exception was made.

"Now, John, you know you don't mean that. Wilson, sit back down. And you"— she turned to me —"wipe your mouth." She thrust a napkin at me.

I crammed the napkin against my mouth, trying to restrain further laughter. Looking around, I saw Mom glaring at Dad, Dad glaring at Wilson, and Wilson taking sips of milk then smiling prissily and making little head shakes, like Percy Dovetonsils.

"Hey, look, this is my last night here," I ventured. "Couldn't we, I don't know, cool out?"

It was as if they all took a deep breath and counted to ten. As if the movie projector went briefly on hold, then started again.

"Will you be in the same dormitory?" Mom asked.

"Yeah, same *room* in the same dormitory."

"With Brad and Isaac?"

I sighed. "Yeah."

"I thought you liked them."

"They're okay. I just don't have much fun with them."

"In a fraternity," said Dad. "That's where you'll find your *real* friends."

"Okay, Dad."

"Or the stamp club," Wilson piped up. "Great guys there."

"Yeah," I agreed. "They really *stick together.*"

"Har-de-har-har," said Wilson.

I glanced at my watch. "You know, I ought to get going. I'm seeing Suzette tonight."

"Oh ho!" It was Dad's French laugh, indicating a certain raciness. "Weel you take her to ze *salle à coucher?*" he asked, leaning his chair back on two legs, waving his wineglass as if at some gay celebration of the liberation of Paris. "*Et coucher* ze leeving sheet out of her?"

"John!"

"Aw, for chrissakes, Dad! What the hell's the matter with you?"

"Ho ho ho!" He rolled his eyes, waggled his eyebrows roguishly — and hit the floor with a crash as his chair went over backward.

"*John!*" Mom rushed around the table to kneel by him.

"*By the Holy unfucked Mother of Christ!*" Clambering to his feet, he threw his wineglass against the wall.

"Stop that!" Mom was not very effective at getting anyone to do anything.

"*You think that's fucking funny? Is that what you think?*" He grabbed the offending chair and slammed it repeatedly into the wall. Wood slivers flew like shrapnel.

"I'm out of here." I stood up so fast, *my* chair went over backward. Departing the dining room, I traversed the hall and grabbed the front-door doorknob.

"*Goddamn fucking son of a bitch!*" More glass smashed.

"John, you stop this right now!"

I burst through the door, my father's voice like a powerful hydraulic device ramming me out of the house, out of my family, and out of Roslyn. I rushed down the front steps and headed down the walk.

There was a tugging on the back of my shirt. "Hey!"

I stopped and turned around. Wilson stood there. "What?"

"Couldn't I go with you?"

"To *Suzette's?*"

"Well, no, I guess not. I just don't want to stay here."

I met his imploring gaze. He looked at the ground. "I hate it when you leave me here. And tomorrow you're going away for a long time."

"Just two and a half months."

"Are you kidding? That's like two and a half years!"

"Aw, Wilson . . ."

"He's getting worse, man. You saw it. I don't know what to do."

"It's not really *that* bad, is it?" In an effort not to let this upset me, I was in severe denial.

"You don't know. You can get away. I'm stuck here. It isn't fair."

I put an arm around his shoulders. "Look, I'll stay in touch. Okay? And we'll write. If it gets too crazy, I'll come down. But, um, Suzette's expecting me so I really ought to —"

"You don't care. You're gonna go up to your fucking college and you won't even think about me."

"No, really —"

"Go see your girlfriend. What do I care?" He started off down the street.

"Where're you going?"

"Maybe I can stay at Gary Smith's."

"Gary Smith's?" The Smiths, in the ramshackle house on the corner, made the characters in Li'l Abner seem urbane sophisticates.

"Yeah. When you're gone, I stay there sometimes. Well, so long. Have a good trip. I'll be okay." Wilson nodded and continued on his way.

For the thousandth time, I wished I could do something to help. But what would such a thing be? Take him up to Dartmouth? Wilson had correctly identified my favorite thing about college, though — it got me away from here. I couldn't *stand* it at home anymore. Living there was like being in jail.

CHAPTER THREE

How's Your Love Life?

SUZETTE'S HOUSE WAS ONLY a few blocks away so I didn't bother with the car. I could use the walk, in any case. What was it with my parents? Domestic life at Froggie's, in idyllic Roslyn Estates, was never like this; graciousness and decorum ruled the day there. Or at Ace's, where his brother played Bach on the piano and his mom recently claimed to be reading T. S. Eliot backward. At Josh's, things were always *haimish* — homey, friendly, and warm — and his mom, Bananabelle, would smile and tell me she was my "Jewish mother by proxy." What did this say about my parents? It was hard to dope out. Because, really, what did anything say about anything?

It was a particularly beautiful night, stars blazing down, fireflies flashing their unbreakable codes to one another. As I headed down Warner Avenue, the suburban dream of the fifties unspooled on either side: the handsome homes, the glimmering birdbaths, the scent of freshly mown lawns. A light breeze stirred my hair. Focusing on none of this, I turned my thoughts, as ever, to girls — specifically, the ones who'd turned me on most in high school. Who were they? The Jewish princesses! Imperious Eunice Levine was, by general agreement, number one on the Hebrew hit parade, followed closely by Sheila Raskin, Sandy Scherzer, and Claudia

Zitzmann. They had fuller lips and bigger breasts than the gentile girls, important qualifications to my way of thinking. Indeed, most of the shiksas looked bland and malnourished beside them.

I had a favorite. Shelly Rappaport sat behind me in American history. How many times had I dropped my pencil in order to bend and, while sloooowly retrieving it, covertly swoosh my gaze up her skirt? Her thighs had a heavenly meaty quality, and above them were these slightly bulging panties. What was that? Bush? How I speculated about what was in there! I didn't know exactly what pussy looked like; it was the ultimate no-show in the magazines. Was it a hairy doughnut? An armpit with a ragged hole in the middle? Fidel Castro's mouth? I'd learned about the labia majora and minora in biology; they were right beneath the ol' mons veneris, the mount of Venus my friends and I had made so many lame jokes about climbing and planting our flags on, but I had no more than a vague idea what any of this looked like. Maybe tonight. Sure.

As I passed Dr. Kasamir's house, the man's Weimaraner, known locally as Cerberus, rushed from the shadows, barking its ass off. I came to a quivering halt. The damned animal had once, a couple of years ago, reared up and bitten me on the butt, and I now knew to repress the urge to run and instead move very slowly, pretending I could care less. Word had it dogs could smell fear. I walked on carefully, trying not to feel afraid, but it was like swimming, trying not to be wet. The animal rushed me, defending its territory with such mega-aggression that I might have been a Russian agent about to release plague germs into the Kasamir front yard. I wished for a pump shotgun to blow the four-legged fuck into hamburger. Dogs were such assholes.

I kept walking, whistling what I hoped would pass as a carefree tune — it was actually "Summertime" by the Jamies — and finally crossed some invisible boundary. The creature gave a dismissive snort and turned away. I heaved a sigh and returned my mind to girls, or girl, actually — the one I was about to visit. Suzette was Jewish, too, but not a Jewish princess. At least, not in the sense the others were, the bunch who strolled the high school halls like Semitic overwomen, not deigning even to notice dumb-ass Jesus-boys like myself. No, Suzette was different. She was, as I saw it, her own person — smart, interesting, and more involved in reading the *New Yorker* and following ballet than in all the usual, silly high school stuff. *And* she had big breasts. Finding myself before her house, I went up the walk and rang the bell.

Suzette opened the door, looking fetching in her plaid pleated skirt, black blouse, and circle pin. A lot of girls were wearing circle pins lately. I wondered if the pins spoke of some secret, subversive women's organization, since they undoubtedly were pussic symbols. Of course, sometimes a cigar was just a cigar, and the circles might simply be circles, for no reason at all.

"Hi."

"Hi."

She turned up her face for a kiss. I liked this, and accommodated her. She wore pleasingly sticky lipstick and smelled great.

"Nice perfume."

"It's Shalimar."

"Then 'Shal' I kiss you again?" I pulled her closer and began snorfling her neck, where the stuff had apparently been daubed.

"Oh, hi, Daddy!"

Yi! I pulled away, flustered. "Hey, hello, Mr. Kornfeld. Swell night, isn't it?"

The man, a robust, rosy-cheeked five foot six, eyed me. "Don't mind me, young man. Just kiss her wherever you want."

"Daddy!"

He turned to her. "Don't misunderstand, honey. I didn't mean *wherever* as in your ear or leg or —"

"*Daddy!*"

It occurred to me that the man was drunk, that *that* was the source of the rosy cheeks. In fact, he was holding a scotch on the rocks, if I didn't miss my guess. Funny thing, fathers.

"Can I kiss her in the kitchen?" I asked.

"You stay away from her kitchen," he said sternly.

We eyed each other a moment, then cracked up laughing.

"Hey!" Suzette glared at us. "That's not funny, you guys."

"Are you watching Bishop Sheen?" I asked.

"Nah, screw'm," said Mr. Kornfeld. "Tonight's Nixon. The moron's addressing the Republican Convention. Want to join me?"

"Well, actually . . ."

He looked without benevolence at me and Suzette. "Okay. Then I guess it's bed for me. Gather ye rosebuds, kiddies . . ." He wandered off, swirling his drink so that the ice went *ting ting ting*.

Suzette put her hands on her hips. "You two think you're so funny."

"Maybe we should do the Sullivan show."

"Stop making jokes. I want to talk to you."

Oh, God, no. Not talk to me. "What'd I do now?"

"The same thing you always do. Can't you ever take anything seriously?"

"I take *you* seriously." I tried to put my arms around her, to get back to where we'd just been.

She fended me off. "You take making *out* with me seriously. I mean, really — making smutty jokes with Daddy."

"Smutty? What smutty?"

"Kiss me in my 'kitchen.' I think that's called a euphemism."

"That wasn't smutty! Euphemism for what?" Though the blues song "Come On in My Kitchen" did suggest certain euphemistic possibilities.

"You know for what. Don't you have any respect for me?"

"Oh, my *God*, yes. Incredible respect. That's why I'm here instead of any other place on the night before I leave for college."

"Well, it's not like you're going to Outer Mongolia or somewhere."

Was she starting to soften?

"I don't know. It's pretty far away. Maybe *Inner* Mongolia?"

"And there's something else on my mind." No, she was not softening. I hated it when she got this way, with all this stupid shit to say. Couldn't I just put my tongue in her mouth?

" 'There is something on your miiinnd,' " I sang. " 'By the way you look at mee-ee-ee . . .' " The song fit the situation perfectly. I wondered if Bobby Marchan was thinking of me when he composed it.

"There you go again. Would it kill you, just once, not to make a joke out of everything?"

"But I often don't make jokes out of everything! Take polio. When's the last time I made a leg-brace joke?"

"Yeah? What about the fish?"

The fish. She was never going to let me forget the fish. "Hey, the fish was funny!"

"It was not. You looked like an idiot."

I'd come up with the fish bit maybe a month ago at a place called Archie's, where you'd go for hamburgers after a movie or basketball game. I'd been with Suzette, Froggie, Robkin, and a couple of others, sitting at a table, eating and fooling around, when the inspiration came. "What's this?" I yelled, flinging myself onto the floor, onto my side, and then convulsing wildly, flipping and flopping desperately. The people at the table began calling out guesses, but no one got it. Finally, I leapt up and said, "A fish out of water!" This brought down the house, or at least the table — with one exception: the large-breasted Yidette currently glaring indignantly at me.

"Froggie thought it was funny."

"Well, Froggie can be an idiot, too."

"So I'm an idiot, my best friend is an idiot, and — who else that I care about? Bo Diddley? Yogi Berra?"

"I'm only saying that sometimes you have to act normal to, I don't know, get along in this world."

"*Conform?* You're asking me to *conform?*"

"It's not a dirty word."

"But . . . but . . ."

"You know, when you come to school in bedroom slippers —"

"They're *comfortable.*"

"And when you pick me up for a date in a cape —"

"I *like* capes. Maybe not every day, but —"

"And when you talk like a Negro —"

"But they talk better than us! They get to say *y'all* and *sho' nuff* and *mofo* —"

"That's what I mean! Listen to you! Can't you ever just be like other people?"

On the verge of a stroke, I made little sounds of dismay, helpless to articulate my towering disapprobation.

"There's spittle on the corners of your mouth," Suzette informed me primly, offering a Kleenex.

I did not like that there was spittle on the corners of my mouth. Even less did I like having to be like other people. Unless it was an accident; that would be okay. I took the tissue. Things sure weren't going the way I'd hoped they would. Why did girls always want to change you when how you were was fine?

We looked at each other awhile. I calmed down. Maybe, it dawned on me, I should give Suzette what she wanted. "Well," I said, in my best cool high school voice, "how do you think the Roslyn football team will do next year?"

"What?"

"I saw this cool 'forty-nine Merc today. Customized up the wazoo. Skirts, spinners, bull-nosed, lowered. Really fab."

She was looking at me oddly.

"I certainly hope we can surpass the Russians in the space race. Too bad about that U-2 business. Is there a flag around here we could salute?"

A smile tugged at the corners of her mouth. She was fighting it, but there it was.

"Read some James Baldwin yesterday. You know, we've got to get those people their civil rights!" I pounded a fist into my palm with a look of great earnestness.

"All right. Stop."

"What will your major be at the U of Chi? I'm personally considering international relations with a minor in Chinese. Still, it would be nice to investigate nuclear —"

"Stop! Okay!" She was laughing. "You win! You're like other people!"

"Then could we go inside now?"

"Of course." Suzette took my hand and pulled me into the living room, reaching to the TV to turn Nixon off. "We'll start over. Would you like anything?"

There were so many answers I could have given. Perhaps you can guess some of them. "I would like," I said carefully, "to be sitting next to you with that three-way bulb at its lowest setting and Miles on the hi-fi and —"

"I know. Same thing you always want." She was standing very close, her Shalimar scaling my chin and slipping into my nose.

"Well, we're going away and won't see each other for a long time, and I really want tonight to be special. You know? You look so beautiful." Where was I getting this shit?

"If you think that *Battle Cry* crap is going to work with me . . ." But there was that melting expression, the one she always wore while dropping the resistance with which these encounters began.

"I wrote a poem for you today," I told her. "Want to hear it? It's real short: 'My dear / Come here.'" I reached out and gathered her in my arms.

"Nice." She allowed herself to be gathered. Her eyelids lowered and her lips parted slightly. And then I was kissing her and was she ever kissing back! Damn, I liked those lips. They somehow managed to be soft and firm at the same time. These qualities had always seemed somewhat at odds to me, but there they were, coexisting right there on those pouty, bee-stung lips. Down in my pleased 'nads, great armies were forming up.

"Let's sit down," she whispered.

"Yuh . . . yuh," I managed.

She began turning off lights, leaving only the desk lamp with its green glass shade glowing softly in the corner. Sitting on the sofa, she cocked a finger at me.

"I've got a surprise for you tonight."

As the mother in the Lenny Bruce bit said, *Surprises! I love surprises!* Of course, in that case, her son was handing her a hidden bomb to bring on her plane. "What is it?" I asked, sitting down next to her.

"You'll see." Placing a hand on each side of my face, she pulled me toward her. Again, those soft/firm lips . . . and then her tongue slipped delightfully into my mouth, like an old friend I hadn't hung out with for a while.

If a bird had flown over, it could have drifted lazily skyward in the hot updraft that now rose from us. I kissed back, and we had a long, soulful smooch that would have been nicely complemented by a Solitaires record. There was sex on her breath.

"Ohhhhhhhhh," she sighed.

Girls made those great sounds. It always surprised me when they did. At first, I'd think, *What? Is she okay?* I myself never made a peep. Was it just me? Did Froggie or Ace make sounds? So much to know. And then there were the body zones. There were places that were okay to touch. Elbows, earlobes, and feet, for instance: touch 'em with impunity, twenty-four hours a day. On the other hand, breasts, inner thighs, ass, and wazoo were *not* okay. You could put your hand on the outside of a thigh, but not on the inside. It seemed as arbitrary as Mexican justice. And the funny thing was, the places that were most forbidden were the very places my hands most wanted to go. Was it *because* they were forbidden? I didn't think so. If my brain were wiped of all knowledge and experience, my hands would still want to go up her skirt. If I were *dead*, they'd want to go there.

Then there were border zones — hip, lower back, knee, and shoulder front, an area I thought of as "overtit." Time to explore some of those, I decided. Kissing her with particular zeal, I put a hand on her knee.

"Ohhhhhhhhhhhhhhhh." Her head rolled back and forth. She sure seemed turned on. Emboldened, I slipped a skillful, almost imperceptible hand six inches closer to her scrantz.

Her head stopped rolling. Her eyes opened. "Don't," she said.

"Okay. Sorry." Keeping it lighthearted, I went to kiss her again, the offending hand held high. This made her smile and she served up the smooch. More tongue, more moaning. If my balls had had mouths, they would have emulated that guy in *The Fly:* "Help us! Help us!" My body — I swear this is true — took over and directed me to ram it into her mouth. Now *that* would be something — a blow job. But such acts from seventeen-year-old girls didn't, in my long-ago sense of fifties reality, even fall into the realm of the possible. It probably wouldn't happen until I was twenty-seven, in an apartment in a tall building in Manhattan, drinking scotch and playing Frank Sinatra records. Now *there* was a disgusting thought. Meanwhile — tonight included — I'd just have to settle for this unending combat, never resolved. I sighed inwardly.

Suzette hit me on the arm. "Hey! Didn't you hear me?"

"Huh?" But for the beating of my heart and the rushing of my blood, I hadn't heard shit.

"I said it's time for your surprise."

"Surprise? Oh, right." I pulled back from her a little so she could give me the gift, whatever it might be. I was betting on a diary. Chicks loved that shit.

But Suzette reached for the top button of her blouse.

What?

Her fingers moved to the second button, and then the third. I sat transfixed, only a foot or so from her gradually emerging jehoshaphats, cunningly packaged in a lacy black bra.

She watched me with a little smile. "You've been wanting them, haven't you?"

"Yuh . . . yuh."

"Well, they're yours. They're my good-bye surprise."

The blouse was open now. I gulped. "So . . . I should just —"

"I wish you would."

My God, what unselfish act of charity had I committed in a former life to be allowed this? I reached out a trembling hand, ran a finger from her shoulder to her ripe, bursting left breast. She didn't pull away! She didn't slap my hand! I put my palm on the front of it, and could feel her hardened nipple pressing against me through the fabric!

"*Eee! Eee!*" Her voice had gone high and squeaky, into mouse levels. Would she mind if I —?

"Yes! Oh, yes!" She sat up straight so I could unhook her bra.

Damn! I reached around her with only the vaguest notion of how to do this. Working blind, I found the clasp and tried to open it in a sophisticated, worldly, *Playboy* magazine sort of way. It proved difficult. I'd hoped for a casual one-handed flip-open, but one-handed flip-opens evidently lay in my future, as all I was doing now was getting a cramp in my thumb.

"Oh, hurry. Please."

With my heart in my throat, I reached around and tore and tugged at the stupid thing with both hands, jerking Suzette this way and that.

"Want me to?" she whispered in my ear.

"No, no, I got it." It was incumbent on *me* to do this, an affirmation of my suavity. Contorting my body around her, I discerned the problem. Three clips! Evidently, her ba-boos were of sufficient heft to require such precautions. With great concentration, I undid the clips one at a time. And . . .

Whooof! The bra flew off her and landed on the bust of Churchill that sat atop the coffee table.

"God. Oh, God. Touch me!"

Yes. Immediately. Working myself back around so that I could see them first, I felt my face droop in awe. Her nipples were all hardened up! Touch them, hell. Guided by some primordial race memory, my mouth went straight to them.

"*Eep!*" she cried. "*Eep! Eep!*" The sounds were now of such high frequency that perhaps only beings from Jupiter could hear them.

My dick had done what dicks do and had, in fact, become so big and hard that I could have beaten an armed intruder to death with it. More than anything in the world, I wanted her to grab it. More than another Yankees pennant, sending men into space, and victory in the Cold War, I wanted her to just snatch up my crank and wrap her little hand around it and squeeze it, just do incredible things to it.

I decided I would make this easier for her.

While continuing to kiss and feel, I was able, with my other hand, to unhitch my trou. My fully expanded johnson burst forth.

Let's see, I thought, *how should I play this? Ask her? Nah. Suggest we play this new game I'd just invented, Gear Shift? Uh-uh. Pledge my undying devotion if she'd only prove her love by, you know, jerking me off? Bad idea. What the hell* — I slammed her hand onto my dick.

Puzzled, Suzette manually explored it a moment. I devolved into primitive, old-brain functions, rolling my eyes up in ecstasy. Whimpering, I began uncontrollably pressing myself against her hand.

"What are you . . . ?" She returned in a flash to normal consciousness. "Oh, my God!" she cried, whipping her hand away. "Gah!" she continued. "Put that away! It's *disgusting!*" she concluded.

My cock recoiled, crestfallen. It happened to think it wasn't bad-looking at all.

"That you would have taken out your *penis!*" she exclaimed. "People don't do that until they're *married!*"

I felt as if I'd entered Eden, for, like, five seconds and been booted out by God. "Okay, okay, I'll marry you!" I snatched up her hand and tried to put it back.

"Awk!" She sprang away like a startled cat, landing beyond the rug. "You're *horrible!*" She grabbed her bra and stuffed her boze back into it. "How could I have ever liked you! Get out! Get out!"

She was actually screaming.

"Hey, shhhhh!"

"Shhhhh, nothing! I should call the *police!*"

"But . . . But . . ." I stood up, and my perhaps permanently hardened dong thrust upward, as if giving her the finger.

"Suzette? What's going on?" At this perfect moment, Mr. Kornfeld barged in.

In an utter panic, I grabbed my jeans, yanking them up so hard I pulled my feet from under me and went over backward.

Mr. Kornfeld stopped. There I was, dazed on the floor, my hard-on lying on my stomach like a log. Then he checked out his rumpled daughter as she attempted to button her buttons, tuck in her tails, and fix her hair all at the same time, her face still wearing the expression of someone who'd just been menaced by giant spider things from the Earth's core. He looked back at me as I was desperately yanking up my underwear and, of course, getting my balls caught and screaming, "Fuck!"

"Daddy, *do* something!"

He did. He burst into laughter. Pointing at me, he laughed harder and harder.

"Daddy!"

The outrage on his daughter's face triggered even greater laughs. Tears rolled down his cheeks. He put a hand on the wall to keep from falling over.

"Th . . . th . . . that's quite a flagpole you've got there, son."

Suzette's outrage increased exponentially. *"Daddy! He made me put my hand on it!"*

It was an effort to speak, but Mr. Kornfeld managed. "W-well, in that case, did you run it *up* the flagpole? Did anyone *salute?*" He contorted in mirthful agony, hands going to his stomach.

Suzette stamped her foot in fury. "Damn it, Daddy. Stop it! Why can't you ever be serious?"

Jesus, she was like a broken record! Seeing my opportunity, I ran for the door, still cinching my belt, and burst outside into the warm summer night. Crickets were cricking, a distant dog barked, the scent of roses floated by. All this I noticed in the back of my mind somewhere, but the foreground was dominated by a single, screaming, physiological need for which there was but one solution. The question was, where? Here, on the Kornfeld driveway? A token of my affection for her to remember me by? But what if Suzette, as threatened, was calling the cops? Never good to be found by the fuzz while flogging the flute. Home, then. I set out.

And ran into an old friend — Cerberus! Unfortunately, this time I wasn't observing a respectful speed limit but flying along like an Olympic sprinter. *Arrrhhhhh!* went the animal, leaping at me, slamming into me with its entire weight, bearing me to the ground. There it stood, paws on my chest, barking like shotgun blasts.

"Hey, come on. I didn't do anything to you." How much more could go wrong on a single night?

Bright lights illuminated the lawn. The screen door of the house whapped open and Dr. Kasamir rushed out, his white hair pillow-mussed. Spotting me, he rolled his eyes.

"Harazzing my dog again. I sought after lazt time you vould stay avay from him."

Lazt time apparently meant the occasion of the animal sinking its teeth into my buttock. I remembered Dr. Kasamir telling the cops

I'd threatened the dog with a cricket bat. That no bat, cricket or otherwise, had been found seemed not to matter. I was a kid and Kasamir was a doctor.

"All right, Hermann, ve vill go inzide." Dr. Kasamir yanked the dog and they went away. I got up, struggling to regain my composure. At a rapid walk, I continued homeward, passing the Methodist church. In what way, I wondered, did a Methodist's method differ from anyone else's? There were so many small-town mysteries. Now I moved past Adelstein's, the sundries store. What the hell *were* sundries anyway? Weird word. Faster I went, running again now, and zoomed past Mr. Kanufsky's candy store, where the girlie magazines were. I had worked there during high school, and Mr. K. had taught me how to make a real Jewish egg cream. And now I went past Mr. Darling's, who was anything but, having stolen at least a dozen baseballs from Wilson and me over the years, whenever one landed in his yard, and now I zoomed between the stone plant holders at 31 Warner, into my driveway, and up on the porch. God, could I ever not wait to get upstairs — I had migraine testicle aches. At the front door, though, I stopped.

My father was still up, listening to Bix Beiderbecke!

Yes, the light was on, and Bix's trumpet, turned up loud, was effortlessly reaching the porch. I hazarded a peek through the window. There was JC Senior, all right, scotch in hand, belly like a watermelon straining at his shirt, nodding to the beat.

The way I envisioned the problem, Dad was a Cyclops perched on an island with a club, guarding the strait through which I had to sail to reach Thrace. There was simply no easy way to get upstairs without being spotted. I could try stealth, opening the door *verrry* slowly and tiptoeing up the staircase in hopes that the giant wouldn't notice. Or I could do the opposite, using such extreme speed as to disappear from sight before the man, lost in his Jazz Age reveries, even looked up. Were there other options? I was at pains to think of one. All right, Plan B. I burst suddenly through the doors and raced up the stairs. I'd almost made the little landing where I could swing right and disappear, when —

"Hey!" The giant, stirred from its stupor, had become sentient. Fuck!

"Yeah, Dad."

"C'mon 'n' hav'a drink."

Now that I was eighteen, my father, always in search of a drinking buddy, would hit on me every so often.

"Kinda tired, Dad. Gotta leave really early . . ."

"C'mon. Geddown here."

Oh, God. Pasting a dumb, amiable smile on my *punim,* I went down and sat with him in the living room.

"So — did Wilson come home?"

"How the hell should I know? Hav'a drink."

I poured a drop of scotch and lots of club soda over some ice and took a hearty swallow. "Mmm. Great!" *For God's sake, beat me off!* my dick was screaming, joining the shrill voices of my balls in a persistent chorus of urging.

"Lissen'a this." The giant somehow managed to get to the Victrola. Dad eschewed 45 or 33 rpm records, extolling the audio quality of his twenty- and thirty-year-old 78s. They had a solid tonal feel, he thought, unlike LPs, which sounded wispy and strange.

Screeeeeee! I winced as the needle flew across the record's grooves. Then, there it was, that damned song:

> *Who's that knocking on my door?*
> *Who's that knocking on my door?*
> *Who's that knocking on my door?*
> *Cried the fair young maiden.*

"Barnacle Bill the Sailor" was the song he listened to again and again. And again. When in his cups — which was to say, every night — he'd put it on automatic.

> *It's only me, from over the sea,*
> *Said Barnacle Bill the Sailor.*
> *I'm all lit up like a Christmas tree*

Said Barnacle Bill the Sailor.
I'll sail the seas until I croak
I'll fight and swear and drink and smoke
But I can't swim a bloody stroke
Said Barnacle Bill the Sailor.

At this point, a great solo by Bix ensued. It *was* very hip, but when you've heard it ten thousand times, even a great solo by Bix Beiderbecke gets tired. The record went on, with more quasi-racy lyrics and a surprisingly hot solo by Benny Goodman, of all people, this being 1929, but here JC Senior's attention grew tenuous and he staggered to the turntable to get back to Bix. I rolled my eyes. This could go on all night. I *had* to beat off.

"Dad, I gotta get some Zs. G'night, now." I stood.

"Aw, stick aroun' awhile."

"No, really, I better go."

"Whussamatta? C'mon!" He looked at me with a pathetic expression, half-yearning, half-Mussolini giving orders. He could still tug on my emotions. What the hell, I'd be splitting in the morning, wouldn't see him for months. Maybe I could spend a few more minutes with — .

Are you insane? my balls shrieked. *Upstairs! Now!*

Jamming my door closed, not bothering to turn on the light, I tore off my pants and fell onto my bed. Grabbing my swollen hog, I thought of tits, asses, tits, inner thighs, and tits. My hand was setting a new land-speed record. Nipples, areolae, bras coming off, and . . . and . . . *ker-whoosh!* I was like an oil well, the recoil practically sinking me into the mattress.

Thank you, breathed my balls.

I just lay there now, mind loose, going back through the day. It was some review. My family was a drag, my (no doubt, former) girlfriend was a drag, life in this stupid suburban town was a drag. All that mattered was Froggie and my other high school friends, and they'd scattered to the four corners of the Earth and were no longer available. So I'd be back with my weird roommates at this supposedly great school where I hadn't made a single real friend in my entire freshman year. I hated my very existence! Maybe I should —

Plurp!

What?

Plurp!

There it was again, something smacking against my forehead.

I turned on the light. Aw, fuck. Long goobers of come were hanging from the ceiling. Vaguely impressed with my own squirtability, I rushed to the bathroom, returned with towels, and cleaned things up. Then, grumbling, I scrunched up in bed. Man, I couldn't wait to get out of there. No matter how lonely and uncomfortable it was, Dartmouth couldn't be worse than this.

CHAPTER FOUR

The Big Green

TO GET THERE FROM ROSLYN, you took the expressway into the city, then swung north through a bit of New York, then a stretch of Connecticut — a grungy, ugly, urban section bearing no resemblance to the upper-middle-class Connecticut of popular imagination — and then, *whoosh,* up through Massachusetts on pristine, gorgeous Route 5. The first thing you knew, you were coming up the hill into Hanover, New Hampshire.

I felt an unexpected thrill driving through the clean, pretty little town; up Main Street to the Inn Corner, then — in as abrupt a presentation as a magician's colorful silk whipped off a newly appeared dove — Dartmouth College. You couldn't see it . . . and then, all at once, you could. It took the breath away.

Not for nothing was Dartmouth known as the Big Green. The color was everywhere — green grass; green trim, roofs, and shutters on the buildings; green trees. Viewed from the air, the college rose up from a very sea of green. Before me as I waited at the light was the great, lawny expanse actually *called* the Green, with its crisscross of walking paths. It was the soul of the campus. Beyond it stood enormous, majestic Baker Library, with its white, skyward-thrusting tower housing a seventeen-bell carillon. To the right was Dartmouth Row, three stately classroom buildings of white wood with green shutters that had looked more or less this way since 1791, when they had been the entirety of the school. And on my left were the tree-shrouded domains of President John Sloan Dickey, Dean of Students Thaddeus Seymour, numerous department heads, and the other feudal lords of this place — Parkhurst Hall and College Hall. A more imposing layout of academic architecture could not be imagined. Supposedly, President Eisenhower had swung by a few years ago and stated, "This is what a college should look like." I saw it as an academic Camelot, the library standing in for Arthur's castle, the other buildings lesser but still exalted quarters of the knights, dukes, and earls.

"Duke duke duke, duke of earl earl earl," sang my Ford's little radio, tuned to WDCR, the college station. I turned right onto East Wheelock, then pulled up behind Dartmouth Row, to Fayerweather Row. There were many rows at Dartmouth. The Fayerweathers were three dorms in a, yes, row. They were three-story structures of brick with more green shutters. My room was on the third floor of Middle Fayerweather. And there was my parking space, right in front, just as the letter from Buildings and Grounds had promised. My own parking space! Feeling empowered, I slipped in and killed the engine.

Getting out of my cigarette-smelly car, the thing that hit me first was the piney tang of the air. It was so *clean* here, far from the sweaty grime of life in the New York City area. Far from everything, really. At Dartmouth, you were in the *woods*, Jim. I stretched luxuriously in the dappled sunlight, enjoying the way things looked. You felt it had been this way for centuries and would continue to be this way for centuries more. It was stuck in time, its rustic-gentry character presiding like a formidable eighteenth-century patriarch with whom you didn't dare disagree. There was no hint of architectural modernism, no aluminum and glass, no Frank Lloyd Wright. There was sameness. Beautiful, gracious, traditional sameness.

Just now, the school was going through its annual coming-alive routine. Not much happened here during the summer, although the New Hampshire countryside was at its achingly beautiful zenith then, its mountains, lakes, rivers, and woods engendering an exhilaration you simply couldn't find on the banal flatlands of Long Island. Most Dartmouth guys weren't up here during the summer months. Now that autumn was upon the land, the three thousand–man student body was streaming back. They marched along the walkways with their crew cuts and healthy Caucasian faces, wearing their Dartmouth jackets and numeral sweaters. The latter were dark green, with the year of one's class in white numbers. Guys on junior varsity teams got them, while varsity players got letter sweaters, with a big, capital *D*. At Hanover's latitude, there was already a crisp fall note in the air. I cherished autumn, and it arrived here a month earlier than in Roslyn. Throwing open my trunk, I found my woodsy red plaid flannel jacket and put it on. The excitement of being back was a physical tingle.

Energized, I lugged my stuff upstairs, past the nest of mailboxes at the dormitory door, past the posters advertising Dartmouth Outing Club hikes and Webster Hall concerts, past the bulletin board already thumbtacked with handwritten notes soliciting used textbooks, football tickets, and rides to the girls' schools, Skidmore, Smith, and Colby Junior. And Green Mountain, a two-year school in Vermont that Dartmouth guys knew as the Groin. At room 302, one arm around a load of books, records, and loose coats, I managed to unlock the door with my free hand. My room! No Isaac, no Brad. Not yet. Since the three of us were again to be roommates, we'd been allowed to leave our furniture there over the summer. Not that it amounted to much: three desks and chairs, supplied by the school; a ratty sofa we'd bought used from an emmet, as the local citizens were called; dressers in the bedroom; the sound system in its place in the corner, gold smoked-plastic cover over the record player; half-assed, cheap speakers hanging in the corners. I opened the bathroom door; yes, there was Doreen, the *Playboy* centerfold, her big breasts spilling from her open ski sweater, the skis themselves nestled in the crook of one arm. When you sat down, there she was, smiling at you. The expression was ambiguous — was she just being friendly? Or was she eyeing your wank?

I unpacked my stuff and stowed it away. Plunking down in my desk chair, I lit a Winston. I did this without guilt or a second thought. Except for a few jocks worried about their wind, every-one smoked. There was my Dartmouth ashtray, sitting by my Dartmouth lamp, here in my Dartmouth dormitory. One thing about Dartmouth — it was very Dartmouth.

As I enjoyed my cigarette, music drifted in from the hall — Ahmad Jamal playing "Poinciana." I would forever associate the song with Froggie and Sandy Shaw. Remembering, I smiled. The previous February, Sandy had been my Winter Carnival date. She went to UNH — the University of New Hampshire — and so did a pal of mine from Roslyn High, Marla Moes, with whom I'd acted in school plays. She'd shown me a picture of Sandy while we were home for Christmas, and to my immediate interest, Sandy had looked like Doris Day. Despite all the dumb, virginal comedies Doris was making at this time, she was still, by my standards, a sexy woman. I knew this because when I saw her movies I wanted to lick her thighs. So when Marla proposed Sandy as a potential date for me, I jumped at the chance. And when Sandy showed up, she did indeed look like Doris Day — younger, slimmer, but definitely in the Doris mode. What was more, she'd very quickly started doing things like linking arms with me as we walked around campus, laughing cheerily at my jokes, and looking admiringly at me as I expounded on some dumb theory. *Wow,* I thought — *I'm going to make out with this girl!*

That night, with Brad at a wrestling tournament and Isaac ski-ing, the room belonged to me. I put the red bulb in the lamp and brought Sandy there. There was a jug of apple cider we kept on the window ledge so it would turn hard. Sandy and I had some and began making out. She made noises and put her tongue in my mouth. When I tentatively felt her up, she actually pressed her boob into my hand. Need I mention that I got excited as shit? She was taking off her blouse when someone knocked on the door.

I freaked. Campus cops? Supposedly, if you were caught in com-promising circumstances, you'd be expelled for failing to behave like a "Dartmouth gentleman." The knock came again. Jesus! I shooed Sandy to the bathroom, made a stab at fixing my clothes, and, opening the door a little, peered into the hall.

It was Froggie! In my state of glandular excitement, I'd forgotten I invited him up for Carnival. But I'd been about to feel Sandy up! What would I do?

Froggie was a true friend. "I'll, uh, go hide. Let me know when to come out." Grabbing my brand-new two-volume, fourteen-pound *Life* magazine history of World War II, he disappeared into the bedroom, closing the door behind him. I released Sandy from the john. She looked around anxiously, holding a towel to her chest.

"Is it okay? Was it the police?"

"No, no — it wasn't anyone. Uh, a little more hard cider?"

Soon, floating on whatever minute amounts of alcohol may have actually gotten into our systems, we were again making out. Meanwhile, of course, there had been music playing, a stack of records I'd put on: *Kind of Blue,* the Modern Jazz Quartet doing *No Sun in Venice,* and the *Poinciana* album. I'd have preferred playing the Cardinals or the Moonglows, but the music of these groups had not yet been collected on LPs. When the MJQ finished, down flopped Ahmad, and that made things even nicer. Froggie was forgotten. I had actually gotten my hand onto Sandy's inner thigh — the lower and less exciting end, but inner thigh nonetheless. She panted and sweated and went *ooh, ak,* and *eee.* Had I been older, I would have recognized the signs — the girl was ready to go. But my innocent, eighteen-year-old, brought-up-in-the-fifties self didn't have a clue. The thought of taking things to the next level, of running into the bedroom, ripping off clothes, and, before the startled Froggie, plunging my great tumescent pole into her eager, glistening gobble-creature simply didn't occur to me. So I continued to make out, with great energy and passion but with no end point in mind other than charging into the bathroom and flogging the hog when I couldn't stand it any longer.

The Ahmad Jamal album, meanwhile, continued to play. An hour passed with "Poinciana" flowing endlessly from the speakers. There was a recurrent, rising melodic fragment — *doodle-oodle-ooh.* And Froggie, ensconced in Isaac's bed, trying to focus on the Wehrmacht's march through Belgium, kept hearing it. The occasional *ook* or *gleep* from Sandy would rise above the music, but mainly he heard *doodle-oodle-ooh.* Over and over again.

Finally, as I had foreseen, my balls went critical, so I ran to the bathroom, gave my dick three strokes, and came like an East German water cannon. Returning, I found that Sandy had suddenly and magically become far less interesting. "You know," I told her brightly, offering her blouse, "we might want to get an early start tomorrow. That ski jump starts pretty early in the morning."

She looked at me in incomprehension. "But . . . but . . . ."

"C'mon, I'll walk you to your room." Ah, the naïveté! Quickly as I could, I brought the crestfallen girl to her lodgings and rushed back to hang out with Froggie, whom I found at my desk with a six-pack of Bud, deep into the Battle of Kursk.

"How you doing, man?"

"Doodle-oodle-ooh."

"How's school? How's life?"

"Doodle-oodle-ooh."

When he regained the power of speech, we spent the remainder of the evening pleasantly, sharing thoughts, digging music, making each other laugh. How nice, once carnal cravings were satisfied, to be doing this instead of that.

WHAM! THE DOOR FLEW OPEN. Isaac clomped in with his skis, his ski boots, his ski parka, his ski haircut, and his ski zits. Throwing his stuff on the sofa, he lit a ski cigarette. That is, he lit up a Salem, which was mentholated.

"Hi," I said.

"How are you?" Isaac asked.

"Fine. How are you?"

"I'm fine."

We looked at each other. This was major conversation for Isaac Andersson. He was tall and skinny, about six four, and maybe his genes had been too busy producing height to have much left over for conversational acuity. His ears stuck out, he wore glasses, and there were braces on his teeth. Gregory Peck he wasn't. I groped for something more to say.

"Uh — how'd your summer go?"

"Fine."

Right. "Well, I haven't seen Brad."

"Guess he's not here yet." Isaac put his skis and boots into the closet. Finding his Salem three fourths ash, he lit another.

I cast about for further linguistic intercourse. Couldn't talk rock 'n' roll — Isaac barely knew it existed. The Yankees? Isaac was from somewhere in California, where there had only been Major League teams for three years — what did he know of the Yankees? Science fiction? Didn't read it. Girls? The subject made him turn red and emit nervous laughs. What else was there? For me, conversation had always been play. You batted words and notions back and forth like tennis balls, dropping witticisms like bebop drummers dropped bombs. For Isaac, conversation was irrelevant. I wanted to be friends but didn't know how to connect. We stood there, a frozen tableau of unease, when happily the door banged open and Brad strode in with his suitcases.

"Hey, you guys! Long time no see! What've you been up to?" He dropped his bags and rushed over to shake hands, exuding cheerful energy like an attar. I relaxed. Isaac and I could now focus on Brad and no longer be like a Swiss mountaineer trying to communicate with a Chinese guy in a rice paddy.

Brad Johnson was something else entirely. Shorter than me but powerfully muscled, he was an unassuming midwestern jock god. Sports pumped through him like amphetamines. He came from a place called Palatine, a suburb of Chicago, and had many friends at Dartmouth — Jack, Biff, Mike, Kirk — also from the suburbs of Chicago, and they talked endlessly about football, basketball, hockey, track, swimming, and soccer, often as pertained to recent performances of the teams at their high schools. To my amazement, Brad knew not only about the varsity teams, but also the JV and even *freshman* teams. "Saw a good twelve-year-old last month," he'd mention to Biff. "Tailback named Wiznarkski."

The three of us went to dinner at Thayer Hall. This was a large, institutional dining room, filled with the murmur of conversation, the clinking of knives and forks, and the crash of pots and pans apparently being flung around the kitchen. There was no music and no art on the walls. The selection of food was limited. Not terrible, just boring. As a freshman, I'd *had* to eat there, or at least pay for meal tickets. This year, no longer bound to Thayer, I'd often head downtown for civilized food at Lou's, Hal's, or the Green Lantern. This generally meant cheeseburgers with too much ketchup.

That night, as we hung out in our room, we were paid a visit by our down-the-hall neighbor Al Heller. Al was a senior. Last year he'd befriended the new freshmen in room 302.

"So — you decided what houses you're going to rush?"

That again. "Well, actually —"

"Um, I, uh —" Brad looked distractedly out the window at the illuminated Baker Library tower.

Isaac groped for a Salem.

Al Heller laughed. "Yeah, it was like that for me, too. Rush sucks. You have to do it, though. Important decision."

"How'd you decide to join AD?" Brad asked.

"Actually, I just went to a random bunch of houses the first night. Some I liked, some I didn't. You could tell when they didn't want Jews. AD wasn't like that."

We looked at Al with serious expressions. Here was a Jew talking to gentiles about that uncomfortable subject you basically didn't mention in high school. Pretty grown-up, this college stuff.

"It sure sounded like you guys have fun there." I was remembering the stories Al told last year. He'd barge in late with beery breath, filled with hilarity at the latest bizarre incident in his fraternity basement. As he told it, the brothers of Alpha Delta Phi had a lively time.

"Well, yeah, that's what a fraternity's for, right?"

"Is it?" said Brad. "I mean, I like fun as much as the next guy, but what about sports? What about meeting people you'll, you know, be in business with later?"

"Hey, we play interfraternity football. You ought to see Otter. He's our quarterback. He plays with bare feet."

Picturing flashing cleats, I winced. "Doesn't he get hurt?"

"Nah, not Otter. He's amazing. You should meet him."

It occurred to me that maybe Al's visit was not just random. In fact, it could be that *all* his visits had been a public relations campaign for the AD house. And with rush starting tomorrow, here, by great coincidence, he was again.

"Listen, wait till you hear this story. We're hanging out at the bar one night —"

"That's how all your stories begin. 'We're hanging out at the bar one night,'" Brad pointed out.

"True, but don't interrupt. All of a sudden, in walk Doberman and Coyote, and they've got a chicken. They stole it from some farm or something."

"A *live* chicken?" I couldn't believe all the animals around here. Live chickens were seldom glimpsed in Roslyn.

"*Yes,* a live chicken. Will you let me tell the story, for Christ's sake? Okay, what Doberman and Coyote have in mind is to eat the chicken at a special dinner they're gonna have on the front lawn of the house, with tuxedos and a candelabra. But first the bird has to be fattened up and they want to keep it in the basement for a week or two. So the chicken moves in, with Coyote feeding it lots of corn. But it keeps jumping out of places, scaring the brothers. And they're finding feathers in their beer. Even worse, the thing is shitting all over the place. It's not real *smelly* shit or anything — it's that white stuff, y'know? — but still, it's *shit.* Now Dobes and Coyote don't live in the house, so they don't know what a drag this is all getting to be. So we grab 'em and say they've got to do something. Doberman comes up with an idea he hopes will satisfy everyone — keep it in the bathroom. So the chicken goes in the bathroom. Only now you can't take a leak without it flying in your face, and the *bathroom* is getting covered with shit. We tell Dobes and Coyote either eat the chicken tonight, or we'll stick their faces in the gutter."

"Gutter?" said Isaac.

"We have a gutter. Down in the bar. You'll see. You're coming for rush, right?"

The three of us hesitated.

"Yeah, sure, Al," I decided.

"What about you two?" Al regarded Brad and Isaac.

"Is this story getting anywhere?" Brad looked pointedly at his watch. "They were going to put the chicken in the gutter, and . . ."

"Okay, okay. Dobes and Coyote look at each other and say, 'All right, tonight we dine!' But first they have to kill it, and no one's up for breaking its neck. Long discussion. Finally, Coyote comes up with the solution. He runs upstairs and comes back with an electric cord he's yanked out of someone's lamp. He's going to *electrocute* the chicken."

"Aggghhhhhh!" we cried.

"So Coyote strips the end of the cord and ties it around the chicken's leg. He's ready to plug it in when Dobes says, 'Wait!' He says if this is going to work, the chicken'll have to be *grounded.* Well, we're all really impressed that Doberman knows so much about electricity. He finds a pan in the kitchen, fills it with water, and puts the chicken in it. 'Now?' says Coyote. Dobes nods and Coyote plugs the cord in. *Bzazzzz!* The chicken goes stiff as a board. They leave the plug in for, like, forty-five seconds, which, having seen movies where guys get executed, they figure should be enough. But it isn't! Not only is the chicken still alive, it goes leaping out of the pan and staggers around the bar. Before anyone can grab it, the back door slams open and Troll walks in. Troll's been humping a nurse in the hearse. He has no idea what's going on, and all of a sudden there's this chicken flying in his face! He throws himself out of the way, the chicken zooms out the door, and everyone goes racing after it. But it doesn't get far, only to the front lawn, where it's now gimping around like it's Long Chicken Silver.

"Meanwhile, up on the second floor, the Man is trying to book for a midterm, and this horrible squawking is messing with his concentration. So he takes his forty-five out of his desk drawer, goes to the window, and *drills* the chicken. *Pow!* Feather explosion! Doberman gives Man a reproachful look, picks up the corpse, and he and Coyote take it upstairs where they pluck it and roast it."

"Did they eat it out on the lawn?" Brad asked.

"Oh, yes. They had it with French fries and a nice Chablis."

"Wow," I said. "That's an amazing story. Did it *taste* any good?"

"Dobes said it was delicious."

"And Coyote?"

"He didn't say. He broke a tooth on the forty-five slug and had to go to Dick's House."

This was the Dartmouth infirmary. I didn't know it yet, but I'd become quite familiar with it. Next door, if you needed brain surgery or something, was Mary Hitchcock Hospital. And a nursing school, attended by a few score thick-calved emmet girls. When Al finally left, it was late, and we hit the sack. Isaac wore his paisley pajamas in the single. Brad jumped to the upper bunk in his Palatine Pumas T-shirt, and I countered in the lower bunk with Hawaiian shirt and boxer shorts. We lay in the darkness like parallel lines, forming a staff for the pealing Baker Tower bells to land their notes on.

"That Al Heller is kind of *weird*," Brad said.

"Whole house sounds weird to me."

Isaac exhaled clouds of mentholated smoke, which reached me and Brad, reminding us he was there.

"What do you think, Isaac?" Brad solicited.

"Yeah, weird. That's what I'd say, too. Weird."

Brad's head looked down at me. "You're actually going to rush AD?"

"Well, sure, I guess. I mean, you know, a courtesy call anyway." There were things called courtesy calls.

"You don't think they're *weird?*"

Brad made it sound like I was about to visit a plague site where infection was certain. I laughed. Brad himself was the least weird person I'd ever met. He was so clean cut, the air squeaked as he walked through it. He had to have been an Eagle Scout but I couldn't bear to ask.

"I want to meet these guys. Doberman. Snot."

"*Why?*" Brad groped for some way to wrap his mind around my strange point of view.

"I thought the chicken story was funny," Isaac offered.

"You *did?*" Brad looked at him, shocked.

I lit a Winston. "Come on, Brad. It *was* funny."

Brad thought a moment. "Well, okay. Yeah. It was funny."

Isaac and I began laughing at him. After a moment, Brad joined us.

"Isaac, you know the story he told us last year that I loved most?" I asked.

His cigarette lighter flared.

I took this for affirmation. "When those girls asked that guy Rat Battles for change of a quarter? And he swallowed the quarter and said *ding ding ding ding ding* and popped five nickels out of his foreskin?"

"Yeah, right. Somebody did that." Brad dripped skepticism.

"Are *you* going to rush AD?" I asked him.

Pause. "Sure, why not?"

We all laughed.

"No, I don't know. The jocks are in Beta. I'm friendly with some guys there."

"Hey," I said, "do either of you ever wonder whether to rush at all?"

Long pause.

"What do you mean?"

"You know — not join any house?"

"What else would you *do*?" Brad was perplexed.

"Plant trees? Write poetry? Make snow angels?"

"Seriously," said Brad.

"Okay, I don't know what else you'd do. But are fraternities, you know, conformist? Do you think they ought to let in guys with beards?"

"*What* guys with beards?"

"Yeah, what are you talking about?"

"I think probably I'm not talking about much of anything."

"You're not going beatnik on us, are you?"

"Look out. I'll recite *Howl*."

"No! Not that!" they cried in horror. I'd sicced it on them last year a few times.

The tower bells went off again. They did this every fifteen minutes. At quarter past the hour, they went *ding-dong ding-dong*. At half past, *ding-dong ding-dong . . . ding-dong ding-dong*. Next they would go *ding-dong ding-dong . . . ding-dong ding-dong . . . ding-dong ding-*

dong, and at the hour they'd go *ding-dong* eight times. Fayerweather Hall was right by the library. The strategy we'd developed last year was to fall asleep quickly, after one burst of bells, to avoid being awakened by the next.

And that's what we did now.

CHAPTER FIVE

Rushing

ACTUALLY, I DID HAVE a rushing plan. I would try to pledge my father's house, Sigma Alpha Epsilon. That I'd never been there and knew diddly about it was no problem, I told myself — I was, after all, a legacy. To warm up, I'd fall by a few other houses, chosen at random, to see what rushing was like. And, yes, I would visit Alpha Delta Phi, a courtesy call for Al Heller.

Dartmouth had twenty-four houses, and I knew very little about most of them. Beta Theta Pi, the one Brad had mentioned, was the famous jock house. My athletic résumé contained a season of soccer at Roslyn High and the ability to dance the slop; for me, Beta would not be a "good fit." Ultimately, I stabbed my finger down four times on the fraternity list in the *Daily Dartmouth*. And here I was at the first of the four, Psi Upsilon, surrounded by guys wearing ties and name tags. The living room, with its leather furniture and burgundy rugs, was crowded. There sure were a lot of madras jackets there.

"Hi!" said a preppy-looking brother whose tag identified him as Tad. "Damn glad to meet you. If you don't mind my inquiring, what's your handicap?"

Huh? "Oh, no, I'm fine. I broke a metatarsal once, but I don't limp or anything."

"I see you have a sense of humor. I mean, of course, your *golf* handicap."

Tad had blond hair that fell halfway down one side of his forehead, a Veronica Lake cut that had lost its nerve. His blue tie bore hundreds of little psis and upsilons.

"Um, sorry, never played golf."

"What *do* you play?"

"I've done Hamlet and, uh, Prince Max Luckyfoot in *The Pirates of Penzance.*"

"What?"

OUTSIDE AGAIN, I felt that never had I been among so many people with whom I had absolutely nothing in common. The Psi Us were from the golf-playing world, wherever that was, and I was — well, I still hadn't *found* my world yet. Maybe it would be at Delta Kappa Epsilon, reputedly some sort of fun-loving party house. Sounded promising. But when I got there, things were quiet. I was one of only five other sophomores currently extant there, and soon I was surrounded by several Dekes, as they called themselves. One of them had an impressive beer belly that hung beyond his fly. The face zits of the guy next to him looked like a connect-the-dots puzzle. Their ties were stained, and their shirttails halfway out. A cool breeze touched the back of my neck through a broken window. Despite the draft, the air held a faint but unmistakable tang of garbage too long unremoved.

"Hey," said a Deke with food in his teeth. "What's this?" He extracted his dong and let it hang. Then he pulled his pants pockets inside out.

No one replied. The dick pointed at the floor, angling slightly to the left. It looked dispirited somehow. Finally, the guy cried, *"An elephant!"*

The Dekes cracked up. They bent at the waist, whooped with delight, and put their hands on the wall to keep from falling over. The six potential pledges, myself included, looked at one another in bewilderment.

The Deke with his dick out tried to explain. "See, the pockets are the ears. And this is —" He stopped. The guy to his right had flicked a booger at him, and it had stuck to his cheek. Putting his dick away, he peeled off the offending item and, after a brief inspection, flicked it back. More laughter, unshared by me.

I FLED AND MOVED ON, shortly arriving at the house universally known as the Tool Shed. It had Greek letters, but nobody used them. If Psi U was preppy and Deke slobby, the Tool Shed was bottom-of-the-social-scale creepy. The fellow who brought me in had breath like the New Jersey Turnpike. In the living room, where testaments to the brothers' academic achievements hung in extremely neat arrangements on the walls, some sort of contest was occurring. While a few curious rushees watched, two slender, bespectacled fellows — pencil-necked geeks, as I would later hear them called — faced each other like gunslingers. When a brother in polio braces called out, "Nineteen to the sixth power over the square root of fourteen hundred seventy-six," the guys drew slide rules from their belts and calculated their asses off. One of the boys was acclaimed the winner. The other was so pissed off he said, "Damn it."

"So what else do you guys do for fun?" I asked a brother who lived in a plastic, germ-free bubble.

"Not much," he replied morosely.

BACK OUTSIDE, Fraternity Row was a bright thoroughfare before me. It was a broad, handsome street, with fourteen fraternities lining its sides, all lit up with Rush Week spotlights — quite a splendid sight. Each house had a flagpole poking from its front, and from the flagpoles hung colorful fraternity flags emblazoned with Greek letters. Kappa Sigma! Sigma Chi! Beta Theta Pi! They were imposing three-story structures, and rather large, as each lodged two to three dozen guys. Maybe they qualified as small mansions; I was vague on architectural terminology. But it was all very impressive, conjuring up Fitzgeraldian visions of my father's time here, with flappers, raccoon coats, and silver hip flasks.

I strolled down the Row, watching my fellow sophomores make their glum transits from house to house. The autumnal snap in the air had only intensified on this September night, and the stars shone without competition from city lights, the Milky Way a brilliant spatter across the sky. The moon stared down like a giant eye. Without depth perception, though, I assumed.

At the end of the Row was my next stop, Pi Lambda Phi. It was situated slightly around the corner, across the street from Dartmouth's other Jewish house, TEP, which Al Heller had summarized as "full of screamers." Pi Lam, however, was the cool New York Jewish house, and since I was mad for anything cool, New York, or Jewish, I was a moth to its kosher flame.

And there were guys I liked here — Bags, Poz, and Tor — my next-door neighbors last year in Middle Fayerweather, where Brad was wont to make fun of their "Jewish accents." Things sure were relative — I hadn't noticed they *had* accents.

Bags Bergman spotted me as I came in. "Poz, Tor, get your asses over here! Look who's rushing!"

Poz and Tor got their asses over. "Hey, man!" they cried, shaking my hand. "Come on, we'll show you around, introduce you to some of the brothers."

Poz was amusingly self-important. Bags was friendly and sort of grooved. Tor had that New York cool, despite being from Florida. His hooded eyes made him look like Lenny Bruce's skinnier younger brother.

"Am I allowed to make foreskin jokes?" I whispered.

Poz, Bags, and Tor laughed good-naturedly and punched me in the arm. I was their pet goy.

This was my first look at more than the living room of a fraternity, and I was curious. Upstairs, there were two- and three-man suites, living rooms and bedrooms, not wildly different from what was in the dorms but way more *haimish*. Pi Lam fraternity paddles hung on the wall, and I could smell Old Spice and English Leather. Someone had Miles's *Sketches of Spain* on a record player.

"Where else you been?" Poz asked.

At the mention of Psi U, they made expressions of indigestion. When I brought up Deke, they belched and scratched themselves and stuck their fingers in their noses.

"What is it with those guys and snot?" I asked.

"It's a house tradition. They think booger-flicking is hilarious," Poz said.

Bags laughed. "They do it to their dates!"

"Get out." It seemed beyond the pale. "And the dates think it's funny?"

"Of course not. They run out crying."

"Kind of lonely over there on big weekends," Tor mused.

"So where you going next?" Bags asked. We were down in the living room now, where a rumble of conversation prevailed.

"What? You're not pledging me here?"

They were suddenly uncomfortable. "Well, but, you know, we, uh . . ."

I laughed and pointed a finger at them. They were my pet *Yideles*. "Just kidding. I'm going to SAE next."

They exchanged looks.

"Well, you'll see what you think," Bags Bergman said.

"Oh, and a courtesy call at AD."

The Pi Lams burst out laughing.

"What?"

"No, nothing. They crack us up, man. We had a great co-party with them last year."

"You did?" This was news.

Bags smiled, remembering it. "There was this guy there, speaking of foreskin jokes: Rat Battles. This girl asked him for change of a quarter and he whipped out his —"

"Yeah, I've heard that one, actually."

AD was a controversial place, at once loved and reviled in the Dartmouth community. Controversy, though, was good. Disorder was stimulating. Anything that outraged squares was prima facie good, I felt.

It was time to move on, so I bade Poz, Bags, and Tor good night and left the Row. SAE was all by itself on top of a hill. It seemed a little larger, whiter, and more resplendent than the others, with at least three spotlights illuminating its broad front porch and fraternity flag. I went up the steps, trying to picture JC Senior at age

nineteen walking into this place with a saxophone case, saying —
what? Did they use the phrase "How's your ass?" in the twenties?
Maybe "Twenty-three skiddoo!"

Inside the front door was an anteroom containing a table, behind
which sat two girls in dresses and stylish coiffures. They fixed me
up with yet another name tag and directed me inside.

Beneath high, vaulted ceilings in the living room, a crowd of SAE
brothers and hopeful rushees attempted to relate. I recognized
some standout members of my class in the crowd — Carl Maves,
with the IQ of 700; Mike Moriarity, the actor; Bill King, the quarterback. The place was full to bursting with alpha-male energy. I
wished I could just relax a little.

Looking around, I found every brother already talking to someone who wasn't me. What were you supposed to do? I sidled up to
one knot of guys.

"I think you'll find most of the real achievers at Dartmouth
choose SAE," a brother was saying to several prospective pledges.
"It's a tradition here. Why don't you tell me something about your-
selves?"

"I'm Bob Wormus," one of them replied. "National Honor
Society. State high-jump medalist."

"Ted Kurtz. President of student government junior and senior
years. Won the Austrian fencing cup in 1959. During summer vacation, I built a house for my family from scratch, starting with chop-
ping down trees for wood."

"Jonathan Lamb. Well, let's see. I won the freshman national
debate title; I'm president of the Dartmouth Young Republicans;
and I recently foiled a bank robbery, for which I was given a thousand-
dollar reward."

They turned to me.

"Ah . . . I got a Buddy Holly autograph! You know, before he
died?"

They looked at me as if I were pus. I had never less known what
to say.

"Yes, and, you know, it's a little-known fact about Buddy, but he
had these terrible teeth. I mean, awful-looking — yellow and

stained . . ." It was true; I'd seen him outside the Brooklyn Paramount.

But my audience had dispersed and could no longer hear me. Fuck. Again with the bad-fit thing! Five fraternities and five bad fits. It was the nightmare scenario that had haunted me: I wasn't going to fit anywhere!

CHAPTER SIX

The Adelphian Lodge

I LEFT SAE, NUMB. To no great surprise, I found my feet taking me back to my dorm. What a washout I was! Ace would laugh — I hadn't even been given a *chance* to sell out. I'd have to make up some story about deciding against fraternities at the last minute so Froggie and Josh wouldn't know of my dismal failure. All that was left was to reach my bed and fetal-ball it under the covers. But then I stopped short. I had to go to the fucking AD house! *Shit!* But I'd promised Al Heller. Sighing, I changed direction.

If the world around me knew the extent of my misery, it gave no indication. A luminous cloud sailed unconcernedly across the moon. A few late-season crickets chirped without noticeable melancholy. I passed Thayer Hall, crossed the Green, and threaded my way through a stand of pines to East Wheelock Street. Wheelock as in Eleazer Wheelock, the preacher who'd come here to educate the Indians almost two hundred years ago, bearing "five hundred gallons of New England rum" and establishing Dartmouth's alcohol-tropism right from the start.

At last, I came to Alpha Delta Phi. It was another grand-looking, lit-up house / mansion, neither identical to nor particularly different from the others I'd seen tonight. It was fronted by a broad lawn and displayed a forest green flag bearing a crisp white alpha, delta, and phi. But as I went up the walk, there *was* a difference — speakers on the balcony were blasting "Mama, He Treats Your Daughter Mean" by Ruth Brown!

This raucous, seminal R & B record was as unlikely a thing to hear on a quiet Hanover street as surf. Tugged a few millimeters out of my dolor, I headed up the walk, onto the concrete porch with its woebegone deck chairs and highway-spool tables, and arrived at the front door. A big guy in Buddy Holly glasses greeted me with a smile.

"Hey! Hello! Welcome to the AD house!" He stuck out a hand to shake with me but discovered there was a can of Bud in it. "Christ!" he snorted, and smote his forehead. Curiously, he used the hand with the beer in it, which struck with a metallic glorping sound. A golden geyser fired up, spread its foamy arms, and fell back on his head. "Oops," he said.

Laughing, he tossed the beer over his shoulder, put an arm around me, and asked, in a breeze of Budweiser breath, "Hey, man. How the fuck's it goin'?"

"Well, uh . . ." I was taken aback.

He wore a sport coat over a pale blue shirt with a frayed collar, and his chinos were beer stained. A stylish spray of newly picked weeds thrust from his breast pocket, upon which had been affixed a name tag reading DUMPTRUCK.

"Come in, come in." Exuding geniality, he pulled the door open.

Bright light dazzled my eyes. A great waft of beer and sweat broached my nostrils. The Ruth Brown song was vastly louder inside, and the guys filling the crowded living room were cheerfully yelling over it to be heard.

"Let's get you a name tag," Dumptruck proposed.

By the door was a card table, at which sat a pair of girls. According to her name tag, the brunette with the red, lipsticky mouth and obvious advanced degree in mammary studies was FAT FRED. *Fat* seemed unkind, though. I would have chosen *voluptuous,* possibly *Rubenesque.* Her eyes betrayed scant intelligence but were nonetheless large and luminous. She had apparently been born under the cow star.

"What are you looking at?" She smiled at me.

I became aware that the little dotted lines coming from my eyes had met in her cleavage. To my surprise, I giggled.

"You're cute," Fat Fred said.

"Torrie!" Dumptruck roared. "Name tag!"

TORRIE TOILETBOWL held up her hand. She was immersed in a copy of *Sexual Behavior in the Human Male,* one of those Kinsey Report books everyone had been making such a big deal about.

She read a moment longer, then looked at me with a wondering expression. "Wow! Did you know ninety-two percent of guys beat off?"

"Uh . . ." I could think of no reply. If you had said *beat off* to Suzette, she would have gone, *"Ewwwww,"* and smashed a vase over your head.

"I could have told you that," said Dumptruck jovially. "There's semen flying all over the place around here."

"Really?" said Torrie. "Could I watch sometime?"

I was into science fiction. I knew what an alternate universe was. Apparently, I'd just walked into one.

Torrie, if I had had to pin it down, was in the Shirley MacLaine mode — sexy in a tomboyish way. Her eyes sparkled with intelligence, her hair was red, her freckles numerous, her breasts . . . well, they were beneath her Smith sweatshirt, so I could make no assessment. I found her instantly likeable.

"So if you could fix this young rushee up with a tag . . . ," Dumptruck prompted.

Torrie crooked a finger. I bent down and she pinned a name tag on me: ELEANOR ROOSEVELT.

"Very good. Okay, Eleanor, let's see what's going on." Grabbing me by the lapel, Dumptruck plunged into the crowd.

We were in a large, rectangular living room, furnished with lush, pleasantly overstuffed green sofas. At both ends of the rectangle were large fireplaces. As we passed one, I saw an AD brother sitting in it. "Crackle!" he was saying. "Crackle hiss!"

"Ah, we're temporarily out of wood," Truck explained. "Come

on — let's go down to the basement. It's the real heart of the house, you know."

"Okay." The room hummed with activity. As we threaded our way through the crowd, a hard rubber ball boinged off my brow and landed at my feet. Shaking my dizziness off, I looked around. A short muscular guy with a thatch of blond hair was waving his lacrosse stick to catch my attention. "Little help!" he called.

Dazedly, I picked the ball up and tossed it back.

"What can I say?" Dumptruck spread his arms. "It's a jungle in here."

The guys with lacrosse sticks resumed their practice, delivering close haircuts here and there. They threw the ball *hard*. Nobody seemed to care.

"That's Hydrant and Magpie," said Truck. "They're on the lacrosse team."

"Where do you guys get these names? Like, why are you Dumptruck?"

"Because that's what I do!" Dumptruck walked here and there, gaily raising and lowering his shirt, serially revealing his great hairy stomach. "Dump!" he cried. "Dump! Dump!"

I stared at him wonderingly. No one else was paying the slightest attention. Definitely an alternate universe.

Dumptruck led me into a small hallway and pointed at a door. "Tube room." He pointed at another. "Sink room." And another. "Back door." He opened and closed it so I was given a brief view of the driveway and the adjoining fraternity, Chi Phi. "And here"— he gestured at an open doorway —"here we have . . ."

"I wanna tell you 'bout ooh-poo-pah-doo," roared a Negro voice up the stairs, and a funky saxophone began to blow.

"Yes," Truck said heartily, "the heart of the house." He headed down the stairs and I followed. The stairway was narrow and twisty, and the walls were fire engine red. On them were portraits of what I took to be life at the Alpha Delta Phi house. The first was of a great pile of bodies, male and female, human and animal, tits and asses and dicks, a tongue licking a nipple, a lizard with a long, erect tail walking backward up an inner thigh, and so on. Beneath it was scrawled *Sod Heap.* The next group of drawings was of Negroes playing instruments, their lips impossibly large and their eyes stereotypically rolling in abandonment. Racist but not mean — these were just happy-go-lucky, old-fashioned black folk, the way white people liked to imagine them before civil rights came along.

Then, all at once, we were out of the dark stairway and right in the middle of the AD bar. Music surged from a brightly blinking red and yellow jukebox. It took a moment for me to place the song. Omigod, it was "Golden Teardrops" by the Flamingos! I'd chased this record all through high school and failed to get it. *No* one had "Golden Teardrops," but these guys did. Then, to my amazement, I saw a line of brothers before the jukebox, making the slow, soulful dance moves I'd loved for years, when the black groups did them at rock 'n' roll shows. But Dartmouth guys? Exhilaration was knocking on my door. I *liked* it here.

A U-shaped bar thrust out from one wall. Perhaps a dozen guys were standing around it, talking, making each other laugh. A short, peppy brother named SNOT stood by the tap system, keeping them in fresh beers. The rest of the basement was one big cavernous room, held up by pillars. Some kind of stone walls. A concrete floor, also painted red. A gutter running around the perimeter, as Al Heller had promised. Mattresses atop wooden platforms providing seating. A phone booth–size bathroom was squeezed in under the stairs. In the back was a dark doorway labeled SEX ROOM. It looked like the entry to some terrible netherworld.

And then I noticed something else — I was the only sophomore in the room. The guys around the bar were the brothers who were too cool for rush! They preferred drinking with their friends to making conversation with dopey strangers. The official rushing things all fraternity upperclassmen were supposed to do, they weren't doing.

Dumptruck clapped me on the back. "Let's have a beer."

"Uh, didn't I read that there's no drinking during rush until Friday night?"

"Monday, Friday, same thing. Now over here we have the much-vaunted Hard Core. A great bunch of guys!" He bellied up to the bar, raising a hand in greeting.

"Hey, Truck," said a guy. "How you doing?"

Dumptruck put an arm around my shoulder. "Guys, this is Eleanor Roosevelt. Eleanor, meet Otter, Coyote, Snot, Black Whit, Giraffe, and Zeke Banananose."

"Hi." So this was the famous Otter, who played football barefoot. He looked affable enough.

"Hi, Eleanor. Hello. Welcome to AD," said the guys, radiating contentment at being exactly where they were, doing precisely what they were doing.

"So," said Truck to them, "how 'bout a beer?"

"Sure," said the guys. And threw their beers on him.

"Aggghhhh!" roared Truck. *"You sons of bitches!"*

The drinkers laughed merrily. Truck removed his glasses and wiped them on my shirt; his mouth, so recently smiling, now turned sharply downward. "I'll get you guys," he said. "Search the shadows. You won't see me coming. I'm going to turn your faces into, like, hamburger. There'll be flies . . . !"

"Fries?" Snot looked over suddenly. "God, I'm starving! Where's the 'wich man? Does he come during rush? What's the —"

"Flies, you asshole! And —"

"Okay, Truck. Go change clothes." Otter smiled amiably. "I'll keep your place warm here."

"Fucking shitheads." Truck lumbered away, wiping his face with his shirttail.

I found myself left with the Hard Core. They projected simultaneous friendliness and danger. Accordingly, I felt simultaneously welcomed and frightened. They had that don't-give-a-shit aura I'd run into here and there in guys, that rock 'n' roll energy that made authority figures wary and women wet. Being here with these guys — possibly becoming a fraternity brother of these guys — produced a similar sensation in my belly to what I'd felt my first time out on a high diving board.

"Here's that beer you heard rumor of." Otter handed it to me. I almost burst out laughing. The guy really did — he looked like an otter. He was long and slinky and had cool buck teeth. In life, there are cool buck teeth and stupid-looking buck teeth. Otter had *cool* buck teeth. He had his own way of moving, zooping this way and that.

A new record dropped on the jukebox. It was "Shopping for Clothes" by the Coasters. I was once again amazed.

"Are you smiling at my volcano zit?" Otter touched the blemish on his nose self-consciously.

"Oh, no, no. I just — I was listening to the song."

"I'm very sensitive, you know." Otter smiled. And it was an *otter* smile. Exactly what the smile of an actual otter would be, if there were an amused one around, six foot two and having a beer. He met my eyes and, in exact synch with the deep-voiced Coaster on the record, said, "Go ahead, try it on, stand in front of the mirror and *dig* yo'self." I laughed happily. I'd gone to school here a year and didn't know about these guys?

Now in a navy-blazer-over-chest-hair ensemble, Dumptruck returned. He no longer seemed miffed in the slightest. "All right, gimme that beer. In a glass, this time." Looking at me, he confided, "I hate this rush shit." The beer arrived and he threw half of it down.

"Me, too," I said.

"Times like this, I wish I weren't Phi Beta Kappa."

I blinked. "You're Phi Beta Kappa?"

"Do you believe it?" said Otter. "Truck's one of our finest." The others dissolved into hysterical, beer-spitting laughter.

"They're not as demented as they seem," said Dumptruck.

"Sure we are," said Otter.

I tasted my beer. The brothers returned to their conversation. The one identified as Coyote was by himself, though, and I went up to him.

"So, you're the guy with the chicken?"

Coyote did not look as much like a coyote as Otter looked like an otter, but close. There was something feral about him, a sense that at any moment he might pounce on a squirrel and eat it. And somehow Dumptruck was very like a dump truck, and Hydrant like a hydrant. The naming process here was inspired. Back at Pi Lam, Poz and Tor and Bags were just plays on the guys' actual surnames. Here, the names were descriptive. Giraffe really looked like a giraffe. Tall, long neck, sort of slow-moving and herbivorous. Even Snot seemed aptly chosen — not that he looked like a booger, exactly. Who knew what a guy who looked like a booger would look like? It was more a personality thing. The guy had irrepressible energy, was always leaping this way and that. The way snot would, if snot were alive and enthusiastic. This was hard to explain, but true.

"How'd you know about the chicken?" He seemed surprised.

James Brown's "Think" came on. One of the dancers by the jukebox did a 360-degree spin and fell into a split.

"Word gets around. You're famous, man."

"Yeah, sure."

"Where's the other guy? Doberman?"

"Gone. Thrown out of school."

"Really?" I was disappointed. "Because of the chicken?"

"No, no, he was down on the Row last spring. He got really drunk at Kappa Sig, came outside at midnight naked except for some girl's bra and panties, and jumped on the hood of a state trooper's car. And he said to the cop, 'Take me home.'" Coyote's Doberman impression featured an imperious, haughty tone, as a lord to his footman.

"Uh-oh," I said.

"If it had been campus cops, they would have let him sleep it off and everything would have been cool. But these were New Hampshire state troopers. You know, real Waffen-SS. Next thing you knew, they charged him with disturbing the peace, lewd acts, and all sorts of other shit. To keep him out of jail, the school had to expel him."

"What's he doing now?"

"Working on a banana boat."

"What?"

"Why, you look amazed, sophomore. Have you never worked on a banana boat?"

Snot, overhearing, sang, "'Day . . . mayza day . . . mayza day-ay-ay-o.'"

The other guys came right in. "'Daylight come an' we wanna go home.'"

MEL ALLEN and the other baseball announcers used to enjoy saying, "How quickly things can turn around." I marveled at how my emotions had rebounded from wormlike despair to happy excitement. My rush agenda would now be AD, AD, and AD.

On Tuesday night, I met Scotty. He seemed to be the house hipster, wearing cool shades, despite the hour, and a small silver bone on a slender chain around his neck. Scotty gave me my first look upstairs. Here there were living spaces, much like those at Pi Lam, only instead of English Leather the scent was, well, probably it was thousand-year-old socks. Scotty brought me to his room and offered me a cigarette.

"Let's see here." Scotty flipped through a line of LPs on one of his shelves. To my amazement, he nonchalantly pulled out the Atlantic album *Rock 'n' Roll Forever* that had the *old* Atlantic material, on the yellow and black label, from before Alan Freed even got to New York, like the *original* version of "Shake, Rattle, and Roll" by Big Joe Turner, and "Drinking Wine Spodie-Odie" and, yes, "Mama, He Treats Your Daughter Mean." This was another record I'd been after for years — it was the Holy Grail of R & B LPs — but it had been relentlessly out of print. Suddenly, to be in its very presence . . . !

"Where'd you get that album?"

"Bought it when it came out, man."

I was stunned by his nonchalant musical coolness. It had come out in 1953 or something! Who knew about rock 'n' roll in 1953?

"Scotty? That's what they call you? How come you don't have a nickname?"

Small smile. "I transcend nicknames."

We smoked our cigarettes, listening to the Drifters sing "Money Honey." I couldn't tell whether Scotty was looking at me or not; the shades' lenses were absolutely black.

"Hey, you know what? You look like George Shearing." The noted blind pianist never appeared without his dark glasses.

"Thanks, man. Someone else told me that once."

I felt pleased to be one of the two people in Scotty's life who'd detected his Shearingness. "One Mint Julep" by the Clovers came on. We listened, not saying much beyond the small, almost involuntary sounds we made at various moments in the music. Suddenly, an hour had passed.

The door flew open and Snot ran in with a crazed expression, waving an ax. "All sophomores out!" He was referencing the fraternity term for telling rushees that they would not be asked to sink — you "axed" them.

Scotty held the door open. "See you tomorrow, man."

SO FAR, SO GOOD. Being asked to come back didn't guarantee you were in, but it was sure a step in the right direction. You didn't find out if you were in until Friday, the terrible valley of decision known as Sink Night.

Back at the dorm room, Brad was sanguine. He'd been able to sink early at Beta, where he'd been the good fit of the year. They'd taken him upstairs to the president's lavish, trophy-strewn room and told him he was in. I was glad for him. Isaac had narrowed his houses down to two. I hadn't heard of either of them. They were called Zeta Psi and Alpha Chi Rho. I had no idea what went on in those places.

"Do you like the guys?" Brad asked him.

"Yeah. I don't know. I guess so."

"Decisive as always," I noted.

"Well, what are they like?" Brad prodded.

"A lot of guys in sport coats, standing around talking."

"Isaac, that's what rushing *is*. You just described every house on campus."

"Huh. Guess so."

"So go back to the guys you met. You must have some impressions of them." My curiosity was aroused.

Isaac thought for a while. "Well, they were pretty short."

"Isaac, compared to you, everyone's short."

"I was making a joke."

Brad and I exchanged a look. We often missed Isaac's jokes.

"What about you?" Isaac asked me.

"Yeah," said Brad. "You haven't said anything yet."

"Well . . . I went to a whole bunch of houses at first, but now I seem to be just hanging out at AD."

"Are you crazy?" cried Brad. "They kill chickens!"

I laughed, picturing the electrified fowl staggering around the basement. Being familiar with the location made the story more vivid.

Isaac leaned forward. "You should really think about this. They're the worst house on campus. The girls from Colby Junior get *warned* not to go there."

"They're sick," said Brad. "They're an animal house."

"I don't know what to tell you. I met a lot of people I liked. Isaac, I met one of the chicken guys. The other one's working on a banana boat."

"See?" Brad shook his head. "The place is *weird*."

"But, listen, I'm actually comfortable there. As in 'relaxed.' Isaac, are you comfortable at Zeta Rho or whatever it is?"

Isaac hesitated. "Well . . ."

"*I'm* comfortable."

"We knew that, Brad."

"Can we go to sleep now?"

Isaac checked his watch, then looped it around the bedpost. "We're very close. Three, two, one . . ."

The Baker Library bells went through their *ding-dong* cycle and then tolled twelve.

"G'night, you guys."

"Yeah, good night."

A moment passed.

"Don't do anything *weird* down there."

"Eat me, Brad."

ON WEDNESDAY, I registered for classes and bought a great, heavy load of books. Brad put a bullfight poster up in the room.

There were a lot of these around. Isaac spent a good hour waxing his skis.

"It hasn't even snowed yet," I said.

"So?" said Isaac.

At the AD house that night, the crowd was smaller. Around campus, both rushers and rushees were narrowing down their choices. My fellow hopefuls seemed like pretty good guys.

Jeff was a short, peppy guy. Everything made him laugh. His friend was Alby. Alby didn't really look like a guy from Dartmouth. What he looked like was a guy from jail — tough and slightly psychopathic, with piercing Paul Newman eyes. You saw him and thought, *Trouble.* But he was funny! When I came up to them, Alby was telling Jeff how much he enjoyed eating pussy. He said girls kept telling him how good he was, and he'd modestly explained it was because he was a board-certified cunnilinguist.

Ned I knew from my dorm. Very intense guy. About *everything.* He looked at you intensely, spoke intensely, probably took a piss intensely. When he laughed, he laughed intensely, folding over in the middle. He was talking to John. Because John had the same last name as Bags at Pi Lam, he was already being called Bags here, too. Balding at nineteen, with large pate, squinty eyes, and a thick, muscular torso, he looked like a cross between a Piltdown man and a giant baby.

Then there was Carl. Carl had instantly bonded with the AD brother known as Frog, who rode an Indian motorcycle and dressed in greasy biker denims. Carl also rode a bike. He basically looked nuts — a guy who might at any moment do absolutely anything. The house drew guys like him and Alby. There were other rushees as well — Fitch, a movie-star handsome guy I'd seen around; Denny Crane, the big-assed sophomore who lived down the hall from me in Middle Fayerweather; Marty, with his glasses and neatly combed hair; Mike; a few others I didn't know yet. These guys would be my fellow pledges, if I got in. They seemed like fun.

On Thursday night, not finding Torrie Toiletbowl and Fat Fred at the reception table, I went looking for them. I was starting to feel they were friends. Well, Torrie, anyway, with her ebullience and wit. She knew how to make me laugh. With Fat Fred, I was mainly drawn to her tits.

I grabbed Snot as he was zipping by and asked him where the girls were. He made exaggerated sniggerings and pointed. "The library!"

I went to the library, a smallish chamber off the living room with bookshelves and a fireplace. Pushing inside, I froze. Scotty, Torrie, Fat Fred, and Dumptruck were playing strip poker. Scotty's ensemble was underpants and a bra on his head, and Torrie, whose bra it apparently was, wore Dumptruck's socks on her tits. I shrank back.

"Hey, rushee," yelled Scotty. "Come in here and play my hand, will ya? I gotta bleed the weasel."

"But . . ."

Scotty tromped by me, out the door.

Enormously self-conscious, I took Scotty's seat on the floor. I couldn't take my eyes off Torrie's oddly clad orbs, though I tried to pretend I was looking elsewhere.

"Nice socks, eh?" Torrie said. "Argyles, I think."

Ears flaming, I examined Scotty's hand and discovered he was holding three eights. I bet heavily. But when Dumptruck called, Fat Fred took the hand with a full house.

Just then, Scotty returned.

"Hah!" Torrie held up the two hands. "Read 'em and weep, Scottso!"

"What?" Scowling, he took off his underpants, revealing a member the size of a baguette. He looked at me. "All right, you've had it!" Grabbing his schlong, he ran straight at me, as if planning to impale my brain with it through my left eyeball.

"*Yah!*" I leapt to my feet, dodged Scotty, and raced from the room, trailed by peals of laughter.

I HAD ALWAYS LOVED strip poker. Well, I'd always loved the *idea* of strip poker, never having actually played it. I'd had a few beat-off fantasies that involved it, but that was all. The idea was just so incredibly sexy. I sure hoped I'd wind up here at AD. Maybe there'd be *more* strip poker. And more of *everything* — all kinds of steamy, erotic stuff I couldn't yet imagine, that these guys did all the time. But first I had to be invited.

I walked into the house on Sink Night, very worried. What if Scotty and Dumptruck and the rest had just been screwing around all week, and tonight they'd bring out the ax? I tried to put my fears aside.

Torrie and Fat Fred gave me naughty looks and pinned on tonight's name tag. It said BIG JOE TURNER. I thought I detected Scotty's hand in this. "Where is everybody?" I asked.

Fat Fred pointed to the basement stairs.

Tonight, finally, beer was legal during rush, and all over campus rushers and rushees alike were having their first alcohol of the week. At AD, on the other hand, this merely meant a continuation of what had been going on for four days now. Just about everyone was at the bar. The air was dense with cigarette smoke, music, and conversations. I finally saw what the gutter around the basement floor was for — guys were taking leaks in it, lining up as if at that huge urinal in Grand Central Station. The piss, smoke, and sweat combined to make a ripe, male perfume.

Magpie took me aside, handing me a beer. "So how're you feeling about the house?"

It was a really tough choice, given my long list of options. "I feel great about the house."

"I know it's hard to decide. When I was rushing last year, I faced it, too. But AD's the only house on campus where you can really piss on your date." He said it with great enthusiasm, as if this marvelous and unique aspect of the AD house just kept giving him pleasure, year in and year out.

As always when you're having fun, time disappeared. Some of the guys by the tap system — Magpie, Hydrant, and a few others — were playing Alphabet Pirates. It was a game they'd made up. "R!" they said. "I, I, Cap'n." "G!" "O?" They stumped about on peg legs. "A-R-R-R, young 'Arkins." "More rum, Purity." And so the night flew by, a blur of weirdness and music.

A hand fell on my shoulder. Looking around, I saw Zeke Banananose. "Hey, rushee. Come with me."

I headed up the stairs with him. "What's up?"

"We'd like you to see the brothers on the back porch."

So — this was it? They were going to ask me to sink? My heart climbed into my throat.

We arrived at the back door. Zeke Banananose held it open for me, and I went out onto the tiny back porch. The door closed. I turned around. There were no brothers on the back porch. I was alone with the stars and pine trees.

My gut flopped over like a sick seal. *I'd been axed!* Why? What had I done? Ace had been so right — I should never have rushed a fraternity.

Nice the way they did it, too. Fuck you, rushee. I'd never liked that Zeke Banananose guy. He was too loud by half and had cheeks like a pizza. But what happened with Otter and Dumptruck and Scotty? I'd thought they were my new friends. Now I'd never get to jump around excitedly with Snot, or piss in the gutter with Charlie Boing-Boing, or moon people from the balcony with Magpie. I'd never meet Doberman! Shoulders slumped, hands in my pockets, I shuffled back to the dorm.

An hour later, my roommates found me in my bunk, still in my sport coat and shiny black shoes. They were all smiles: Brad was officially a Beta and Isaac had done the unexpected — he'd sunk Pi Lam!

I roused myself a little. "But you . . . you're not . . ."

"They said I had an outcast mentality and that was good enough. Poz and Tor sunk me."

I was amazed. I'd never thought of Isaac as having any particular mentality at all. Sighing, I told them of my rejection at AD. To my surprise, they leapt to my defense.

"You didn't want to be in that house anyway," Brad said. "Fucking chicken killers."

"Maybe I can get you into Pi Lam," suggested Isaac.

"Sure, maybe." I doubted it. Probably my rejection had already been disseminated on some sort of interfraternity grapevine, and all over campus they'd now be talking about me. I was damaged goods.

As we lay in our beds, I wanted only to sleep. Sleep was great that way — unconsciousness beat misery every time. But Brad and Isaac were so jazzed by *their* evenings that they kept talking.

"You okay, man?" Brad asked me after a while.

"I wish I were dead."

"Oh."

That shut them up. I rolled over and jammed my eyes closed so that, as Bo Diddley put it, "sleep could slip up on me." But sleep seemed far away.

CHAPTER SEVEN

The Pinto Is Spotted

HOW LONG, I WONDERED, could a person feel misery of this magnitude before his emotions simply melted down like some errant nuclear plant? Brad and Isaac were snoring now, leaving me alone with my feelings. Which was probably just as well, since who wants to hear about the degree to which some guy hates himself?

Wham! Wham wham wham!

"What the fuck?" Brad sat bolt upright.

Isaac rushed to his dresser and lit a Salem.

Wham wham wham wham wham! Someone was pounding the shit out of our door.

"I don't know who that is," Brad simmered, "but he's gonna wish he wasn't." He stomped from the bedroom, the angry wrestler in his boxer shorts.

I hastened to follow, Isaac bringing up the rear. Brad tore the door open. In burst Dumptruck, Otter, and Scotty in his shades. They were profoundly drunk, falling all over themselves.

"Drop your cocks and grab your socks!" roared Scotty. He looked happily at Otter. "I've always wanted to say that."

"All right, Adelphian Rangers on patrol. Is there a new fucking pledge around here?" Otter peered exaggeratedly around the room.

"Yeah, where the fuck . . . ? Hey, there he is." Rushing behind me, Dumptruck enfolded me in a bear hug. "C'mon, pledge, we're going places!"

I was utterly confused, and Brad and Isaac were too. What was happening did not follow from what had happened before. These guys shouldn't be here — I'd been axed. Two different movies had somehow been spliced together.

"You must be the roommates," said Scotty brightly. "How the fuck are ya?" He strode up to Brad and hugged him warmly. Brad yanked away, repelled.

Otter produced a bugle. Pressing it to his lips, he blew vast quantities of alcohol breath through it, making horrible sounds.

"We're out of here!" Scotty shouted.

"I'm in my pajamas!" I cried.

"What's that, pledge? Is something wrong?" Scotty put his face an inch from mine.

"No, nothing, I'm cool." I smiled broadly to demonstrate the carefree truth of my assertion.

"*Au secours!*" Otter cried gaily, pointing to the door with his bugle.

"No, man, *au secours* means 'help.'" Scotty shook his head long-sufferingly. "I keep telling you. You're trying to say *allons-nous!*"

Otter looked stubborn. "Fuck if I am. I *like* saying *au secours*. Has that hard *c* sound."

"Otter, I used to be into hard *c* sounds too. *K* sounds too. But I graduated to *l*s. *Allons-nous* has a nice *l* sound."

Aquatic mammal eyed small canine with disdain. "*L* sounds are for chicks. Can you imagine a guy named Lilly, for instance?"

"*Could we please get the fuck out of here?*" Dumptruck roared. Still grasping me from behind, he lifted me as if I were paper and began a bowlegged quick-walk for the door. The others, shrugging, fell into place behind us. Like a totally inept military unit, we marched from the room.

My roommates stared after us.

"Guess he's in," I heard Isaac say.

"I'm not sure I like the looks of this," Brad murmured.

• • •

THEY HUSTLED ME DOWN the hill behind the Fayerweathers, then down a farther small hill, detouring around the great stone mausoleum known as the Sphinx — some mysterious secret society for seniors — and onto the AD lawn. I had to know what was going on. Either I'd somehow been sunk after all or they'd decided they hated me enough to kill me.

"Hey, uh, what is this? Have I been sunk or something?"

"Of course you're sunk." Otter regarded me with surprise. "Zeke Banananose didn't tell you?"

"He sent me out to see the brothers on the back porch. Only, uh, no one showed up but me."

"What?" cried Scotty. "That asshole!"

"Got him mixed up with that guy Denny Crane, didn't he?" Otter said. "Now I understand. He sank Denny and bounced you. What a fuckhead!"

"Somewhat inebriated, I expect," said Scotty.

"Anyway, I guess now we're stuck with both of you."

I looked at him uncertainly. Otter gave me the grin.

"So . . . I'm in?"

"Sure, man." Scotty socked me in the arm. "Any fan of Big Joe Turner is a worthwhile —" He stopped, struck by a thought. "Hey! You got any Clovers records?"

"Sure. 'Lovey Dovey,' 'Blue Velvet,' 'Little Mama,' 'Hey Miss Fannie' . . ."

"*What is the fucking matter with you guys?*" screamed Dumptruck. "*Don't you want to drink?*"

"Patience, big fella," Otter counseled.

"This is great!" I was full of happiness. "Really, you guys — thank you."

"Don't thank us yet, pledge." Scotty laughed dangerously. "First, you have to get through the *terrible AD pledge period.*" He cupped his hands around his mouth to say it with an echo.

"And the Fires," said Dumptruck casually.

"The Fires. What's the Fires?"

They laughed merrily.

"You'll see," said Scotty. "But tonight's for fun, so 'Come on, baby, let the good times roll,'" he sang, in a fair impression of Shirley and Lee. Well, of Lee, actually.

The action was still in the basement. The jukebox was blaring the Isley Brothers' "Shout," which competed for aural dominance with the spirited whooping of happily drunk young guys. I spotted Alby, Jeff, Ned, and several other sophomores I'd seen rushing here.

"Happy Sink Night, pledge!" Charlie Boing-Boing wove up to me and booted on my foot.

My jaw dropped. My foot had never been booted on before. This was new territory.

"Tisk," said Otter. "Such unpleasantness. One grows faint." He took my elbow and brought me to the bar. "Cold frosty for the new pledge!"

Ten cold frosties later, my pajamas soaked, a pledge pin glistening on my chest and a warm fraternal glow suffusing me, I felt that I'd never been happier. That bit about not knowing where I belonged? Maybe this was the place. Otter was dancing to some Chuck Berry record, his head bobbing to the beat, forward and back, forward and back — an extremely otterlike mannerism. Snot was again by the tap system, laboring to serve the clamoring masses. Carl was in a belching contest with Coyote. It was as if they were attacking each other with static. Alby and Jeff were cheering them on, raising their fists high, hooting like strange, fucked-up birds. Oh, boy, was this great! It was the way life was meant to be lived, high on music, alcohol, and friendship, as continuously as possible.

Someone pulled the plug on the jukebox. Voices were raised in protest but quieted as four AD brothers stood together in the U of the bar and sang what was apparently a house song. It was slow and lovely, in four-part harmony. I strained to make out the words:

> I love my girl, yes I do, yes I do,
> I love her truly,
> I love her ruby red lips,
> And her lily white tits,
> And the hair around her asshole

I'd eat her shit
Chomp chomp chomp chomp
If she asked me to.

I found myself having an easier time with the song's sweet glee-club voicings than its memorable lyrics. I guess I wasn't quite ready for the hair around women's assholes. It was bad enough they had assholes. The song reached its second verse, but I realized I'd have to miss it — my need to whiz, which I'd been trying to ignore, had become overwhelming. Not comfortable yet with just whipping it out and going in the gutter, I joined the mob in front of the little bathroom and finally made it inside.

Here, the urine odor — a mere accent in the bar — was vastly more concentrated. There was urine on the floor, urine on the toilet seat, urine in the sink. Maybe this was why it was called Sink Night. Well, who was I to stand aloof? Whipping it out, I began to pee. On the walls and ceiling had been carved a hundred nicknames, of brothers both recent and stretching into the misty, mythic past. Flea. Oblamov. Black Mike. T-Bear. Once again, I mused that Adelphian nicknames reflected some kind of formidable group genius — they'd been so incredibly *right* for all the guys I'd met. I asked Otter what my nickname would be. As far as I knew, no pledge had gotten one yet.

"Takes time, man," Otter advised me. "Gotta get to know you first."

I hated having to wait. Once I had a name, I could carve it in the ceiling, right up there between *Monk* and *Gland*. Oops, piss splashing on the floor. I redirected my stream. So that was the explanation for the stench in here — people kept reading the walls and whizzing all over the place.

Wham! The door flew open. It was . . . Terry No-Come, if memory served.

"Hey," Terry said. Shouldering up to me, he took out his meat and commenced a serious urination in the sink. "Ahhhhh," he said.

We whizzed, side by side, me a little self-consciously. After a while, Terry opened his eyes. Glancing idly at my dick, he did a take.

"Whoa! What's the *story*, pledge?"

I sighed. I'd been through this interrogation a thousand times but had yet to feel comfortable with it. What Terry saw was that the skin of my dick was two different colors. To wit, flesh-colored and brown, mingling softly like camouflage.

"Uh . . . well, I was swimming at this beach and there were these rafts with tar on them. It went through my bathing suit and got on my dick, and when my father cleaned it off with turpentine, I, uh, had a whole new look."

Terry became excited and inspired. "Umm . . . Two-Tone! No, too obvious. Marblecake? Not quite. Pinto! That's it! Fuckin' A! All right, pledge, from now on you're Pinto."

"Pinto?" It didn't sound like much next to Black Whit or Mag F. Pie.

"C'mon!" Terry yanked me out of the bathroom. "Hey!" he called to the room. "Check this out!"

A crowd gathered around them. I had just put my dick away. Was I supposed to take it out again?

"Drop trou," Terry whispered.

Worse yet. Did I really have to do this? I supposed I did.

"Undertrou, too," ordered Terry impatiently.

"Okay, okay."

"Whooooa," said the crowd. "Damn! Holy shit!" They stared at my unit as if it were some strange new insect.

Hydrant stroked his chin. "Vanilla Fudge?"

"No." Terry was calm as could be. "He's Pinto. I've named him and it's final."

The brothers looked at one another. "Pinto," said Otter, trying it on for size. He smiled the Otter smile. "Bitchin'," he said.

A roar of approval went up. *"Pin-to, Pin-to, Pin-to!"*

I liked it. Not flamboyant or mythic, but cool, because it was a private joke shared only by me and my fraternity brothers. From now on, for better or worse, I was Pinto.

But who was Pinto? I wondered.

CHAPTER EIGHT

Nine Ways to Excite Your Date with a Garden Hoe

WILLY MACHINE OPENED HIS MOUTH to start the annual pledge orientation lecture, and then closed it again as the door rammed open and Alby rushed into the living room, twenty minutes late for the Wednesday-night house meeting.

"God, am I sorry, Brother Machine! You won't fucking believe what just happened! Somebody robbed the liquor store on Main, right while I was actually in it, and by the time the cops —"

Mouse, employing his wide-flung, pinkly translucent ears, had heard enough. "Put a sock in it, sophomore! You don't come late to major pledge meetings like this. Better shape up or you're gonna be sorry. Especially on . . ." He glanced at the other brothers in the room.

"The night of the seven fires," they chanted in spooky unison.

The pledges exchanged nervous looks. They had no idea what the Fires was — just that it was the famous, scary AD hell night, and *they* had to go through it. They kept asking for particulars, but the brothers wouldn't talk. Otter did offhandedly mention something about "Stalingrad with kegs." This did wonders for the pledges' peace of mind.

Allegedly, every Dartmouth AD since butter churns had gone through the Fires. Even avuncular old Al Dickerson, the dean of freshmen, was supposed to have gone through them when he'd been an Adelphian in the twenties. Of course, he'd been in a coma for a year afterward, Scotty informed them, but, hey, small price to pay. The pledges nodded with frozen smiles.

The entire membership, forty guys strong, had shown up for the house meeting tonight and there wasn't a seat to be found. Alby shrugged and threw himself down on a sofa already holding Bags, Pinto, and Rhesus Monkey. The three reacted in surprise, alertly holding their beers away. Happily, not a drop of precious amber fluid was lost.

"Alby, get the fuck off me," growled Bags. The squished three were doing their best to show no emotion, concern, or even surprise. They were learning the zeitgeist here. It was perfectly normal for some 190-pound guy to suddenly land on you out of nowhere. Happened all the time. You had to take things with equanimity.

Alby made a grab for Bags's beer. "Yog. Gimme that." Bags avoided the grab and immediately chugged what was left, triumphantly crying, "Ha!"

Bags was now Yog, too — short for Yogi Bear, the cartoon character. Not that Yog was particularly like Yogi Bear. In fact, he was nothing like Yogi Bear. Yogi Bear was not a scowling, patrician troll with browridges. But the inspiration for Yogi Bear had been Yogi Berra, Pinto's all-time baseball hero, to whom Bags bore a vague resemblance, so he liked Yogi. Recently, someone had offered yet another possibility: Centaur. It might have been the most inspired of all — you could see Yog with hooves — but as a late entry, it didn't get far. Indeed, the consensus had by now solidified around Bags. To the best of anyone's knowledge, no rule forbade there being two Dartmouth Bagses at the same time. Pinto thought it was fine, too. It was hard to explain, but Bags looked like a Bags.

"*Goddamnit, will everyone shut the fuck up?*" Mouse glared from pledge to pledge.

Willy Machine continued to stand patiently facing them. He was preternaturally calm, imperturbable as a Buddha. As the pledges quieted down, he began. "Alpha Delta Phi began in 1832 at Hamilton College in Clinton, New York."

Charlie Boing-Boing threw his drained beer glass into the fireplace, where it shattered pleasingly. "Remember this shit," he told the pledges. "There'll be a test."

"The guy who founded AD was a student there," Willy continued. "He started it as a literary society and later it turned into a fraternity. His name was Samuel Eells. No, Alby, I'm not shitting you. Now, from what I've read on Samuel Eells, he mainly seems to have been sick all the time. He had pneumonia, consumption, and, well, whatever the fuck else they had in those days. I don't know how much fun he would have been to drink a keg with, but you know, everyone in this room owes ol' Sam a debt. Without him, no us."

It took a moment for this to work its way through the part of Pinto's brain that figured out what the fuck people were talking about. But, yeah, seemed right.

Charlie Boing-Boing took the floor. "Now, what they did in this literary society was write things — you know, essays and poems and shit — and then read them to each other."

"'Kin' A." Mouse spat in the breast pocket of his shirt.

Charlie looked at him oddly and went on. "We current ADs feel a deep bond with our brothers of yesteryear. Yes, they may sound like a bunch of simps, but now that I've gotten to know you guys a little, I'm sure they'd think you were assholes, too."

Pinto blinked. The brothers thought they were assholes? Or was this name-calling merely part of hazing ritual, as traditional and stylized as Kabuki? Who knew? Maybe they *were* assholes.

"Anyway, because of our deep respect for these dipshits, and in keeping with our literary traditions, each of you will write a paper and read it to the brotherhood."

The pledges groaned.

"It has to be at least a thousand words, and don't think you can just write drivel, either. You're gonna get graded, and if you fuck up, we do terrible things to you."

"Oh, sure," said Alby. "Like what?"

"Well, like last year we made a guy clean the gutter with his tongue."

Alby's face drained of color.

Charlie Boing-Boing tugged a list from his shirt pocket. "Okay, here are your topics. Huck Doody, we'll start with you." This had quickly become Ned's nickname, for who could deny that he looked at once like Howdy Doody and Huckleberry Finn?

"The title of your paper is 'Sniffing Mommy's Panties.'"

"What?" Huck leapt to his feet and went into a stunned crouch. The other pledges exchanged uneasy looks. They'd expected the standard stuff —"My Personal Commitment to the Alpha Delta Phi" or something.

"I'm not writing that!" Huck declared.

"Sure you are. Pinto."

"Here."

"'Three Ways to Bite Off a Girl's Nipple, and Five Good Uses for It Thereafter.'"

Pinto found himself speechless. But at times like this you were supposed to be cool. "Ah . . . you know, I'm going to use this opportunity to try to really say something meaningful." That drew a few snickers from the brothers.

"Rhesus Monkey."

"Hey!" Huck Doody said. "Didn't you hear me? I'm not writing about my mother's panties! What, you think I went through her dresser drawers?"

"You could go through Fat Fred's purse," Scotty offered. "I think she keeps an extra pair in there."

"Fat Fred appears to have a fine bouquet," contributed Dumptruck.

"Shut up," said Scotty.

"So what's the problem, Huck?" said Charlie Boing-Boing in overly solicitous tones. "You want a new topic?"

"Fuck, yes."

Boing-Boing and Mouse stared at him awhile. Someone coughed. A plane went by overhead.

"Stirrin' up the weather again, mistah," said Rhesus Monkey. This bit of wisdom came from an Adelphian janitor, septuagenarian emmet Al Clark, who believed jet planes were having an adverse effect on local meteorological conditions.

Charlie turned to Willy Machine. "Do we have something else for Huck?"

Brother Machine consulted the master list and looked up. "Why, yes. How about 'Finger Painting with Your Own Shit'?"

"Okay, Huck?"

Huck opened his mouth.

"They'll keep getting worse," Mouse warned.

Huck slumped. "Okay, as long as my mother's not in it. I *hate* writing about my mother." He glared at the seniors.

"I'm glad we could address your concern, pledge Doody." Charlie Boing-Boing took the list of topics from Willy Machine. "Next — Rhesus Monkey."

At the bar a few nights ago, Snot had decided Jeff looked like a monkey. Pinto could see it — he was small, limber, and quick, and his features had a certain simian cast. Of course, he could also squinch his eyes and look like Charlie Chan, but a brother from the class of '58 already had that name. Furthermore, Snot insisted that he didn't mean just any monkey, but, specifically, a *rhesus* monkey. Everyone knew rhesus monkeys; their strange little faces had been all over the newspapers and TV for years, due to their use as test animals in polio research.

"Okay, you get . . . 'Using Afterbirth in a Waldorf Salad.'"

"You know, it's amazing," said Rhesus Monkey. "I must have a dozen recipes."

"Next, Y. Bear."

Pinto couldn't believe it. Bags was now Y. Bear, too? He had more names than God.

"Yog, your paper is 'My Sensations at Birth.'"

The process went on, everyone getting their topic. Pinto's mind wandered. He was blowing off serious homework to come here tonight. In the three weeks since he'd joined the house, his fraternal activities had been devouring his study time like Henry VIII gobbling a plump capon. He envisioned himself in a political cartoon, walking a Road of Life, with happy-go-lucky ADs waving James Brown records on one side, and boring schmucks in suits on the other. The boring schmucks were labeled SECURITY.

Normally, Pinto didn't think much about the future. He was a real in-the-moment guy. But, as the essay topics droned on, he tried looking ahead a little. He had a life coming up — what should he do with it? What, for him, truly mattered? He'd long and passionately believed that if people had more fun, a new and better world would emerge that would do away with war and poverty. He knew it sounded silly and sophomoric, but he truly believed that if people would just unclench a little more often and enjoy themselves, stop taking everything so seriously, a lot of the world's problems would blow off like fog.

It was working in corporations that messed people up, he felt. Yes, this assertion was very Ace Kendall, but Ace was right about some things, and corporate robots was one of them. Pinto wasn't going to be the man in the gray flannel suit — no way. But he didn't feel drawn to the folk songs and getting-to-know-Negroes crowd, either. He had nothing *against* getting to know Negroes; he just didn't want to make an official goal of it. So how could he make a living outside the corporate culture, spreading fun? He meant *real* fun, too, not the safe, plastic shit people on *Father Knows Best* did. He meant drunk as shit and knee-deep in pussy! Okay, true, he hadn't *been* knee-deep in pussy yet, but he had a great imagination. He became decisive — henceforth, he would dedicate his life to the pursuit of fun and pleasure. For the good of all mankind, of course.

And if this were to be his destiny — to become Johnny Happyseed, wandering the byways of life, tossing fun this way and that from a burlap shoulder bag — where should he go to learn the ropes, one of those airless, chair-filled rooms in Dartmouth Hall, where the clock never ticked, or here at the AD bar? Pinto was wide-eyed and wonder-struck with AD: the amazing characters, the flood of new friends. It was just too cool not to be down here every night. He knew he should take his classes more seriously, but his classes were horrible, boring and soul-crushing. How could Money and Banking, Advanced Calculus, and Government 21: Delaying Civil Rights Legislation help him with his goal of jollying up the world? Yet these were the courses upon which his father had insisted. JC Senior felt that, in life, you could be a doctor, a lawyer, or a businessman.

All other careers were suspect, possibly of communist or homosexual origin. So he thoughtfully guided Pinto to course choices that would prepare him for all three. But how was, say, today's lecture on the check-processing system of the Federal Reserve Board going to stand up to the sparkling conversations about tits at the AD bar? The place was a nightly workshop in spontaneity and nonlinear thinking, albeit adding little to your college transcript.

His hippest course was French 4, thanks to the teacher. Pierre Astier was extremely cool in the soulful Gallic manner. He had them reading *The Fall* by Albert Camus, using it as a jumping-off point for extended meditations on, oh, the intractability of fate, the meaninglessness of existence, and all the other cheerful stuff existentialists went on about. Pinto dug the concept that actions were all that mattered, that they alone defined us. He felt a wild, romantic yearning to fight with the Loyalists in the Spanish civil war, who had, unfortunately, been defeated twenty-two years earlier.

In the evenings, you sometimes saw Mr. Astier with his trench coat and a Gauloise, leaning against the lamppost before the bookstore, observing the passing scene. With his tilted fedora, he was the most soulful, Humphrey Bogart–like guy around. The way he smoked was *better* than Bogart. Did Frenchmen have some special gene? The way the smoke drifted from his mouth and nose into moody curlicues during his unhurried, world-weary exhalations fascinated Pinto, who felt he couldn't be that cool in a thousand years.

A big laugh brought him back to the room. Carl's topic had just been named, and Pinto had missed it.

"And, finally, Goosey Gander." Boing-Boing smiled. "We saved this one for you, Goosey." They'd hung this name on Denny Crane earlier today. It was his long neck, which gawked and swayed, that had inspired the sobriquet. Denny wasn't crazy about it, but what had he expected? Falcon? Barracuda? He was lucky he wasn't called Pube Hair.

"Goosey, you have the honor of composing 'Nine Ways to Excite Your Date with a Garden Hoe,'" said Charlie Boing-Boing cheerfully, as if handing him a swell gift.

Goosey's mouth fell open. Him write that? He couldn't think of *one* way to excite a date with a garden hoe. Had he made a mistake pledging AD? So often he felt like the odd man out here. Well, maybe normal man out.

"All right, pledges," announced Snot. "Next on the agenda, the world-famous Alpha Delta Phi statue!" Making cowboy whoops and whistles, Charlie Boing-Boing, Snot, and Mouse herded them over to the little nook at the foot of the stairs, the rest of the membership falling into place behind them. There, on a scuffed and stained wooden pedestal, stood a heavily tarnished bronze statue, about two feet high. It portrayed a pair of World War I soldiers, the less wounded one helping the really fucked-up one clump forward against all odds. The two doughboys, Snot divulged, represented the United States and Canada, and the solidarity between the Adelphian chapters of the two countries. They were known as Vic and Harry, and the formal name of the statue was *The Brothers*.

"Too much, daddy-o," murmured Scotty.

Pinto gave him a curious look.

"I was being ironic," said Scotty.

The statue might have been one of the great Alpha Delta Phi traditions, on prominent display in all twenty-four chapters, but Pinto couldn't work up much enthusiasm for it. Who wanted to look at two wounded, bleeding guys every time you went for a beer? People put cigarettes out on it — it was *ugly,* man. But there was a curious thing about it. The more ambulatory soldier wore an actual AD pledge pin on his uniform, right there on his chest amidst the blood and trench schmutz. The pin and the area immediately around it were brightly polished — you could easily make out the AD star and crescent on the pin's gleaming surface. The rest of the statue probably hadn't seen metal cleaner since the Coolidge administration, but the pin shone like a star.

There was a reason. Every time a pledge entered the house, he had to *call in*. That way, if a brother needed shit work done, he'd know the free labor had arrived. So what you had to do, Willy Machine said, was go straight to the base of the stairs and loudly announce your presence, all the while vigorously rubbing the soldier's pledge pin. That's what had made it gleam — a thousand Adelphian thumbs.

"All right, gentlemen, downstairs for boot training!" yelled Mouse.

The pledges wailed in protest. Again? They'd done boot training twice already!

"Hey, we just want you to be ready for the Fires. This is for your own good, guys," Dumptruck assured them.

With a profound lack of enthusiasm, the pledges shuffled downstairs.

The first boot practice had been held shortly after Sink Night. Magpie was this year's boot coach, and had immediately introduced them to a stunning new concept — recreational vomiting. The pledges had exchanged uneasy looks. Boot on purpose? Because you *wanted* to? It was an Adelphian tradition, 'Pie explained. Once you conquer the basic horror of regurgitation we all start with, he said, it becomes fun! Whole new dimensions of play and athletic endeavor open up for you!

Yeah, right, thought the seventeen pledges.

Life-size pictures of Dorothy Kilgallen and Arlene Francis — annoying television personalities noted for their nonpulchritude — were hung over a portion of the gutter. Mouse paced ten feet from the wall and drew a yellow chalk line on the floor. You stood at the line and chugged until you booted. The goal, Magpie said, was learning to power boot. Power boots were the home runs of throwing up. A good power boot, in this case, would fly smartly from the mouth, travel the ten feet, and strike Arlene and Dot with a healthy *splat.*

The pledges were busy pretending they weren't scared. Even Alby and Bags were suspiciously quiet. Seventeen minds were thinking, *Wow, this sure is sick! Can I actually do this? If I want to be an AD, do I have a choice?* The answer, of course, was no — though it was but one daub on the larger AD sickness palette, booting was a must. "Pledge AD. Boot AD," as Snot put it.

Somehow, they all hung in. Each of them made his peace, more or less, with booting on demand. And they did try hard, but they couldn't hit the targets because they couldn't get any distance. They tried and tried until finally some of them had to go pass out on the mattresses, but all they produced were *spit boots* and *dribble boots,* as the brothers identified them. *Women* did spit boots and dribble boots, they added. Meanwhile, Arlene and Dot stood there, unbesmirched. The problem, Magpie thought, was the pledges' inexperience. *Power boot* was just an abstraction to them. He tore up the stairs.

"I don't want to do this anymore," whispered Goosey Gander. "Couldn't we just collect money for orphans or something?"

Pinto knew what he meant. But no whining for him. He was going for an A in booting. Or, in Dartmouth talk, he wanted to ace it.

Magpie returned, followed by Dumptruck and Zeke Banananose.

"All right, pledges, pay attention. Truck and Bananascrotum here are gonna show you how it's done."

Truck and Bananascrotum stepped without noticeable dread to the chalk line. Indeed, they were like cocky, big-league pitchers taking the mound. Hydrant handed each a huge, freshly drawn mug of beer, full to the top, foam running down the sides. As the pledges watched in awe, each junior poured the entire contents of his mug down his throat! Just poured this incredible amount of beer directly down their gullets, never having to swallow! Were they cool, or freaks of nature? Well, both, Pinto supposed.

The pledges now witnessed their first power boots. Almost simultaneously, Dumptruck and Zeke opened their mouths and brought forth great, golden arcs of beer and foam that would have traveled twice ten feet, had not the happiness girls gotten in the way. Truck and Zeke slapped palms twice, as if they were Miles and 'Trane approving of each other's solos. "See you guys later," they called, heading back up the stairs. If they were the worse for wear, they didn't show it.

"All right?" said Magpie. "You see?"

The pledges could only nod.

Pinto, credulous naïf of his generation, may have been the only pledge to believe Magpie's declarations. Clearly, if Magpie said so, booting *could* be enjoyed; you just had to do it right. It would be like learning to swim — some coughing and choking at first, perhaps, but in the long run a wonderful hobby. And you could do it anywhere! Learning how, that was the tough part. He did, that night, unleash one power boot, sort of by accident, that eclipsed Arlene Francis's lower face and won a round of pleased snaps from the brothers. Encouraged, he kept plugging away. But finding booting fun was no piece of cake.

As the class proceeded, the basement filled with rank puke odors, intense enough that if someone had delivered a pizza, he would have died. Magpie, of course, had known it would be like this when he volunteered to be boot coach. Sometimes you had to do shit for the greater good, though. Tonight, he actually felt encouraged. Bags and Alby were starting to hit the targets. Fitch and Round were showing improvement. Even Huck Doody was catching on.

After each boot practice, two pledges were selected to clean up. The coda, Scotty called it. Tonight, the lucky pair was Pinto and Rhesus Monkey. In an act of unaccustomed charity, Magpie let them wait until morning. Always good news when you're going to pass out any second. In the morning, though, the boys learned a lesson — when your boot classroom marinates for twelve hours, the smell gets worse! Horribly, unimaginably worse! Nobody had opened a window or the back door. It was like walking into a sick person's stomach. They tried to avert their noses, but there was nowhere to avert them to.

"This is kind of World War One," Pinto muttered.

"Mustard gas at the Marne," said Rhesus Monkey. "I'm hip."

They went to the mop closet and took out hose and squeegees. There was a standard way of cleaning up on such occasions — you stood at one end of the basement and, with the nozzle set on high, blasted the floor-crud across the room, sweeping it with waves of water and the squeegees into the gutter. Soon, the gutter was abrim with boot soup. Then you had to hose the gutter itself until everything went down the big drain at the end of the bar and was lost to mortal man.

At last, they finished. After hosing each other's nude selves down, they put on the fresh clothes they'd brought and went upstairs.

Great gales of laughter were coming from the tube room. Curious, Pinto and Rhesus Monkey checked in. They found a dozen brothers high-spiritedly marching around the room, over tables and sofas, to the theme music of the *Rocky and Bullwinkle* show. They were playing invisible instruments, Snot doing an energetic trombone. It was the Sunday Morning Bullwinkle Club, and the enthusiastic members were like carefree leprechauns romping in a pumpkin patch.

Pinto had never encountered a cartoon character as lovable as Bullwinkle Moose. Forever cheerful, delivering surreal dialogue in his cool, goofy voice, the moose seemed eternally without restraints, capable of doing absolutely anything at any moment. No wonder the ADs liked him.

Rocket J. Squirrel had a charm of his own, often reminding Pinto of Snot. Snot, like Rocky, was small, peppy, and unflaggingly cheerful. Actually, lots of ADs were like cartoon characters. They didn't just walk up the stairs; they darted merrily up them. They didn't laugh; they chortled with glee. There probably wasn't a single AD who didn't wish he could go up on one foot and, with a cloud of dust and the sound of a bullet ricocheting, get from point A to point B in nothing flat. How cool would that be? So, limited only by the laws of physics, they came as close as they could to the moves of Bugs, Daffy, and the Road Runner, as well as Bullwinkle, Boris Badenov, and Dudley Do-Right. What cartoon characters and AD brothers most had in common, Pinto thought, was their exuberance. He pictured Wile E. Coyote and Elmer Fudd, smashed, chatting amiably while whizzing into the gutter.

OCTOBER BEGAN; around campus leaves exploded with color, while the ones on the ground smelled spicy when you stepped on them. They sure knew how to throw an autumn here. Inevitably, along came the Yankees in the World Series. Pinto had been a fan forever. Some sort of deal had apparently been struck with them for his soul, back in the misty recesses of his childhood. The circumstances were now obscure, but evidently it was for life — his happiness was inextricably tied to the fortunes of his team. Happily for him, they almost always won.

So far, some series! AD's baseball fiends — Scotty, Alby, and Hardbar — were saying it might be the best ever. Of course, they were drunk. But then, so was everyone else, had been all week. World Series games were played in the afternoon in those days, and it was necessary to start drinking early. Today's keg had gone on tap at 9:30 a.m. Well, today's *first* keg.

The 1960 World Series was special not because it was perfect, sparkling baseball, but because of its utter wildness and improbability. The Yanks had won, 16–3, 10–0, and 12–0. It was the most incredible offensive display ever seen in a Fall Classic. You couldn't keep up with the records being broken. Never had one team so dominated another. Except, weirdly, *only in three of the games!* The rest were won by the Pirates with normal, workaday scores of 6–4, 3–2, and 5–2. Who could explain? And so, the season had "come down to a single game," as Yankee announcer Phil Rizzuto, in his excitement, wouldn't stop saying. And hence, here was Pinto in the jam-packed AD tube room on a Thursday afternoon, burning with baseball fever, holding a giant sixteen-ounce cup of Budweiser like a security blanket.

Horrible, toxic tobacco smoke enwreathed them. Zippo lighters kept clinking closed. Pledges strode in and out with trays of fresh beers, distributing them to the thirsty brothers. The air was rent by partisan shouting. Strictly speaking, there were no Pirate fans there — only Yankee lovers and Yankee haters. It was impossible to say who was louder. Like the series, it seesawed back and forth.

Alby apparently decided it would be fun to sit next to Pinto and shout excitedly in his ear every time the Pirates did something. And he had plenty of opportunity as, through the first half of the game, the Pirates scored four times while the Yankees managed a single, measly run. Pinto was distraught. Alby was more jaunty and smug by the minute. And then, out of nowhere, Mickey Mantle knocked in a run! And then Yogi Berra — *Yogi Berra!* — smashed a three-run homer. Pinto gloated at Alby, who feigned interest in the head on his beer. The Yankees, at last, had the lead.

You couldn't hear yourself think — the noise was as loud as a motorboat in a phone booth. By the bottom of the eighth, the Yanks were ahead 7–4, and Pinto had relaxed. A three-run lead with Shantz in relief? No sweat. He noticed Alby shifting around a lot next to him.

"Getting worried, are you?"

"Worried? There's a spring up my ass!" The absurd green sofa on which they sat had apparently, at some stage in its career, been thrown off Mount Everest.

Then, tragedy. Bottom of the eighth; man on; a Pirate grounded to Tony Kubek. As Tony reached for the ball, it took a bad hop! Hit him in the throat! Knocked him to the ground, where he lay writhing in pain! *And now, instead of a certain double play, the Yanks had Pirates on first and second with no outs.*

Alby, to his credit, did not give Pinto the unmitigated shit he expected. But around the room, brothers were reacting according to their preferences, screaming like buyers at a commodities market. Dumptruck, a stalwart Yankees man, was eye to eye with Zeke Banananose, who hated them — spittle flew between their faces. Snot looked ready to reach up and punch Giraffe in the stomach. Scotty and Hydrant didn't care who won and bellowed random obscenities just to make a contribution.

"Cocksucker!" Scotty yelled. "Ass! Blow job!"

"Motherfucking son of a bitch!" cried Hydrant. "Nipple!"

By the time the Yanks got the Pirates out, they'd scored five runs. Pinto was like an orphan whose new toy has just been snatched away by the sadistic lesbian attendant. The Pirates led 9–7 going into the ninth.

The room was in sports nirvana. No one could believe this game.

"Two runs mean nothing!" Magpie yelled. "These are the Yankees."

"Eat my potato shit!" countered Bags.

And then, the Yanks tied it up! RBIs by Mantle and Berra! Perfect!

Guys were hoarse, limp. Pinto was close to burnout. Being a baseball fan in October was *hard,* man.

And then, the bottom of the ninth was played. If an asteroid had crashed into the Earth vaporizing India, he couldn't have felt worse. Bill Mazeroski came up. The guy was a good-fielding second baseman with a lifetime batting average of around .250. He should have grounded to short. But no. *Bam!* Home run. Game over. Season over. As Pirate fans flooded the field, Pinto descended into sadness. For the first time anyone could remember, Phil Rizzuto didn't utter a sound. Possibly, he had run off to boot. The most exciting homer in World Series history, and it had to be at Pinto's expense!

The room was going wild. A hundred glasses seemed to shatter in the fireplace. The Yankee haters jumped up and down until the place shook. If someone had been using the sex room, directly below, he would have lost his hard-on.

Alby gave Pinto a sympathetic look. "Look at it this way, man. The Yanks set new records in hits, runs, and RBIs. Whatever World Series hitting marks exist, they broke. In the future, they'll say the Pirates won by accident. Come on, man, the Yankees were great!"

"Yeah," said Pinto. "I guess they were. Thanks, Alby."

"Sure, man." He snuck a look at Pinto. *"Your team lost, you fucking loser! Loser, loser, Pinto is a loser!"* He danced in delighted circles around him, crowing at the top of his voice.

Pinto grabbed him. "Alby, we're getting the fuck out of here. I'm buying you dinner at the Green Lantern." It was almost a plea.

Alby considered. "How about the Hanover Inn?"

"That's fucking expensive, man!"

"Hey, Pinto, what kind of assholes blow the World Series while breaking every offensive record known to man? Huh? Huh?"

"Okay! Stop! Hanover Inn! But we gotta go now!" It was like being trapped in a pen of hysterical cattle on diet pills. "Go! Move!"

They grabbed sport coats from their rooms. Al's had an armpit rip.

"So what?" he said combatively.

In the crowded, white-linened Hanover Inn dining room, they disappeared in a sea of patrician alumni and professors in ties. Alby, with great gusto, consumed a rib eye steak with béarnaise sauce that cost Pinto twenty dollars. Pinto ruefully ordered a chicken salad sandwich. Alby demanded a beer, too, but they carded him. "Fucking New Hampshire," he complained. "Why isn't this New York so we could drink?"

The dinner actually wasn't bad. Pinto enjoyed himself, and the entire time they were there, not a person belched, bellowed, or booted.

It was *weird*.

THE ADELPHIAN NICKNAME machine continued to spew forth monikers, but so far, no one had come up with a good one for Marty. Bivalve was suggested and Pinto thought the name funny. However, as it was merely clever with no discernible connection either to Marty's appearance or personality, it did not gain footing.

Pinto liked hanging out with him. You had to get past first impressions, though. He looked like the solemn little boy at Sunday school, with black-rimmed glasses, neatly buttoned shirt, and perfect, prissy haircut. He also gave an impression of great intelligence; you would have chosen him for your academic decathlon in a second. In fact, Marty *was* very smart, but also painfully shy and insecure, inclined to believe himself the least worthy person in the room. It was hard even getting him to talk.

When he was sober.

But a fascinating transformation would occur as the night wore on and successive beers were consumed. It wasn't Mr. Hyde that came out, exactly. More like Jack Lemmon on the fourth day of a beer binge. That is, Marty magically became friendly, funny, confident, outgoing, witty, and weirder than shit. Alcohol, it seemed, brought forth his inner hot-shit.

One Saturday night, as Pinto and Marty were at the bar, Pinto thought he heard a crackling sound. What? But then it went away.

They talked a while longer. Then there was the sound again. Crackling. What the fuck *was* it? This time, an acrid odor accompanied it. Marty was on the other side of the bar top, wearing an innocent expression. Pinto bent over to look.

Marty was burning his bush.

His pants were around his ankles and his shirt was pulled up. His pubic hair was in flames! Pinto looked at Marty in amazement. Marty smirked, running the flat of his hand over the little blaze, putting it out. Pinto could find no words. Realizing his mouth was open, he closed it.

Still with the little smirk, Marty did it again. Lighting his Zippo, he brought it to his bush, which again blazed up. *Crackle, crackle, crackle!* Again the sweep of the hand and the fire was out. He was able to do this so quickly that little of his bush was actually consumed, allowing him to pull the trick repeatedly.

Pinto burst out laughing. He knew he was supposed to be cool, but he just couldn't help it.

"Hey! Yo! Check this out!" Pinto pointed both index fingers at Marty's dong.

People came over. Fat Fred was down that night, as were Whit and Pam. Soon, a small crowd surrounded Pinto and the bush burner, wondering what was up. Marty noticed that Pam and Fat Fred were discreetly checking out his joint. He preened, tightening his butt muscles so it stuck out more. Thinking, *Cool, this is the male version of what high heels do to pussy.*

Pam wolf whistled. Fat Fred gazed with apparent approval, although you never really knew with her.

"Come on, Marty!" Pinto urged. "Show 'em!"

The small smile returned. The Zippo flashed, the bush flared up.

"Ohhhhhhhh," said the crowd, as if viewing a particularly gorgeous firework.

At that moment, Dumptruck entered the basement. He'd been booking and was completely sober. "Jesus Christ!" he roared upon seeing the fire. Racing to a pitcher of beer, he hurled the contents into Marty's crotch.

"Yah!" cried Marty. *"You son of a bitch, that's freezing!"*

Hisssssssssssssss . . . Vile smoke rose. The brothers laughed and laughed.

Terry No-Come, he who had invented Pinto's name, was at the

non-jukebox end of the bar. Though he had eschewed the mob, he had not missed Marty's pyrotechnics. He stroked his chin . . . and smiled.

"Moses! His name's Moses!"

There was a singular lack of dispute. A roar went up from the two dozen guys and the pair of chicks, as well.

"Moses, Moses, Moses . . . !"

Magpie turned to Snot. Remembering the origin of Pinto's name, he said, "What is this — the year of the dick nicknames?"

"The year of the dicknames!" corrected Snot, raising his glass in pleased acknowledgment of his own razor wit.

MOSES'S RISE TO LEGEND status occurred soon after. Autumn was in its bare-trees-in-the-moonlight phase, and on a dark Halloween night Moses joined the basement crowd around nine thirty with a jack-o'-lantern he'd found somewhere. He set it on the bar, where Pinto appreciated its jolly, flickering company. Jack-o'-lanterns were fun.

Beer followed beer. Bo Diddley and Jerome quarreled on the jukebox. Goosey Gander passed out early. After a while, so did Fitch and Zeke Banananose.

By beer number nine, the "real Moses" had appeared. He bent over to examine the jacko. Using his fingers to stretch his mouth wide open, he tried to return its huge carved smile. He looked like a dental exhibit. When he removed his fingers, his lips plurped back to normal. He thought a moment. Then he tossed away the pumpkin's little hat and the candle. Next, he put a fist through the pumpkin's bottom. Grabbing a steak knife from someone's encrusted dinner dish, he sliced through the pumpkin's rear.

Assessing his handiwork, he nodded with approval. Then he stripped. By this time, Moses's hairy ass was not exactly new to anyone, but his flying underpants did draw some attention, and a growing crowd watched as he pried the pumpkin open. Grinning at them, he wrapped the jacko around his waist, as if it were a bath towel. A strange new nose emerged.

Nothing matches the laughter of pure delight. Clearly, this was the best jack-o'-lantern ever seen. People cheered and whistled. Moses made the Hard Core on the spot.

Pinto wasn't sure who had the idea first, but suddenly everyone was yelling it at once. Marty *had* to go trick-or-treating.

Whooping and making Little Richard screams, fifteen ADs thundered up the basement stairs and out the back door, where they stood blinking a moment at the real world. Stars, pines, all that Dartmouth beauty. And before them stood the handsome home of the neighboring fraternity Chi Phi. The ADs got along well enough with them, and guys from the two houses would sometimes drink at one another's bars. But they were sort of straight, seldom eating their underwear or sticking their dicks into girls' ears. They said they saw no point in doing these things, and for that the ADs felt they were like the benighted European sovereigns who'd seen no point in bankrolling Columbus.

While the ADs hid behind bushes and pine trees, trying to stifle their laughter, Moses marched up to the big front door and slammed his fist on it. After a pause, an irritated Chi Phi brother looked out.

"Trick or treat!" Moses cried merrily.

The guy's gaze lowered and his jaw dropped. "Jesus Christ, man, get out of here! Dean Seymour just . . ."

Indeed, he had just walked in, having been invited there that night by the Chi Phi brothers — *with his wife* — for a decorous, kiss-ass dinner, including candles and linen napkins and everything. With cries of dismay, the ADs grabbed Moses and got him out of there before the dean could turn and catch him red-handed, or red-dicked, to be scrupulously accurate.

Having dodged the expulsion bullet by a razor-thin margin, the brothers figured Moses might want to call it a night. But, no, he declared he hadn't even gotten started yet, this was a great thing to do, and besides, he really wanted the candy.

"Hey, man, we're talking about townies." Hydrant had a worried look. "You could get in trouble."

"So fucking what, man?" Moses wielded his beer pitcher with carefree abandon. "You think anyone'll have Hershey's Kisses?"

"But they could put you on pro," Otter said.

"Pro? Me? *Pfagh!*"

Otter made the otter grin and chuckled. "This young pledge thinks he has it all figured out. Tell you what, Moses — I'll bet you ten bucks you wind up in the cell at the cop shop." This was where the campus cops hung out, a small, unpretentious structure in the shadow of the Giant Smokestack.

"You're on!" Moses pulled his pumpkin up and looked around at the crowd. "Well, here I go. Who's with me?"

Silence.

Moses couldn't believe it. "*No* one's coming?"

Alby cleared his throat. "Important song I'm waiting for on the jukebox."

"Gotta book," said Hydrant.

"It's too cold out here." Magpie's pointy chin drew minuscule lines in the air as his teeth chattered. "I'm going the fuck in."

"Sissies." Moses, in pumpkin, socks, and glasses, started off, giving them a glimpse of his ass through the rear pumpkin flaps.

"I wonder where he plans to put the candy," said Alby.

IN THE MORNING, the townspeople of Hanover were in an uproar. A dozen of them had been paid a visit the previous night from some naked guy in a pumpkin. They were all for Halloween, but this was going too far — it was one of those damned college kids again. In a couple of cases, children had even answered the door and encountered Moses at dick level. The campus cops were looking for him, and the town cops, too.

When three days passed without a break in the case, the Hanover municipal fund even offered a small reward. The police interviewed all the victims a second time and the victims patiently looked at pictures of every guy currently attending Dartmouth. They shrugged. No one could remember his face.

CHAPTER NINE

There Were Giants
in Those Days

AT NINE P.M. EXACTLY, on a Tuesday night in mid-November, with a raw north wind whistling across the Hanover Plain and most Dartmouth men ensconced in their vaguely warm rooms, booking for midterms, Pinto decided that going down to the AD house would beat the shit out of wrestling any longer with the incomprehensibility of the prime rate. Accordingly, he flipped his Money and Banking textbook closed, placed his Winstons in his pocket, shrugged into his B-9 air force parka, and headed for the door.

"Uh-oh!" Brad crowed. "There he goes again."

"All work and no play," called Pinto musically.

"Yeah, well, more like almost all play and hardly any work, in your case."

"It's just for a couple of beers." Pinto was gone before Brad could say more.

"Couple of dozen is more like it." Brad winked at Isaac, who made no reply.

OUTSIDE, THE WIND was like a spray of freezing needles in the face. Hastening down the hill, Pinto ran into Huck Doody, headed in the same direction.

"I really shouldn't be going to the house tonight," he grumbled. "I should be booking."

"Yeah, me too, I guess."

"I probably won't stay long."

"Okay."

"I never planned on joining a fraternity, anyway, and this is exactly why."

"So why *are* you going to the house, then?"

A maniacal smile spread across Huck's face. "Because I wouldn't miss a minute of this wonderful shit!"

AD stood brightly against the night, lights in every window. Throwing the door open, the boys went in. The living room was deserted but for Fitch's cat, who was batting an empty Trojans box across the floor, then leaping on it like a fearless predator. The boys crossed to the AD statue and began calling in. Placing his thumb on the soldier's shiny pledge pin, Huck threw his head back and bellowed, *"Most unworthy neophyte, Huck Doody, from Rochester, New York, begs to announce his most humble presence at Alpha Delta Phi!"*

Down the stairs galloped Mouse, his face a mask of fury. "Anh!" he cried. "Anh! Anh!" This little cry was ubiquitous around the AD house. It could mean many things. Black Whit would use it as an expression of delight. But more often there was a negative connotation. In this case, Mouse was clearly appalled.

"What are you doing?" he screamed at Huck, racing back and forth, making little jumps.

"Uh . . ." Huck was taken aback.

"You don't know your own name?" Mouse shrieked incredulously.

Huck did not like being yelled at. This was wearing thin. "What the fuck are you talking about?"

"It's *Huckleberry* Doody, you douche bag!"

"Oh, for Christ's sake!"

"Do it again!"

"What?"

"Do it the fuck again!"

Huck's teeth ground. "Most unworthy neo—"

"*Yell it!*"

"*Most unworthy neophyte, Huckleberry Doody, begs to announce his most unworthy presence at Alpha Delta Phi!*"

Mouse's eyes bugged out, so vexed was he. "You asshole! You fucking asshole!"

"Now what?" Huck's fists were balling and unballing.

"You didn't rub the badge!"

Huck's lips drew back in a snarl, but he went to the statue and rubbed the badge. "*Most unworthy neophyte, Huckleberry Doody, begs to announce his most unworthy presence at Alpha Delta Phi!*" He glared at Mouse, daring him to have a problem, any problem at all.

Unlike Huck, Pinto didn't let this stuff bother him. It wasn't abuse; it was tradition. He began rubbing the badge. "*Most unworthy neophyte —*"

"Oh, shut up, Pinto. Come on, let's go drink."

The boys shrugged and followed Mouse down the stairs, emerging into the noise and blaze and glory of the AD basement. The jukebox was closed for renovations — someone had thrown a keg at it — but the radio was on, and Ray Charles was singing "Night Time Is the Right Time."

"Asshole pledges!" called Hydrant from the clump of guys at the bar.

"You shitheads!" barked Dumptruck.

"Fuck!" yelled Zeke Banananose vaguely.

The shouts were pro forma harassment, nothing to worry about. The two pledges went with Mouse to the bar. Also among the drinkers was the junior known as Hardbar, whom Pinto hadn't gotten to know yet, and several sophomores, including Alby, Rat, and Round.

"Fucking pledges," Alby greeted Huck and Pinto cheerfully.

Dumptruck slapped the back of his head. "You're not allowed to say that. Behave yourself, neophyte."

"You better look out after I've had fourteen beers," Alby warned.

Truck was not too worried. "Hey, Pinto and Huck. Chips to me."

So it was Truck who had supported the keg. They each gave him a dollar. Pinto got a beer and went to stand with Round. One of Pinto's new pals, the jolly sophomore was round as can be, shaped like one of the gnomes in the Oz books. If he'd had three holes in his ass instead of one, you could have rolled a strike with him.

"What's happening?" said Pinto.

"Good timing, man. Tanzi just dropped the keg off." Dartmouth fraternity guys for generations had bought their kegs from Tanzi's, the ramshackle grocery on Main.

Pinto waved a hand. "Hey, 'Drant! Beer?"

Cigarette clamped in his mouth, Hydrant took a glass from the formation on the towel and drew Pinto one. "Here you go, my man!"

It tasted great, so he drained it and wiped the foam from his mouth.

"Hey, Pinto." Rat, on the far side of the bar, checked in.

"Hey." Rat's hair was short as a marine's, his belly hung over his belt, and he wore Dumptruck-type glasses, big with black rims. He'd gotten his name last week. The Adelphian naming thing had worked again — he resembled a big, bloated water rat, creeping out of some Amsterdam canal, dripping with stuff you didn't want to know about.

Round, looking natty with a food-encrusted fork worn through his lapel like a boutonniere, smiled blearily at Pinto. He'd evidently consumed immoderate quantities of tonight's malt offering, Narragansett. This was a thin and nasty New England beer whose sole virtue was its price. Still, it did the job, and Round was three winds to the sheet. Throwing a friendly arm around Pinto, he spoke with deeply felt *in beero veritas:* It was *killing* him not to be a member of the Hard Core. The guys who gained membership in the Adelphian psycho elite, Round felt, were the samurai of the beer world, and he should be among them.

"I think the problem is, you haven't done anything to stand out," Pinto said. "Neither have I. Fuck, I want to be in the Hard Core, too. There must be something we can do to get noticed."

The bar clamor swelled as Scotty and Fat Fred came in. She was wearing a fluffy, fat sweater, loud green in hue, that in no way de-emphasized the heft of her wazooms, which rumbled about pleasantly beneath the mohair.

"Hey!" Pinto yelled to Scotty, pointing at the radio. "All Ray Charles!"

"Outstanding!" Big grin.

Pinto returned to Round. "Okay, what about this? We moon the governor of New Hampshire. We could lie in wait for him in Manchester, or wherever the fuck he is."

First, of course, they'd have to learn that gentleman's name. It was a rare Dartmouth man who could have told you the name of the governor of New Hampshire, or knew diddly-squat about what passed for politics there. The school was like an American base in a Third World country.

Round pushed up his glasses. "Good idea, Pinto. Very practical."

Ray Charles was singing "I'm Movin' On," and Scotty and Fred were dancing with enthusiasm, Fed's ba-boos bobbing and weaving like Sugar Ray Robinson. Hydrant refilled beers. And now Pinto got to check out Hardbar, AD's famous masturbator.

Hardbar, Pinto had heard, beat off more than anyone who'd ever lived. He was sort of good-looking, but also scrawny and pale, resembling perhaps Montgomery Clift recovering from a terrible beating. Tonight, he was excited about a new scheme. It seemed that he utilized, well, accessories. Skin mags, sure, but D. H. Lawrence and Henry Miller, too; he was gourmand and gourmet at the same time. He also had a variety of personally produced tapes of sexy music, and even a furry glove he pulled out on special occasions. He revered whatever was erotic but insisted it live up to his high standards. Women's breasts, he often opined, should be meaty and full.

On the bar next to him was the Wollensak tape recorder he'd brought. Pinto, who made mixed tapes of his favorite tunes, had worked with them. They were nicely designed and metallic-looking, very German and efficient. And they had pause switches. The plan was to set it up in the sex room, and then be able, with the touch of a finger, to start it recording some guy's lay. He planned to station the microphone three quarters of the way down, to pick up the actual *squirsh squirsh squirsh* sounds. The tape would be a great new vector for his frequent gratify-Pepé sessions, he believed.

"Hey, 'Bar, I think now's the time." Dumptruck nodded at Scotty and Fat Fred, who had supplanted dancing with norgling, a Dartmouth term that implied hot making out with lots of tongue down the throat. They stood center-floor, his hands cupping, nay, clutching her posterior, as she gave him fingertip tingles on the back of his head. Surely, the beast with two backs would be next.

Hardbar vaulted the bar with the Wollensak and made for the sex room. Shortly thereafter, he came out, whistling innocently. But Fat Fred had noticed. "Don't set it up on our account," she called out. "I'm having 'my friend.'"

The wind left Hardbar's sails. Slouching like a question mark, he returned to the bar and took a desultory hit of beer.

Rapid clumping from the stairway presaged the entry of Fitch. Everybody liked Fitch. Another of the pledges, he was a buff, good-looking guy with a great smile gleaming out of a ski-tanned face. Pinto always enjoyed his company. But it was the damnedest thing about Fitch — he was accident-prone. Really, truly accident-prone. If someone entered the house by kicking the door open, Fitch would be on the other side. If you were putting on your coat, his face would magically float to the exact spot where your fist came out of your sleeve. He bought a lot of first aid supplies.

On this occasion, he emerged from the stairwell with hands swathed in bandages. *Uh-oh*, Pinto thought. Fitch shouldered through the growing crowd, hands held high, and requested a beer, which he had to drink pressing the glass between the bandages and wincing a lot. Nonetheless, he downed the beer and got another.

"So what happened to your hands?" Hydrant asked.

"Well, I was driving back from Skidmore." Fitch had a girlfriend there. "I'm coming back on Route 4, I'm almost home, and I get a flat. *Flubba-flubba-flubba,*" he added, helpfully re-creating the sound the tire made as he pulled over. "I get out and jack the car up but all of a sudden it starts to wobble."

Uh-oh, Pinto thought again. The guys at the bar exchanged wary looks.

"I saw it was about to fall, and so I, well, I just did what anyone would have done."

"What was that, Charlie?"

"I caught it."

No one spoke for a moment.

"You *caught* it?" said Huck.

"You caught the *car?*" said Pinto.

"Yeah." He chuckled self-deprecatingly. "Seemed like the thing to do at the time."

"Charlie?" Alby said.

"Yeah?"

"Anyone *wouldn't* have done that. Only *you* would have done that. *Are you fucking crazy?*"

Fitch wanted a cigarette, but of course his hands wouldn't fit in his pockets. He smiled gratefully as Hydrant put a lit one between his lips.

"Do they hurt?" Pinto asked, looking at his great white mittens.

"Actually, they gave me Darvon." He smiled blissfully. "No pain, Pinto. Hey, say that ten times fast: No pain, Pinto. No pain, Pinto. No pint, piano. Oh, wait —"

He had them laughing again. Their horror at his brushes with death always gave way to merriment, which in turn seemed to increase everyone's thirst. There was something about a brush with death that would do that to you, even just hearing about it. Hydrant had fresh beers waiting. Pinto marveled at how smoothly he performed the Adelphian tapping ritual, with what skill he set the glass before you filled just so, with a precise half inch of head.

Scotty and Fat Fred were now seated on the bar facing inward, their feet hanging over one of its inner thighs, as Otter called them. Hey, where was Otter anyway? Pinto loved it when lots of ADs hung out here at the same time, each contributing his flavor to the stew. He wanted to keep up with all the conversations at once, not miss a single laugh.

"Hey!" called Scotty sharply. "Listen to this!"

The chatter died and you could hear an announcer on the radio.

". . . From the State Hospital for the Criminally Insane in Mathis, New Hampshire. There is an all-points bulletin . . ."

A dangerous, homicidal nut had escaped and was now leading all the cops in a five-county area on a wild chase along winding two-lane roads. No one spoke for a moment. Then Scotty said that since he considered *himself* a dangerous, homicidal nut, he was going to drink a toast to the fucking guy, and who'd like to join him? A mutter of assent went up. One and all raised their glasses high. Twelve columns of foamy yellow disappeared down twelve slick throats as Ray Charles returned and burst out with "Yes, Indeed."

"You know, speaking of cops," said Coyote, who seemed to have sidled in from somewhere, "did you guys ever hear about the Man and the campus cop?"

The pledges shook their heads. This could be good. The Man was Ronn Remington. Yes, with that extra *n*. He'd been an AD senior last year, or maybe it was two years ago — it was hard keeping track of these guys. He was, by all accounts, rich, handsome, and athletic, with women hanging off him like monkeys. He would play soft jazz on the living room piano at faculty 'tails parties, and abruptly go into some Christmas carol as if played by Jerry Lee Lewis. And, of course, he had famously shot the chicken.

"So one night," Coyote began, "the Man was in his room — the one at the top of the stairs that Scotty and Hydrant have now — with Tatiana. She was this rich chick who went to Vassar. Six feet tall. Beautiful but scary.

"So they're in Man's bed, okay? Of course, the college would throw him out in a second if they even caught him with her on the second floor. Girl on the second floor of a fraternity? Out of school, ipso facto — that's the way they think. But there the Man and Tatiana are, naked as shit. The house is quiet; everyone's at a basketball game. They're doing the horizontal watusi when the Man hears the door open downstairs. He goes out in the hall and looks over the banister. It's a campus fucking cop."

The pledges listened, wide-eyed.

"There's no time to get dressed. There's not even time to *explain.*

And, meanwhile, the cop is coming up the stairs . . . and all of a sudden the Man bursts out of his room with a six-foot-tall naked woman over his shoulder, and as he runs down the stairs, he knocks the cop cold! And he's out the door. Still nude, but that's okay — they finish up in the hearse."

The pledges looked at him in shock.

"You mean . . . he hit a *cop?*" This was outside the realm of Pinto's experience.

"It was a short right, pledge. Knocked him cold." Dumptruck shook his head. "The cop almost brought legal action against us."

"Yeah, yeah, but the Man won," said Scotty. "If the cop had gotten a decent look at him, he'd have been out. Not graduate from Dartmouth for the sin of *getting laid?*" Scotty drew himself up in outrage. "How dare they run that on us? We pay their fucking salaries!"

"Now, Scotty." Dumptruck gave him a fresh beer. "Be at peace."

Scotty gave him a look. "Fucking bleeding heart."

"Fascist stooge."

They clinked and mutually chugged.

Alby was hopping from one foot to the other. "Hey, my back teeth are floating! Finish the fucking story. What happened with the Man?"

"Oh, right. Well, nothing! He got his diploma and made a lot of dough in mining. Guess it was worth it, slugging that cop." Coyote grinned ferally.

Pinto's eyes were starry, hearing about the "ooooold ADs," as the brothers referred to their forebears. He loved these tales of a fabled, earlier time when the AD house was at some kind of crazed behavioral zenith and outrageous Adelphians strode the earth like depraved gods, doing whatever they felt like, and the good times never stopped. "The Man," they called the guy. As if he were a template for all other men, the model you had to live up to.

"Hey, I got a story for you." It was Magpie, newly arrived in his 1962 numeral sweater. Pinto enjoyed watching the handsome junior talk. (Or "tawk," actually —'Pie had a strong Long Island accent.) Which he sure could do. He got his nickname while jabbering on and on during a card game. "Jesus Christ, John, you chatter like a magpie!" Downey had cried in exasperation.

"This story's about Cuntwolf," he said.

"There was a guy named *Cuntwolf?*"

"Oh, yes, pledge Pinto. He was a 'fifty-eight. Fine fellow, but he had some funny habits. Ate dog food, for one thing."

Pinto, Round, and Huck exchanged looks.

"Anyway," said 'Pie, "Cuntwolf's walking by the Hanover Inn one day and the bus from White River Junction comes in. The driver goes inside for a cup of coffee. Cuntwolf sizes up the situation, shrugs, and steals the bus. He puts on the driver's cap, yells out, 'Lebanon, New Hampshire, next,' and off he goes."

"Wait a minute," said Alby. "There were *people* in the bus?"

"Oh, yeah. Like, ten of them. So Cuntwolf drives them to Lebanon, parks by the town square, and walks away. He hitchhikes back to the house."

"Jesus Christ!" cried Huck Doody with his usual intensity. "People must have gone batshit!"

"You know, they didn't. I think everyone — the school, the bus line, the passengers — felt so, you know, *stupid* about the whole thing, they just kept it quiet."

"But . . . he *kidnapped* people." Pinto couldn't believe any of this.

"You'd be surprised," Scotty said, "at how things work here. The school and the town have sort of an understanding. Boys will be boys, right?"

"Hey, Hydrant. You want to fill me up?" Pinto stuck his glass in 'Drant's direction.

"For fuck's sake, pledge, don't you ever draw your own beer?"

Pinto cast his eyes down. "I don't do it right. I make too big a head and it runs down my hand."

"All right, come on in here." Hydrant lifted the hinged section of the bar and beckoned.

Pinto felt a leap of excitement. To be allowed *inside?* Into the inner U of the bar, where the tap system was? Cool!

The tap system was the house pride and joy — a gleaming,

stainless-steel *assemblage* treated with near reverence by many of the brothers. The lower part was a refrigerator that held two half-kegs, one on tap and the other in reserve. Above were two taps, worked with colorful plastic toggles. One read SCHAEFER BEER, the other said ASK THE MAN FOR BALLANTINE.

Most ADs preferred Schaefer. Budweiser was next best, and then Ballantine. If you wanted something you could both drink and use to clear a clogged drain, you went with Narragansett. A quarter-keg of beer — enough for two dozen guys to have a fine evening — could cost you from $7.50 for 'Gansett to $12 for Bud. Later, Tanzi's would collect the empties in their pickup truck. For more important occasions, you ordered a half.

"Okay, Pinto, look. The whole secret is — tilt the glass!" He took one of their standard eight-ounce glasses, flipped the tap on, and brought the glass up under it at a tilt. The beer ran in, and as it approached the top Hydrant leveled the glass and shut off the tap. Perfection — nearly full with a half inch of foam.

"Now you try it."

Pinto was nervous. He had a tendency to klutz things up at key moments, like his high school graduation when he shook the diploma and tried to leave the stage with the principal's left hand. He took a glass, tilted it beneath one of the taps, and brought the toggle forward. Lovely golden fluid flowed. He did what Hydrant had, leveling off the glass at the last minute. To his amazement, he had tapped a perfect beer, and on the first try!

Hydrant was cool. "Good work, pledge Pinto."

"Unhhhhhh!" yelled Ray Charles.

"Unhhhhhh!" the Raelettes replied. Pinto loved the Raelettes. Their voices made his spine tingle.

"So I did okay, huh?"

"You did. In fact, I'm entrusting *you* with the bar!"

"What?"

Hydrant vaulted out, rammed through the crowd, and started dancing with Scotty and Fat Fred. Pinto stared after him.

"Pledge, gimme a beer!" Coyote held out his glass.

"Come on, come on," complained Magpie, holding his out, too.

"Hey, what the fuck's the delay?" yelled Zeke Banananose.

Pinto sighed and began filling glasses.

Huck Doody looked at Coyote. "How did we *get* this way?"

"Well, pledge, when two people love each other very much and get married, the X and Y chromosomes . . ."

"No, man — the AD house. The sickness thing. Twenty-three houses here don't eat their underwear. And then there's us."

"Good question, pledge. Well, it started with the class of 'fifty-six. They began as freshmen here in 'fifty-three, so they were the first class with a lot of vets from the Korean War. By the mid-fifties, this house in particular was full of ex-marines and shit."

Truck nodded. "Yeah, and they'd been in a *war*, right? They're over twenty-one and they've been out there fucking and killing and eating dogs. When they got here, what were they going to do, turn back into nice, middle-class college boys?"

"Fuck, no!" spake Rat blearily. He was a dependable blitherer.

Coyote gave him a bland look. "That's correct, pledge Rat. In fact, they were the wildest bunch of guys Dartmouth ever saw. You know, with those tattoos: 'When I die, I'm going to heaven — I've spent my time in hell.' And those silk jackets, big *Korea* on the back, with a fire-breathing dragon."

Pinto had seen a few of those. Some of the Roslyn hoods' big brothers had brought them back. Bright contrasting colors, totally cool.

"So they got the ball rolling. There were probably a dozen in all — the first Hard Core — but the ones you keep hearing about are T-Bear, Black Mike, and the first Rat — Rat Battles."

"Rat Battles could power piss," reminisced Mouse. "One day, we were having a smooth faculty 'tails party and Rat drank nineteen glasses of punch and power pissed twenty feet into the fireplace. It was horrible! Oh, did I mention there was a fire in there at the time? This bank of piss-steam rolled out."

"*Agggggghhhhhhh!*" cried several in the audience.

Mouse sighed. "No one's grades improved that day."

"So what's the story with this guy Doberman?" asked Pinto. "Is he really on a banana boat? Is he ever coming back?"

Great whoopings and yellings from Rat, Zeke, and Fitch, who were playing football with a watermelon, made it hard to hear.

"Doberman's all-time, man," said Magpie. "Remember Princeton?"

"Not likely to forget." Coyote smiled fondly.

"What'd he do? What'd he do?" Alby was impatient when a good story was at hand.

Magpie laughed. "He gets this power wheelchair. It just has a little motor, so he replaces it with one from a motorcycle. We put it in the hearse and bring it with us to the Dartmouth-Princeton game."

"We wrap bandages around his head and put a blanket around him . . ." Coyote began.

"But wait." Pinto needed more background. "What kind of guy is he? What's his favorite music? What's he look like?"

"Oh, he's a big happy guy, kind of a slob."

Huck Doody registered surprise. "No shit? I thought he'd be kinda lean and mean."

Coyote laughed. "Huck, his nickname doesn't come from Doberman, the dog. It's that character in 'Sergeant Bilko.' Doberman! The dumb, lovable slob!"

"Hey!" said Alby. "What happened with the fucking wheelchair?"

"Okay. So Coyote and Otter are pushing Dobes around in the wheelchair. It's great — the crowds part like the Red Sea for them. They actually wind up on the field. Otter and Coyote act like they belong there and wheel Dobes right near the Princeton bench. Dobes is trying to look mentally deranged — not all that big a stretch — while Otter and Coyote are his responsible, caring buddies who selflessly wipe his drool, happy they brought him to this special game. Actually, the poor guy had been going to *play* for Princeton, they confide to a cop who comes over, having been a major star in high school, but then got paralyzed in a terrible motorcycle crash."

"Get out," said Huck. "They went for that?"

"Are you shitting me? They *loved* it. The people there would have done anything for Doberman. So there they are, the three ADs, watching the game from the sidelines, right next to the players, the coaches, and the guy dressed up as the Princeton Tiger."

"Pretty soon it's halftime," said Magpie. "Out comes the Princeton marching band. They start doing all this John Philip Sousa shit and, you know, making these images you can see from the stands of American flags and eagles and so forth. That's when Doberman turns on the motor."

Coyote cracked up. "The chair peels out like a drag racer. He's on the forty-yard line. He's heading straight for the band."

"Otter starts yelling, 'My God, help! He's comatose, he's comatose!' And Dobes, in the chair, is doing *this*." Dumptruck rolled his eyes up so only the whites showed and let his mouth sag like the mouths of zombies in movies.

"The band's in the middle of 'The Wolverine March' when the bass drum guy notices Doberman is coming. *Hey,* he yells at the other guys. *Look!*

"But they can't hear him. And then — *wham!* — Dobes hits the clarinet section going thirty-five miles an hour. Scatters them left and right. Then he hits the trombone section and they go over backward and hit the drummers, and the drummers go over! It's the domino theory!"

"I was watching from the stands," said Magpie. "The whole Thanksgiving turkey formation just vanished like a TV picture fading out."

"And then the pièce de résistance," said Dumptruck. "The wheelchair's still zooming around, the band's in chaos, cops are closing in — Doberman's trying to get away but the wheelchair hits a tuba. The wheelchair stops but he doesn't. He lands, does a forward roll, and comes up throwing his arms wide. The blanket falls off — and he's naked!"

Moses, Pinto, and Round, standing side by side, looked like a Three Stooges joke as all their mouths fell open at once. Public nudity was somewhat rare in American life at that time.

"What happened then?" Alby demanded.

"Dobes is doing a broken field run, trying to evade the cops. They finally tackle him on the twenty-yard line. The crowd leaps up and applauds. Dobes takes a bow before the cops drag him away."

Ka-tunk ka-tunk ka-tunk. The unmistakable footfalls of Y. Bear sounded from the stair, his usual sequence of double jumps on stumpy legs, an aural ID as reliable as fingerprints. He was arguing with someone.

"Of course they do!"

"You're telling me that the same label beer tastes different in different places?"

"Of course! Everyone knows that."

Out came Bags and Moses. "How can it taste different? Schaefer beer is Schaefer beer."

"Ah-ha! No! Because everywhere they make it, the water's different!"

Moses was stunned. "You're saying . . . *water* makes beers taste different?"

Bags, having already sufficiently specified this, disdained a reply.

"But how can *water* taste different? It's all H-two-O, right?"

"Moses, you moron . . ."

The brothers at the bar spoke up. "Fucking pledges!" "Sophomore assholes!" "Stupid neophytes!" With the brief ritual over, the guys turned back to their beers, and the sophomore assholes joined them. Bags, popular among the brothers, received many greetings.

"Hey, Yog." "Hey, Bags." "What's up, Y. Bear?"

A stogie stuck from his mouth, and he wore, as usual, a day or two's growth of beard. He seemed to be mining the Broderick Crawford mystique. "What the fuck are you waiting for, Pinto? Cold frosty for me and the Bushman here." Throwing a friendly headlock on Moses, he dragged him to the bar.

Pinto hopped to it, and shortly handed each a beer. Moses was looking at Bags reproachfully, combing his hair back into place with his fingers. Give him another five or six of these, Pinto thought, and his hair would look like the Bride of Frankenstein's.

And then, from the corner of his eye, he saw Fitch's latest accident occur, right from the top, as if in slow motion. Rat threw a drunken pass with the watermelon and *ka-splat!* Fitch slid on the slime and suddenly was doing that back-and-forth thing with his body, that last, desperate attempt to find balance.

"*Yah!*"

Slam!

Everyone turned to look. Fitch was down in the beer puddles and cigarette butts. "My back!" He was performing a strange circle dance, hands on his back, legs driving him round and round.

There was a group sigh. Again?

Pinto panicked and grabbed Bags by the shirtfront. "We're all totally drunk here," he cried. "Tell us what to do!"

"Drink more?"

"But we have to do something!"

"Pinto, leave me alone. I'm drunker than you are."

"Oh." Pinto let Bags go.

"Yahhhhh!" cried Fitch.

"I guess Pinto's right." Truck sighed. "All right, let's get him to Dick's House."

The college infirmary had gotten its name when some guy named Dick in the class of '27 died of polio, and his parents built the place and named it for him. As an AD, you wound up seeing a lot of it.

"Hey, Rat, help me put him in the hearse and we'll drive him over." Zeke Banananose went to Fitch, gesturing for Rat to help him.

"Is that a good idea?" Pinto whispered to Scotty. "They're pretty drunk."

Scotty looked thoughtful. "Could be interesting."

Zeke took the shoulders and Rat the ankles. Zeke counted down from three — some were surprised he could do this — and they lifted Fitch.

"Aaaaaaagh!"

Bags went up to him. "Everything okay?"

Fitch opened an eye. "I was playing for sympathy. I need a beer."

One was brought at once. Zeke and Rat paused so Fitch could lift his head and quaff it. "Thanks," he said, out of breath. Moses got the back door for them.

"All right, you guys!" Rat shouted. "We'll be right back. Don't finish that keg!"

"Are you sure we should be letting them do this?" Pinto asked Scotty.

"Not at all."

"But —"

"Pinto, think of it this way. Fitch gets hurt a lot but he always survives. As for Zeke and Rat, if they got hurt, who'd give a shit?"

Pinto looked at him dubiously. But Scotty and the others here had to have dealt with emergencies before. Trusting drunken morons like Zeke and Rat to take a wounded brother to the infirmary must have been an okay, even time-tested method. Pinto was very trusting.

Moses closed the door after them.

"So — what was Flounder like?" Pinto had been reading the bathroom walls again.

Dumptruck pondered. "Class of 'sixty. Big guy — he could do a great Charles Laughton. His father owned half of Wyoming and was rich as shit."

"Funny," said Pinto. "I was picturing this sort of hapless yet lovable fat guy who was always getting in trouble."

Magpie laughed. "That's not *our* Flounder. He was fat, but big, impressive fat, you know? Like Winston Churchill. Actually, he could do Winston Churchill, too."

Ray Charles was singing that incredible live version of "A Fool for You" from the *Live at Newport* album. The piano chords were like black church music. Hey, maybe one of Ace Kendall's churches, where he was meeting all those great black people! Wouldn't it be a pisser if Ace wound up seeing Ray Charles? Wait, that train of thought made no sense at all. How many beers had he had?

Speaking of Ace, he'd written to him at Grinnell a few times, and finally gotten a letter back. Actually, a poem, the thrust of which was that Pinto was an asshole for joining a fraternity, and that he — Ace — would have no more time for him. Fucking guy — Mr. Tolerance had none for his friend.

Pinto started to get angry, but then imagined Ace somehow wandering in here and witnessing Dumptruck and Zeke Banananose demonstrate the art of power booting, the look of utter incomprehension that would be on his face, and he cracked up. But why was Ace being like this? Pinto tried to ignore his hurt feelings. Figuring,

Fuck him, I've got lots of friends now. But the hurt feelings did not dutifully go away.

Crackle-crackle-crackle.

Pinto sniffed the air. "Moses, knock it off."

Moses looked at him with concern. "There's not much left. It's like a forest fire went through it."

Alby whistled piercingly. "Yo, listen up!" He pointed at the radio.

". . . At speeds in excess of ninety miles an hour! The driver, now identified as Leroy Glutch, seventeen, was incarcerated last year for rape and unnatural acts with . . ."

"Hey, did you guys hear?" said Round. "He's headed this way."

It felt a little weird. What had been just a radio story was threatening to invade their lives.

"Well, fuck this mortality shit, right?" said Pinto with great jollity. "Come on, you guys — cheer up!" He offered them fresh beers but was ignored. The plight of Leroy Glutch seemed to resonate for the ADs, and there was a sense of doom in the basement. But then things took a turn for the better as Troll and Donna Daley came in. Troll was a tall, fun-loving guy, looking festive in his brown Russian greatcoat and red scarf. Pinto didn't know him too well, but liked him. And Donna . . . Donna was red-cheeked and delicious in her shiny blue ski parka that matched her eyes. She was so *cute!* Pinto wasn't crazy about that word, but in this case it was inescapable — she was small, animated, pretty, and built. She was a third-year student at the Mary Hitchcock School of Nursing, and Pinto had a major crush on her.

Hardbar exited the bathroom. He did a double take at Troll and Donna, and dashed into the sex room.

Pinto brought them beers. He loved it when girls were in the house. Something changed in the social dynamic then. The ADs certainly did not tone down their behavior — they even seemed spurred to greater heights of sick creativity — but it was a classier, more elegant sickness somehow.

The AD bar was quite special, although Pinto wouldn't fully know that until it was gone, replaced by a standard issue one in '62.

What made it special was its U shape. A sociologist could perhaps have drawn diagrams of the conversations that were made possible. There were people on one side, on the other side, and in the middle. On a good night, the talk was three-dimensional, enriched by overlap. This is how it was now. Eighteen guys plus Fred and the divine Donna, elbows on the bar, everyone having a ball. WDCR even played Ray doing "Rockhouse."

"Hey, you pledges hear about the time Otter had to get up a chip lay?" said Coyote.

"No," said Huck, "but I think we're about to."

"Yeah, Otter and some other guys — Flea, Dog, Gland — they road-tripped to Saratoga Springs, only they weren't going to Skidmore."

Knowing laughter from the older brothers. The pledges exchanged blank looks.

Dumptruck looked at them patronizingly. "He's talking about Congress Street."

No light dawned in the pledges' eyes.

"It's where you go to dip your wick." Magpie looked at them. "It's where the *whorehouses* are!"

"Ohhhhhh," said the pledges.

"I had a date at Skidmore once," Dumptruck offered. "Her name was Babs Clumper."

The brothers regarded him as if possum wastes had been placed beneath their noses. They were reacting to the name, however — not Truck.

"No, really. She had a car so we went parking and made out." He sipped his beer, and mentioned casually, "She had zits inside her mouth."

"What?" cried Huck.

"Like, all these little pimples and things, inside her mouth."

"Where exactly?" asked Coyote. "Between her lips and teeth? On her inner cheeks? Her tongue . . . ?"

"All those places," said Dumptruck. "There was a panoply of them."

"Or a plethora," said Alby. "So — the chip lay?"

"Right," said Magpie. "We get to the whorehouse and after all that driving no one wants to actually go in. Except Otter. But he comes back because he left his wallet at the house, and has to take up a chip."

A new concept under the sun — the chip lay. Everyone laughed, picturing Otter standing there with his hand out to the open car window.

"How much does it cost?" Pinto was very interested.

"Ten bucks for a half 'n' half." Bags chewed his cigar. "That's standard."

"Half 'n' half?"

Bags rolled his eyes. "First they blow you, then you get laid. Half 'n' half, get it?"

"Ohhh," said Pinto.

Bags knew everything, as he often pointed out. Such was his fate on Earth.

"Anyway, they get up the chip and Otter goes in and gets laid. He said it was a good time." Coyote got a fresh beer from Pinto. "Oh, did I mention that all the girls on Congress Street are black?"

"*Black?*" cried Huck, Round, Pinto, and Moses.

"Sure," said Bags. "Once you try black, you never go back."

"Hey, Truck," said Pinto. "I had a date with a girl named Zarne Pearlswig."

"Gah," said Truck. "That's terrible. Did she have zits inside her mouth?"

"Nah," said Alby. "In her pussy."

Around the bar, the men shuddered at the thought.

"I could get an unguent for her," said Donna Daley.

"Pussy zits are common enough that they make unguents for it?" Mouse looked alarmed.

"Well, it's more a lubricant, I suppose." Donna smiled demurely and winked at Pinto. *Wow!* Pinto thought.

"Hey," said Fat Fred to the pledges. "You guys ever hear about the time Rat Battles put quarters in his foreskin and —"

"*Yes,*" cried the pledges.

"*I* have a story." It was Hardbar. "The other night I was with this girl, Veronica. Man, she had big tits, at least three hogans per."

A hogan was a measure of breast size. It had something to do with how many hats a tit could fill. Or maybe how many tits would fill a hat. Pinto had never fully understood.

"So there we are in bed. I lick her tits; I squeeze her buns. I've got my finger up her. Man, is she wet!"

This was the best story of the night by far. Pinto, Alby, Dumptruck, and Round were getting hard-ons.

"Okay, so then she grabs my crank. She's running her fingers over it, giving it little kisses. Then she just plunges it into her mouth."

Hardbar's audience was rapt. All other conversations had died away.

"Man, she's licking me all over. I get big as a commuter train. I'm ready to pull into her station, but then — incredible! — her sister, Chloe, comes in. She does a slow strip and then gets into bed with us."

Pinto's jaw dropped. This was the very sort of stuff he hoped to experience often in his life. It was great knowing that an actual AD had done this stuff.

"Well, then the sisters start kissing each other. Real French ones, you know? And *then* — they kiss each other with the head of my dick in the middle!"

"Really?" cried Pinto, Huck, and Round at the same time.

"Yeah. Chloe's also tickling my balls, and —"

"Hardbar!" protested Dumptruck. "Stop! You're killing me!"

"I'm getting a reltne!" cried Magpie. A reltne was a hard-on so big it stretched the skin tight on the rest of your body, pulling your facial features into a weird rictus.

"I want a date with Chloe," called Scotty.

"Hey!" said Fat Fred.

"You can come, too."

"Always do," said Fat Fred.

"And then *I* came!" Hardbar announced. "It was beautiful."

People digested this a moment.

"So — you came with them, like, licking your German helmet," said Round.

"Yeah, well, in essence," said Hardbar.

"What do you mean, in essence?"

"Uh — you guys do realize this is a beat-off fantasy, don't you?"

"What?" cried Alby. "You son of a bitch!"

"Uh, I'll be back in a minute." Dumptruck ran up the stairs.

"What the fuck's the matter with you, Hardbar?" Magpie asked.

"I thought you knew. You think I really *do* stuff like that?"

"Hold up! Listen!" It was Mouse, by the radio. The same excited WDCR news guy was back. He said the car containing the escaped nut had gone into a tree at ninety miles an hour, *right outside of Hanover!* There would be no need for an ambulance.

The guys looked at one another. The escaped nut story had turned out to be a real downer.

Round filled his glass. "See you later, men." He headed out.

"Hey," said Pinto, alertly jumping to the tap, "who needs a refill? Night's young, right?" He wanted to stem further defections.

Perhaps due to Pinto's ministrations, or perhaps because Ray Charles now sang "I Got a Woman," the good humor and playfulness slowly returned. ADs were nothing if not resilient. Scotty and Dumptruck did a side-by-side whiz in the gutter. Bags declaimed to Pinto on the superiority of Chuck Berry to Elvis, saying it was Chuck who should really be known as the king of rock 'n' roll. He was preaching to the choir.

It was late enough that the radio could pick up WOV from New York, so they switched over and found Jocko playing "Bewildered" by James Brown. Several unworthy Caucasoid voices rose to sing along.

Suddenly, Zeke Banananose and Rat walked out of the stairway, smiling and excited.

"Wow, man, cool movie!" Zeke drew a beer. *"The Magnificent Seven.* There's this guy who can throw a knife so fast he —"

"Wait a minute," said Pinto. "Movie? What happened to Fitch?"

Zeke and Rat exchanged blank looks.

"You assholes!" said Scotty. "Fitch! You were taking him to Dick's House."

Zeke and Rat stood there. "Oh, yeahhhhhh," said Rat finally. He looked at Zeke. "Remember?"

"Uh . . ." Zeke wasn't completely sure. He was a couple of years more deteriorated than Rat.

Magpie threw his hands in the air. "Where's your fucking car?"

Pinto, Zeke, Rat, and some others went upstairs with him. In the parking lot behind the house was Zeke's Pontiac. Pinto ran up and looked inside. Fitch was fast asleep in the backseat.

Magpie faced Zeke and Rat. "You morons!"

"I guess we should take him to Dick's House now," said Zeke.

"*Yes!*" screamed 'Pie. "*Immediately!*"

They watched the car depart and returned to the bar. Truck came back down, looking relaxed and pleased with himself. Then Otter, reigning Duke of Adelphia, entered with regal hipness, nodding to one and all with a small otter smile. On his arm was his girlfriend, Gay Fallopian. In some unknown fashion, Otter had reworked the last name into Tabiggatits. That was pronounced "Ta-bigga-tits." Gay Tabiggatits! She went to Smith, a dark, attractive young woman of Armenian extraction whose tits were no tabigga than anybody else's.

Otter did a head bob or two, looking over the assemblage. "Well, boys, what have you been up to tonight?"

"Heard some great Ray Charles," said Scotty.

"Told dirty stories," said Fat Fred.

"Injured Fitch," said Alby.

Otter nodded sagely. "Just another bitchin' night at the ol' AD bar."

"Hey, Troll," said Donna Daley. "Weren't you going to show me the jizz room, or whatever you call it?"

"The sex room, yes," said Troll. "That's it, over there." He pointed at the battered entryway with SEX ROOM scrawled in red paint across the top.

"Be right back," Hardbar called over his shoulder as he vaulted the bar. "Think I left my, uh, *cigarettes* in there."

"So you have it handy to the bar, eh?" Donna nodded. "Very good location."

She and Troll turned back to their beers.

Hardbar returned, waving a pack of Camels. "Found 'em." He took a spot next to Troll. "Room's free."

"Huh?" Troll had been named Troll because Terry No-Come said he looked like he lived under a bridge.

"Oh, we don't want to go *in* there," said Donna. "I just wondered where it was." She did a double take. "Hardbar? Is that a tear?"

A cowbell rang from atop the stairs. "Sandwiches!"

Excited shouts went up, and the ADs swarmed up the stairs and swept into a practiced circle around the 'wich man, a bespectacled freshman who always seemed taken aback at the depth of the Adelphian nightly hunger. His wicker sandwich basket was filled to the brim with delicious, irresistible sandwiches on white bread! Oh, boy, all Pinto's favorites: Tuna fish! Chicken salad! And, especially, peanut butter and jelly! He grabbed one of each, and two chocolate milks.

The crowd quickly reformed at the bar to down their eleven-o'clock supper. For several moments, no one spoke, and all you could hear was chewing and swallowing.

Round returned. There was a merry twinkle in his eye as he pounded the bar for attention. "Hey, remember that guy who hit the tree?"

Several guys nodded.

"He sounded like house material, wouldn't you say?"

The brothers shrugged good-naturedly. "Sure, Round," said someone.

"Well, good! Because I brought as much of him as I could scrape off the windshield back with me."

He set his beer glass on the bar. Inside, with the fork sticking out of it, was a column of gray, pulpy brains.

People froze with their sandwiches in their mouths. Bending forward, they took a look. Steeling themselves, they took a closer look.

Gay Tabiggatits emitted a little cry. Fat Fred and Donna Daley blanched. The women were gone from the room like dewdrops from a hot car roof.

The ADs exchanged looks. A moment passed. Smiles began tugging at lips. And then a great roar of disgust and approval went up, and the room rang with raucous male laughter. The brothers were floored by Round's boldness and audacity. It made the pledge-class blob seem a little . . . dangerous, all of a sudden. They raised their glasses and inducted him into the Hard Core on the spot. The induction ceremony was that they drank the beer in their glasses.

The music coming up from New York was cool and the keg was still strong, but something now went out of the room. After the cheers died down, no one had much to say. Guys' eyes kept straying to the brain glass. Uneaten sandwiches littered the bar top.

After a safe fifteen minutes, Y. Bear and Moses remembered an important movie that was on *The Late Show.* Huck Doody muttered something about a fucking eight-o'clock class and followed them up the stairs. Rat had to go boot. Zeke Banananose was asleep on one of the mattresses. Hardbar dispiritedly went into the sex room to turn off the Wollensak, and didn't come back.

In this manner, the bar crowd dwindled. Finally, only Round, Pinto, and Alby were left, and the latter two were working on their own excuses for leaving.

"Jeez, I'm really surprised."

"Why's that, Round?" Alby looked at him fishily.

The fat pledge picked up the brain glass. "Because I felt sure someone would drink a beer out of this."

And he did.

CHAPTER TEN

Road Trip

PINTO EMERGED FROM his Saturday Nuts 'n' Sluts class no more enlightened about schizophrenia than ever. The one opinion he'd formed was that as long as schizophrenics were going to be picking up radio transmissions in their heads, they should try for New York stations. Ordinarily, finishing his last class of the week brought joy, since it meant he could race to the house, turn up the jukebox, and think of nothing but fun till Monday morning. Not this weekend, however. No, this fucking weekend he was going to try, against all odds, to catch up with his schoolwork. Somehow it was already mid-November and finals were less than a month away.

"Pledge Pinto!" Scotty strode up, smiling broadly. "Today is your lucky day!"

Uh-oh, thought Pinto. "Scotty, listen, man, I'm booking out of control —"

"Now, Pinto. What we have here is an opportunity for you to broaden your horizons, learn new skills, and see the world."

"We're joining the navy?"

"We're going on a road trip!"

A road trip? Great! But . . .

"Pinto, you have your whole life to catch up on your work. Is that what you want on your tombstone? 'He was always really caught up with his work'?"

"No, but I could get into trouble if I don't —"

"Oh, I see. You want it to say 'He stayed out of trouble. He was a good boy.'"

It was impossible to talk to Scotty at times like these.

"And anyway, Coyote couldn't go so we need your car."

He'd wondered about his sudden popularity. Okay, that left him three choices. Tell Scotty to take the car — which was unthinkable — or lie, saying the battery was dead, or actually allow himself to be dragooned into going.

Road trips were an important part of the experience up here — guys had been hauling ass out of Hanover since the beginning of cars, chiefly because, except for getting drunk and breaking things, there was nothing to *do* at Dartmouth. Because there were no girls! Well, there were a few — nursing students, like Fat Fred, and hospital personnel, like Pam and her physical therapist roommates — but the good ones among that small group had long since paired off with cool guys like Scotty and Black Whit. And that was it. The nearest girls' school, Colby Junior, was an hour away, or forty-five minutes if you were drunk and heedless of death.

"When would we be leaving?"

"Now!"

"But I don't have any gas."

"You'll buy some."

"Scotty, I'm broke."

The junior was taken aback. "What? You asshole! All right, we'll need another man. Come along."

"I didn't say I was going."

"Sure you did. Body language." Scotty towed him by the scarf toward the house.

They found the AD living room deserted but for Moses, who was lying on the floor with Fitch's cat asleep on his stomach. Scotty marched up to him, Pinto in his wake.

"Moses, this is your lucky day!"

"It is?" Moses peered up at Scotty, his magnified eyes wide behind his glasses.

"Yes, *you* have been selected to join the Great Adelphian Weekend Road Trip!"

Moses sat up fast, the cat leaping off. "Me? Thanks! Uh, where we going?"

Pinto had been wondering that, too.

"To Smith. I have plans to coincide with Torrie Toiletbowl tonight." Scotty regarded his fingernails.

Pinto was confused. "I thought you were going with Fat Fred."

"I'm not 'going' with anyone. I don't 'go' with people, pledge Pinto."

"But I see you two together —"

"Sometimes. When we choose to be together." This was sounding a little like Ace. "And this weekend I'm choosing to get together with Torrie."

Scotty watched Moses looking at him through his thick glasses. Every so often, when the light was right, they'd go opaque. Suddenly, you'd be relating to only a nose and a mouth. "So, does Fat Fred know?"

"What a crass question!" Scotty regarded Moses with disdain.

Moses quickly went to pieces. Someone wasn't approving of him! "Oh, God, I'm sorry." He wrung his hands. "Can I still come?"

"Sure. And what's more, I'm going to let *you,* a mere pledge, make the most vital contribution to getting us there!"

"Fuckin' A! How?"

"By paying for the gas!"

Moses looked at him sidelong. Before he could frame a reply, the door to the library flew open and Alby, who'd been inside, masturbating to his psychology textbook, stuck his head out. "Hey, if I can come, I'll give my unit a break and hope for a hand job later."

A hand job! Pinto's heart leapt. Well, actually, his dick leapt; there was a palpable quiver. Imagine getting an actual hand job!

So they split. No toothbrushes, no second sets of underwear, no overnight bags. They just took a flying leap out of their lives without a second thought, without dogs to feed, ovens to turn off, or children needing sitters, and diddy-bopped happily out to the Ford. Moses and Alby jumped in back while Scotty took shotgun. Excited at the prospect of madcap adventures, Pinto headed down the driveway.

As he reached the end of the shrubbery that clung to the house like a fallen sock, a figure stepped from the shadows. Pinto stamped on the brake. It was Otter! He rolled down the window.

The Otter grooved over, bobbing his head, grinning his grin. "You boys wouldn't be going to Smith, by any chance."

"We sure are, Otter!" Moses cried from the backseat. He wanted Otter to like him. Well, actually, every guy in the pledge class wanted Otter to like him.

"Bitchin'." He opened the shotgun door and gestured Scotty over with his ass. Scotty sighed and shifted to seat-center, where it was less comfortable.

Departing town involved certain preparations. First, they went to the Gulf station and filled Pinto's tank. Grumbling, Moses forked over the $3.50. Scotty strode off to get beer. And there was one other thing. Otter placed a hand on Pinto's shoulder.

"Hey, how 'bout doin' me a favor?"

"*I'll* do you a favor," said Moses.

Otter ignored him. "You see, Pinto, based on my phone call with Gay, tonight will bring an erotic encounter and yet here I am without a supply of prophylactic interventionaries."

"What?" said Alby, Moses, and Pinto.

"I'm gonna be humpin' her and I'm rubberless! Now — pledge Pinto — your contribution to the road trip is a pack of Trojans for the fun-loving Otter, so he may disport himself with carefree abandon."

All Dartmouth men knew the unpleasant little shop on Main Street, beneath the shoe store. You were apprised of the existence of Fletcher's by your upperclassman dorm proctor your first week there. At a school of three thousand guys, it served as vital a function as the library or the gym.

With apprehension, Pinto made his way down the steps and

pushed inside. As usual, Fletcher — no one knew his first name, nor was he called Mister; just Fletcher — was with his all-emmet entourage. They turned to look at him, puffing on pipes. Fletcher had a big fleshy face and thinning hair, and chewed gum with his mouth open. The men projected attitudes of amused tolerance for the pinheads, as emmets called Dartmouth guys.

"Ayuh, mistah! What kin we do ya faw?" As if he didn't know. There were a few shelves bearing dusty brushes, combs, and Barbasol but they'd probably gone untouched since the retreat from the Chosin Reservoir. Guys came here for one reason only.

Pinto shuddered. The men were disgustingly mature, with forty-year-old bodies, arm zits, stained teeth, and moles. Talking to them, even glancingly, about his sex life was like drinking from a spittoon.

"Ah, two packs of Trojans, please." He'd get one for himself, too. Who knew?

"What size, mistah?"

"Huh?"

The emmets laughed merrily.

"Just funnin' ya. Here ya go." Fletcher set the unmistakable packages on the counter. His colleagues gazed at Pinto, leering, as if imagining him nude and wearing one of the things.

Back outside, the fresh air was wonderful. And then he saw Scotty coming toward him with . . . a *keg?* "That's the beer you went to get? I thought we were getting a couple of six-packs!" He was appalled.

Scotty laughed. "It's only a pony keg. I'm figuring eighty-five glasses in one of these, which, divided by five guys, means about eighteen glasses per guy. That ought to get us down there."

"I'm not drinking eighteen beers driving to Smith! Are you crazy?"

"Oh, wait," said Scotty. "That was for twelve-ounce glasses. We have eight-ounce ones, so that'd be, oh, twenty-six beers per guy, give or take a glass. We're covered."

"Good, Scotty. We don't want to take unnecessary risks."

"My sentiments exactly."

"But if we got stopped by a cop —"

"Pinto, I've been on dozens of road trips. Not once have I been stopped by a cop. God protects fools and sailors."

"And ADs?"

"Well, we're fools, aren't we?"

Whistling the sax break from "Charlie Brown," he headed for the car, and Pinto forlornly followed. Shit, he wanted to be as irresponsible as everyone else. Why did *he* have to drive? Fuck!

GOING SOUTH FROM DARTMOUTH, you came first to White River Junction, Vermont. As a place, it was distinguished by its undistinguishedness. Nothing seemed to go on there and the men all wore baseball caps bearing the names of motor oils. As they crossed the Depression-era metal bridge into town, the White River roaring over its rocks fifteen feet below, Pinto's riders were sucking down beers, the keg now perched on the backseat. Pinto, not to be left out, was taking hits from a glass Scotty had thoughtfully offered to hold for him. It was then they heard the siren. There, in the rearview mirror, was a motorcycle cop.

Pinto froze. Was he speeding? He jammed on the brakes. The contents of six beers hit the ceiling with a *splat.*

"Pinto!" they howled in protest, beer stalactites descending onto their heads. He was always splashing things against ceilings!

The cop had mirror shades, a broad, impassive face, and a big white helmet. Pinto rolled down his window, movies about Nazis coming back in a rush. Beer fumes arose from the boys' hair like a fetid mist.

"Uh . . . yes, Officer?"

He regarded Pinto impassively. "I stopped you because this is a suspicious vehicle."

"A 'fifty-four Ford is a suspicious vehicle?" Scotty took no shit off cops.

"You got something to say to me?" the officer barked.

"Nah, I'm cool."

"Hey! What the hell is that?" He pointed to the pony keg.

"It's a pony keg!" Alby announced cheerfully. "What'd you think it was?"

Pinto dropped his head onto the wheel.

"All right. You college kids better come with me."

He got on his bike. Gesturing for them to follow, he started off. Pinto pulled out behind him.

Otter looked puzzled. "Hey, correct me if I'm wrong, but does this strike you as normal police procedure? Asking your prisoners to follow you?"

He had a point, but Pinto wasn't about to make trouble. There were plenty of other guys in the car who could do that. They drove out of White River Junction and onto a country road. Then, gesturing to the shoulder, the cop pulled over. Pinto dutifully followed.

"Why did he take us out here?" asked Moses, peering anxiously around. "Is he going to shoot us?"

"You moron," said Alby. "He's not going to shoot us."

The cop dismounted and came again to the window.

"For college boys, you sure are stupid." Off came the helmet and glasses.

The cop was Carl.

"Seal?" said Otter in amazement. Carl had finally gotten his nickname. He indeed looked like he could play "The Star-Spangled Banner" on squeeze-bulb horns.

Angry phrases barraged out the window at him as they realized who he was.

"Seal, you asshole!" they cried. "Are you fucking nuts, man?"

Pinto heard the Otter laugh begin. "Uh-heh-heh-heh-heh . . ."

The others paused. Actually, what Seal had done was pretty cool. But what if a real cop had come along? Although now that Pinto looked, Seal's cop outfit was seriously cheesy — he was wearing a sheriff's star and had a cap pistol in a silly western holster. But wasn't pretending to cophood a felony? Even among crazies, Seal stood out. Many ADs talked the talk — he *did* shit.

Seal seldom altered his bland expression and did not do so now. Putting his shades back on, he asked, "So where the fuck are you guys going?"

"Smith!" Moses announced. "I'm going to get laid, maybe!"

Seal observed him a moment. "All right, this could get hairy. I better tag along."

"Jeez, with the keg and all, we're a little full," Pinto fretted.

The faintest of smiles crossed Seal's face. "That's all right. I'll keep up." In a roar and expulsion of exhaust, he sped southward, dwindled to a dot, and was gone.

With a gulp, Pinto put the Ford in gear and sped after him.

ROUTE 5, DARTMOUTH men agreed, was a great road. Perfectly engineered and beautifully designed, lined on both sides with pretty Vermont woodlands, it took you most of the way to Northampton, Massachusetts, where Smith College was. The bizarre thing was, the road was always almost empty. Maybe you'd see three cars in twenty minutes. To have constructed the world's best road for three cars every twenty minutes seemed a bit ahead of the curve to Pinto, but it sure was fun to drive on.

By the time they passed Bellows Falls — known to generations of Dartmouth men as "Fellow's Balls"— a state of joyous inebriation prevailed in the car. Pinto, along with the others, had put a good dent in his twenty-six beers and was laughing along as Otter and Scotty coached Moses in basic automotive sickness.

"All right," said Scotty. "Since we don't know when the next car is coming, you're going to moon that pine tree over there."

"Where?"

"Right there, you gork! Next to all those other pine trees." Scotty pointed it out.

"Oh." Moses looked dubious but his body remained poised to perform.

"Now remember: When I say, 'Go!' open your belt and pants and zip down your fly with your left hand while opening the window with your right. Okay? Then you slide the pants down *as you rise from the seat* and plunk your ass out the window."

Pinto was looking around for cops. So this was mooning.

"All set?"

"Belt and pants, fly down, pants down *as I rise from the seat*, out the window," Moses muttered. "Belt and pants, fly down . . ."

"Go!"

He opened his belt and pants. He zipped down his fly. He slid down his pants *as he rose from the seat* — and pushed his naked ass hard against the closed window.

"Oh, man," said Scotty. "That's not a moon, Moses; that's a pressed ham!"

His self-esteem plunging, Moses reached between his legs and rolled the window down. The intense wind shear flung his balls about like wind chimes.

"Hey, get those things away from me!" cried Alby.

"What's it called when a girl does it?" Pinto asked Scotty. "A pressed hamette?"

"Well, if she bends over far enough, it's a glazed clam."

"*Ew,*" said Moses, having slid his pants up *as he was sinking* into his seat.

"*Ew?*" said Otter. "Pledge, ADs do not say 'Ew.'"

"Sorry, Otter," said Moses. "I won't do it again. I promise."

"Hey, Otter!" said Alby. "You're right next to a window. Whyn't *you* show us how it's done?"

Scotty grinned like a hyena. "Yeah, Otter, whyn't *you* show 'em?"

Otter coughed into his hand. "Settle down, boys."

"What a great idea!" Pinto was in the full flush of his alcohol high. "Come on, Otter!"

"Aw, you guys. Look, I'm just going down to see m'girl."

"I know! Give him another beer!" Pinto was delighted to have formulated the solution to all Otter's problems.

"Hey, who knows what a double hogback growler is?" Alby asked.

Silence.

His eyes twinkled. "That's when you drop trou, tuck your cock and balls between your legs, bend over, and fart."

The car rocked with laughter.

Alby ran down the etymology. "The hogback is your dick coming out between your legs, your balls are the double, and the growler is —"

"*The fart!*" yelled Pinto, Scotty, and Moses.

"Hey, what if you *came* after you bent over?" suggested Moses "Then it'd be a *spitting* double hogback growler."

Scotty and Otter exchanged looks. Not bad.

A horrible, disgusting Paul Anka song dripped out of the radio grille. "*Yah!*" Pinto spun the dial.

"There're no other stations around here. Just the one." Scotty seemed angry at the state of Vermont for allowing this.

Pinto kept twirling, but Scottso was rightso.

Scotty turned to Otter. "What's the matter, big boy? Getting settled down? Not throwing so many moons anymore?"

Otter was annoyed. "I've thrown more moons than the rest of you put together."

"Oh, dear," Scotty lamented, "wedding bells are sucking the coolness out of that old gang of mine."

Otter shook his head and laughed.

Regular girlfriends bore an ambiguous status at AD. On the one hand, if she was cool and shared in the group ethos — like Pam — you adored her. If she tolerated things with an embarrassed smile and was adorable — like Magpie's girl, Nancy Manhattan — you liked her. But for the ones who screamed and ran merely because someone whipped out his schlong or lit his fart, you felt only contempt. Most reviled of all were the girls who kept their boyfriends *away* from the house. Woe betide the brother who allowed himself, in his pursuit of nooky, to be lured into domestication. Despite his great coolness and unassailable membership in the Hard Core, Otter had lately been missed at the bar, too often off with Gay Tabiggatits somewhere. In fact, he hadn't even told her she *was* Gay Tabiggatits — that was how compromised he'd become.

"Hey," said Moses. "Ever notice that when you're watching the credits of a movie and it says 'music by'— you always notice the music?"

There was no immediate reply.

"Hey, look!" Pinto pointed out his window, at the opposing lanes of traffic.

Seal was roaring by, one hand held high, doing a wheelie. He was like a cowboy whose horse was rearing up.

"The fuck's the story on that guy?" asked Scotty.

"Uh . . . no one knows," Pinto said. "The pledges have been wondering that, too."

Alby was jealous of the attention. "Hey, ever hear about the girl who drank beer at the beach and got sand in her Schlitz?"

"Pinto! We need a whiz stop!" Otter had had eleven beers since the last such stop.

Ahead, the shoulder was wide. Another car was already there with its hood open and some guys standing around. Pinto parked about thirty feet in front of it. The Ford emptied out. Pinto, Otter, Scotty, Alby, and Moses stood five abreast, whizzing into the grass at the edge of the highway — an outdoor version of the Adelphian gutter.

The other guys were wearing Dartmouth jackets. No AD had *ever* worn a Dartmouth jacket. To do so was so far removed from the Adelphian sense of style that the ADs felt discomfort even thinking about it. The guys had to be douche bags.

Then Seal roared into the guys' midst, throwing up dust and pebbles. As the delighted ADs watched, the Douchemouth guys spoke earnestly to him, pointing to their open hood. Seal nodded amiably. Like a kindly country doctor making a house call, he stepped up and peered under the hood. Then he took out his dick and began peeing on the engine. Steam billowed up.

The guys sprang away from him as if he'd turned into a werewolf. As they watched in confusion, he gave his dong a shake and zipped, then jumped on his bike — all of this without the slightest expression — and roared off. And threw a little salute to the ADs as he flew by.

It was the whiz stop of the year.

THE SURPRISE FOR PINTO at drive's end was that they didn't head straight to Smith but instead pulled into Amherst, where his friend Froggie went. Smith, Amherst, and Mount Holyoke, another top chick school, formed a little triangle of literacy in the North Massachusetts wilderness. They were aristocrats among colleges, abounding in prestige and excellence, part of that network of elite

New England schools to which Dartmouth also belonged. You could go to Colgate or Harvard or Wesleyan or Hamilton or Williams or Yale or Middlebury or Brown or Tufts or Bates or Bowdoin or Colby, and the men you'd meet would look, dress, and sound much the same. And then they'd go out to run the world. As would the women at Smith, Holyoke, Radcliffe, Vassar, Wellesley, Skidmore, and Wheaton. It was the Greater New England College Club, and *everyone* wore crewneck sweaters and maroon penny loafers.

Pinto was itching to run over and see Froggie at the DU house. But first, there was business. It seemed that Amherst had a chapter of AD and Scotty had arranged beds there for them. Impressed by such resourcefulness, Pinto parked in the AD lot. Finding a pair of French doors standing open, the boys went inside.

It was beautiful! There were no broken windows or dents in the wall. The furniture looked great, without slashes or beer stains. There was even a chandelier.

"Okay, we're looking for Amherst Bear," said Scotty. "Maybe they're downstairs drinking."

They located the stairs to the basement.

"Sure smells weird." Moses sniffed the air. "What is that?"

Pinto got it. "It's clean air — no beer or piss or boot."

"Holy shit!" said Scotty. "What do they do here — have meetings of the stamp club?"

"Yeah, they really stick together," said Pinto.

Scotty looked at him oddly.

They checked out the depressing basement, with its absence of normal olfactory markers. "There's no jukebox!" cried Scotty and Pinto together.

"*Hey! Anybody here?*" Alby yelled up the stairs.

No answer. This was stretching out and Pinto wanted to get the fuck over to Froggie. "Hey, can I meet you guys later?"

They made arrangements and Pinto split, excited to see Amherst Frog, as you were supposed to call him these days. Pinto had visited him at Amherst Delta Upsilon on several occasions, hitching down from Dartmouth to do so. Froggie had been a pledge since some point in his freshman year, the first of the high school gang to join a house. While Amherst DU was no Dartmouth AD house — there was only one of those — Pinto liked a lot of the brothers there.

For the most part, Amherst DUs were not named for animals, vehicles, fireplugs, or anything, really. Mostly, they were Ted, Tom, and Mike. They were clean cut — JC Senior would have approved. They did not particularly subscribe to amused cynicism about all human activity or Dadaistic displays of sociopathic behavior in public spaces. Like Chi Phi, they were a good house but hadn't even heard of double hogback growlers.

After a pleasant if unmemorable afternoon — that was the drawback of normal societal values — Pinto returned to Amherst AD. It was a handsome edifice, in the classic, white-pillared New England mode. At the door, he looked inside. A guy was coming down some stairs.

"Uh, hi! I'm one of the Dartmouth guys? Are they around somewhere?"

The guy eyed him apprehensively. Pointing a finger, he said, "In there."

Thanking him, Pinto went into the big living room. There were the ADs. They'd brought in the keg from the car and tapped it on the piano, everyone apparently still working on their twenty-six beers.

It must be said they were shitfaced. As Pinto had quaffed several frosties of his own at DU, he was staggering about in the same territory. He looked around.

"Where are all the Amherst guys?"

Moses and Alby exchanged looks and chortled.

As best as Pinto could piece it together, Alby had been first to discomfit the Amherst ADs when he'd crouched before a radiator and, having announced, "I'm butter!" slowly melted. But when Moses stood on the coffee table and burned his bush, reciting the Ten Commandments at the top of his voice, the Amherst guys had gone nuts! Their *girls* might see him, they said. They believed Moses to be a mentally ill individual whom the Dartmouth ADs had brought along to inflict on them as a cruel joke. To dispel this notion, Alby and Scotty had burned *their* bushes, too. (By now, these were being called brush fires.) This had made apparent the basic conflict in belief systems between the two AD brotherhoods, and the Amherst guys had gone to some safer part of the house, wondering how big a mistake it had been to offer these guys beds.

Pinto was sorry to hear it. He'd figured on getting to know some of them.

"You have to take these things in stride, Pinto." Otter clapped him on the shoulder. "If you wanted guys like them to like you, you should have joined SAE."

"I did try," said Pinto.

"*What?*" cried Alby, Otter, Scotty, and Moses, all turning at once.

"Kidding. So now what?"

Otter grinned. "Why, now it's time to meet the ladies."

"Okay. Well, *you'll* be meeting one."

"Now, now, pledge. We'll scrape something up for you."

"Gee, thanks."

"For real, Pinto. Gay said she'd get dates for you, Moses, and Alby."

"Really?" said Pinto and Moses. They looked at each other in amazement.

"Does mine have a good ass?" Alby asked. "It's axiomatic that my dates have a good asses."

"Well, we'll just have to see, won't we?" Otter grinned and bobbed his head a time or two.

They set out for Smith, which was twenty minutes away in the impressively ugly little city of Northampton.

"Hey, Otter." It was Moses. "If I can get laid tonight, will you lend me a rubber?"

"Moses, you're not going to get laid." Otter regarded him with amusement.

"Lend?" said Scotty.

"Sure. I'd, you know, give it back."

"*Bleahhh!*" cried Pinto, Scotty, and Otter.

Alby shrugged. "What's the big deal?"

Alby and Scotty had been chuckling over a story in the *Sophian,* the Smith College newspaper, and kept referring to an Ann. Maybe an Ann with full lips and ample gazongas who was advertising her willingness to bounce on his pole, and they were headed to her dorm now so she could do exactly that.

He was partly right. They did go to Ann's dorm. It was fronted by a fire hydrant, so they parked directly before it, reasoning that if the Ford suddenly caught fire, there would be all that water *right there.* Al and Scotty headed inside and Pinto tagged along.

"So Gay's in here?"

"No, Gay's across the street. Otter's over there getting her."

"Then what are we doing *here?*"

"Just having fun."

Pinto shrugged — fun was good. They went to the girl behind the desk, whom a sign identified as GRETCHEN POTATOES. She was dressed *perfectly.* Everything she wore was tasteful, understated, and showed off her good looks. Each hair was in place; every eyelash curled just so. *How'd she do that?* Pinto wondered.

Alby handed Pinto the *Sophian,* winked at Scotty, and turned to the fetching Miss Potatoes. "Hi, I'm here to pick up Ann Montana, please?" He smiled charmingly.

She returned the look coldly. "Is this some kind of joke?"

"Joke? What do you mean? Just tell her I'm here, okay?" He fixed his Paul Newman eyes on her. Like so many women before and after, she fell instantly and involuntarily in love with him. You could see it happen — the part of the lips, the hand to the chest.

"But, listen. The thing is — Ann died this week."

"*What?*" said Alby. "Died?"

Pinto stole a look at the newspaper. The headline said JUNIOR ANN MONTANA SUCCUMBS IN BICYCLE ACCIDENT. Holy shit!

"I'm sorry. She passed away on Monday."

"Shit!" Alby threw up his arms in exasperation. "Now what am I going to do for a date?"

This was meant to be the punch line, the triumphal moment of the scenario, after which they'd race back to the car, laughing about how sick they were. There were no ulterior motives. They weren't trying to get dates. It was sickness for sickness sake.

Scotty couldn't hold it in anymore. He made one of those laughter-preceding snork sounds that happen when you're trying your best to resist. "Sorry," he said to Gretchen Potatoes, pretending the snork had been a sob. "This comes as quite a shock."

"I'm sure." She returned to Alby, meeting his eyes levelly. "So *I* might be free tonight."

Alby was amazing. This happened to him *all the time.* He was very handsome, and his pale blue eyes could melt ice, as they just had. When women fell in his arms, he shrugged and enjoyed himself. No lingering virginity problems there.

Gretchen asked to be excused, and then, to everyone's surprise, returned with dates for Pinto and Moses! Pinto was confused — wasn't Gay getting them dates? But when Gretchen introduced him to Mindy Disbro, as his date was named, he forgot all earlier arrangements. Damn, a pretty blonde with fine, healthy wazook-ies! A side effect of his pictures in the safe at home was that every girl he actually met was immediately compared to them and usually fell far short. But Mindy, albeit not up there with Eve Meyer or Bettie Page, to name two of his favorites, was good-looking. True, there was something slightly, well, *vapid* in her expression, some sort of vacancy where character was supposed to be, but that was probably true of most college students, including himself. And, anyway, who cared? She had wazooms!

Moses was presented with a tiny, bespectacled brunette. She was full of bubbly enthusiasms and beliefs, just like Moses. Indeed, almost everything about them matched — she was the female him. Pinto didn't get her real name but she almost immediately became known as the Digit.

By this time, Torrie had shown up to meet Scotty. Pinto was always glad to see Torrie, with her freckles, merry laughter, and general coolness.

"Hey, Scottso!" she called out. "How they hangin'?"

Scotty, going in for a suave cheek kiss, hesitated. How do you suavely kiss a chick who's just asked how they're hanging?

Gay was not pleased to find Pinto, Moses, and Alby already with dates, as the girls she had chosen for them had taken showers, done their hair, put on makeup, tried on several outfits, and applied perfume.

"Well, put 'em out on the street, then," Alby suggested cheerfully. "Make a few bucks toward tuition, right?"

Gay failed to see the humor in his remark.

"Scotty? How are we going to get everyone in the car?"

"Six in back, four in front. Keg in the trunk."

And so it was done.

Pulling from the curb, Pinto asked, "Where should we go? I hear there's a place called Rahars that's pretty good . . ."

"Oh, Rahars is great!" contributed Mindy.

"Sure," said Scotty, "if you like fireplaces, smooth make-out music, really nice mixed drinks, and a subdued atmosphere with comfortable armchairs and sofas. You know, square shit like that."

Pinto had been about to yell, "Let's go!" "Yeah, fuck that shit!" he snorted ruefully. What kind of schmuck would want to be drunk, comfortable, and making out?

Scotty offered directions to somewhere else. The nice dorms and tree-lined streets gave way to body shops and ancient, factorylike structures of filthy red stone. Could this be right? Scotty told him to park by a, well, *tavern* probably described it best. The sign said CITY CAFÉ. It was a serious *bar* where blue-collar guys threw down boilermakers and grumbled to one another. Of course ADs liked it — no other Dartmouth man had even *thought* of going there.

The group extracted itself from the Ford and stood in the chill evening, the girls shaking the wrinkles from their toggle-button car coats. The welcoming host, Scotty held open the door to the café, and they marched inside. Gay was regarding Otter with displeasure. Moses and the Digit continued their colloquy. Alby and Gretchen couldn't keep their hands off each other. Torrie went in last, hooking her finger through Scotty's collar and pulling him along. Scotty's eyebrows went up. Torrie sure wasn't Fat Fred.

Inside, the air was cool and slightly damp, the room lit mostly by the dozens of beer signs on the walls. Bar, stools, cigarette machine, shuffleboard — the bare essentials, no more. A jukebox sounded from the back room but Pinto wasn't encouraged, based on the polka currently playing.

"Hey, Stan!" called Scotty. "How's your ass?"

The big Polish guy behind the bar looked up. "Ah, jeez, not you guys again."

"Come on," said Otter. "You love us."

"Fuck I do," he muttered.

"Hi, Stan." Torrie managed to look totally preppy and extremely sexy at the same time. It was she that ruled the clothes, not the other way around.

Stan's expression changed. "Heyyyyyy, girl — how you doin'? Siddown, have a Schlitz."

"Don't get sand in it," Alby warned quickly.

"I ain't seen you, Torrie. Gettin' too good for us?"

"Trying to get educated, Stan, so I don't piss away the family fortune." Torrie Toiletbowl's dad owned the Mahler Toilet Company. She bent over the bar to kiss Stan's cheek. Stan blushed and stammered something.

"So, give you a hand tonight?" Torrie suggested.

"Your spot's always open back here, Tor. You know that."

Grinning, she went behind the bar. Stan seemed tickled as a kid at Christmas. Otter told Pinto later he'd never seen Stan let *anyone* behind the bar but Torrie. He said that the ADs had been repairing to this, their favorite blue-collar redoubt, for many years and that Stan got on the rag sometimes but Pinto should cut him some slack because the big Polack was okay.

"What'll it be?" Torrie asked brightly, holding up a beer glass.

Soon, everyone but Scotty and Torrie had squeezed into a couple of booths in the back room. Two other booths were occupied — one by local guys with packs of Camels rolled up in their sleeves, the other with three Saturday-night-date couples.

Pinto sat with Otter and Gay.

Otter looked at her solicitously. "Is your beer the proper temperature?"

"What if I said no, it's three degrees too warm? What would you do?"

Otter displayed his teeth charmingly. "I'd ask if you meant Fahrenheit or Celsius."

It wasn't the answer she wanted. "Fahrenheit," she snapped.

"I'd drink it myself, being less picky than you."

"Swell."

"And then," he assured her, "I'd give Stan shit about keeping his refrigerator too warm. I'd put bottles in an ice bucket. Then you could dip them in and out, and maintain just the right temperature."

Gay glared at him. She sure wasn't buying his playful bullshit.

"Okay, what's the matter?" Otter asked.

"What happened to that dinner we were supposed to have?"

Otter's face fell. "Oh, jeez. Fuck! Uh . . . Stan has a jar of really nice hard-boiled eggs . . ."

"Never mind!" She took an angry sip of beer, then chugged down the rest and slammed the glass on the table. "Get me another! And it better be the right fucking temperature!"

Pinto hated it when guys and their dates didn't get along. And speaking of dates, what was the story with his, perched inoffensively next to him, sipping her whiskey sour?

"So, uh, what are you majoring in?"

"I haven't decided yet. I'm just a freshman, you know."

He hadn't known. Finding himself the elder of the pair made him feel empowered and cool. But he undercut this by admitting, "I haven't decided yet, either. I was going to be a chem major but when I saw those organic molecules I switched to English. Maybe that's what I'll major in."

She was gazing fixedly at him, hanging on his words as if the boring shit coming from his mouth was somehow wonderful and profound. She seemed *enthralled*.

"So, uh, you like rock 'n' roll?" he asked.

"Of course."

"Really? Who's your favorite group?"

"Well, I love Bobby Rydell."

Pinto choked on his beer. Searching for a napkin and not finding one, he fell back on his sleeve. Why couldn't she say Bo Diddley? Just *once*, why couldn't some girl say Bo Diddley?

On the other hand, non–Bo Diddley–loving dates could make out as energetically as any other, he supposed, and their doo-wah-diddies were no less appealing. How should he approach it? Feed her drinks? He flashed on himself as Lee J. Cobb, plying a tart in a cheap hotel room. Didn't want that. But hazarding a first kiss was so, you know, *scary.*

"Pinto?" She tilted her head back. Her lips parted.

Holy shit! He *was* going to get some. How much remained to be seen — Alby's hand job mention had stuck in his mind. Man, to have some girl actually jerk you off! It was an idea so sexy he almost passed out. Instead, he kissed her.

"Ohhhhh," she moaned with feeling.

Pinto was surprised. That was some pretty energetic moaning for one measly kiss. Her face hovered in front of him, lips moist. He tried again.

"*Ohhhhhhhh!*"

He jerked away. Everyone in the room was looking. Maybe he *was* a great lover who'd just bloomed thirty seconds ago. But more likely the girl was *weird*. Maybe her glands were broken. "Um . . . why don't we just drink some beer awhile, okay?"

A great roar outside caused heads to turn. Roaring up on his big Indian was Seal, the streetlights glinting from his mirrored shades, a gorgeous blonde behind him, laughing at something. She too wore shades, and sported a black leather jacket that set off her near-platinum hair as it blew back like a flashlight beam in the night.

"*Hey, you fucking assholes!*" Seal bawled. "*Everything okay in there?*"

The ADs threw Seal thumbs-up signs, grinning through the window at him, holding up their beers in salute.

The blonde whispered something in Seal's ear. Seal smiled. With a wave at the guys, he spun the gas and sped off in a cloud of noise and exhaust.

Across the table, Moses and the Digit paid attention solely to each other.

"So, see," Moses was explaining to her, "water tastes different in different geographical regions, and since they use water when they make beer, the beer tastes different. Milwaukee Schlitz tastes totally different from Los Angeles Schlitz."

"Amazing. Say, why don't we have some Northampton Schlitz?"

"The guy who explained this to me is Brother Bags. I saw him take a sip once, spit it on the floor, and yell, 'Albany Schlitz!' in this really disgusted voice."

"As for me," said the Digit, "I knew a guy in high school who could piss over a garage."

"Wow!" Moses was greatly charmed.

Otter, coming back from the head, stopped off to see Scotty and Torrie at the bar. "So what's up?" he asked them.

"Oh, we fine," Scotty said. His eyes were like little circles spinning around.

"Wish *I* were fine." The serious talks about the future that he and Gay had been having were clearly getting him down. Fun, in his life so far, had always come first. Now, though, he was thinking about law school, and then marriage and family. Yet his heart still yearned to piss on someone's mother's leg! Fuck, he felt so *torn.*

"You're just in time, man. Torrie's gonna tell a dirty joke."

Otter glanced over at Gay. Her arms were crossed and she stared stonily at the wall. "Guess I better get back."

Scotty felt sympathy. He'd been where Otter was. Once. Now he followed a policy of All Women Are Slaves. Though it would be hard to think of Torrie that way.

Pinto had had enough beers since leaving Amherst to supersede his fading previous high with an even higher, happier one. "Otter, this is great! You guys do this all the time? Fuckin' A!"

Otter smiled weakly.

"I'm calling Froggie," Pinto decided. Getting to his feet, he started off, then came back. *"I'll be right back!"*

"I can hear you," said Mindy.

Oh. Right. Not deaf. *Dumb,* that's what she was.

Boy, he felt great! He went to the pay phone, found a dime, and dropped it in. When they answered at Amherst DU, there was music coming at Pinto from two directions. Better at DU, actually, since Hank Ballard and the Midnighters sure was better than Connie Francis.

"Froggie!"

"Pinto!"

"What's going on?"

"I'm drunk as shit!"

"Me, too!"

"Hey, whyn't you guys come over here?"

"We're drinking purple Jesus punch!"

"Yeah, but it's great here. They have shuffleboard and beer and —"

"What? Hello?"

"Jesus. You will not believe what I'm seeing."

"What?"

"Alby's getting a hand job!"

"He's what?"

"Right here in the City Café! I'm looking at it. She's got her hand just *wrapped* around his *schvantz*." In his excitement, Pinto had lapsed into Yiddish.

"You mean, his dick's out?"

"No, no — it's in his pants. Her hand's wrapped around the pants that're wrapped around the dick."

"Oh, okay."

It was true. While Moses and the Digit chattered away, oblivious, Alby and Gretchen were entwined like snakes on Spanish fly. And, yes, seen by Pinto alone, Gretchen's hand was squeezing Alby's stiffened crank with brio.

"This is the best time I've ever had in my life!" Pinto blurted.

"Did you wind up with a date? Are you getting any?"

"Oh, uh, jeez. Yes and no. Okay, call you later."

He tried to walk straight back to Mindy, but if Arthur Murray footprints had trailed him, they would have described a broken field run by Crazy Legs Hirsch. He noticed the tables of Massachusetts emmets had also seen Al and Gretchen's crotchic activities. The girls at the one table were blushing furiously, repressing giggles.

The boys had no such compunctions, but elbowed each other, guffawing openly.

"What's the matter?" Pinto called to them. "Never seen a hand job before?"

Otter, Moses, and Alby swung their heads. Pinto was not known for sudden outbursts to drunk and possibly dangerous townies. But they gave him a look and turned back to their dates. Alby swiveled his head to Gretchen, whose tongue poked from her mouth, ready to continue. Otter and Gay returned to not communicating, and the Moses-Digit conference about everything in the world recommenced.

Pinto made for Mindy. "Hey!" he shouted suavely. "Wanta dance?"

"Oh, yes." She came into his arms, pressing tightly against him. What was the story with this chick? Why did she act like he was her dream lover or something? Was the Pinto she beheld somehow different from the schmuck he saw in the mirror every morning, with the coated tongue and granulated eyelids? What if this were the way she acted with all her dates, taking on, as an example, the entire Amherst lacrosse team behind the Laundromat each Wednesday? As they twirled slowly to the jukebox, the room lights seemed to grow comets' tails. He brought his nose to her neck.

"Shalimar!"

"Oh, my God, you're right! That's amazing!"

"I know my way around necks."

"Tee hee hee hee hee!"

Moses gazed at the Digit, desperate to be understood. "But *think* — if it's beating the meat for boys, it has to be called something for girls. Clubbing the clam?"

The Digit winced. "Are you crazy? Clubbing? We don't do it that way."

Alby reeled from the men's room and draped himself over the back of Moses's seat. "Hey, man — if someone shot off one of your balls, would you be called Mose?"

Otter glowered at Gay. The bitch stood between him and a cool life. What the fuck was so great about this relationship shit, anyway?

Gay sighed. Dartmouth AD had been great for a while but she'd hoped Otter had moved beyond the boot-in-some-girl's-cleavage stage. He just couldn't resist. But he was far too adorable to let go of.

Pinto was in Yankee Stadium. Yogi was up. The count was three and two. The stands began to rumble. An earthquake? Newcombe pitched. The rumbling increased, flinging him around. What?

Mindy was shaking his shoulder. "Silly! You fell asleep but just kept dancing. It was sort of amazing, really."

"Just resting, pal." This was the standard AD response to an accusation of passing out. ADs did not pass out, they rested.

"Pinto!"

"Hah?"

It was Froggie! And Bush, who was peering about puppylike for poon.

"Mario!" Pinto ran up, arms wide.

"Angelo!" Froggie and Pinto hugged each other like hearty Italian immigrants. This bit was left over from high school.

It seemed like all the world was happy and drunk. Even — who was that on the jukebox? — Julius La *Rosa*? Good God, where did they find this stuff? But it didn't matter, because he sounded like Fats Domino. Wait a minute. Julius La Rosa like Fats Domino? Had he thought that? No, it was an alcohol hallucination, he was fairly sure.

Seal flew by the window on the gleaming Indian, doing seventy, never looking over. His chick's hair lit the night.

Pinto loved the world.

Moses loved the Digit.

Otter said to Gay, "I'm having a beer with Scotty," and went to the bar.

Gay sighed and dug in her purse. Finding her Bawds and Strumpets of Elizabethan England textbook, she flipped it open and began reading in the candlelight.

Scotty was feeling fine and mellow but wondered if he was going to get anywhere with Torrie tonight. Though the more he watched her merry performance behind the bar, filling glasses, joking around with the customers, the more his erotic plans were deflected and he felt something subversive. Like . . . friendly? He wasn't used to this. She was what he thought every girl should be — smart, sexy, and without all that wilting, passive shit, like Pinto's date. And she could hold her own with the ADs. During a recent visit, Seal had waved his dick and yelled, "Hey, Torrie, ya know what this is?"

"Why, it looks like a penis, Seal," she'd replied coolly. "Only shorter."

In fact, Scotty realized, he *respected* her. And it was getting in the way.

In the back booth, Gretchen gave it one last stroke. *"AIIIII-IEEEEEE!"* Alby's hard-on screamed and spat forth a Halley's comet among ejaculations, creating a great, growing stain on his pants. He lay back in total peace.

"Now me," Gretchen said.

"Huh?" He looked at her in surprise.

"HEY!" PINTO SAID to Mindy, shouting over the swell Lawrence Welk song that currently played. "Wanna see my car?"

"I've already seen your car." Looking confused.

"I mean, uh, how it looks when there're just two people in it." He was trying to be suave and rascally.

Her eyes became luminous. "Actually, I'd love to see that."

This was so *cool!* Pinto gallantly held her coat for her and then the door. He noticed Scotty and Torrie grinning, working their index fingers rapidly in and out of their other hands. His laugh was like an explosion.

The night was colder. Pinto could feel each chill inhalation go straight to his medulla oblongata. It was after eleven; the streets were deserted. The clacking of the traffic light was like the giant ants in *Them.*

At his car, they climbed into the backseat. Gazing at him, eyelashes lowered, she tittered. Jesus, who did her material, Lillian Gish? But it didn't matter. They didn't need to talk about Shakespeare. She had a good heart, as did he. Their hormones bubbled like jukeboxes. *Ow!*

And so, the mechanics of it all, his arms around her, the lips zorping in, the kiss. Boy, did he like lips! His dick, at that moment, chimed in by turning hard as uranium.

"Oh, *my!*" Her legs were opening and closing like the jaws of a cartoon alligator. Wafts of funk arose. If there was ever going to be a girl who wouldn't stop him when he felt her up, this was the one. He brought her close and put a hand on her breast beneath her sweater.

"ANHHHHHHHH!" She thrashed her head back and forth. Did all girls do this? Head-thrashing. It was so . . . *abandoned.* He switched his hand to her other breast. "GNAAH! ZORT!" she cried.

When he pulled away a moment, she straightened and peeled off her sweater, and then, well, out they came, and then — there they were! Pendulating in front of him like kitchen gadgets! "How do you like my, uh . . . ?" She cupped one in each hand and bounced them. *Flubbida-flubbida,* they went.

"I *lubbida-lubbida* them!" Hey, were those areolae spinning? He placed a hand on each. They hardened against his palms. Excited, he felt her up as thoroughly as he could figure out any human way to do, her relentless shrieks of pleasure like the cries of wounded animals.

BACK INSIDE, Moses had been thinking about kissing the Digit for several beers now. She had a small, round face, a spatter of freckles across the nose, and very red lips, glistening with whatever lipstick she used. If she'd just shut up for a minute . . .

"Oh-*kay!*" he said with the sudden gaiety of a cruise-ship director. "It's ten fifteen! Everyone do their Mona Lisa impression!"

The Digit broke off in midsentence to look at him oddly. Shrugging, she clasped her hands at her waist and smiled enigmatically.

There! He moved in quickly, before some new topic could arise, and then, when his lips were almost touching hers, hesitated, breathing in her mingled scents: perfume, beer, maybe a little cold cream, and the lipstick added a note, too. Ravished by her vest-pocket pulchritude, hoping he wouldn't screw it up, he kissed her.

Joy fell from the heavens like shiny Christmas tree decorations. The Digit so admired his intelligence, his wit, his idealism. And, uh, looked like a pretty good putz down there, too . . .

Their nearly identical lips pressed together; their tongues met. Bliss.

PINTO HAD PROBABLY gotten more tit in the last ten minutes than he'd gotten in his entire life so far. He'd felt the living shit out of her fabulous white mounds, and licked her sweet nips until he became concerned he might lick them off. But, oddly, this activity, this thing he'd longed for forever, was already growing old. He wanted *more*.

So next, according to his intellectual understanding of these matters, would be the insertion of the, ah, central finger up her, well, yes, that. New to wazoos, he had no operational understanding of this, but, yes, he was pretty sure that would be the move to make, in fact now, if he could just fucking stop all this *thinking* about it and, instead, *do* it. Certainly Mindy was ready. Her head was back, her eyes closed, her rapidly panting breath like Art Blakey on the hi-hat.

So he brought his hand up her leg, pausing to savor her *inner thigh,* and then on to higher, more tropical climes. "KLURT! EENK!" Shrugging, going totally on instinct, he poked a finger forward . . . and went into her so readily he felt *sucked.*

"GNARR! FNORK!" She lay there, eyes shut, apparently acquiescent to his every vagrant whim. She seemed to have entered some remote but wonderful alternate universe. Her incessant noises remained behind, however; he needed a pair of those headphones they used at pistol ranges.

He had a sudden epiphany. Of *course* making out in high school had been so grim — *he hadn't been drunk!* He happily zorped his finger this way and that, as if she were a swimming pool and his finger an overheated fifth-grader just released from piano practice.

OTTER WAS ENJOYING Scotty and Torrie's company. Life was so much better when things were cool. He bought the next round of beers and told the story of how on a road trip, Doberman had crawled onto the hood of the hearse and licked the bugs off the windshield, explaining to Flea, who was driving, "I just wanted to make sure you could see." And how one night in Boston, he had asked some brothers to wait while he went back into the joint they'd just departed so he could give the bartender a tip. Which he did by throwing up on the bar. Ah, halcyon days!

ALBY INTERMINABLY MASSAGED Gretchen's groin. How long was this going to take? His arm hurt and he had to piss. It would be so easy to just walk away. But, no, he felt, under these circumstances a real man makes his chick come.

"Oh, yes." Gretchen sighed. "I'm sooo close."

Right. You've been saying that for twenty minutes. But he didn't say this out loud.

MINDY'S SCREAM WAS SO PIERCING Pinto briefly imagined the car windows shattering. Her body, arching up from the seat, fell back. "Now you," she said, smiling.

So maybe his special dream for this road trip — that thing men called hand jobs — was about to happen. Great! If only his head hadn't started spinning three seconds ago.

GRETCHEN'S ORGASM WAS LONG and sweet and ended in a giggle. She gave Alby a kiss, then took his hand and tugged him outside so he could relieve himself of his last thirteen beers. Leaning against a telephone pole, Alby managed to whip it out and aim for the gutter.

"Here, let me." She brushed his hand away and replaced it with hers. Alby was surprised but pleased. She was able to direct his stream and write on the pavement *Al & Gretch*. Her hair, her mouth, her clothes — all were still pristine. Neither the drinking nor the making out had marred her perfection in any way. She was surrounded by an invisible Gardol shield, as Alby would later contend. She could hold your dick while you pissed, crawl through the muck, have sex in any and all settings, and not acquire so much as a speck of dust.

PINTO SHOOK HIS HEAD, hoping to clear it. He had to rally — this would be the worst time in the world to boot. He peered around groggily. Holy shit, she'd worked his hard-on out of his fly! It was right there, sticking out of his lap like an alien! Wrapping her fingers firmly around it, Mindy began jerking it off.

"*Ohhhhh!*" cried Pinto, to his surprise.

"Listen to you!" she said with a laugh. "Okay, what else shall I do?"

"Else?" Jesus, what she was already doing was heaven. What else was there? Tickle it with a peacock feather?

But actually there was something.

She put it in her mouth.

The world stopped. Pinto's brain became a faster-than-light spacecraft that circumnavigated the galaxy and returned to Northampton trailing stardust. He stared in almost religious awe at Mindy's mouth as her lips moved up and down his manhood. This had to be one of those pots of gold said to be at the ends of rainbows.

And then, even as he luxuriated in his blow job, a retrograde thought slipped in. Hey, his brain *noodged* him — what happened to the hand job? Because he'd been waiting for one of those his whole life, so shouldn't he actually *have* one before he moved on?

Yes, there he was, Mindy blowing him, and all he could think about was this hand job that hadn't actually happened because she never finished it! It was supposed to be in the clear, not merely a prelude to something. Later, at a time of mutual convenience, they could reconvene and she could suck his dick all night. But having his first time for both sex acts fall within the same five minutes . . . He felt obscurely cheated.

Mindy, knowing nothing of his stupid ruminations, cheerily sucked away. This made him laugh, and he surrendered to the experience. My God, in a single, sudden onrush he was getting to do all the things he'd dreamed about his entire life, all those gross and wonderful things he'd imperfectly pictured while firing those trillions of sperms into the void. Wow! *If only he didn't have to boot!*

SEAL, WITH CLEO behind him, whooshed down the breezeway. She tongued his left ear and the wind slipped a chill into it. He laughed and shivered. If he could make a carpet out of all the tongues in all the ears down all the years — he had to think about this a minute — well, actually, he'd probably be put away somewhere.

Seal glimpsed his future. It would be a life of rigorous spiritual discipline and meditation, within which he would perfect himself. But that time was not yet. He whooped and rode over the roof of a Volkswagen.

MINDY LIFTED HER HEAD to remove a hair from her mouth.

Pinto's dick felt the coolness of the air. "Don't stop!" he cried in dismay.

How could you describe the feeling of a blow job? You could say it was warm and wet and that you could perceive a tongue performing pirouettes all over your German helmet but once you'd said that you still hadn't said shit about *how incredibly great it felt!* And part of the greatness was seeing them do it! *Actually put it in their mouths!*

Mindy smiled and got back to business. His dick rewarmed. Indeed, his erogenous zones were like the cowboys in *Red River,* whooping exuberantly and waving their hats.

Happily, his whirlies were gone. He was back in space again. Hey, weren't those the Pleiades? Hi, girls! Man, this was the life! Getting drunk with your buddies *and* a blow job? In one night? Forget it!

Sounds reached him — women's voices and a door opening and closing. Grumpily, displeased at being yanked back, he opened an eye.

The door in question was right outside his window and from it emerged a line of beefy babes with bowling bags. Huh? He caught sight of a sign in the window — tonight, it seemed, had been the finals of the Northampton Polish Women's Bowling League! They lumbered by, inches away, a herd of mastodons making for the water hole. The window condensation blocked their view.

Perhaps this was when he became a true AD. Seized by an antic impulse, he opened the window fully. In his lap, Mindy was going *glorp glorp glorp*. He whistled.

The nearest women looked over. Winking, Pinto pointed to his crotch. The women, shifting their bowling balls uncertainly, peered inside.

Later, Pinto wasn't sure what he'd thought they'd do. Shit, they were, you know, *women* — he guessed he'd expected a few screams of horror. He sure hadn't expected them to burst out laughing.

"*Wmff?*" Mindy peered upward, little lines appearing between her eyebrows.

"Oh, uh, everything's cool. In fact, things couldn't be more perfect." Wow, he realized, what a concept! How could something be *more* perfect? "Please don't stop."

But she lifted her head to look around. Great, broad-cheeked, peasant-stock women were leering at her through every window.

"*Anh!*" She cowered against Pinto.

"Whassamatta?" He was sooooo tired. Not sick to his stomach anymore; just needed a few months' sleep. If he could close his eyes, only a minute, he'd be fine again.

"Pinto, who are all these *women?*"

"Huh?" His dick down, he wrestled it back into his pants. "They're just a bowling league. They're okay."

She was trying to get her blouse buttoned. "Pinto, I want to go, okay?"

"'M gonna do that in just a . . ."

"Pinto!"

But Pinto was resting.

CHAPTER ELEVEN

Alby Takes a Dive

HE WAS DREAMING ABOUT EATING Mindy. Now that she'd done him, his dream self felt, it seemed only fair for him to do her. With great apprehension, he tied on his lobster bib and moved toward her. She lay nude on a rug before a fire, legs apart. He was finally going to get a good look at *it!* But no matter how close he came, he couldn't quite see *it.* Then his face went too close and an incredibly powerful scent zorched up his nostrils, all smoky and sharp, and his eyes flew open. Alby was holding a bottle of Jack Daniel's beneath his nose.

"What're you doing?" Pinto whimpered.

"Using bourbon as smelling salts," Alby said proudly.

"Where am I? Where're the girls?"

"You're right the fuck where we found you — in the backseat of your car."

"Huh?" But it came back. He'd been getting blown! And then the women came out, and, well, he didn't know exactly what happened then. But he quickly deduced what *hadn't* happened, as he became aware, through the medium of his swollen groinal mechanisms, that he had blue balls once again.

He sat up abruptly. "Who's —"

"Scotty's driving."

"Hey, Pinto! How's your ass?" called Scotty cheerfully from the front seat.

His ass was grass. Someone had apparently driven a Frankenstein's monster bolt through his temporal lobes. And what could those demons of nausea think they were doing down in his unhappy lower trunk? Perhaps he should boot.

His whole relationship to booting had changed. Whereas it had formerly seemed one of the ultimate bad things that happened in life, now it was no bigger a deal than blowing his nose. So easy, once you gave in to it. He rolled down his window and executed the Technicolor yawn. The air rushing though his sweaty hair felt great.

Refreshed, he sat back down.

"Your knee went in my balls," Alby told him reproachfully.

"Where the fuck are we?"

"Headed back to Amherst," Moses said excitedly. "Pinto, I'm in love!"

Otter and Gay had hammered out an eleventh-hour truce, which, if somewhat shaky, was nonetheless in place. But that didn't mean Otter had to listen to this shit.

"Hey, Moses?"

"Yes, Otter."

"Suck one cock." It was the punch line from some forgotten bar joke, used now by the ADs as an all-purpose invective. "Talk about something else, okay?"

"Sure, Otter." He went close to Pinto's ear. "I'm going to have her up to school. After Thanksgiving and finals and Christmas and shit. I'll have her up for Carnival."

"But what happened to Mindy?"

"Dropped her at the dorm with the other girls. She said to tell you she had a wonderful time, except for the bowling women."

The car hit a pothole, which jounced them about.

"Fix this road, you asshole!" Alby yelled.

"Hey, Alby — where'd that bottle go?" Pinto did not feel like drinking bourbon — it would be like licking Archie Moore's toe jam — but he was suffering from toxic lag and sometimes there were things you had to do to put yourself right. Pinto believed his natural fallback condition was elation, and if life did not constantly provide it, he would just have to create it himself.

The bourbon flavor made him wince. No wonder the Confederates lost the fucking war, he thought sourly. But the next swallow was better, and after one more Pinto had begun to smell magnolias and hear the jaunty strains of "Dixie."

"Where's Seal?"

"If you had his date, would you be here?"

Right. Made sense.

"I bet the brothers just can't wait for us to get back there to ol' Amherst AD." There was an edge in Scotty's voice. "And you know what? I can't wait either."

Pinto felt a chill. The Amherst brothers had seriously pissed Scotty off. And now everyone had been drinking all night. Were they going to rumble? Normally of jovial disposition, Scotty could be induced to high dudgeon by certain circumstances. As, for instance, when Kennedy "stole the fucking election" last week. The Amherst ADs had outraged him, too. They had no soul. They kept telling them what *not* to do. He himself believed in green lights, all the way. Do any damn thing you wanted and, assuming you weren't hurting someone, be left the fuck alone!

The Amherst ADs, Scotty felt, had not shown the Dartmouth contingent respect. After all, wasn't Dartmouth AD the capstone of the whole fucking twenty-four-chapter national? The others just marched in lockstep, embracing the Adelphian status quo. Or so Scotty saw it.

Dim lights showed through the curtains of the living room as they pulled into Amherst AD's little side-of-the-house parking lot, and you could see through the open French doors guys in madras jackets, chinos, and bare feet, slow-dancing with their dates to Johnny Mathis.

"What a bunch of Amholes!" murmured Alby wonderingly.

Scotty nodded. A visceral, monsoonal rage was blossoming in his solar plexus. Oh, wait, that was indigestion. He gunned the engine and edged forward.

"Hey!" Pinto pulled himself up. "Where the fuck are you going?"

Scotty put on his shades. "To the belly of the beast!"

Lights dimmed, they advanced without detection, nosing through the French doors. The children of the ruling class twirled to "Wonderful, Wonderful" in the firelight, holding each other tightly.

Scotty hit the headlights. The dancers froze like fawns. He laughed. It was, Pinto felt, a fairly *scary* laugh. An image entered his mind of himself happily crawling into bed with a good science fiction book. He'd read a chapter and then, after releasing the multitudes of restless sperms currently cluttering his balls, fall wonderfully asleep and dream of, oh, desert cactus. There'd been that great magazine, *Arizona Highways,* in the doctor's office when he'd been a kid. The images of the strange green barrels thrusting from the desert sands had stayed with him. Yes, he'd like dreaming about those.

Scotty, not being telepathic and hence unaware of Pinto's pansy-assed fantasies, edged the car inexorably forward.

They began to be noticed. *"Eee!"* screamed several girls. "Hey, you sons of bitches!" roared some guys.

Scotty didn't precisely want to *kill* anyone, at least not consciously; what he *wanted* was to be a giant, industrial-strength cleansing device, sweeping away these people's entire *scene!* However, and despite the alcohol he'd consumed (which was urging him to squash the preppy bugs), his higher consciousness opted for a certain classy restraint. That's why he didn't simply peel out and send Amholes flying. He just kept creeping inexorably forward.

"Play some decent music!" he yelled out the window, honking the horn.

The crowd parted like a roadful of Korean refugees before an important courier in a jeep.

"Scotty! Hit that guy!" Alby pointed at the priggish Amherst AD he'd encountered earlier in a disagreement about washing hands after urination.

Scotty swung the wheel this way and that. When he banked right, a wave of dancers swept off that way. When he went left, same deal.

"You Amholes!" Alby yelled.

The Amholes were pounding on the hood like Central American

leftists. Time for the better part of valor. Scotty veered for the front door.

They barely fit through. After Scotty sort of, you know, *widened* it a little. *Skreek!* Then they were outside and bumpity-bumping down the broad front steps, the AD front door falling away crazily on one hinge.

Pinto was being hurled around the car. "Jesus! Scotty, take it easy!"

"Inner stillness, Pinto. The worst is over." He hung a left onto Main Street and calmly drove away.

Since there were no more beds at Amherst, they returned to Northampton. There was an AD refuge there — a mortuary, as it turned out. The place was owned and run by the father of a Dartmouth guy, a particular friend of the ADs named Czeluzniak. He was a Kappa Sig and he came down to the house a lot. His father ran the Northampton Home for the Dead or whatever it was called. Indeed, on one or two occasions, Czeluzniak and the ADs had driven to the City Café in the company hearse with a stiff in the back. Tonight, Scotty said, they would be able to crash there, no problem.

The dead-body area was downstairs. At the bottom of a stairway, and along a hall, was the Adelphian Suite, a trio of rooms Czeluzniak said would always be there for them. Pinto went to the head, booted a couple of times, blew his boogers out, threw cold water in his face, took a piss, jerked off, combed his hair, and came back out, a new man. Alby glided mischievously up, offering a quart bottle labeled FORMALDEHYDE.

"Are you crazy?" said Pinto. "Get that away from me!"

Alby shrugged and took a swig. "Ahhhhhh!" he said, with no visible detriment to his being.

Pinto snatched it away and sniffed its mouth. "Hey! This is gin!"

"Did I say it was formaldehyde?" He retrieved the bottle and had some more.

It wasn't long before the boys were ready to rest. The clock was striking three and the only thing left on the radio was marine hymns. Otter showed him the bunkhouse. It was a showroom for coffins. And that was where the ADs racked out, peaceful as babes, each in his own silk-lined casket.

• • •

THE DARK SIDE of road trips was that they ended. Tired and hung over, mottled with odd bruises and abrasions, Dartmouth guys at Skidmore and Wellesley and Vassar and Endicott marshaled themselves on Sunday mornings to face the long schlep home. As for Pinto, he was awakened by the sound of his coffin lid slamming. He opened his eyes to find darkness.

"Hey! Get me the fuck out of here!"

The lid lifted. Alby smiled down. "You rang?"

Pinto did not think he was funny. If he hadn't been supposed to not show his emotions, he really would have shown his emotions. Out he came, wrapped in a horrible leather shroud of hangover symptoms. Matters were not helped when the ADs, having pulled themselves together, went upstairs and found rain falling. The malevolence of the New England winter cannot be overstated, and it was a real pain in the ass faced five months a year by all local college students unable to teleport. Pinto sighed; he sure was going to enjoy driving through this shit.

After a nutritious breakfast of a Coke and a slice at the Boss Nova Pizzeria in Amherst, the ADs hit the road.

"Hey, why don't we play Geography?" cried Moses. "Alabama!"

"*Shut the fuck up!*" yelled Scotty, Otter, Pinto, and Alby. It was weird. The beer would take you sooo high. And then, like the waters of Old Faithful, down you'd inevitably come. It dissuaded one of God's existence. Ingmar Bergman was right.

They retraced Friday's route, albeit with less exuberance. Alby was drunk for the occasion but no one else had bothered. They were thinking about Monday classes. Alby shrugged and took personal possession of the dwindling Adelphian beer supply. Pretty soon they were at the entrance to Route 5.

"Aw, look at that poor guy." Moses meant the shit-for-brains in a Dartmouth jacket who'd stationed himself by the entrance. The stupid gork was huddled there, wet and miserable, sticking out his thumb.

"Should we pick him up?" Moses asked.

"Fuuuuuuck him!" said Scotty, Otter, and Alby.

Pinto wanted to seem generous-spirited and a good guy, but really didn't want the schmuck drenching his backseat. He said nothing.

"Come on, you dipwipes! Look at the poor guy! Pull the fuck over."

Pinto sighed. As no one made major objections, he stopped, and the poor guy clambered gratefully into the back. Alby drew away from him in distaste.

He was a freshman from Richardson Hall. His name was Rick or Steve. Moses tried to start a conversation but couldn't get much going.

"Come on, Scotty," Pinto whispered. "Be nice. Maybe he'll rush next year."

Scotty snorked.

Seal, roaring through the rain, spotted the Ford and came in fast and at a tilt, throwing a great wave of water against the windshield. He laughed at Moses's surprised face peering through the window.

Moses stuck his head out. "Hey, Seal! How's your ass?"

"Moses," said Seal, "this is your lucky day."

Moses felt a quease of anxiety. "Why?"

No cars were about. Anyone with any sense was home with a fire in the fireplace.

"Because I'm giving you your first motorcycle lesson!"

"Me? I . . . don't know what to say." Moses did not want a motorcycle lesson in the freezing rain, seated behind a maniac. But you had to be cool.

"Come on, man. We'll outrun the raindrops."

"Great!" Stoically, Moses reached for the door handle.

"Are you crazy?" cried Pinto. "You'll die!"

He managed a casual laugh. "Don't worry so much, man." He got out and climbed on the bike. "C'mon, Seal, let's see what ya got!" he cried, with a show of lightheartedness.

Seal took off, sending Moses's head flipping back. *Oh, my God,* Moses thought as the enormity of his mistake sank in.

"Gonna be a long day for the boy," Otter observed.

Soon they were on Route 5 North, apparently alone in the universe, the freshman in back eyeing Alby apprehensively. By now the weather was as nasty as Pinto's diarrhea had been that morning, if less brown. The temperature was poised a few degrees above freezing.

"Okay," Alby announced, "I've got a new stupid game."

They regarded him warily.

"In this game, we have to figure out how to use all the states in the Union in a sentence."

"Alby, what are you talking about?" Otter, having slept a whole three hours, was back in the pink.

"Okay, take North Dakota. Now listen: The further you go North . . . Dakota it gets."

Otter and Pinto looked at each other.

"Here's another. There's this guy and he tells his roommate he's got a date and he'll be out all night. The roommate wishes him luck. But the guy comes back in a half hour with a broken nose and a black eye. 'What happened?' the roommate asks. 'Well,' the guy says, 'everything was going fine but then I asked for a blow job.' The roommate shakes his head. 'You idiot! You Nebraska that on the first date.'"

Otter and Pinto found themselves laughing. Scotty would not be cozened into any such display.

The car flung itself northward. Alby continued sucking down beers and soon stated that he badly needed a whiz stop.

Pinto peered through the windshield. The weather made it an alien world out there.

"No, Pinto." A contrarian mood sometimes took Scotty, and one just had. "Keep driving. Alby, you have to hold it."

Alby shook his head and laughed. "Hey, Scottso? Kiss my pledge ass!"

Pinto felt dread. How would Scotty react to such outright mutiny?

Scotty laughed back. "All right, you don't have to hold it. Here. Do it in this." He stuck an empty Budweiser Imperial quart bottle at Alby.

"Swell." Alby resigned himself to the no-stop policy and took the bottle. The freshman eyed him warily as he clumsily pried out his member with his other hand.

The mouth of the bottle went in and out of focus before Alby's eyes, a gateway to an alternate universe. He pointed his dick and let go. In his urinary system's advanced state of readiness, the pee leapt forth with an exuberant gurgle that rose in pitch as the bottle filled.

Scotty had been following this through the rearview mirror. With a laugh, he grabbed the wheel from Pinto and began swerving the car left and right.

"Hey!" said Pinto.

"Whoa!" cried Otter.

"Jesus, cut it out, will ya?" Alby's pee stream had ceased to thread the needle.

Scotty continued to swing the car from lane to lane. Alby, abandoning all hope, fell back on the seat, laughing helplessly. His penoidal extension, left to its own devices, spun round and round like a lawn sprinkler. And though he didn't get much altitude, he sure got dispersion.

"Anh!" Little zaps of pee were striking the freshman's shoulder, chin, and socks. *"Stop!"* he screamed suddenly. *"I have to get out!"*

"Are you nuts?" said Scotty. "It's the planet Venus out there."

"Let me out!" the freshman screamed. *"I gotta go!"*

Otter and Scotty exchanged a look and shrugged. "Pull over, Pinto."

The guy sighed in relief as the car slowed.

"Listen, you've made a great impression," Otter assured him. "We hope to see you in the fall."

The guy repressed a hysterical laugh. "Right. I'll be there for sure."

They stopped atop a slushy hill. Route 5 continued to be nearly deserted. The guy could wait a long time before someone came along. Until he turned into a snowfreshman at the side of the road. But out he went, and began walking away as quickly as possible.

"Come back, Shane!" Alby called.

"Damn, that was one good helicopter job, Alby." Otter seemed pleased.

"It was?" said Alby.

"Is that a term we should know?" Pinto asked.

"Well, sure, if you want to. I mean, I just made it up, but yeah! What do you think, Scottso?"

"Fine term, Otter. The next time I see someone's dick spinning around, I'll know just what to call it."

Pinto pulled back onto the highway. The driving was bad but not horrible, and the Ford was able to chug along without skids or other mishaps.

"So, which fire are you going to be at, Otter?" Scotty asked.

"Oh, I thought I'd welcome the boys at the first fire. You know, make 'em feel cared about." His eyes went to Alby, Pinto, and Moses, and he laughed nastily.

"Why is that funny?" Alby looked anxiously back and forth at them.

"And you, Scotty?"

"Oh, I thought I'd do the final fire. You know, the survival cooking class?"

They laughed even more nastily.

"Why is this funny?" Alby cried. "What aren't you telling us?"

Pinto went over the crest of a hill and started down. Drizzle fell in veils. An upcoming bridge traversed a deep ravine.

Pinto continued forward without concern. But there were things people didn't know, down there in the suburbs of New York City. And one of them was that *bridges freeze first*. Because, as temperatures fall, the still-warm ground keeps roads from freezing while bridges ice up in a few seconds.

They hit the bridge. The car didn't have a chance. It shot forward, out of control, twirling like a ceiling fan.

"*Yahhhhhhhh!*" The guys clutched one another.

The skid took forever and no time at all. And then they slammed into the railing about four fifths of the way across and caromed off, spinning much faster now.

"*Whoooooooa!*" The ADs' eyes were like saucers.

Blamp! They went off the central rail, back to the east rail, and came to rest.

Four doors flew open.

"Holy fuck!" cried Pinto. "My car!"

"Holy *fuck!*" cried Alby. "The hill!"

They looked up the hill. Another fool was coming down too fast. He'd do the same thing they'd done!

"Run!" Otter cried.

Omigod, Alby thought, *he's gonna hit me!* He vaulted over the side of the bridge and fell thirty-seven and a half feet to land on his ass on a pile of rocks. The wind knocked out of him, he lay there, gazing at the stars, which the clouds had just obligingly revealed, the weather now, at this absurd moment, clearing.

Meanwhile, the other guys had leapt in all directions. Pinto had thrown himself — Steve McQueen–like — behind his car, then, realizing what a dumb schmuck he was, run like hell for the end of the bridge. Scotty and Otter were hot on his heels.

The oncoming car hit the ice like a suddenly released bowling ball, zooming straight for them. Happily, it hit the railing a good hundred feet in front of them, the ice on the bridge having become only more slippery. The car boinged back and forth between railings and came to a stop in its turn. A man and a woman burst out in consternation.

And now another car barreled down the hill, in blissful ignorance of its fate.

ON THE NEWS that night, it was called a "freak twelve-car pileup." Things took forever to sort out. A cool state trooper brought them coffee. Well, Pinto didn't have coffee, as he felt coffee tasted like the constipated shit of gibbons mixed with hyena piss. The other guys had coffee. They'd been having such a great time! He hated when things took a turn away from fun. Fuck the car — what happened to their carefree Sunday afternoon?

There was a distant cry.

"Did you hear something?" Otter asked.

It came again.

"Was that *Alby?*" said Scotty.

"Hey, where the fuck *is* Alby?" Otter said. "I haven't seen him since the crash."

The wind had shifted and you could hear better. "Hey, guys! I think I'm hurt!"

They sprang to the rail. There was Alby waving to them, a Rorschach blot on the rocks below.

An ambulance came and took them to the Brattleboro hospital. Pinto, Moses, Otter, and Scotty sat around the lobby without much to say. Scotty called the house and ninety minutes later Dumptruck showed up in Coyote's corroded station wagon.

They filed out of the local cop shop: Pinto, in his torn, stained sport coat; Moses, with no shoes; Scotty, smoldering over this most recent interface with the Man; and Otter, wondering how much longer he was going to think this shit was cool.

"What happened to you guys?" Truck asked wonderingly.

No one leapt to respond.

"Seal and Moses were just pulling into Hanover as I was heading out. Quite a ride in the rain, I guess." He eyed them. No reply. He shrugged and drove the rest of the way home in silence.

CHRISTMAS BREAK WAS FUN, especially since Pinto managed a "gentleman's C," in his father's words, in all his courses. He did Christmas stuff with his gentile friends and Hanukkah stuff with his Jewish friends. Ace, he didn't see at all.

The biggest treat was the trip into the city to see John Coltrane at the Village Gate. This was one of New York's premier jazz clubs, on Bleecker Street in Greenwich Village, and going there, you felt very cool. He and Froggie paid the scowling black woman in the dashiki and decended the stairs to the Gate's cavernous interior. Somehow, they wound up with seats right by the stage.

At nearby tables were lots of chicks with dark eye makeup and great, unbrassiered tubes bouncing against their peasant blouses. Pinto was impressed. They were like Bennington girls, only more *city* somehow. And all the black cats in shades — how did they get around this dark room without barking their shins? There were also a few Beats — scruffy, bearded white guys with torn sweaters and annoyed expressions. Their era was winding down.

At length, Coltrane came out with his group. He seemed very serious in his dark well-tailored suit, not making jokes or being playful with his bandmates. Indeed, there was a certain air of distraction about him. Maybe, Froggie said, he was listening to music that his brain constantly generated. Wow, Pinto thought, how would you get any sleep?

The pianist was McCoy Tyner, a skinny, dapper dude, and the bassist's name was Jimmy Garrison. The drummer was a revelation. Elvin Jones ranged over his kit like a man possessed, churning out rhythms and polyrhythms that made Pinto's head spin. He was like some great natural force, a tornado (for Pinto) and storm-tossed waves crashing on a shore (Froggie's metaphor).

And then there was 'Trane. Here, the comparison switched to volcanoes erupting, or maybe stars going nova. Never in human history, Pinto felt, had a man projected so much energy from the mouth of a horn. He wasn't just running chord changes, like Dexter Gordon and a host of other modern jazz tenor players. Instead, he could blow notes so quickly that he could play arpeggios containing two or three chords within the space of a couple of seconds. It took Pinto a while to get used to what he was doing. At first, it was just noise. But when he *listened* . . . Wow!

When 'Trane played the great "My Favorite Things," which went on for twenty-three minutes of uninterrupted gorgeousness, Pinto opened his eyes and watched. 'Trane had picked up an instrument that looked like a fat clarinet and turned out to be a soprano sax. It gave the music a strange, foreign sound, like it might have partially come from India or Egypt.

Pinto was looking up at a sharp angle, but he got a great view. 'Trane's whole face scrinched up when he blew. His eyes squeezed shut, a vein bulged on the side of his neck, and another at his temple. His sweat flew around in the spotlight. Pinto had never been so impressed with anyone.

He went home with a revolutionized sense of life. If 'Trane could do what they'd just heard him do, then a person could do anything!

No limits! That's what the implied message was. Pinto felt inspired to take something to the limit, too — be like 'Trane. Unfortunately, he had no idea what that something might be.

WHEN HE GOT BACK to school for second term, winter had stormed into Hanover like a wrathful frost giant. Snow blanketed the buildings and the Green. Streets and walkways had been cleared somewhat but every other topographic feature was buried. The bright winter sunlight bounced off the snow to create a blinding glare; you had to wear shades. And it was freezing, the temperature seldom rising above twenty. Altogether, a recipe for serious physical discomfort that would not go away until April. But that was Dartmouth.

Suddenly, everyone was walking around with skis on his shoulder. Isaac came into his own at this time of year, heading out every other day to Stowe or Sugarbush or Mad River Glen or even, if he was squeezed for time, the Dartmouth Skiway, just to be up on those lengths of wood, flying down a hill. Pinto thought skiing looked great — from a distance. He had this weird aversion to compound fractures.

His first visit to the house was for the Wednesday-night meeting. For some reason, Black Whit's car, in the AD parking lot, was a wreck. The windshield was shattered, the fenders were deeply dented, the tires were flat. Perhaps it was a fashion statement.

At the meeting, Dumptruck took the podium. Filthy Phil was president, but since he never came to meetings, here Truck was with terrible news. He glowered down at the membership like an Old Testament God. "Welcome back!" His voice dripped sarcasm. "So glad to see you all. Well, here we are in second term. And weren't we all ready to have a good time! Carnival's coming, the Fires, too. But oh, no — *five hot-shits* came back yesterday and now we're in trouble again!"

This was terrible news. But what had happened was no big deal, really. Whit, Alby, Zeke Banananose, Fitch, and Hardbar had gotten drunk in the basement. Whit had stated that he *hated* cars, that humanity would be better off without them. The rest agreed, and, well, they'd merely heeded their feelings and gone to the parking lot, where they attacked Whit's black Packard with a baseball bat, bricks, and the sharpened tip of an umbrella.

"How can you be in trouble for destroying your own car?" Whit asked indignantly. "Isn't that unconstitutional?"

Dumptruck was not interested in the constitutionality of the Interfraternity Council Disciplinary Committee's ruling. He took a deep breath.

"Let's review the basics. The first time they caught us — remember Rat and that chick in the furnace room? — we got a college warning. Now they've caught us again, for what they're calling *wanton fucking destruction of property,* and we're getting a *second* college warning!" He regarded the miscreants balefully. "They met last night."

There was a terrible silence.

"But we're still okay," Scotty said. "Right? We're not on probation or anything."

Truck laughed. "If someone *farts* the wrong way, we're gone. As we all know, they've been looking for an excuse to shut us down for years. So I guess we're all going to behave like Dartmouth gentlemen for a while."

"Hey, Scottso — get us a string quartet for Carnival!"

"Yes, we could serve iced tea. How about a poetry reading?"

"Hey, cool!" Truck wanted to have funny ideas, too. "We'll turn the sex room into a play space for poor emmet kids!" He remembered he was mad. "You think this is a joke? Well, I think it bites!"

Pinto thought it bit, too. Big Brother was always watching them, just because they had a better time than the other houses. Meanwhile, time was passing and Winter Carnival was around the corner. The AD hell night had to be coming any day now. The pledge class braced themselves. When would it be?

CHAPTER TWELVE

The Night of the Seven Fires

"PINTO! WAKE THE FUCK UP!" CRASH! WHAM!

His eyes popped open. The clock said 6:00 a.m. Brad's face was hanging down from the top bunk. "This has got to stop!" it was screaming at him.

Pinto stifled a laugh. Upside down, Brad's scowl looked like a smile.

"You think this is *funny?*" Brad's anger was so great it seemed to make his head expand.

"No, *you're* funny. Upside down, you look like a being from another dimension."

"I'll give you another dimension. Get your fucking fraternity brothers out of here or I'll throw you out the fucking window!"

"Okay, okay." Pinto threw back the covers, ran across the chilly room, and ripped open the dresser drawers.

"Pinto! Pinto! Pinto!" The voices were chanting it.

"I can't believe this!" Brad cried. "When is this going to end?"

"Today, I think." Pinto pulled pants, turtleneck shirts, and sweaters over his long underwear. "It's the Fires; it has to be."

"Oh." Brad thought a moment. "If you die, can I have your records?"

Pinto had managed to get enough layers on that he stood a fifty-fifty chance of not instantly expiring when he went outside. Their window thermometer stood at 7 degrees. Fucking New Hampshire. He raced from the bedroom to the front door and threw it open.

Dumptruck filled the doorway like an enraged Kodiak bear. With a great *"Ahrrrrr!"* he grabbed Pinto by his parka flaps and yanked him into the hall.

"Have fuh-unnnnn!" Brad called after them.

TRUCK AND SCOTTY marched Pinto toward the house, flanking him like a military escort, the clouds of their breath like ghosts trying to escape from their heads. Inhalation was a drag in weather like this. Your phlegm froze. Once, when Pinto had had a cold, mucus had dripped from his nose and formed a snotsicle.

"Hup two three four!" barked Truck.

The sun would not be up for another hour. They clumped through the darkness and cold and up onto the AD front porch. Where it was pristine, the snow reached midthigh. This was typical. Inside, they found a crowd of brothers having coffee and doughnuts.

"Cool!" Pinto grabbed a mug.

"Are you bent?" Scotty shrieked. *"Get the fuck in the tube room, pledge!"*

Pinto jumped and raced for the tube room. So this was how it was going to be. Inside, he found Rhesus Monkey, F. A. Mac, Goosey Gander, Huck Doody, and Moses strewn about the furniture. Alby was on a sofa. Pinto dropped down next to him.

"Hey, man. You awake?"

Alby regarded him coldly. "Now I am."

"The brothers gave me this nice cup of air." Pinto took a sip.

"Yeah, I don't see why we can't have coffee." Rhesus Monkey's eyes were slits worthy of Ming the Merciless.

The door opened briefly and Bags was propelled inside.

"Hey, you guys." He was as casual as if they were meeting for a quiet breakfast at the Inn coffee shop. Grace under pressure, that was the thing. Today of all days.

Of course, one pledge was always reliably graceless. "Does anyone know what they're doing to us tonight?" Goosey Gander fretted.

"I hear that if you're not circumcised, they use ice to numb your foreskin and then cut it off with a Swiss army knife," said Rhesus Monkey.

"Yeah. Supposedly it doesn't hurt all that much," said Alby.

As was well known, Goosey possessed a hooded hog. He grabbed his crotch in horror.

Now Round and Rat were thrown into the room. Round bowed grandly. Rat fell down and seemed to doze off.

Finally, a short wait later, Fitch clumped in, on crutches once again.

"Aw, Christ!" Alby rolled his eyes. "*Now* what?"

"Greenstick breaks in the forth and fifth metatarsal. There was this manhole —"

"Never mind!"

"Whoever does the Fires with Fitch, look out for falling rocks," the Monkoid warned.

"You think they'd make me do the Fires on crutches?" Fitch regarded him with amusement.

"I think they'd make you do them in a *wheelchair*," said Rhesus Monkey.

Their conversation was interrupted as Mouse and Charlie Boing-Boing kicked open the door, making everyone jump. "All right, you assholes, you're all accounted for but Seal, and when we catch him —"

"Yo! Here!" Yawning hugely, Seal separated himself from a heap of blankets and overcoats by one of the bookcases.

Mouse tried to hide his amusement. Seal often took his rest in the tube room after a good bar night. To the seniors, he was the Great Sick Hope for the future of AD. "Okay, you guys — first you have to take the AD pledge test!"

The pledges evinced neither delight nor enthusiasm at this announcement.

Snot and Terry No-Come handed the test out. The *questions* covered five pages. The pledges had been told to bring their own blue books, but Pinto now wondered if two would be enough.

"So I hope you guys paid attention to Brother Machine's lectures," said Charlie Boing-Boing. "Now, what was that founder's name again? Let's see . . . Samuel Crabs? Samuel Manta Ray?"

The pledges searched their memories. What *was* that guy's name? This did not bode well. Grumbling, they let themselves be moved to separate rooms, a stratagem the brothers had developed to discourage cheating. Pinto sat at Scotty's desk and read through the questions, half of which seemed to concern aspects of AD that had never even been mentioned. The fraternity *creed?* How were you supposed to answer a question you knew nothing about? *Oh, right — bullshit,* Pinto remembered. He *had* learned something at Dartmouth.

Alby couldn't stand having to sit still so long and soon found himself suffering from anal itching. Bags sputtered indignantly at each new question, which just made the brothers laugh. Fitch, naturally, kept sustaining paper cuts. Rhesus Monkey laughed at the questions and wrote whatever came to mind — his opinion of recent movies, his taste in beer, his mother's operation. No one would ever read it, he was sure. Goosey Gander sweated bullets, trying to frame answers that would please the brothers. Seal burned the test in Dumptruck's ashtray, leafed through a couple of his skin magazines, beat off, and took a nap.

When the time was up, the brothers collected the blue books. Next on the agenda, Willy Machine informed them, was the reading of the pledge papers. Pinto had been working hard on his, the one about biting off girls' nipples. He was hoping the guys would enjoy what he'd written.

By four, the brotherhood had moved to the bar so that beers could be drawn. Pinto and the others got their hopes up, but Otter announced that, for now, only brothers could imbibe. Indeed, several of them seemed to have been drinking all day, or all their lives, for that matter.

"Okay! Shut the fuck up!" It was Hydrant. "First we have that star of stage, screen, and girls' locker rooms — Huck Doody!"

Huck made a cautioning expression around the room, like an infielder looking a runner back to second. He'd brook no interruptions or inane commentary. Clearing his throat, he began.

"'Finger Painting with Your Own Shit. For me, it began early. The artistic impulse struck for the first time shortly after I turned one and a half. There seemed to be all this stuff in the back of my diaper, so I pulled some out. I didn't know what it was yet — I was too young — but it was brown and smelled pretty good. As I squished it pleasingly through my fingers, I was struck by an idea. Standing in my playpen, I began wiping my hands on the wall. To my wonderment, gorgeous swirls of brown appeared.'"

Huck was getting laughs and groans. His intonation became more passionate.

"'Pretty soon, I'd covered a quarter of the wall. This was the first panel of the triptych I was planning, *Burnt Umber Sunset*. But before I could move on to the critical central section, my father came in and started screaming. He *hated* my painting! I grabbed another handful of my pigments and threw them at him.'"

Huck looked up with a grin. "'So he spanked the shit out of me.'"

Guys were laughing and applauding. Huck favored the room with two stiff bows and, yes, a shit-eating grin.

"All right!" called Charlie Boing-Boing. "Next, F. A. Mac."

Mac was the straightest pledge, except maybe for Goosey Gander. He had a crew cut and wore horn-rimmed glasses. He'd been with the same chick — Beverly — since before they were conceived. He was going to be a pediatrician. He was the nicest guy Pinto had ever met.

F. A. Mac stood apprehensively.

"Don't be nervous!" Magpie shreiked.

"'Sex with Multiple Amputees. When having sex with the limbless, you should strive to find a woman with good humor and an open attitude. Having myself had sex with many four-stumpers, I was most fond of Susan. My friends and I used to screw around with her often. And *around* is the operative word, as we soon discovered that the best way to work things was to place her on a revolving platform, so that she could suck my wang while my friend

Bob had his face in her crotch. Then we would rotate, and now I would sample her candy box while Bob's boogie became the focus of her oral attentions. It struck Bob after several rotations: what we had here was truly a lazy Susan!'"

More laughter. This torrent of sickness from the mild-mannered, bespectacled future children's doctor was almost shocking.

Bags was next, discoursing on "My Sensations at Birth." His essay opened with a great line: "When I began my life by crawling from a vagina, little did I realize that I'd spend much of the rest of it trying to crawl back in one." Yog got a major round of snaps for that one.

Next up was Seal.

"Oh, uh, I meant to mention: I can't find my pledge paper."

"*What?*" cried Mouse.

"I dunno — I had it all done. It was in one of my notebooks, but I guess I left it somewhere. It was pretty good, too."

The brothers looked at one another. What should they do to him? Shave his entire body? Introduce paint thinner to his rectum?

"Okay, Seal," Otter said, deciding. "We're going to get you tonight."

"Yeah," said Mouse. "We'll give you some material for a *new* pledge paper."

"Whoopee." Seal made little circles in the air with his index finger.

"Goosey Gander!"

It was the moment Goosey had been dreading. The brothers regarded him cynically. This would probably be the worst paper of the day.

"'Nine Ways to Excite Your Date with a Garden Hoe. One might begin by inquiring what other sort of hoe there is. A concrete-parking-lot hoe? A gymnasium-floor hoe? But never mind.'"

The brothers took hits off their beers, bored.

"'But if you really want to excite your date, I'd throw away that garden hoe. Put on some soft jazz and undress her slowly, taking the time to plant small kisses on her flesh as you reveal it. Especially, caress her nipples lightly and watch them come to ruby hardness. When she's nude, stroke her all over, gradually bringing your hands to her Triangle of Excitement. Part her legs and pour warmed maple syrup so that it runs over her belly and into the cleft of her sex.'" All this in Goosey's strange, reedy voice. Dumptruck once said he sounded like an oboe.

The brothers' boredom had vanished. This was sort of . . . *hot*. What had happened to Goosey Gander?

"'It is often good to part the pussy lips with a gentle thrust of one's slippery chin. Then, later, your dick will slide in fine. And speaking of your mighty prod — your personal garden hoe, as it were — you may now thrust it into her well-lubricated motorcycle repair shop.'"

Motorcycle repair shop? Truck mouthed to Scotty.

Scotty shrugged.

"'Now, pull it out again, because the next seven ways involve your tongue.'"

"*Ow!*" screamed Truck.

"Tell it, bro'!" piped Hardbar.

To spare the reader a possibly inconvenient self-gratification, the rest of Goosey's pledge paper shall go unreported here. When he finished, dead silence ensued. Then Hardbar began to applaud. Then the whole room applauded, Dumptruck and a few other guys actually standing. Then Pinto realized the reason they were standing was to run up to their rooms for a minute. This was the ultimate compliment; Goosey grinned shyly. No one could fathom how he'd done it, but Goosey Gander had somehow just scored the first major points in today's competition for the Adelphian pledge prize.

When the guys returned, Willy Machine shouted, "Pinto! Your turn!"

Pinto gulped and stood. This was like following Little Richard. Well, he'd just have to make the transition from sublime to revolting as pleasant and breezy as possible. Act like a nice guy, not the pervert the subject required him to be. "'Three Ways to Bite Off a Girl's Nipple, and Five Good Uses for It Thereafter. Biting off a girl's nipple is always a splendid thing to do, but as with most human effort, there is a downside. Principally, the blood that bursts forth at the moment of dentation —'"

"*Agghhhh!*" cried Dumptruck.

"'— will spatter your face and clothes. You will need a basin and warm water. But I digress. In the first nipple-biting method, which was originated by Rube Goldberg, you fasten your teeth around the nipple in question. Holding your jaw with your hand, you place your elbow over the foot of a guy being hit on the knee by a doctor with a rubber mallet. Pung, zip, bite! Remove nipple from mouth and dry on paper towels. Wash face in basin.'"

"*Agggghhhh!*" cried Truck and several others. It was a sound of affirmation, like the crowd at a bullfight going "Olé!"

Pleased, Pinto continued. "'Technique number two. Once the nipple is between your teeth, walk her into a meat freezer. Your teeth will soon chatter violently and voilà. Method number three: paint the circumference of the nipple with ground chuck and thrust her mammalia into a cage of starving coyotes.'" Pinto winked at Coyote, getting a laugh out of him. "'The nipple will soon be removed but may be difficult to retrieve unless you wear long padded gloves.'"

"*Agggghhhhhhhh!*" cried Dumptruck. "This is fucking sickening!"

"'Now, as to the five uses — one might stretch the nipple and wear it as a beach hat. Or use it as a Frisbee! Another possibility — you could put in on a baby bottle.'"

"Hey!" said Scotty. "That's redundant. You can't use a nipple as a nipple."

"All right. A doorbell?"

Scotty considered. "Yeah, okay."

"Come on! Two more uses!" Magpie hated it when things bogged down.

"Right. 'Fling 'em sideways so they skip across a lake. And, finally, graft them to the foreheads of the Japanese, so there'll be an actual reason for calling them nips.'"

That got a huge laugh. Pinto might not have won Best Pledge Paper, but he walked away with Most Disgusting. At AD, this was meaningful. The brothers had just informed them there was a pledge prize this morning. The guy that threw the overall best show today would get it, and Pinto was determined to be the one.

Although how he could ever win, with wild men like Seal and Alby around, was an open question. But he was going to try.

Around seven, the pledges were released for their pre-Fires dinner. "Nothing too hard to boot," Otter advised them. "Spaghetti's best."

Minaciello's was Hanover's sole Italian restaurant. Hanover's sole non-American food purveyor of any kind, actually. It was a big, friendly place with red-and-black-checkered tablecloths and clusters of straw-wrapped Chianti bottles dangling from beams. The pledges helped Luigi and his wife pull tables together, putting four of them in a row.

When Luigi pulled out his order pad, seventeen guys yelled, "Spaghetti!" So he brought out a huge bowl of the stuff and set it before Rhesus Monkey. As he poured tomato sauce liberally over, the Monkoid began tossing the pasta with his hands, loudly singing, "Oh, Marie."

New Hampshire liquor laws being what they were, the boys had to settle for Cokes and root beers with dinner. This necessity was unpopular.

"Why aren't we in New York?" Alby lamented. "Why aren't we attending Cornell or Hamilton or somewhere?"

"Yeah!" said Rat.

"Fuckin' A!" Fitch waved his crutch.

"You know what, you guys?" said Huck Doody. "I think you're going to get all the beer you want in a little while."

"I want to propose a pact." Goosey Gander was full of surprises today; everyone looked at him. "The pact is, we're going to help each other not die tonight. Because I don't know about you guys, but I'm scared shitless."

Few would have admitted it but almost everyone was scared to some degree — if not shitless, then, certainly, with a much smaller quantity of shit than usual. Pinto was buzzed on adrenaline. Alby's leg was bouncing up and down. Huck Doody was laughing too hard.

Dinner was nice. The boys were beginning to feel like a team. Whatever the Seven Sacred Watch Fires of the Alpha Delta Phi held for them, the pledge class would meet it together. They were ready.

Well, as soon as they got totally shitfaced down at the house, they would be.

Marching back together, they were in a considerably better mood. Light snow drifted down. Snow was so quiet. Pinto was knocked out by snow. When they got to AD, they found the parking lot devoid of cars and the house bereft of brothers.

Except for Filthy Phil, who greeted them jovially in the basement.

Pinto hardly remembered the house president; he hadn't seen or thought about him since Sink Night. A hotshot engineering student, all he did was book, or so it seemed. But on tonight's solemn occasion, in order that the rest of the brothers could go prepare the bonfires, he had left the engineering library long enough to come down and, in effect, shoot the starter's gun.

"Boys," he said, "we have bought you a keg. I've been through the Fires twice, and here's some wisdom I've acquired: the drunker you are, the less you feel the cold."

The pledges climbed all over one another to get to the taps. Soon, music was blaring and beer was running continuously through them and out their dicks. But this was nervous drinking, more functional than fun. They were like a line of cars at a gas station, filling up for the hazardous trip ahead.

Filthy Phil looked at his watch. It was ten p.m. "Gentlemen, zip your parkas."

A shiver of anxiety ran through the pledges. This was it.

Filthy Phil explained some things. They would go out in pairs, carrying mimeographed maps. The maps would take them to a remote spot called Balch Hill, which they would ascend until they found the first fire. Also, when they were walking to the various fires, brothers in cars would be cruising the road, trying to catch them. Anyone they caught would have to return to the house and start over. Even if they were almost done. "So don't get caught," Filthy Phil advised, having a look at his clipboard. "Here are the pairings. Moses and Round, Alby and Fitch —"

"Hey, you're kidding, right? I mean, I'm not going out there, am I?" Fitch pointed to the cast on his foot.

"Pledge, we wouldn't think of doing the Fires without you."

Fitch went pale.

Rhesus Monkey sniffed. "Told you."

"Okay, next we have Huck Doody and Y. Bear —"

Huck and Bags nudged each other and laughed like rascally cartoon criminals. They'd show the brothers.

"— F. A. Mac and Seal —"

F. A. Mac could see the logic — straightest guy in the pledge class paired with the most bent — but he sure wished they'd put him with someone safer. He thought a moment. There *was* no one safer. He sighed; years from now, over port and cigars, he'd probably laugh merrily about this.

"— and finally, Goosey Gander and Pinto."

Pinto's jaw dropped. The last guy in the world he wanted to go through the Fires with was Goosey Gander. He wanted to be with one of his friends; Goosey, he hardly knew! He'd never felt *motivated* to know him. The guy's presence in the fraternity was an anomaly, due solely to Zeke Banananose's error during rush. The nickname was, as usual, perfect — Goosey looked like that comic book character Baby Huey, the giant duck in diapers. Six four, but with a lot of his weight having apparently sagged down into his ass, Goosey was like a sofa cushion that hadn't been shaken for a year.

Bags and Huck Doody were dispatched first, out the back door into the arctic night. They looked grim.

Pinto was throwing down beer after beer. Goosey watched in incomprehension. "With all they're going to make us drink, you want *more?*" He himself would drink as little as possible. Sadly, he had no choice.

When Pinto had demolished another two beers, Alby and Fitch exited, Fitch clumping out on his crutches, throwing back resentful looks at the brothers. And after another two . . .

"Pinto! Goosey Gander! Front and center!"

Filthy Phil inspected them. He held the basement door open. A gust of howling, freezing wind greeted them.

"You guys?"

Pinto and Goosey looked back at Filthy Phil.

"This won't go by again. Enjoy it."

Pinto filled with unexpected exhilaration. He'd wondered for weeks how he'd feel when it came time to embark. Now he knew — he was psyched!

Goosey just gazed hollowly straight ahead, as if viewing distant disasters unfold. Why had he joined AD?

HUCK DOODY AND Y. BEAR headed across campus for Lyme Road, which would take them out of town. They walked solemnly down the middle of the plowed street, the snow heaped high on both curbs like gloomy cliffs. The sky had cleared, and apparently the brothers had arranged for a full moon, for there one was, illuminating the frozen campus with silvery light. The tableau was hushed, white, and serene. Leafless trees, coated with ice, clattered in the wind.

The boys passed the libes and the chem building. Bags strode along as if he owned the night, a squat, dense figure, chin thrust forward like Mussolini. Huck scampered like a cat, eyes restlessly searching for any sudden appearances of cars.

"Hey, Yog."

"What?"

"Heard much about the seventh fire?"

"Not really. Why?"

"I don't know. There's a rumor they're planning something really sick up there."

"Swell. I thought they were planning something really sick at *all* the fires."

"Well, yeah, but they say the seventh is really, *really* —" Huck cut off. A car was coming, small and white — it could be Terry No-Come's MG, ready to take them back to the house! "Bags! Over the top!"

Bags didn't quite make it. Instead of going over the drift, he went *into* it, leaving a Bags-shaped hole. For his part, Huck went over the top like an Olympic drift jumper. When he landed facedown on the other side, however, a submerged, invisible bush slashed his forehead. Huck felt blinding pain and saw stars. *Jesus Christ.*

The car contained merely a tired English professor and was an Austin, not an MG. Yog emerged from the snowbank, brushing himself off. "Huck? Where are you?"

"I'm here, I'm here." He landed beside Bags.

Bags drew back. "Hey! There's blood all over your face!"

"There is? Shit."

Bags took a closer look. Several nasty rips across Huck's brow were enthusiastically welling gore. "You asshole! All right, let's get you to Dick's House."

PINTO AND GOOSEY took Lyme Road without mishap. Civilization gave way to wilderness; on either side of them, deep pine forests now loomed. The temperature when they left the house had been ten above, but out here it felt like twenty below. The boys' boots on the snow sounded like squeezed bags of cornstarch.

"Pinto, this is crazy. It's total wilderness! *Anything* could happen!"

"I think that's the point, Goosey. The way I look at it, this is a rare chance in life for some truly insane behavior without an authority figure in sight."

Goosey regarded him, at a loss for words. But Pinto wasn't his problem. And did he ever have a problem! The Fires were going to be horribly worse for him than for the other guys.

Pinto saw the look on his partner's face. "Hey, whoa, what's the matter?"

Goosey couldn't keep it to himself anymore. "Pinto, I've never told this to anyone. *I can't boot.*"

Pinto didn't know what to say. Within the Adelphian belief system, it was like admitting to impotence or chicken fucking. Well, actually, the ADs might have liked the chicken fucking. But poor Goosey — what a terrible dilemma! "Don't give up, man. Booting is a normal human function. You'll catch on."

To Pinto's surprise and great discomfort, Goosey began to cry. "I've never been able to boot. Even when I was sick with the same virus that had everyone else booting their guts out, I couldn't boot."

"But we had those practices. How did you — ?"

"I pretended. I made noises and spat a lot. Pinto, I've never booted in my life!"

A stunning admission. His sympathy for Goosey deepened. It must have been terrible, slogging through the years of childhood viruses and stomach flus without being able to boot. But he couldn't let these sympathies take over his night. Priority one was having a ball. Well, priority one *always* was having a ball. Next on the list was winning the prize. Priority *three,* he supposed, was keeping an eye on his hapless pledge brother.

They started forward again.

THE DOCTOR FINISHED sewing up Huck Doody's forehead, which hurt like a motherfucker. "I'd go sleep it off now, son," he said.

Outside, Bags eyed Huck's dome of white bandages and said, "So, we're going to your room?"

"Are you kidding?" said Huck. "I need at least twenty or thirty beers for the pain." He pulled the laughing Bags with him, in the direction of Balch Hill.

THE WAY YOU could recognize the turnoff was that a bunch of cars had turned off there. The narrow roadway, which was old and riddled with potholes when not blanketed with snow, wound up the side of Balch Hill. Where Pinto came from, hills were mild, inoffensive things; to his mind, the great hump ahead should have been called Le Balch Massif. It stretched up before them, a tree line about a hundred yards ahead. From there on was pine forest.

"Okay, let's go. Maybe they'll *make* you boot. They're experts, right?"

Pinto's attempt at comforting Goosey went over like one of those dumb rockets the air force tested that flew up a little way, made a U-turn, hit the ground, and exploded. Shrugging, Pinto resumed his slow progress up the hill.

After another ten minutes of hard slogging, they penetrated the tree line and made a sharp environmental transition to dark, hushed forest. The map, examined in the light of Pinto's Zippo, said they should just stay on the old road, so they did, dwarfed by the enormous pines, peering with trepidation into the great darkness on either side.

And then, as they rounded a ridge, they saw the first fire! It roared upward, primitive and terrific, making a golden oval of illumination amid the trees. Several figures were silhouetted. They headed toward it.

Soon, voices could be heard, and then laughter. Among the laughs was "Uh-heh-heh-heh-heh."

Pinto felt himself grinning. "Come on, Goosey. This one shouldn't be too bad."

They closed in on it. The firelight created a ring of crazily dancing tree shadows, a display of powerful human mojo to spook the boogedy-boogedies of the night. Perched on a stump was a pony keg, gravity tapped, and there Otter was, along with Mouse, Terry No-Come, and Pale Pete, drinking beers and discussing the universe.

"Hey, Otter!" Pinto shouted. He barged toward them.

The brothers spun to glare at him with Parris Island–like fury. "What did you say?" shrieked Charlie Boing-Boing, leaping out from behind the fire.

Pinto opened his mouth.

"*Shut up!* Say nothing! You come in here on your *knees,* pledges!" Mouse screamed.

Pinto stole a look at Goosey, who was stoically going to his knees.

"*You heard him, Pinto!*" Charlie Boing-Boing's voice was so high and piercing, Pinto was concerned it might dislodge precarious snow above, burying them all. "*On your knees and call in!*"

Surrendering to the process, Pinto joined Goosey, and they began calling in. "*Most unworthy neophyte, Pinto/Goosey, begs to announce his most humble presence at Alpha Delta Phi!*"

"What? What?" Mouse was aghast. "Did you hear that?"

"Tisk," said Otter. "Appalling."

Pinto and Goosey looked at them blankly.

"*This isn't Alpha Delta Phi!*" Charlie Boing-Boing yelled. "*You fucking assholes!*"

Oh. Right. Pinto and Goosey began again. *"Most unworthy neophyte, Pinto/Goosey, begs to announce his most humble presence at the Adelphian fires!"*

The brothers considered a moment, drinking their beers and smoking their cigarettes. Snow fell from a branch, hitting the ground with a great *ker-flump!* The air smelled like electricity.

"Actually," Otter decided, "you need to say 'at the *first* Adelphian fire.'"

"Most unworthy neophyte, Pinto/Goosey —"

"Shut the fuck up!" screamed Mouse. *"We know who you fucking are!"*

Otter smiled and shook his head at the silliness of it all. "Gentlemen, you may approach the first fire."

Pinto and Goosey went to stand with the others. Terry No-Come handed them each a beer. "Ha! Gave both of you your names, didn't I?" he observed.

"Hey, that's right. I think we should drink to Terry, don't you?" Otter asked Pinto and Goosey.

Pinto was set to chug, but Otter spoke up. "No, no, Pinto. This one's a gentleman's beer — for Terry."

They drank a gentleman's beer. That meant you took a minute or two with it, enjoying it in a quasileisurely manner — like a gentleman. In the fire, Pinto noticed embers that looked like a terrified face.

"Now, boys," said Otter, "how about saying hello to my girl."

"Hi," said a voice, and venturing from behind the fire, dressed in a pert blue ski parka with a furred hood, was Gay Tabiggatits! Pinto couldn't believe that it had even *occurred* to Otter to bring her.

"Hi, Gay," he said.

"What is this, a fucking cocktail party?" Charlie Boing-Boing screamed at him. "Knock off the chitchat!"

Mouse returned the pledges' cups, filled to the brim again.

"Thank you, Meesedip." Otter turned genially to Pinto and Goosey. "All right, gentlemen, now that you each have a beer, why don't you chug them?"

They raised their glasses and began to drink. The frosty fluid made a ribbon of cold down Pinto's throat.

"Two more beers for the boys," said Otter.

Terry had them waiting. That they were in sixteen-ounce cups, holding twice the volume of the glasses they customarily used at the bar, wasn't bothering Pinto at all. He chugged his beer and belched loudly.

"Oh!" Gay clapped her hands to her hood. "You have sullied my ears!"

"Please apologize to my girl, Pinto."

"I'm sorry for sullying your ears, Gay."

Terry gave them two more beers. Again they chugged. This time Pinto overtilted and twin rills of beer made icy lines against his cheeks.

"Asshole!" cried Mouse and Charlie Boing-Boing. "Asshole! Asshole!"

"You're supposed to get it all in your mouth," Pale Pete explained.

"Well, enough preliminaries," Otter said. "It's time we got down to some serious booting. Don't you think, honey?"

Gay forced a smile.

"Good. Terry, give Pinto a fresh beer."

Dependable Terry returned with another beer.

"Now, chug!" ordered Charlie Boing-Boing.

Pinto swung the cup to his mouth and began swallowing deep drafts. He wished he could just open his throat and pour the stuff down, the way Truck and Zeke Banananose could. Someday he'd be brave enough to try that. To think he'd once doubted what Magpie said, that all this could be fun. He was having a *great* time. The brothers were so cool. Otter was terrific. Terry was terrific. They were *all* —

Glorp! Something thick and goopy went down his throat and caught there, like a giant wad of phlegm. Pinto gagged — and booted. He booted everything he'd had to drink all night in a single great arc of roaring foam and twining pink spaghetti strands that narrowly missed Charlie Boing-Boing's left ear and splatted spectacularly against the trunk of a tree.

"All right!" exclaimed Mouse.

"Outstanding!" cried Charlie Boing-Boing.

"Wow, tight pattern!" enthused Terry No-Come.

"Uh-heh-heh-heh-heh-heh." Otter looked at Gay, who managed a giggle. She had gone quite pale.

Pinto spat several times and cleaned his mouth with snow. "What the hell was in that?"

"A raw egg," said Pale Pete. He was the house nice guy, always ready to lend a hand or clear a confusion.

"Now, Goosey!" Otter announced jovially, as if introducing the next contestant on a game show.

Goosey swallowed and turned to Otter. "Put in two, okay?"

"All right, pledge Gander!" The surprised-but-pleased Otter bobbed his head forward and back, grinning the old Otter grin. Everyone else smiled, too, though they did not bob their heads forward and back.

"How about some warm-up beers first?" said Charlie Boing-Boing. "Get him rolling."

Great, thought Goosey. He took the proffered beer from Terry and, swallow by swallow, drained it.

That selfsame brother Terry No-Come came back with another glass.

Goosey drained that one, too.

"Come on, Goosey!" cried Pinto. "You can do it!"

Terry, like a machine doing the same thing forever, handed Goosey another beer.

Goosey tiredly drank it down.

The time had come. Mousedip handed the beer with the eggs to Boing-Boing, who passed it like a sacred chalice to Goosey Gander.

Goosey looked into it with trepidation, but began to drink. It wasn't that he didn't feel the disgusting objects traverse his boot zone. It wasn't that he was somehow immune to physical revulsion and nausea. Just, in his case, they did not trigger vomiting. And so, experiencing profound revulsion all the while, he chugged the beer and eggs down and set the cup unsteadily on a stump.

"*Anhhh!*" Charlie Boing-Boing walked disgustedly into the woods, where he could shortly be heard taking a leak.

"No boot?" said Terry. "Gee."

"Boooo!" Everyone looked at Otter. "Boooo!" he repeated.

"Penalty!" yelled Mouse, leaping up and down. He and Boing-Boing handed Goosey another cup of beer, this one laced with cigarette butts. They were just trying to help.

Goosey shuddered but drank that down, too. This time, he actually gagged — but he didn't boot. Turning green he was, but boot he did not.

"You should take lessons from Pinto," Pale Pete advised him. "Pinto booted very well."

"Yeah, fuckin' A," said Terry No-Come. "Pinto, have a gentleman's beer."

Pinto felt a warm bloom of acceptance. But instead of sipping the beer, he amazed himself by pouring it down his throat, just as if he'd always known how. Then, crumpling the cup, he threw it in the fire. His grin met with big returned grins of the brothers. Goosey sighed.

ROUND AND MOSES were released from the house at nine forty-five. It was so cold their eyelids stuck to their eyes. Crossing the Green, they clumped past the growing Winter Carnival snow sculpture. It was thirty feet high so far, but you still couldn't tell what it was going to be. That was a surprise they'd spring during Carnival week.

Round, still pursuing a spot in the Hard Core, was looking forward to a jovial evening of sickness during which he hoped to establish himself as a Henry VIII for our times. Like Pinto, he wanted to display a stylish improvisational insanity and, of course, get drunk as shit. Maybe it was actually a Falstaff for today that he wanted to be.

Moses, though, was looking lost and terrified. How was someone like him going to get through a night like this? he asked Round. He was a guy in thick glasses who played chess! Maybe he'd die. Maybe he'd puke so hard pieces of his stomach would fly out of his mouth.

"Moses, cheer up!" Round, in all his globular corpulence, grinned at his pledge brother. "We'll show those guys some tricks."

Moses looked mournfully at him. "But something's wrong. I don't feel right."

Round thought a second. "Moses, how many beers did you have tonight?"

"I don't know. Three or four."

Round looked at him in exasperation. "That's not enough. You're still Marty. You're not Moses yet."

Moses looked thunderstruck. "You're right. I was so busy worrying about the Fires, I forgot to drink. What am I going to do?"

Round sighed. He'd been planning to drink the brandy himself, later on when he got really cold, but what the hell? He pulled out his silver flask and handed it over. Moses's eyes lit. Stammering thank-yous, he gurgled down half the contents.

"Damn!" he observed. "Not bad."

"It's Rémy."

"Cool!" Before Round could reach for a sip of his own, Moses quaffed the rest. "Wow, man, that did it. I feel like myself. You're a great guy, Round. Thanks."

They proceeded out of town. Round smiled. He'd helped his AD pledge brother.

Moses smiled, too. He'd faked Round out and now was drunker than ever.

WATCHING FITCH STUMP along beside him, his fucking crutches keeping them to a crawl, Alby tried to quell his impatience. He'd never particularly liked Fitch. He wasn't sure why. Viewed superficially, they were much alike. Their capacity for alcohol was greater than anyone's in the pledge class, except Rat. But then, Rat could have outdrunk W. C. Fields, Dean Martin, and a giant sponge all at once. The problem was that fucking Fitch kept getting injured! How could you respect a guy who broke a bone a week? He was just looking for attention. His mommy had ignored him or something.

At length, they arrived at the second fire, where the presiding brother proved to be Hardbar. *Oh, Christ,* thought Alby and Fitch at once, *he's going to make us beat off!* Also present were Flea, Tiger, and Monk, among whom, Alby feared, not a man jack would make the slightest move to prevent such ignominy. But, no, all they had to do, Monk told them, was drain the beer from a condom. Big fucking deal — drain a condom. But it was hard! Alby couldn't figure out how to get the beer in his mouth. And the rubber, being wonderfully flexible and stretchable for modern sex, must have held a half gallon. Alby finally stuck the open end in his mouth, bit down, raised the rest with his arms, and then unbit a little. He was able to regulate the flow of beer into his mouth thereby, and soon had chugged it down.

The brothers were pleased with Alby, though not nearly so much as he was with himself.

Tiger ran beer into a second condom. When it was great and bulging, he offered it to Fitch. Propping his crutches under his arms, Fitch took it. He tried a few ways to drink from it, but none worked. Then he spilled half.

"Whooooop!" cried Flea, re-creating the sound of a nuclear war air-raid siren. *"Penalty, penalty, penalty . . ."*

"Aw, shit." Fitch was not pleased with the situation. "What's the penalty?"

"You have to drink this." Hardbar handed him a new condomful of beer.

Fitch tried, but the crutches made him awkward. He spilled half the new condom, too, and dropped the next one on the ground, where it burst with a total loss of beer.

Tiger was losing patience. "Fuck, pledge, you're a total incompetent! Haven't you ever drunk beer out of a scumbag before?"

"It's these crutches, man."

"Well, then — fuck 'em!" Tiger yanked them away and threw them in the fire, where they burst into flame. Fitch fell over with a surprised yelp.

"Shut up!" comforted Hardbar. "But we will take account of your handicap. Lie back and open up."

"Okay, good idea." Fitch did, and the brothers poured a rubber's worth of beer into his mouth. He managed to swallow half. Another 40 percent ran down his cheeks, and 10 percent went up his nose. It was that 10 percent that made him cough and then boot high in the air like a fountain.

The brothers cheered in unexpected delight. Alby felt the momentum in the win-the-pledge-prize competition shift instantly to Fitch. *Shit,* he thought.

PINTO AND GOOSEY trudged on through the pristinely-beautiful-but-implacably-hostile-to-life landscape, up the trail, in search of the third fire. It was so cold that if you touched your eyebrows, they broke. Against the northern horizon now danced flamboyant aurorae borealae. Pinto grabbed his nose and twisted it, feeling the phlegm glaciers within break up and breathing return.

"So, Goosey," Pinto said. "How do you feel?"

Goosey looked at him fretfully. "Like I drank a bathtub."

This did not augur well. Pinto tried every way he could think of, but he couldn't make it augur well. In fact, he didn't even know what *augur* meant.

"What'll happen?" Pinto asked him. "Will you explode?"

"I don't know. This has never happened to me before. It's probably never happened to *anyone* before." His face scrunched up. "How can I *not be able to boot?*"

Pinto was moved by Goosey's plight. He himself often felt like an outsider. But how did you help a guy boot? Run headfirst into his belly? As for Goosey's chances of surviving the night, Pinto felt it could go either way. They had moved into new and unknown regions — the Lewis and Clark of puke.

Ahead, a swarm of sparks rose to drift across the sky. And now you could see those spookily waving tree shadows again. There, behind a hump of snow, blazed the third fire. Pinto and Goosey fell to their knees.

"Most unworthy neophyte —"

"Hey, knock off the yelling, you shitheads! Get in here!"

The boys leapt up. Awaiting them were five brothers under the leadership of Willy Machine, in his World War I German greatcoat. Nestling in the snow were numerous gallon jugs of cheap red wine.

"Pinto and Goosey? We thought you were Bags and Huck Doody."

Bags and Huck Doody hadn't been there yet? That was strange. They'd left twenty minutes earlier than he and Goosey. Where were they?

"Well, no matter." Willy, with his usual absence of affect, took a stick and inscribed a circle in the snow. "Pinto, you get to sit in the throne."

Pinto hadn't heard about any thrones. Still, with his parka and many layers of clothing beneath, he was pretty well insulated. He started to sit.

"Oh, and drop trou first."

Each fire, Pinto was realizing, took on the personality of its head brother. Whereas Otter's had been genial, playful, and beneficent, Willy Machine's would be cool and efficient. Bracing himself, he dropped his various trou and eased his ass into the snow. Twin flowers of cold blossomed on his buns.

"Goosey, you take this"— Willy handed him a huge mug of wine —"and stand right there between Pinto's legs. Pinto, get your legs open. Now, we're going to play a little game. What's it called, men?"

"*Boot in bush,*" chanted the brothers.

They'd formed a wolfish semicircle around Pinto and Goosey — Coyote, with his feral grin; Embryo, chortling with cowboylike good humor; Snot, caught up in another of his energy vortices, bouncing up and down like an excited basketball. There were no girlfriends.

"Okay, Goosey, I want you to start chugging this wine," Willy Machine said. "And when you boot, I want it to go square in Pinto's bush."

"Yeah, none of this turning your head away stuff," said Snot.

Pinto experienced an almost unbearable urge to bug out. This was truly depraved. But he took a deep breath and the crisis passed. Nothing they could dish out was going to be too sick for *him*.

"When I boot, huh?" Goosey's words were slurring. It struck

Pinto that his own continuous booting was keeping most of the alcohol out of his system. Goosey, on the other hand, was getting hammered. No one had ever seen him drunk. What would he be like?

"Pinto, I'm really sorry about this. I —"

"Will you hurry up and boot in my bush? I'm freezing my ass off down here!"

Goosey gulped, shut his eyes, and began chugging as fast as he could. The brothers leaned forward eagerly. Now that Goosey was on wine, Pinto couldn't believe he'd continue not booting. He could almost feel the steaming cascade blasting about his genitals.

"*Yurch!*" went Goosey. "*Blurg! Hurch!*"

Pinto cringed, waiting for the splash. When one didn't come, he opened his eyes. Goosey was jackknifed over his groin, gagging like sixty, but all that was coming out were two long strands of saliva boot, dangling like pale, glistening worms in the firelight.

"Goosey, come on already!" Pinto's butt had gone numb.

"*Boot boot boot,*" chanted the brothers.

Goosey straightened with difficulty and resumed chugging, but more slowly now, taking several swallows, then stopping and weaving a bit, then swallowing again. Suddenly he dropped the mug and bent violently at the waist. The brothers leaned forward. Pinto cringed. Goosey made a terrible set of sounds . . . and nothing came out.

"*Asshole asshole asshole,*" chanted the brothers.

Abruptly, from the rim of the clearing: "*Most unworthy neophyte, Bags/Huck Doody, begs to announce his most unworthy presence at the third Adelphian fire!*" A pair of figures parted from the darkness and walked toward them.

"Why, hello, boys," purred Willy Machine. "Stop off for a few drinks?"

"On your *knees*, pledges!" barked Snot. "You crawl in here! You're late!"

Bags and Huck traded exasperated looks. Pinto got the feeling they weren't getting off so well on the degradation aspect of things. Then he noticed Huck's bandage.

Bags made a play for sympathy. "Sorry, guys. Little stop at Dick's House."

"Yeah," said Snot, "and I had to jerk off in my grandmother's hat. Goosey and Pinto *beat you here!* Pinto, stand up and get those trou back on."

With a gasp of relief, Pinto jumped to his feet, drawing layers of clothing over his poor frozen cheeks. Willy Machine found a fresh patch of snow and drew side-by-side circles in it with his stick. "Bags, Huck, drop trou and sit your asses down right here."

"What?" rumbled Bags.

"Jesus Christ!" Huck's head hurt and he wasn't in the best of moods.

"*Hit it!*" Willy's stick pointed unwaveringly at the thrones.

Radiating indignity, Huck dropped trou and sat. "*Holy shit!*" he said as his ass met snow. Bags took his time about dropping *his* pants. You had to let the brothers know you weren't scared. Without comment, he settled himself into the throne next to Huck's. The snow pushed up his scrotum, and his stublike penis pointed at the stars.

"Snot, mugs of wine for Pinto and Goosey." Willy Machine prodded Goosey with his foot. Goosey tiredly arose.

"*Double boot in bush,*" chanted the brothers.

Pinto was delighted. He took his wine eagerly and positioned himself by Goosey over the wide-open legs of Bags and Huck Doody. They began chugging.

"Hey, what is this?" said Huck, with dawning comprehension.

"Goosey!" bellowed Bags. "If you boot in my bush, I'll kill you!"

Pinto paid them no mind. He'd almost drained his mug when the wine caught in his throat, triggering a gag. A red parabola sailed from his mouth to Huck Doody's groin, where it splattered with great violence.

"Pinto!" howled Huck. "*Jesus Christ!*"

Goosey, meanwhile, seemed to be full. Really, completely full. No place for further wine to go. He looked at Willy Machine helplessly.

Bags, thinking himself saved, turned to laugh heartily at Huck

Doody, who was frantically wiping his lap with handfuls of snow. Pinto saw another opportunity. "Snot, gimme more! Quick!" Shortly, a second boot blew forth, a spray boot this time that covered Yog's entire being.

"*Good Christ!*" Bags thundered. "Pinto, you son of a bitch!"

The brothers cheered. Snot darted here and there with his invisible trombone, playing "The Stars and Stripes Forever."

Pinto beamed. He was doing okay.

SEAL SPED THROUGH the woods. It seemed to him that if he could go fast enough, he'd be able to run on top of the snow.

"Seal! Where are you going?" It was the cautious one, Mac, they'd sent with him. "We better stay on the trail. We'll get lost."

Seal ran back and laughed. "How can anyone be lost?" Overhead, every star was sending its own extremely narrow beam at him. The moon said nothing. It was beautiful but dumb as shit, like a Persian cat he'd once had.

"Hey, isn't that it? Up there?"

Seal saw the fire. Its great thermal energies — all those squiggly lines — made him howl. Bunching his leg muscles, he sprang.

"Hey!" Mac ran after him.

"*Awhoooooo!*" Seal keened. Branches flew by. The clearing came closer, figures looked up in surprise, and he dove, moving in slow motion, doing a perfect swan, to float on the golden pool . . .

Whash!

Troll jumped a foot. The body had bolted from the woods, screaming, and thrown itself dead center into the fourth fire. With a great burst of flying embers, the logs and brush collapsed and scattered like the lost tribes of Israel. There was no fire left! After he, Gland, Einswein, and Snake had spent an hour building the fucking thing!

"It's Seal," realized Gland. "He's fucking nuts!"

F. A. Mac arrived at the scene. "Seal, what are you doing? Get out of that fire!"

Laughing, Seal rolled to his left, onto clean snow. The parts of him that were burning went out. Smoke rose from his coat but his mien was blasé.

"Hey, guys! How the fuck are ya?" He leapt up and held out his hand.

"You asshole! You son of a bitch! You fucked up your pledge paper and now you fucked up our fire! Where are we supposed to find more wood?" They began throwing chunks of debris at him, as if he were a sinner in biblical times.

Fuck! Seal spun and ran. Apparently, malign spirits had taken control of his brothers.

F. A. Mac heaved a tired sigh and raced after him.

MR. MOON HAD SAUNTERED a good way across the sky. Rhesus Monkey was totally shitfaced. He clumped toward the fifth fire, dead ahead, one arm around Moses and one arm around Round. The two had caught up with him sometime recently. He was having a grand old time.

Eventually, they arrived at Giraffe's fire. It was the only case that night in which the brother in charge was taller than the fire he'd built. With him were Pig Pen, Guinness, Downey, Sow, and Mole. They had a giant block of ice they'd hauled up in Pig Pen's pickup, and you were supposed to drop trou and sit on it until you'd chugged your weight in ounces. This sounded vaguely fatal to Rhesus Monkey. In his case, of course, since he weighed less than a box of Saltines, it would be no big deal, but for Round?

"Welcome to the fifth fire," Giraffe said. "Why don't we start with a gentleman's — uh, where's Rat?"

Rhesus Monkey, Round, and Moses looked around vaguely. "Weren't you his partner?" Moses asked the Monkoid.

"Yeah, uh . . . well, I don't know. Was he with me when you guys caught up?"

"Shit, maybe," said Moses. "I don't know. I don't talk to him much."

"All right, this is fucked up," said Pig Pen. *"Where the fuck is Rat?"*
No one knew.

• • •

F. A. MAC WADED THROUGH the woods, frantically trying to keep Seal in view. It almost looked like he was running *on top of the snow.* But that was impossible; he had to be seeing it wrong. It was pretty dark. He wondered if he wasn't dreaming the whole thing. "Seal! Wait! No one's going to hurt you!"

Seal's voice called back. "You could be the Under Lizard!"

What? Mac pressed forward. He was catching up — he could see Seal clearly now. And then, he wasn't there! Mac couldn't wrap his mind around it. Then he heard Seal yell his name and ran forward desperately, only to stop short. He was on the bank of a stream or river or something; he could hear it and smell it.

Another bellow. It was coming from below. Seal had fallen in! F.A. didn't even stop to think. He rushed down the bank.

RAT STAGGERED THROUGH the woods. He couldn't remember why he was here. That was all right; he couldn't remember most of the last five years. In fact, what was his name? Well! Damn fine night. He wished his dog were here. Oh, wait, he didn't have a dog. He had a wife. *She* was a dog, some said. He sure was thirsty. He ate some snow. Tired as shit, he looked around for a spot out of the wind. He'd only rest a minute.

F. A. MAC SPLASHED into the river and felt a flood of relief as he realized it was ankle-deep and no wider than a driveway. Seal was perched on a flat rock in a lotus position. Mac burst out laughing. He pulled Seal to his feet. "You fucking asshole!" This was rare language for F. A. Mac, but he had to express his delight.

"I think this is the World River, Mac. It flows from Asgard out into —"

"Good, Seal. Now, listen —'cause I'm pre-med, remember? — we're wet, and if we don't get warm soon, we'll die."

Seal nodded. "Cool."

"*Extremely* cool."

They crossed the little stream and kept going. With no idea

which way anything was, this direction was as good as any. At least they were headed downhill.

PINTO AND GOOSEY reeled along. What fire was next? Pinto had lost track. He sure had booted a lot. After tonight, all future booting would be trivial.

For Goosey, something interesting was happening. His head had gotten sort of fuzzy, in a very pleasant way, and all sorts of jollity was bubbling up in him. If this was what being drunk was, no wonder the guys liked it.

Pinto misinterpreted Goosey's expression as another cry coming on and tried to cheer him up. "Hey, Goosey. Your pledge paper was great, man." It felt funny, calling Goosey Gander "man." But Pinto had seen him bear up under some pretty intense punishment tonight. And he hadn't quit.

"Yeah? You liked it, huh?"

"Fuckin' A. But, Goosey — uh, by the way, do you hate that name?"

Goosey considered. Until now, he basically *had* hated it. But tonight was different. If there were guys in the house willing to be called Mouse and Snot, what was the big deal about Goosey?

"I've kind of gotten used to it."

"Imagine *my* delight when they named me after my dick." Actually, Pinto was full of shit. He *loved* that they'd named him after his dick. "So, Goosey, tell me — how did you manage to write that pledge paper? Did you sniff glue or something?"

Goosey giggled. "Promise not to tell anyone?"

"My lips are zipped."

Pinto had magically transformed into a totally great guy, someone Goosey could trust with his life, so he didn't mind telling him. "Hardbar wrote it for me."

Of course! It made perfect sense. The writing had been so Hardbar. Pinto laughed, and Goosey joined him.

"You can't tell anyone, now."

"I promise. What did you have to do for him?"

"Nothing. He said he just wanted to watch everyone shit when I read it."

Pinto's respect for Hardbar went up. "They shit, all right."

They clumped on. Had to be a fire up there somewhere.

PIG PEN AND GIRAFFE had managed to get the hearse turned around, and now they were headed slowly back down the hill with the three pledges in the backseat, Giraffe manipulating the spotlight.

"Poor Rat." Rhesus Monkey was very worried. "I hope he's okay."

"He better be." Pig Pen was deadly serious now.

They drove slowly on, five pairs of eyes searching. Unbearable guilt racked Rhesus Monkey. He hadn't taken care of his pledge partner. Rat might be an asshole — indeed, a good case could have been made for throwing him down a well and leaving him there — but the Monkoid should have looked out for him.

"Well, look who the fuck it is!" Pig Pen pointed. And there Rat was, curled up in the snow at the side of the road, fast asleep. The minute Pig Pen braked, Rhesus Monkey was out of the car, running to his side.

"Nice to see a guy who really cares about his pledge brother," Giraffe observed.

"You fucking asshole!" Rhesus Monkey began kicking Rat vigorously.

"Hey! Wha — ?" Rat stirred and sat up.

Four sets of lungs exhaled. Rat was among the living.

The Monkoid left off finally, out of breath, and held out his hand. "Come on, get up, you stupid cocksucker!"

"Yeah," Pig Pen said to Giraffe. "It's nice when they get along."

F. A. MAC SPOTTED IT FIRST. "Seal! A road!"

They were shivering like sheep exposed to nerve gas. Clambering down the steep hillside, they slid the last ten feet and landed on the road. Mac had no idea where they were, but it was great to see something that bespoke people and civilization. The road had even been plowed.

"Mac." Seal pointed ahead. "Beady red eyes!"

The beady red eyes were the taillights of a Cadillac sitting on the shoulder. Exhaust plumed from its rear. Someone was in there!

They hit the car at the same instant. The windows were completely fogged. They began pounding on them. "Help! We're freezing out here! Please let us in!"

There was a pause. A rear window rolled down slightly and a pair of eyes peered out. *"Mon dieu!"*

After a moment, the door opened. The boys piled inside, feeling the warmth envelop them. Greeting them with an existential smile was Pierre Astier, the French professor. Smoothing her clothing was a young woman named Cybele. There would be time later to think about how weird this was; for now, relief was all.

Astier inspected them. *"Zut!* You are the polar exploraires, eh? Come on, I take you back to town."

"Hey, honey," said Seal to Cybele. "Wanna see my tattoo?"

ALBY WAS SIMPLY THRILLED to be serving as Fitch's crutches. Ever since Tiger burned the real ones, Charlie had had to fling an arm around his shoulders in order to limp along. They were just like the fucking AD statue.

"You asshole!" Alby yelled. "Why must you be *wounded* all the time?"

"Wish I knew. Been like this all my life. Mom says I'll probably die young."

"Hey, you guys!"

They saw Round and Moses hurrying toward them. "Hey, how's your ass?" Round inquired.

Fitch was exuberant. "Great! Havin' a ball!"

Alby threw him on the ground. "Well, have it down there for a while!"

The boys used time-honored American methods to figure out the disposition of labor regarding Fitch: they threatened one another. Alby was through carrying Mr. Disability around, he declared. Moses passionately defended the useless asshole's right to be a useless asshole. Finally, proceeding with the obvious, Fitch

202 · *Chris Miller*

flung an arm around both Moses and Round, who would spell Alby until the next fire. Five down, two to go. Hup two three four.

PINTO AND GOOSEY, tired and cold — yet somehow still ahead of all other pledge pairs — spotted the seventh fire.

"Last one, Goosey." Pinto licked his chapped lips. "Then they make us brothers."

Goosey's rosy alcohol glow had begun to fade slightly. "Assuming we live."

"Come on, you're doing great. All ADs have to go through this. Dean Dickerson went through it. Dr. Seuss went through it, when he was here in the twenties."

"Dr. *Seuss?*"

"Yeah, he was a class of 'twenty-five; didn't you know?" This much was true; his name had been Ted Geisel then. That Dr. Seuss had done boot-in-bush at the Fires, well, possibly it had happened in some alternate universe where Bishop Sheen sucked buffalo dong on TV.

"*Hey, you assholes! Hurry the fuck up! We're sick of waiting for you!*"

Goosey gulped. This one wasn't going to be nice, like Dumptruck's. The sixth fire had proved to be one long gentleman's beer.

"You gonna be okay?"

"Oh, you know, I weigh a thousand pounds, but other than that, I'm raring to go."

He'd made a joke! It wasn't a very *good* joke, but the thought was there. Grace under pressure! Pinto was impressed.

Holding each other up, they entered the clearing. The seventh fire was a smaller fire, with a smaller contingent of brothers, but they were the very sick heart of the junior class: Scotty, Black Whit, and Magpie. And another guy was there, too, a most unusual-looking stranger. He seemed as genial and full of fun as Santa Claus. No beard, but his cheeks glowed redly in the firelight, and his features were cherubic.

Pinto looked at him in wonder. Where had they found this character?

Magpie stepped up. "Pinto, meet Rat Battles."

Pinto froze. Rat Battles? The original Adelphian Rat, class of '57, who'd anteceded the dumb slob version they had now? The legend who'd dispensed nickels from his foreskin? Who could power piss twenty feet? It was like meeting Babe Ruth.

"So, how'd it go at the first six?" Scotty asked chattily.

Pinto was so enthusiastic in his descriptions of the night's rigors that the brothers laughed. "Pinto is definite house material." Rat Battles grinned. "I say we take him."

"Hear that, Pinto? You're a brother." Black Whit slapped him on the back.

Pinto couldn't believe it. Just like that? Wouldn't he have to kneel before this Adelphian prince and be tapped on the shoulder with a dildo or something?

"How's the night going for you, Goosey?" Magpie asked, with bright cheerfulness.

"Oh, uh, very consistent."

"Good. Well, we want you guys to know that you don't have to drink any more."

We don't? thought Pinto and Goosey.

"Nope," said Scotty. "We figure you made it this far, you've demonstrated your drinking prowess. But we did think, after all that booting, you might be *hungry.*"

Rat Battles nodded. "So we brought you a midnight snack."

Midnight snack? What was this? Pinto examined their faces. Something had changed. The smiles were still in place, but they'd become leers.

Goosey didn't notice. "Thanks, guys, but I can't eat anything. Not a chance."

"*You'll eat, you fucking asshole pledge, or you won't leave this fire alive,*" shrieked 'Pie. "Scotty, where's the hot dogs?"

Scotty plucked a pack from the snow and handed Pinto and Goosey each a wiener. The boys regarded them uncertainly.

"So, all we have to do is eat one of these and we're done?"

"That's all," said Scotty.

Pinto shrugged and brought the frank to his mouth.

Black Whit slapped his hand away. "Whoa, that thing's frozen solid! You want to break your teeth?" He smiled. "You have to heat it first."

"Drop trou, Goosey, and spread your cheeks!" shrieked Magpie.

Goosey's jaw dropped. "What? *Why?*"

Rat Battles placed a companionable arm around him. "You're helping prepare food for your fellow pledge under emergency conditions, with no matches or lighters. Pinto has to hike out of the wild. He needs the energy from these hot dogs. It's a survival situation, Goosey, and they're not gonna thaw on their own."

The wind howled and blew snow in their faces, as if to offer proof of his words.

Suddenly, Goosey got it. He realized exactly what was expected of him, how he was supposed to help Pinto thaw his hot dog. *Oh, my God,* he thought. His asshole cinched shut like a stick-poked anemone.

Pinto blinked. He wouldn't have believed Goosey could look worse than he already did, but his pledge partner had just gone gray as death.

"Please," Goosey pleaded. "It's a one-way street down there. My mom couldn't even get a thermometer in."

"Ah-ha!" said Rat Battles. "But she didn't have *this.*" He drew a jar of Hellmann's Real Mayonnaise from his parka pocket and displayed it dramatically.

"Hey, cool idea," said Scotty.

"Now drop trou and spread 'em!" screamed 'Pie.

Goosey rolled his eyes in despair, too sick and semiconscious to resist further. With slow, heavy hands, he dropped trou and spread 'em.

Scotty dipped Pinto's hot dog in the mayo and handed it back, topped by a generous dollop of white. "Go ahead, man. And leave it up there until it's warm enough to eat."

Goosey's cracked ass was not the most inspiring sight Pinto had ever beheld. The sphincter looked too tight and tiny to admit a knitting needle. This was grotesque. He wished it were 1945 and he was digging Bird at the Onyx Club with a blonde on his arm. Any time or place other than now and here.

• • •

ALBY, ROUND, AND MOSES slogged forward, Bataan-death-march style. They were drunk, sick, and exhausted, and just wanted the fucking night to end. They'd been good ADs and drunk everything handed them. They'd booted repeatedly, and in prodigious quantities. All that remained was the seventh fire.

Hup two three four.

PINTO POISED THE HOT DOG before Goosey's anal port. Could Dean Dickerson really have done this? Well, he supposed he'd better get it over with. Sighing, he pushed the frank forward, and —

"Pinto, okay!" Black Whit yanked Pinto's hand away.

"See, he would have done it. I told you he was sick," crowed Scotty to Black Whit.

Black Whit pumped his hand. "You're a sick fuck, Pinto!" The other guys gathered round to slap him on his parka back.

Relief flooded Pinto. He threw the hot dog into the woods.

"I can stand up?" On Magpie's okay, Goosey straightened and pulled up his trou.

Rat Battles now addressed him. "You were good and sick, too, man. You're an AD brother. Congratulations!" Rat threw his arms around Goosey and gave him a mighty Adelphian bear hug.

"Blooooooorp!" went the surprised Goosey.

It was an impressive *cri d'estomac.* 'Pie, Scotty, Black Whit, Pinto, and Rat Battles took a step backward.

"Gloooooooooo!"

The sound was louder this time, the cry of a moose having its testicles ripped off by screech owls. Pinto and the others huddled, seeking the imagined safety of the herd.

And then Goosey booted.

His liquid contents left his body like the exhaust of a Sabre jet. Indeed, the recoil was so great it flung his head back so that the boot cut a dark path through the fire and then whipped skyward as he now booted straight up into the air, and then that, too, fell back on the flames, with many a *snap, pop,* and *sizzle.* A cloud of foul vapor went up.

At this moment, Alby and his three automaton-like companions emerged from the trees to trudge toward the fire, scarcely registering their surroundings. And stepped into the vapor cloud. Round later said it was like being run over by a smell truck. Alby screamed and threw himself sideways. Round went down heavily and Moses bent sharply at the waist and started to boot all over again. Suddenly unsupported, Fitch went over sideways. "Hey!" he yelled, and then he, too, dissolved into a choking fit.

Scotty whooped and slapped Goosey's back. "Fuckin' A, man! That was fantastic!"

"Four with one boot!" cried Black Whit excitedly.

"And look," said Rat Battles. "He actually cut the fire in half. That's never been done before."

Indeed, Goosey's mighty stream of beer puke had created a *cordon sanitaire* through the heart of the fire. The toxic vapor, snatched by a breeze, now moved off. Alby, Round, Moses, and Fitch pulled themselves to their feet, trying to maintain a semblance of dignity amidst the peals of laughter.

"Well, I don't know about you guys," Scotty said to the other brothers, "but I think we have our prizewinner."

Six pairs of pledge ears perked up. Pinto's heart went into his throat.

"You mean . . . ?" Rat Battles asked.

"Definitely. For the greatest single boot ever thrown by an Adelphian, Goosey Gander wins the prize."

"Huh?" Goosey looked at Scotty in amazement.

"You decked four guys!" enthused Black Whit. "You're a hero!"

Pinto's heart fell from his throat to somewhere halfway down his left leg. He'd wanted that prize so much. He took a deep breath and let it go. Maybe he wasn't cut out to be a star.

THE SCENE IN THE BASEMENT of the AD house at 2:00 a.m. was very Hieronymus Bosch. The brothers had ferried the pledges back from the woods and now they lay everywere, their faces pale, their clothing bearing witness to their dinners. Some were passed out, others too drunk to move. Rat was asleep with his chin in the gutter, its liquid muck ebbing and flowing from his half-open mouth.

Pinto, Alby, Rhesus Monkey, Rat, and some of the others had managed to get the keg back on tap, despite its total illegality at this hour. While pleasant postregurgitory conversations held sway, snores blasted from the mattresses. The night was finally winding down.

Or so they thought.

Unfortunately, Goosey Gander had other ideas. The Fires had uncorked something dark and dangerous from his soul. So he walked downtown and attacked the Hanover Inn with heavy chunks of ice, smashing its big front windows to bits.

The campus cops came at him from three directions and wrestled him to the ground. It took four men to hold him down, and then a half hour to transport the screaming sophomore to the cop shop, where they happily threw him in their little cell.

After a while, one of the campus cops came over and eyed him as if viewing a used condom on a clean beach. "Well, hey, man," said Goosey. "Loosen up. It was just a fraternity initiation."

That did it. The campus cops reported Goosey's statement to the dean's office, where Thad the Dad — as we sometimes called him — was unamused, and suddenly AD was in trouble again. Of course, the ADs knew that, behaving as they did, they had to bear up under punishment from time to time, but that it was Goosey who had put them over the line beggared the imagination. Although it might not have been Goosey's fault at all. How good an idea had it really been to force beers down his throat, a guy in no way part of their bar culture? Rat's collapse in the snow had been scary, too. It could have had tragic consequences. (*Did* have tragic consequences, some said, in that he lived.) The house was going to have to be much more careful when forcing their pledges to throw up in the future, everyone agreed.

For a week, they waited nervously for the other shoe to drop. Then Filthy Phil received a summons to the dean's office.

"Mr. Oehler," Dean Seymour said, "we have to stop meeting this way."

Filthy Phil looked at the floor and shuffled his feet. The upcoming weekend was Winter Carnival. They were going to be put on pro for Winter Carnival.

Dean Seymour never quite knew what to do with the AD house. He'd been an English professor before he became dean. His faculty adviser and mentor, an older gentleman named Edwin Booth, was a Dartmouth AD from the thirties, when it had been pretty much the decorous, sincere literary society Samuel Eells had intended. Sweet, old Professor Booth *adored* his fraternity, and talked of it often to Thad. So, now, whenever the ADs got caught doing something, it was as if they were the beloved but troubled sons of a dear friend, always getting in trouble. He sighed.

"Here's my offer," he said. "I won't put you on social probation if you will make me a solemn promise."

Filthy Phil looked at him uncertainly. Did he have honor? He supposed he did. Half the reason he spent so much time down at the engineering library was so he wouldn't know about the stuff the guys did at the house. He wished he were alone in a clean, well-lighted room with a slide rule and some problems. "And what would that be, sir?"

The unholy deal was entered into: The ADs would sustain the first triple warning in the college's history, which placed them a millimeter away from pro but not quite on it. Able to have Winter Carnival. But, in return, Phil had to swear the notorious Seven Fires would be ended forever.

And so, Pinto's Fires were the last ones ever held. Oh, there was still an initiation each year, a hell night for AD pledges sometimes called the Fires, but forevermore it would now have to happen *inside* the house, where no one could fall asleep in the snow and the only fires were in the living room hearths. The Fires that he and Rat Battles and perhaps even Dr. Seuss had had to endure ceased to exist.

AFTER SLEEPING TWENTY-FOUR HOURS, Pinto woke up and felt at least as well as the average poisoned lab animal. What was it, Monday? Carnival coming this weekend. Should he get a date? It wasn't too late to call Mindy down at Smith. Still . . .

He went down to the bar that night to see who was depraved enough to still want any beer. He found the Rats there, drinking together. It was a frightening sight, an interface between finesse and *feh!* Music was playing and guys were enjoying it again. Scotty and Dumptruck were arguing about Cuba. Things had apparently returned to normal.

Pinto took a beer and stood next to Otter.

"I detect a certain wan dispiritedness about you, no-longer-pledge Pinto."

"Maybe it's postbootum depression."

"So Zeke Banananose told you, right?"

"What? No."

"Zeke Banananose didn't tell you?"

"No, Otter, I haven't seen him."

"Well, okay, then I guess it's up to me. Pinto, as a result of your great good humor during the Fires, and in recognizance of your exemplary booting prowess, I hereby declare you a member in good standing of the Adelphian Hard Core."

Everyone in the room turned to Pinto, raised their glasses high, and cheered.

Pinto was flooded with happiness. These really were the greatest bunch of guys in the world.

CHAPTER THIRTEEN

The Mardi Gras of the North

Wednesday

PINTO HEADED DOWN East Wheelock Street on his way to the house, looking with affection at the towering Winter Carnival snow sculpture in the middle of the Green. It had wound up just short of forty-two feet. Since the official Carnival theme for 1961 was Prohibition Blues, the sculpture portrayed a mean-looking Uncle Sam shaking a puritanical finger, and was entitled "Mr. Prohibition."

Pinto loved the snow sculptures. There were additional, smaller ones all over campus, since each dorm and fraternity had built one. Several were inspired by *The Untouchables*, which much of the campus watched every Monday night; Zeta Psi's, for instance, was called "Eliot's Mess," and showed a mobster shooting a tommy gun at a beer stein, the beer streaming out the bullet holes in arcs of ice made yellow with food coloring. Some of the statues were pretty clever, Pinto had to admit, but none, in his opinion, came up to Alpha Delta Phi's, which portrayed a pair of strange, skinny arms and hands rising from the snow to reach for a crude female torso with enormous snow breasts. The sculpted words beneath said THE UNTOUCHA-BELLES.

Winter Carnival had started in 1910 as a ski competition but quickly became an annual social event of great magnitude. Indeed, for the last five decades it had been the most famous college party weekend in the country. The Mardi Gras of the North, the media called it. And to three thousand Dartmouth men suffering from six weeks of monastic deprivation in a deep freeze, the arrival of women was like bloody meat tossed before hyenas.

Other things went on — ski jumps, hockey games — and Pinto supposed some people went to them. But, in the end, what mattered was getting drunk with your buddies and then taking your date to your room and *getting some*. Girls poured in from everywhere. They came on trains from New York and Boston. They came by plane and car and bus from California and London and Bangkok. Last year — an actual census had been taken — more than *two thousand* dewy young things had shown up. What percent held their date's dick while he urinated was not recorded.

Just about everyone in the house had invited someone up for the weekend, but Pinto had dithered and procrastinated, and now, for better or worse, he was dateless. But here was the thing: he'd had a date for Houseparties and it had been a drag! Houseparties was the big fall weekend, with football, colored leaves, and nonstop celebration. To his dismay, Pinto quickly learned that the girl Bags fixed him up with expected to be fed and paid attention to. Glasses of beer were not her cup of tea. Trying to be responsible, he'd taken her for meals at Hal's, but his legs at every instant tried to carry him back to the house. Nothing against her; he just wished she didn't exist. Big weekends were multicourse feasts of experiences and he couldn't stand the thought of missing a single one; even having to go to the bathroom for thirty seconds produced anxiety. So Carnival would be different. This time, no girl would weigh him down.

Pinto trotted up the stairs for the Wednesday-night house meeting. Yesterday, the yearly AD elections had been held, and now, suddenly, Dumptruck was president. Scotty had been elected social chairman, the job he was born for. From here on, he would possess the keys to the liquor cabinet, control the AD social fund (he could buy house kegs!), and book the bands for big weekends. The rest of the jobs were boring, but someone had to do them. Hydrant became recording secretary, Magpie vice president, Hardbar corresponding secretary, and Black Whit treasurer, although some questioned the wisdom of entrusting substantial funds to a guy who couldn't piss if the bathroom door was open.

In the goat room, the brothers jittered and buzzed. Excitement was building for Carnival; testosterone emanations seemed to press against the roof and walls. There was a sort of raised lectern in front of the room, where whoever was talking stood during meetings. On benches arrayed before it sat the membership. A pair of battered filing cabinets in a corner held term papers o' yesteryear.

Things went quickly. Scotty announced the bands: Lonnie Youngblood and the Redcoats Friday, Carl Holmes and the Commanders Saturday, and — he paused dramatically — on Sunday afternoon the Five Royales! Pinto gasped. The Five Royales were actual, recognized black vocal group legends! Alan Freed hadn't played them much, but Pinto had gotten to know them listening to Dr. Jive, who included southern R & B on his playlist. Their first big hit, "Baby Don't Do It," had contained the immortal line, "If you ever leave me, baby, I'm like bread without no meat."

Then it was Truck's turn. "All right, listen up. Now that the buck stops at me, here's what I have to say. We've got a triple warning, right? Only one in the college's history. We have to be *extremely* careful — if the administration catches *one bad hair* coming out of our nose, we're on pro."

"If we fart within *five miles* of Parkhurst Hall," shouted Hydrant, "we're on pro."

"If we say *fuck* on campus over *one* decibel, we're on pro," said Black Whit.

"If we suck *one* cock —" Scotty began.

"All right, shut up, you assholes. Just remember, if we do go on pro, there'll be no beer, no girls, no nothing. All the house'll be good for is sleeping in. So stay in touch with your higher brain functions and don't fuck things up for your brothers, okay?" Dumptruck regarded them seriously.

No one spoke. A sobering admonition indeed.

Truck smiled benevolently. "And now, let us drink."

With a roar, forty brothers hit the stairs and seemed to transport instantly, in one of those cartoon character jumps, to positions around the bar, looking like they'd been there all along. At AD, Carnival began on Wednesday night. Although at AD it was hard to name the moment when the last party trailed off and the next one began. Like towns in Southern California, they ran together with no discernible boundary. And now someone kicked the jukebox to life and James Brown picked up where he'd stopped the night before, completing a fine, soulful scream.

The weekend had begun.

Two hours flowed by like golden beer from the tap. The room was electric with the joined excitement of so many brothers in the same place at the same time. Guys you hardly ever saw, like Balch and McCamy and Ed the Head, had come out of the woodwork. Even Filthy Phil showed up for a beer.

The guys by the jukebox were attempting to perform the moves of the James Brown band, walking in little circles, rocking up and down with invisible saxophones. But they never attained coordination and hence resembled a horribly broken threshing machine.

The boys stayed up till one, when the keg had to be turned off, and then went to Otter's room, where several six-packs had been stashed. At some point, Pinto wandered back to his dorm.

Thursday

HE WAS DREAMING he'd won a radio contest and his prize was a free brain expansion. At the hospital, under the brain-expansion beam emitter, he felt himself getting smarter and smarter. But then his brain expanded too much and started to come out of his ears and nose like awful gray toothpaste. The pain was incredible.

He woke up. The brain expansion was his 9-on-the-Richter-scale hangover. Oh, God, he shouldn't have had those last twenty beers! Or that final pack of cigarettes — he felt like he'd smoked a jet plane. He managed to get out of bed and stand. The room began to spin so he grabbed the top bunk to steady himself.

Brad breezed in. "Uh-oh. It lives."

"Mmp." Grimly, putting one foot in front of the other, Pinto made it to the bathroom. To his relief, he didn't have to boot. Possibly he'd booted last night; he couldn't remember. Now he just stuck his head under the cold water. His timpani-level headache reduced to a mere conga-drum one. He went back to the bedroom and looked for his clothes. Clearly, he was suffering from toxic lag and needed to get to the house and drink something. Scotty had said they'd be on tap all day, which made sense, since it was, after all, *Thursday of Winter Carnival.* Pinto whooped reflexively, then gripped his head anew.

"Ah, the sweet life!" said Brad. "What's up for today? Peeing on nuns?"

"Maybe. How about you? Cross-country run with full backpacks? Squeezing coal into diamonds?"

Brad laughed. It was a good thing they shared a sense of humor or they'd probably have hated each other. Pinto put on a sweater and parka and his Bugerelli boots and took his hangover outdoors.

Yahhhhhh! cried his hangover.

He made the frigid run to the house. In the basement, Rat, Fitch, and Zeke Banananose were already at work on the day's first keg. Pinto chugged three glasses and felt his head go from jittery conga drum to the smooth, happy pulsing of the Basie band. All right!

One hastens to point out that Pinto didn't always live like this. Just most of the time. And big weekends were special. All the usual rules — your own as well as the school's — seemed to blow away with the north wind and you were free to, well, express yourself. And, though Houseparties had its charms, and Green Key was easily the most beautiful big weekend, Winter Carnival was the party of the year.

More ADs showed up, tromping snow into the house; as noon approached, Otter and Gay made an appearance. To Pinto's amazement, Gay actually drank a beer. When Otter took her to breakfast at Hal's, Pinto realized he was starving and tagged along. Pleased, he noticed Otter and Gay hold hands all the way over. When they got along, they got along. Well, there was a statement worthy of Yogi Berra, but it was true.

Over heaps of scrambled eggs and sausage, Pinto asked Gay about her morning beer. She and Otter smiled at each other.

"Gay and I made a deal. I get to be sick till the end of school . . ."

"And next year he has to shape up. Law school! Wear a tie! We made an agreement."

Pinto was taken aback. "So Otter can moon and boot and eat his underwear until June and it's okay?"

"I wouldn't go that far." Gay noticed Otter giving her a look, and sighed. "Well, I guess I'll just have to grin and bear it."

When Gay went to the ladies' room, Pinto asked Otter, "Is this for real? You're going to stop eating your underwear next year?"

"Who knows? But at least I don't have to put on a tie yet. Pinto, before the deal, she wanted me to take her to some classical music show at Webster Hall tonight and wear a suit!" Otter had been in a high school rock 'n' roll band and didn't wear many suits to many classical music shows.

About two, Pinto began to feel like beer and company, so he went down the house. That's how people said it —"down the house." At the AD bar, he found the crowd had grown to about twenty, including several dates. Alby was having a beer with Large, the giant Chi Phi he lived with in Topliff Hall.

"Where's Gretchen Potatoes?" he asked Alby. He liked using the full name. It had a certain poetry.

"On her way up from Smith, supposedly."

The afternoon passed pleasantly. Alby, for his part, was sucking down beers at a record pace. Having spent many evenings with him, Pinto had become familiar with his rhythms. During his first fifteen beers, he was endearing and funny. The next five brought out the asshole who hit people. From beer twenty-one onward, he inhabited strange, hallucinatory worlds, and it appeared as if he was headed for one right now. Pinto had seen Alby spend entire weekends in this condition.

• • •

NOW HYDRANT'S DATE ARRIVED, a cute little blonde from Aruba named Christie. Hydrant immediately got on her good side by taking her for a romantic meal at the Thayer dining hall conveyor belt. That is, he took things from the abandoned trays that were going by and handed them to her. She looked dubiously at the Salisbury Steak and Orange Cake with Extremely Thin Icing. "That's my dinner?"

"And wonderfully balanced nutritionally, too," he said, spearing an attractive chicken leg as it went by.

Their date was short.

AT THE HOUSE, Charlie Boing-Boing yelled for Alby to come to the sink room — Gretchen was on the phone. This small room at the back of the house held mops, snow shovels, a pay phone, and a sink. Alby pushed in as Boing-Boing went out, handing off the receiver. The ADs loved the sink room because you could take a call and a whiz simultaneously. Accordingly, Alby cradled the receiver between his neck and shoulder, whipped out his Magoo, and began a seven-beer piss into the sink.

"Hi, Gretchen."

"Alby, you're supposed to wait until I'm there to hold it for you!"

Alby looked at the receiver in surprise. How could anyone hear pee going into a sink? The woman was amazing.

"So when are you getting here?"

"Oh, Alby, not until tomorrow. Jenny can't leave until then."

"Why the fuck not?"

"She's having her period."

"*What?*" Why did they have to have periods?

Gretchen laughed. "Just kidding. She needs chains for her tires. Meanwhile, think about me when you're beating off, okay? Have me doing really lewd things."

The minx certainly knew how to deflect a fellow's anger. Hanging up, Alby thought a moment. It was about seven thirty. He wondered what they were doing over at Phi Gam. Off he went, and was not seen again that night.

• • •

SNOT NEVER MISSED an Ingmar Bergman movie, and *The Virgin Spring*, the great man's latest, was no exception. For once, though, Snot wasn't thrilled as he and Fitch left the Nugget after the show. The flick had been ugly, lingering over the rape and murder of a pretty young girl by depraved goons. That Max von Sydow eventually killed them hadn't helped — that had been ugly, too. Why do a movie about ugliness? After such great recent flicks as *Wild Strawberries*, *The Magician*, and *The Seventh Seal*, Bergman had fucking blown it.

"You know what I liked?" said Fitch suddenly as they headed up the sidewalk. "The guy with no tongue!"

The tongueless guy was one of the goons. The movie was set in the fourteenth century, and the goons were peasants in little more than rags. Someone had ripped out one of their tongues.

"Yeah, when he talks, he goes, like, '*Gnssshhhhrrgh*.'"

Fitch cracked up. "You got it perfect!"

"*Rrrrgggghhhrsshhh*," said Snot, twisting up his face to look more like a fourteenth-century Swedish peasant with his tongue ripped out.

"And the other guy *translates* for him."

The other guy was the tongueless one's brother. He alone understood what the horrible sounds meant, and could translate them.

"*Grrrrrggrr*," said Snot.

"My brother says he would like to put his head up your dress, young miss," said Fitch.

They cracked up, discomfiting the Phi Psis behind them, who were trying to talk about the movie seriously. At the Inn, they headed down East Wheelock. Snow had begun to fall. How original, Snot thought.

"Hey!" cried Fitch.

The sudden glee on his face was catching. Snot grinned back. "Yeah?"

"Listen: my new girlfriend, Carol, is coming up on the train, and she's bringing her friend Sandra. Sandra needs a date. Have you got one?"

"Yeah, with Tonto here." Snot held up his right hand.

Fitch chuckled evilly. "I've got an idea," he said.

COYOTE AND MAGPIE, in their B-9 parkas with the hoods up, were also on the prowl. Having spent several hours at Phi Delt, drinking with the irrepressible, rock 'n' roll–loving Oscar Arslanian, they were now headed back to AD.

"Fucking cold," Magpie grumbled. He was from Long Island, for chrissakes; what was this arctic shit? They took one of the diagonal walkways across the Green, and this brought them to "Mr. Prohibition," all lit up with spotlights. 'Pie felt inspired.

"Hey, you know what?" he said. "Let's give Uncle Sam bad breath."

"Okay." Coyote squinted through the wind at him. "How do we do that?"

"Follow me."

Magpie dug his boot heel into Uncle Sam's left pant leg experimentally, then began shinnying up it. Coyote paused, wondering if his dad's Blue Shield was paid up, but followed Magpie. It was no easy climb. A lot of the statue was ice. But they hung in and pretty soon were at the top of the leg, which, Coyote figured, was fifteen feet right there. Stretching, they could now touch the bottom of Uncle Sam's waistcoat. Proceeding a clothing item at a time, with ten more minutes of perilous, agonizingly slow ascent, they managed to get over the big bow tie and into the great figure's open mouth.

They were thirty-five feet above the Green. A nice view, but it was cold as outer space. "Okay, now we give him the bad breath." Magpie nonchalantly dropped trou and squatted. "C'mon, man." With a pleased grunt, he squeezed out a dump.

The idea was too classy to resist. Coyote shoved down his trou and his butt felt the chill kiss of the night. Then he realized — he didn't have to go! This was embarrassing.

"Unh!" he grunted. "Unh!" And then, "Ahhhh!" He hoped Magpie would be fooled. He'd never faked a dump before, and he didn't know whether to feel shamed or amused.

"Hey! Ouch!" cried 'Pie. "What the fuck was that?"

Zing!

Something slapped Coyote's left buttock. He peered out of the statue's mouth. Below were what appeared to be three Hanover High School guys. Noticing that Uncle Sam's mouth contained people, they'd begun winging pieces of ice at them. Evidently, they were the school's highly talented pitching staff, for the ice shards zipped into the mouth with great accuracy, ricocheting about, finding their exposed skin with regularity.

"Fuck!" yelled Coyote as another piece bank-shotted off his ass. "Hey, you dipshits! Knock it the fuck off!"

They just laughed. *Whizzz! Wing!*

"You know, Magpie," Coyote observed, "this is a hell of a way to take a shit."

Friday

PINTO'S HANGOVER was less noticeable this morning. Probably, Pinto reflected, it was because he'd put *so* much beer into himself yesterday that the alcohol was backed up at his liver, as yet unprocessed and hence still in operation. Yeah, that was probably it. Pinto, the great bioscientist, had solved another of life's riddles.

He put yesterday's clothes back on. No one would see them anyway — they'd always be covered by sweaters and parkas. And he didn't particularly smell yet, said Mr. Nose. Isaac had gone skiing at Sugarbush, and Brad was off with his date somewhere, so he had the room to himself for a change. Marge, Brad's high school girlfriend, had turned out to be a cute and perky midwestern cupcake who dimpled every time she laughed at one of Pinto's jokes. Not unsurprisingly, he made as many jokes as possible. She was like a toy that, if you pushed a button, smiled or peed.

Ah, Winter Carnival. Why couldn't all of life be that way?

NOTICING LIGHT AGAINST his eyelids, Alby decided it was probably daytime and considered waking up. Unsure about the damage he'd done to himself last night, and wary of standing suddenly and having his head explode, he decided to stay where he was a moment. Wherever that was. Waking up was always an adventure. It'd been the Pi Lam basement yesterday. And today it was . . .

He opened an eye — and espied a really nice ass, inches from his face! He was lying under a white sheet and morning light was coming through luminously. He extended a finger and stuck it into the center of a buttock, where it made a giant dimple.

The buttock's owner giggled and rolled over. The front of her looked pretty good, too. Okay, let's see what I've gone and done this time, Alby decided, and brought his head from under the covers. He found himself in the spare bedroom at Whit and Pam's, on a mattress on the floor — with a seriously good-looking girl.

"Good morning," she said brightly.

He hoped he'd gotten it up last night. He assumed they'd at least tried. "How you doing?" She had long brunette hair and classically beautiful features. He was in awe of his own taste.

She giggled again.

"So what's your name?" Alby asked.

"Go on! You remember my name. You gave it to me."

"I gave you your name?"

"Sure, my Winter Carnival name, you said. Were you too drunk to remember?"

"No, actually aliens came while we slept and erased certain memories. What name did I give you?"

Giggle. "Cheesa Berger."

"Excuse me?"

"Everyone said I looked like that Austrian actress, Senta Berger. So you started calling me Cheesa Berger."

Alby amazed himself. If only there were some way to record his amusing experiences, so he could enjoy them, too. "So, Cheesa, how'd you like to have me for breakfast?"

She smiled. "My stomach's growling."

They weren't wearing shit, so it was easy to begin.

AROUND ELEVEN, the annual caravan of cars left Hanover for White River Junction. The girl train was coming! At the station, the crowds were Calcutta-like in their density, and all male. But cheerful, very cheerful, and much better fed. You could have floated a truck on their happy energy.

Magpie parked by the tracks. His girlfriend, Nancy Manhattan, was coming. They'd been together since high school on Long Island. They were a great couple, everyone agreed. He couldn't wait to see her. He wondered how she'd like the outfit he wore. Wouldn't be long now.

Rhesus Monkey had begged a ride from Bags, who'd imperiously driven him to the station like Patton closing in on the Rhine. Bags, in fact, was the source of his blind date, who would shortly step off the train. Her name was Stephanie — Stevie to her friends — and, so far, Rhesus Monkey had only talked to her on the phone, during which conversation he had fallen preposterously in love. With her voice, anyway. He didn't have huge numbers of dates. He felt he was the opposite of his buddy Alby, who really knew how to handle women. He just hoped she wasn't too awful-looking.

In his horribly scraped and dented Buick, Fitch drove Snot to the station. He'd thoroughly briefed Snot on his role. The prank they'd cooked up was pretty cool.

And here came de train, whistlin' roun' de bend. The Dartmouth guys held their breath. And the train hit them! It was horrible! Some of their bodies were carried half a mile! Oh, God, the screaming and the blood —

No, no, that was just Pinto's overheated imagination. The train pulled in without incident, containing 93.7 percent nubiles, as ready to explode with party energy as the Dartmouth guys who awaited them. The other 6.3 percent were some guy sleeping, two drunk French-Canadian men, and a rabbi who'd gotten terribly lost. The train doors opened. The Dartmouth guys leaned forward like waves in a Japanese print. Girls poured forth, so many you couldn't believe it. They were like the clowns coming out of the little car at the circus.

Rhesus Monkey was in love with them all, in their parkas and Frye boots. They had a fresh, natural beauty. He wanted to play leapfrog on them.

"Hey! Stevie!" Bags called.

The Monkoid swiveled his head.

"Hey, Yogi!" The best-looking girl Rhesus Monkey had ever seen hopped off the train steps. Wow!

Seeing the look on his face, Bags shook his head. "Forget it, pal. No one gets to first base with her." He spoke with great certainty and finality. But then, Bags spoke that way about everything.

Stevie walked right up to the Monkoid and gave her tumble of black hair a shake. "You must be Jeff. Hi!"

It took him a moment. "Oh!" He laughed self-consciously. "I'm Rhesus Monkey now."

"But that's too long! How about Monk?"

"Uh, there was a Monk Bancroft in 'fifty-seven. How about Doc? I've always wanted to be called Doc."

"Let's make medicine, Doc." She linked an arm in his. "Where's the nearest drink?"

Rhesus Monkey grinned. Y. Bear betrayed a hint of annoyance.

"OKAY," SAID FITCH. "See Carol coming out? The girl next to her, in the red parka? That's your date."

Snot peered through the crowd, and then picked her out. She was cute! He hadn't expected cute.

Carol saw Fitch and raced over. She threw her arms around him, still carrying her handbag, and he came in for a kiss that put his head in exactly the right spot to be smacked by the bag. They laughed — just another rollicking day in the comedy that asked, "What happens when you mix accident-prone with drunk?"

He brought the girls over to Snot. A Winston dangled from his lips, the smoke mixing with the vapor of his breath to create a mighty cloud of white. "Carol, Sandra, meet my friend and fraternity brother Snot. Uh, that's what everyone calls him."

Sandra offered her hand. "Hello. I'm Sandra Sloan."

He took the hand. *"Grsssshhhhrrr,"* he said.

She recoiled. It took all Fitch had to keep from laughing. The look on her *face* . . . Carol was no less frozen by the gnashing, spittle-throwing sounds emerging from Snot. The four were an unmoving island in the teeming crowd.

"Sandra, he says he's happy to meet you," said Fitch, translating Snot's guttural sounds. "And he hopes you have a really good weekend at Dartmouth."

"*Zsssshhhhrggrr!*" added Snot.

Again, Sandra flinched at the sheer, cheerful volume of the horrible sounds. She looked at Carol helplessly.

Carol pulled Fitch aside. "All right, what's going on?"

"Well, uh, Snot has a bit of a problem."

"No kidding! And this is who you got for Sandra?"

"Calm down, honey. It happened just last week, some mishap with a sharp utensil, I think. There's going to be an operation, but"— he couldn't think of what to say —"they're waiting for a donor."

"They're waiting for a *tongue* donor?"

"Baby, it's cold out. Come on, he's just got a little handicap is all. Luckily, I can understand what he's saying." Taking her arm, he rejoined Snot and Sandra. "So, getting acquainted?" he asked brightly.

"*Rarrrrgghhhhshl!*" cried Snot, smiling like a guy in a toothpaste ad.

Carol went to Sandra and whispered in her ear. Sandra looked from Fitch to Snot. Her shoulders slumped in resignation.

"*Snargrrrr.*" Taking her arm, Snot headed for the overwhelmed parking lot.

NANCY MANHATTAN CAME OUT the train door, lugging her paisley suitcase. She scanned the crowd anxiously, looking for Magpie. Oh, there was his car! And there was Jawn, getting out of it. And . . . there was Jawn, standing up, in a clear plastic raincoat — *beneath which he was naked!* She shrieked and rushed over to push him back in the car as he roared with laughter.

CHARLIE BOING-BOING was on the far side of the station with his date, Brasilia, waiting for the crowd to thin a little. The train seemed to have emptied out entirely by now and was doing its pre-departure huffing-and-puffing routine, steam pouring in profusion from beneath the engine. But then he glimpsed a bulky figure exit with a suitcase, someone who looked strangely familiar.

"Honey, wait here a minute, will ya?"

The guy was some distance away, obscured by the surging crowd. Boing-Boing plunged in, caroming from Dartmouth guy to Dartmouth guy, working his way closer. And then he was sure. It was the last person he would have expected. Holy shit, this Winter Carnival was going to be memorable!

ALBY WAS HEADING ACROSS campus with Cheesa Berger, wondering how best to sunder their brief tie, when a burly Kappa Sig strode up. Alby couldn't remember his name.

Cheesa gasped. "Kirk!"

"Mumbles, you son of a bitch! You snaked my date!" His fist flew into Alby's face. The familiar burst of stars, popularized by cartoonists, surrounded his head. He hit the snow, watching from a cat's-eye view as Kirk marched Cheesa away.

He thought it over. He could attempt to kick the guy's ass and heroically retrieve the woman he'd slept with last night. On the other hand, hadn't he just wanted to get rid of her? *Thanks, man,* he decided. Getting up was not as easy as it normally was, but he managed. Okay, back to the house.

IT HAD GOTTEN TO BE five thirty and ever-larger numbers of brothers were assembling. Pinto was trying to be everywhere at once. Downstairs, the jukebox blared and the tap ran continuously. The energy was gathering. Tonight, the band would play and the party would be incredible, but that was still to come. For now, being on the upward slope was just great.

He got a beer from Whit and Pam, who were presiding over the tap, and rushed upstairs. Shit going on up there, too. Some emmet guys were setting up the rented sound system. Mouse and Round rolled up the rugs as Rat and Zeke Banananose created a sort of earthwork out of half-kegs that would surround the band, giving them the illusion of safety. Then Zeke seized the microphone and made earsplitting race-car noises until he'd pissed off the entire house.

After Scotty chased Zeke away, Pinto wandered over to the piano. It was a baby grand and sat to the left side of the Adelphian north fireplace. Apparently, that class of '60 guy, the Man, had at one time pressed thumbtacks into all the hammers, trying for a "more honky-tonk sound." The tacks were gone now, however, and Pinto had become fond of going to the battered instrument and playing one or another of the little piano bits Froggie or Josh had taught him.

At the moment, he contented himself with "Earth Angel." A few guys and their dates drifted over to sing along, and then a few more. They did "Lonely Nights," "Diamonds and Pearls," and "Daddy's Home," all of which, luckily for Pinto, used exactly the same chords. He was having a great time. How terrible it would have been if he'd had to take some girl to dinner at this moment.

The living room was a tapestry of conversations. More and more people drifted in. Whatever reservations Dartmouth men may have had about AD at other times, the house was widely acknowledged as peerless in the big-weekend-party department. The normally disdainful were suddenly their best friends. All these *strangers* wandered about.

At the piano, some dippy chick sat down next to Pinto and began singing with him. He hadn't invited her. He didn't know her. He didn't like her. He sighed.

Luckily, among the brothers leaning against the piano was Tiger. He was an ooooold AD, from the class of '59, who'd made it up from Chicago. Pinto didn't know him but had heard he was a cool guy who got laid a lot. He proved also to be perceptive, detecting Pinto's discomfort with the too-familiar girl.

Then she pushed Pinto aside so *she* could play. She could do all these fancy runs and arpeggios. She began singing "You'll Never Walk Alone," which was probably not the ideal choice for the room. The crowd began to drift.

The energetically singing girl was hitting the climax —"'You'll nev-er walk aloooooone . . .'"— when her right hand, tinkling up the keyboard, touched a strange, soft piano key. Why, it was Tiger's dick, laying right there on high D! The girl's voice jumped an octave as she screamed, then scrammed. It was a smashing way to conclude the song, everyone agreed.

BOING-BOING PAUSED on the stairway to the bar with Brasilia and the surprise visitor. Peering in, he saw lots of brothers. Perfect. "Come on, man — let's go."

With utter nonchalance, the three strolled into the basement. People were involved in their conversations and didn't notice right away.

"Three beers!" roared Boing-Boing.

"Yeah, yeah, keep your shirt on." Black Whit drew the beers and walked over to them. As if carefully braking for a stop sign, he came to a slow but total stop.

"*Doberman?*"

The conversations trailed off as heads turned all around the bar. Boing-Boing laughed at the expressions on their faces.

"It's Doberman!" cried Otter. "Holy shit!"

For it *was* him. The legendary madman of Alpha Delta Phi was back.

"Dobes!" Mouse went over to express his happiness at seeing his old drinking mate by punching him as hard as he could in the arm.

"Ow!" said Doberman.

"Dobes! Dobes!" A crowd of the older brothers formed a circle around him and added their fists to Mouse's.

"Ouch! Hey! Stop!" Doberman shielded his head. At length, the show of delight ran its course and everyone asked questions at once.

Pinto looked on in wonder. So this was the famous Doberman! He'd heard so many stories that he'd expected a Bunyanesque figure. Instead, Doberman was simply a big, friendly guy who resembled neither a god, a dog, *nor* the character on "Sergeant Bilko."

Since Doberman was a '61, the seniors knew him well. The juniors had been with him only a few months before his sudden departure owing to the unfortunate incident with the ladies' underwear and the state troopers, but they'd seen him in action, and he had their utmost respect. The pledges were wide-eyed and curious. What would this wild man do, now that he'd come back?

ALBY WAS AT SOME ROADHOUSE where the bartenders were all from sixteenth-century England. He was reciting lines from *The Magnificent Seven* to anyone who would listen.

"'How can you talk like this? Your gun has got you everything you have. Isn't that true?'" This in a Mexican accent. Then, in the tones of Steve McQueen . . .

"'Yeah, sure. Everything. After a while, you can call bartenders and faro dealers by their first name. Maybe two hundred of 'em. Rented rooms you live in — five hundred. Meals at hash houses — a thousand. Home — none. Wife — none. Kids — none.'" Long pause. "'Prospects — zero.'"

He got both voices right. No one paid attention. He peered among the patrons. Hey, was that Ted Kluzewski? No, wait. It was Killer Kowalski! He'd known it was some kind of K-ski. No, hold on, it was his friend Large. Then he had a moment of clarity. These sometimes occurred in the midst of even the most ambitious drunks. Alby perceived that he wasn't in a roadhouse at all, but a fraternity basement. There was no gutter running around the floor, so he wasn't at AD. Where the hell did you piss around here? He peered behind doors until he spotted porcelain. With relief, he went in and began to pee.

"Oh!" said a voice.

Alby had neglected to close the door. A Bennington girl stood there, checking him out. You could tell she was from Bennington by her long straight hair, dramatic eye makeup, and black leotards. He alertly stretched his dick to make it look longer.

"How you doing?" he asked cheerfully, continuing to blast his heavy stream of whiz into the toilet.

She thought a moment, then hummed a tentative note. She adjusted it slightly, then sang it aloud. The note harmonized with Alby's pee! She grinned at him.

Alby fell deeply, if temporarily, in love.

• • •

AT THE HOUSE, Bags's date arrived. She immediately insisted he take her to the Joan Baez concert at Webster Hall. This was the liberal chick he'd been hearing about, who sang about labor unions and peace. Bags, whose politics resembled Himmler's, thought unions akin to roach nests and peace only a boring pause between wars.

He introduced his date to the brothers as Gross Kay. This was because her name was Kay Gross. In fact, there was nothing remotely gross about her. "Come on, sweetie," she said, tugging his arm. "We don't want to miss the beginning. Joanie might sing about coal miners."

"Oh, God." Bags was dragged out the door.

ABOUT EIGHT-THIRTY, a pair of vans emblazoned with LONNIE YOUNGBLOOD & THE REDCOATS pulled into the parking lot, filled with frazzled black guys who'd had to find this remote educational outpost while dealing with all the two-lane roads, icy conditions, and unintelligible honkies in gas stations saying *cah* instead of *car.* Lonnie couldn't decide if this was racism or just inbreeding. He was a formidable motherfucker and took no man's waste products.

Pinto ran out to greet them. Actual Negroes in Hanover! The vans were painted with purple and mint-green flames. Out came seven guys. They sure were black. A couple of them wore do-rags, and the bass player had a gold tooth with a little diamond in the middle. Pinto was swooning with negritude.

"Hi! Welcome to the AD house!" He took them inside and showed them where they were going to play.

They weren't terribly interested. "Hey, man, where the do-it fluid?"

Do-it fluid! Yes! Scotty had explained. This meant gin. Pinto gave them the brown paper bag and was rewarded with a brief flash of the gold tooth, whereupon the guys retired to the library to compose themselves.

Now the house was really filling up. There were Black Whit and Pam, making out behind the bar. Turnip stood against one wall, dateless, morosely pushing a wet sponge in and out of a beer glass to simulate the liquid sounds of love. Tiger, Goose, and Flea were doing impressions of their animal selves, roaring and honking and, in the case of Flea, sucking blood from a passing date.

Moses stood with the Digit at the bar.

"Oh," she said, remembering. "What do you call it when you stick your head up a girl's skirt and she farts?"

Moses looked at her blankly. "Rejection?"

"No, silly. It's a wind tunnel."

Moses coughed up his beer, inflicting sprays of it on several mildly annoyed neighbors.

"Okay, I heard one the other day." Moses tried to remember it all, get the wording right. "You're in bed with someone and one of you farts. You pull the covers over you. What's that?"

She looked at him blankly.

"A Dutch oven."

The Digit cracked up.

"And then there's a motorboat." He took a step closer, with a leer.

She regarded him, at a loss. "All right, what's a motorboat?"

"You have to lift up your sweater."

The Digit gave him an are-you-nuts look, but then shrugged and did as requested. There were her knob-o-ronies, riding their bra like little round cowboys.

"Okay, ready?" said Moses.

"Sure."

Several brothers and their dates watched the proceedings with perplexity.

Moses stuck his face in her cleavage and went *"Bwrrrrrrrrrr,"* swinging his head rapidly back and forth. Everyone cracked up.

The Digit, freezing, pulled her sweater down. "That's a motorboat?"

Moses smiled. "It is now."

AT NINE THIRTY, the band made its way out of the library and through the crowd to the bandstand. The do-rags were gone; the guys now wore aqua tuxedos with ruffled white shirts and black cummerbunds. Pinto gave Scotty a thumbs-up. They looked cool as shit.

Lonnie Youngblood was a handsome, soulful man in his early thirties. A saxophone hung from his neck. To Pinto, the coolest thing in the whole world was a black guy with a saxophone hanging around his neck. When Lonnie blew a few tentative runs, Pinto got chills. For Houseparties, Otter had gotten them a white bar band from Boston called the Vi-Kings. They'd been okay, but what was about to happen musically here was of a whole other order of magnitude. To hear actual R & B from, like, two feet away was astounding to Pinto.

Lonnie tapped one of the mikes. "Tasting . . . Tasting . . ."

It happened all at once. With a great *ker-whump* on the drums, the band was playing "Last Night," the rocking Mar-Keys' instrumental. Pinto's entire body filled with joy. He leapt to his feet and began doing the slop. The music drew people from all over the house and very quickly the dance floor was jammed.

"Jeez, I hope the sound system's gonna hold up," Scotty, the worried social chairman, muttered.

"Scotty, forget the sound system. Have fun!" Scotty's latest girlfriend, Barbara, poked her boob in his arm. Scotty liked 'em big, and Barbara was nothing if not that.

In response to her words, he jumped in the air with a Little Richard *"Woooooo!"* and came down into a full split. He made a face. Maybe *too* full a split; his left ball was crunched between his pants and his leg. Barbara laughed and held out a hand. She yanked him up and they began to do the mashed potato.

At the finish of the first number, Scotty went to one of the mikes and yelled, *"Are you ready for star time?"*

A great scream of affirmation broke over the room. Lonnie blinked at the intensity. Little early for spirits that high.

"Then let's greet Lonnie Youngblood! And the Redcoats!"

The band kicked right in with "Fanny Mae," and its immense, rocking beat threw the room into frenzied gyrations. The dancing of all these white guys and their dates looked a little silly next to the cool moves of the band, but nobody cared. The crowd could not be called sober and had needed no warm-up.

Dancing like it's midnight, Lonnie thought. *This could be either really good or really ugly.*

Dumptruck rumbled up the stairs from the basement, a pitcher of beer in his hand, an expression of jollity on his face. Pausing, he took a deep, satisfying draft. *This is what it must have been like when the gods drank mead,* he thought rapturously.

He began to walk on but, glimpsing movement through the partly open tube-room door, stopped and went in. It was quiet and dark in there, a musty refuge from the madness without. The wind had blown the snow into identical configurations on the window-panes. On one of the torn green leatherette sofas, someone's date lay. Truck smiled. He knelt and checked her out. She appeared to be sleeping. He stood, dropped trou, knelt back down, and waved his dick in the girl's face.

She just lay there, snoring softly.

Truck giggled helplessly. He wasn't known as one of the major sick guys in the house, but he liked to commit the occasional socio-pathic act. He put his dick about six inches from the tip of her nose.

"Hello!" he made his dick say. "My name is Batiste. I am from Haiti. Uh . . . do you favor foreign aid?"

The girl's eyes suddenly opened.

Holy Christ! He yanked up his pants and ran, whipping his glasses off, raising his collar, and messing up his hair. This would disguise him, he thought, with the whipsaw logic of the totally drunk. Of course, if she *did* recognize him, he'd be the last to know, since now he couldn't remember what *she* looked like. She could be any of the girls in the room. Fuck!

ALBY WENT UP TO the long-haired Bennington chick. You just knew she'd memorized every song Pete Seeger ever sang. Those deep Jewish eyes — Alby was a fool for Jewish chicks. Well, Alby was a fool for Jewish chicks, Czech chicks, Nepalese chicks . . . But he was the opposite of political. When talk turned to anything even *resembling* politics, he split, booted, or threw a punch.

So he struck up a conversation with Liz, as her name proved to be, and before anything political could come up, he let it slip that he wasn't a Dartmouth guy at all but a pitcher for the Minnesota Twins named Dick Stigman. He was at Dartmouth only because he was going to have surgery to correct a rotator cuff problem at Mary Hitchcock Hospital.

Alby watched it happen. As the words *Major League pitcher* left his lips, her entire demeanor changed, and you could smell the sex on her breath. Well, how cool was that? The Bennington chick dug baseball!

BACK AT AD, Snot burst into the basement with an arm around Sandra. Fitch and Carol followed. Snot strode up to the bar in his short, peppy way.

"*Grrssshhsk?*"

"Sure, man." Hydrant drew two beers and handed them to Snot, who passed one to Sandra. She managed a smile.

Snot's good cheer was unrelenting. Damned if being maimed was going to get the best of *him.* The shapes Fitch's mouth assumed in its efforts not to laugh were hilarious in their own right.

WHEN THE BAND TOOK A BREAK, Pinto anxiously rushed down to the bar. Had he missed anything? Goddamn, it was hard, being everywhere at once. Drawing a beer, he looked for someone to drink it with. He espied Doberman, the god himself, in the inconspicuous cul-de-sac at the far end of the horseshoe bar. The great AD legend didn't seem exactly to be partying his ass off. In fact, his expression could have been called somber.

Pinto introduced himself, feeling shy, but Doberman was friendly as could be. He had that easy-to-be-with quality you find in people with nothing to prove. They fell into a conversation that ranged from Buddhism to Garnet Mimms and the Enchanters. Pinto really liked him. But where was the wild man he'd heard about? The guy hadn't so much as eaten his underwear yet.

As if reading his mind, Dobes spoke up.

"Listen, Pinto, you seem like a good guy. I need to talk to someone. Can I confide in you?"

"Um, yeah. Sure. I guess."

"Well, see, this is kind of a second chance for me at Dartmouth. I worked a lot of my craziness out on the banana boat, and I don't want to fuck up again. I'll always love the house, but I guess I'm going to be kind of a spectator from here on."

Pinto felt terrible disappointment. "That sounds great. Yeah, I could see how, after the experiences you've had, a guy might start taking things more seriously."

Dobes winced. "Sounds awful, doesn't it?" He indicated the full beer on the bar near him. "I'm not even drinking, Pinto; just holding the glass. As soon as I take a drink, it'll start all over again. Look, don't say anything about this, okay? I'm not exactly advertising it."

"Sure, okay." What a sad case Doberman had turned out to be!

UPSTAIRS, SNOT, SANDRA, FITCH, and Carol were watching the band play "Do You Love Me," the great Contours song.

"Mgork?" said Snot to Sandra, offering his hand.

Fitch translated. "He says, do you want to dance?"

Sandra froze. Carol elbowed her. "Uh . . . sure, of course." With palpable effort, she let the beaming Snot take her out on the floor. Snot could do a mean Lindy, and soon he was whirling the startled Sandra this way and that, calling out happily to her in his broken garble. Wildly drunk crazies were flinging themselves about on all sides of her, howling and bellowing. The music was so loud she thought she'd go deaf. What terrible hole had she stepped into, to have fallen into this awful netherworld?

"Greegle!" Snot cried happily.

PINTO CAME UPSTAIRS and wormed his way close enough to the band for their sweat to engage his olfactory functions. They were really cranking now. Having just completed "Money," they roared into "Finger Poppin' Time." Pinto was in a state of ecstasy. The amplified sound had turned his gut into an additional speaker that resonated powerfully with each bass note.

Lonnie sang and played the sax breaks. He was of the King Curtis school, with that yakety-sax style. The guitar player and bass player rotated this way and that, their synchronized guitar necks reminiscent of swans. The drummer smiled and sweated. Before them, the sea of white kids danced their asses off.

In 1961, there were many dance steps to know. There was the Lindy, the bop, and the slop, left over from the fifties. No one did the stroll anymore. But now, in the new decade, there was the frug, the mashed potato, the mess around, the continental walk, and the bacon fat. And a new one — the twist — that had the advantage of being extremely easy for white people to do. All of these dances and more were currently on view.

Yes, there they were, the leaders of tomorrow, writhing and leaping about like maniacs. It was a sight to see. Pinto noticed Scotty and Barbara seated on the keg barricade, grooving to the music, and sat down with them. Eyes closed, head bobbing, he spent the rest of the night enjoying his ecstasy.

HUCK DOODY AND HIS DATE, Judy, were sitting with Turnip, Moses, and the Digit at the Four Aces Diner, in White River Junction. It was after midnight, and all were thoroughly drunk and sated from tonight's great party. But soon they became aware that a drunk emmet guy in the next booth was making rude remarks, using the term *pinhead* repeatedly.

As was the case at most schools, the relationship between the local guys and the college guys was somewhat strained. This was not surprising, as the Dartmouth men would go on to run the world, and the emmet guys would go on to run gas stations. For the most part, to Dartmouth guys, emmets were invisible.

But not tonight.

Huck Doody had a temper. He and the emmet got into a classic verbal battle.

"Fuck you!"

"Oh, yeah? Fuck *you!*"

"Not fuck me! You fuck!"

It got more intelligent from there. The next thing anyone knew, Huck and the emmet were facing each other in the parking lot, with the other emmets yelling for their guy and the ADs yelling for

Huck. Judy couldn't believe this shit. Why did she always get stuck with the drunks on these weekends?

The two guys slammed together and wrestled, lost their balance, went over sideways into a car, got up, wrestled again. Turnip and Moses yelled excitedly when Huck threw the emmet, then moaned with dismay when the emmet threw Huck. After a snarling ten minutes, the two guys, as if by common assent, simply stopped. They stood, breathing heavily, looking at each other.

"Name's Bill," said the emmet guy.

"I'm Huck."

Exchanging respectful nods, they walked side by side back into the diner. Moses, Turnip, Judy, and the other emmets shrugged and followed, mingling without animosity. Inside, it seemed like a good idea to have a few beers together.

What no one had noticed, least of all Huck, was that he had fought the entire fight without shoes, which he'd left back in the diner.

After a beer or two, Judy did a double take at the floor. A pool of red was forming. As it seemed to be emerging from the region of her date, she became alarmed and made sounds. Huck pulled his chair back. The blood was originating from his feet. The well-plowed asphalt parking lot, it seemed, hosted a diamond mine of broken glass, and the soles of Huck's tootsies now resembled squished raspberries.

"Eyew! Gross!" cried Moses. The others gave him pained looks.

A rescue mission of Judy, driving Huck's car and him, with a three-car escort of Moses, the Digit, Turnip, and the emmet guys, who were now the ADs' best friends, sped in the direction of Dick's House. No one, it may be unnecessary to add, was anywhere close to sober. While Huck once again enjoyed the sewing skills of the kindly white-haired doctor, the rest of them were summarily ejected. The ADs took Judy and the emmets over to the house, where they drank together with great good cheer until the keg had to be turned off.

This occurred at 1:00 a.m., at all the houses, and peace and quiet returned to the Hanover plain, like liquid that had been spun out to the edge of a centrifuge now flowing back. The bands packed up their instruments, and the tap had to stay off until tomorrow morning. The college would land on you like an avalanche if you didn't obey this strict dictate. Friday night of Carnival was over.

On big weekends, fraternity guys cleaned up their rooms for their dates to occupy and found somewhere else to sleep. For the length of the weekend, no male was allowed upstairs — it was girl country up there. The ADs had tried to be responsive to their dates' needs and had thoughtfully placed a cardboard carton with a slot cut in the top and the label PUT 'EM HERE in the second- and third-floor bathrooms. These were known, in Adelphian parlance, as the rag boxes.

So the girls went upstairs and the boys headed off to sleep in motel rooms, in the homes of locals, and on sofas in the sophomores' dorm rooms. Best of all, Scotty, Barbara, Mouse, and some others went off to spend the night at Whit and Pam's place in town, where male and female could cohabit without harassment.

The only brothers allowed in the house after one a.m. were the ones standing fire watch. It was a college rule: someone had to remain conscious to guard against a fire starting and toasting the dates. Staying awake was a bitch after you'd partied all night, but what could you do? Tonight, it was F. A. Mac and Goosey who'd stay up, the sophomores getting the shit jobs once again.

Outside, clouds blew in front of the moon and a postcard-beautiful snow drifted down like feathers, and fell on and on; as the men of Dartmouth slept, heedless and mostly dreamless, deep in their alcohol-enhanced slumbers, the world acquired a thick, new layer of white.

Saturday

ALBY AWOKE SHORTLY AFTER dawn to find himself in the embrace of Lizzie Leftist, as he'd begun thinking of her. Best-looking commie *he'd* ever seen. Her red hair reached the middle of her back, and her body was like roses and cream. All in all, a terrific chick. But Gretchen Potatoes would be here soon and it wouldn't do for him to be entwined with Lizzie.

Poking his head out of the sleeping bag they'd somehow both gotten into, he discovered that they were in the gloomy confines of the Adelphian hearse. No wonder it was so fucking cold. Obviously, someone had forgotten to turn on the ambient heating last night.

Lizzie's head popped up next to his. "Hi, Dick! Boy, you sure hit a home run with me last night!" Her *h* sounds sent a cloud of morning breath into his face.

Okay, time to get serious. How was he going to get rid of her?

WHIT AND PAM'S APARTMENT was actually Pam's, which she shared with two other physical therapists. They worked at Mary Hitchcock Hospital. When Whit had crashed on skis last year, Pam was assigned his case. It was a terrible multiple fracture, and Whit had to wear a cast up to his crotch and get about on crutches for months. But Pam was the silver lining, and she and Whit had been together ever since.

Pam was pretty and Whit was cool and both were absolutely nuts, which was what Pinto loved about them. They blew off social conventions with such nonchalance that he was awed. At this time in linguistic history, *hippie* still meant a white jazz geek who tried to cozy up to cool black musicians, so Pinto wouldn't know until much later that he had met his first hippie couple, in the modern sense of the word. They were great. And now he'd been invited over for Winter Carnival breakfast!

He ran up the rickety outside stairs to the second-story apartment. Going into Whit's was always an experience, as you sashayed into a totally other zone. In the vestibule, Pam had hung sheets and lace tablecloths and whatnot around the place and fixed the lights in a certain way so that you walked into a luminous white labyrinth. This led to the living room, with the overstuffed sofa and highway-spool table and brick-and-board bookcases stuffed with well-thumbed books of poetry and Green Lantern comic books, and, on the wall, some of Whit's oil paintings of mournful ghosts. There was always music playing, often jazz. At the moment, it was that cool Brubeck album with all the strange time signatures, *Time Out*.

Having negotiated the labyrinth, Pinto found mattresses covering much of the living room, with people on them just waking up. Scotty and his new chick, Big Barbara, were seated companionably side by side on the sofa; they waved to Pinto. Mouse was just stirring; no date in his case. On another mattress, someone was writhing about violently under the sheets, going, "Oh, oh, ohhhh-hhh!" Pinto was shocked, then laughed when the sheet was thrown away and it was only Hardbar, pretending to make out with his date, the centerfold from the new *Playboy*.

Pinto pitched in and they got the mattresses leaning against the wall and the room vaguely cleaned up. And then, in from the kitchen came Pam, wearing only a tiny French apron. "Breakfast," she cried cheerily, holding out a tray of coffee and Danish.

Pinto's eyes bugged. There were her ka-hogas, coming right out the sides of the little garment. Damn, life sure was interesting over here. Whit now entered with his arms around the two roommates, in their bathrobes, all grinning. And then Hawk and Brunella fell by, with their little girl, Cordelia, named for the good daughter in *King Lear*. "Blue Rondo À La Turk" played. A delightful repast was enjoyed by all.

THE CLASSIC BREAKFAST SPOT in Hanover was Lou's. It was on Main Street, flanked by Campion's, the clothier, and Tanzi's, the beer emporium. As you walked in on a winter morning, you were enveloped in warmth and the scent of cinnamon buns and coffee. There was a counter and tables, and a host of bustling emmet waitresses. The place was warm, noisy, and fun.

At a table sat Snot, Sandra, Fitch, and Carol. They seemed somewhat subdued. Fitch's hangover was punishing him and he badly needed a beer, but, of course, you had to feed your fucking date first. So he feigned well-being and said, "Okay, what'll we do today? Hockey game with Princeton at eleven? Ski jumping at the Vale of Tempe this afternoon? And, hey, they're doing *Pajama Game* at Robinson Theater tonight. What a treasure trove of fabulous options!" He made a great, insincere smile.

The girls concentrated on their bacon, sausage, and pancakes.

Snot shrugged. *"Splort!"*

A guy at the next table winced.

"Rrrrgrrr," Snot went on.

"Can't you stop doing that?" the guy at the next table asked irritably. "Those sounds are disgusting!"

To everyone's surprise, Sandra spoke up angrily. "No, he can't, okay? Why don't you mind your own business." She put a protective arm through Snot's.

The guy at the next table shrugged and returned to his breakfast bun. Snot looked in surprise at Sandra's arm and back at her. Fitch and Carol exchanged a glance.

Sandra spoke to Snot. "I'd love to see the ski jump. Could we go?"

"Flrrrgg!" Snot was delighted.

UPON RETURNING TO THE HOUSE, Pinto found thirty or so ADs and dates standing in the front yard, behind the snow statue, periodically breaking into applause and cheers. Curious, he went to take a look.

He found Tiger, Monk, and Mouse standing in a line, peeing an artwork into the snow. In color! They had consumed food dyes a few hours ago and now were emitting streams of red, green, and blue.

"What's the picture of?" Pinto asked Goosey Gander.

"Hiroshima," Goosey whispered back.

Pinto looked at him in surprise. Goosey laughed. "Got you."

Since the Fires, Goosey had turned into Loosey Goosey. It was quite a transformation. "So — what is it?" asked Pinto.

"Actually, they're trying to do a de Kooning."

To Pinto, the multicolored, steaming artwork looked more like a cow and a red barn, but he kept his opinion to himself.

Inside, the house was half empty. A lot of people had gone to the ski jump. Downstairs, he found Doberman surrounded by a worshipful group of sophomores. The jukebox was deeply into bird vocal groups; the Robins, the Swallows, the Penguins, Don Julian and the Meadowlarks, and the Orioles went by in a row.

"Hey, Dobes," said Rhesus Monkey. "About that bra you were wearing — what was the cup size?"

Big laugh. Doberman managed a smile. "I don't remember. My titties were bigger then."

"So what was that bit in Boston — you booted all over some bartender?" Moses gazed at Doberman dreamily.

"Well, not exactly."

"Hey, need another beer?" Rhesus Monkey looked ready to swing from tree to tree to get it for him.

"Nah, I'm good right now."

The poor guy was a captive of his own reputation, Pinto realized. He went to the bar, found a glass, and reached across to tap his own beer. Not caring to appear like a suck-up, as the rest of them did, he stood there, listening to "The Door Is Still Open" by the Cardinals. Alby and Round were trying to impress Doberman with stories about how sick they were. The story of Round and the brain glass surprised and amazed him, and he forgot his resolve for a moment and roared, only to catch himself and return to his remove. It was as if he were fighting a craving for drugs. Indeed, Pinto saw his eyes wander repeatedly to the tap, accompanied by wistful expressions. Poor Dobes.

"HOW THE FUCK DO YOU SPELL Baez?" Alby didn't know who Lizzie was talking about.

She patiently spelled it out. "Joanie's playing again this afternoon, just, you know, spontaneously. In College Hall, around three."

"She's *scheduled* to be spontaneous? What's she got on for tonight? Rigidity? Concupiscence?"

Lizzie looked at him oddly. How did a pitcher know these words?

Alby saw the look and tried to stupidify himself. Crouching a little, he pretended to be chewing gum. "All right, I'll meetcha at College Hall."

"At three."

"Yeah." He was ready to go. Beers awaited at the house.

"Oh, one other thing. I'm sorry, but I sort of forgot. What team did you say you played for?" She blushed, embarrassed. "I know I should remember but I don't."

"I told you," said Alby. "I'm Jack Kralick of the Minnesota Twins."

Lizzie smiled and nodded, then paused and looked at him oddly. "Wait a minute. That's not right."

Uh-oh. "It isn't?"

"No. Wait, I remember. You said you were Dick Stigman!"

Fuck. Now what could he say? "Uh, well, I'm having an identity crisis."

Alby laughed at his little joke, but Lizzie did not join in. "You son of a bitch! You told me two different names!"

"Well, Jesus, what does it matter? They're both Major League pitchers!"

"Shit, I *liked* you, too. You asshole!" Lizzie spun on her heel and walked away.

Alby sighed. Lizzie was cool — too bad she was walking away mad. But now Gretchen wouldn't catch him with her. He yawned. He'd been fucking girls for two days straight with very little sleep and oceans of beer running through him. Tired, he headed for the house.

"NOW, BARBARA, JUST RELAX. I know what I'm doing." Scotty tossed back the rest of his fifth stinger and hefted the ski pole.

Barbara, in her bra and panties, was standing against the wall in Whit and Pam's place. Their hosts were present, as were Rat Battles, H-Drant, Mag F. Pie, Nancy Manhattan, and Hawk Satterfield with the ever-present Brunella, who looked like the woman doing a dance to spring in the annual Jules Pfeiffer comic strip. On the table, the crème de menthe and brandy bottles stood three-quarters empty. The "Charlie Parker at Massey Hall" album was playing. Hawk, an aficionado of bebop, had brought it. Bird's deft, soaring solos were something to hear.

Barbara was trying to be cool. "All right, all right, go ahead."

Scotty wound up and threw. The ski pole sproinged into the wood three inches from her head.

"All right!" said Barbara, stepping briskly away from the wall. "Boy, that was fun! Now what'll we do?"

Scotty embraced her. "You were really cool, honey," he whispered. She felt herself blush.

• • •

AT THE SKI JUMP, guy after guy from Dartmouth, Middlebury, Colgate, Williams, Bowdoin, and Brown zoomed like spacecraft from the lip of the jump, high into the sky, and then down on the polished snow, executing those smooth, kneeling landings. Snot was knocked out by what they could do. There was a story that in the early fifties, an AD went off the ski jump when there was no snow. In a baby carriage. And lived. Snot was knocked out by that story, too. He was *really* knocked out by Sandra, if you wanted to know the truth. He was dying to share his thoughts with her, but the minute he talked normally, the cat would be out of the bag. She'd hate him for making a fool of her, and he wouldn't blame her. What a bizarre fix this was!

Another skier soared off the jump. "Aren't they amazing?" said Sandra. "They're like birds."

"*Zglornk,*" he replied sadly.

BY SEVEN, the house was more packed than Pinto had ever seen it. AD's reputation had brought the usual flood of outsiders, as well as every brother imaginable, past and present. Even Al Heller, the guy who'd early-rushed him, was there, having flown back to Dartmouth from his semester in France. He greeted Pinto warmly and made disparaging remarks when he found out where Brad and Isaac had pledged.

"Hey, Pinto!" called a voice.

At the foot of the circular staircase, he looked up. The Digit dropped a pair of panties in his face.

At eight, Gretchen Potatoes arrived and grabbed Pinto by the arm. But Pinto didn't know where Alby was. Gretchen searched, threading her way through the mass of people, for some time before finding him asleep in the sex room. As the room was otherwise unoccupied, she smiled and curled up next to him.

"Mmmmmrrr," said Alby.

Gretchen held his dick.

"*Mmmmmrrr!*" He sat straight up.

"Hi, baby." Gretchen gave him a kiss.

"Oh, hey. How you doing?" Alby stretched and yawned, wondering where he'd woken up this time.

"Miss me?"

"Oh, mm, yeah." He was bone-tired.

"Al-beee." Her tease voice.

"Hah?"

"Why aren't you getting *hard?*"

It was a difficult question to answer, given the unsuitability of the truth. "Jeez, Gretch, let me wake up, okay?"

She pouted. "Sorry. Guess I'm really horny. I want to make love with you all night long. Doesn't that sound great?"

Alby marshaled a smile. "Oh, yeah."

TONIGHT'S BAND was Carl Holmes and the Commanders. Carl was a cool-looking young black guy. He played guitar and was a lighter-hearted presence than Lonnie, who tended to smolder. Behind him was the usual four-black-guy backup band: drums, bass, organ, and sax. They kicked off with "The Twist," and the entire room began gyrating its ass off.

Pinto, too. He grabbed Gretchen from Alby and twisted before the band with her. You had to do a stay-in-one-place dance because if you made a real move in any direction, your elbow banged into a tit. As he dipped and shook, he saw the front door open and Troll walk in. And who was with him but the divine Donna Daley!

"Hey," said Gretchen. "Put your tongue back in your mouth."

"But, my God, she's like candy!"

Gretchen laughed. "Somebody's hor-ny."

Pinto had to agree. He hadn't expected to hear from his glands today, but here they were, screaming, *"Donna! Donna!"* Why did Troll have to be around?

"NOW, ALBY?" Gretchen gazed at him from her perch on the bar.

Alby cleared his throat. "Not yet. I'll tell you when." He'd better be able to get it up soon, or he'd have a hell of a time explaining himself.

• • •

AT EIGHT THIRTY, Seal made his first appearance of the weekend by driving his motorcycle down the basement stairs. Pleased at the noise and chaos, he decided to consume a few brews. *Rrrrr* went the bike as he gunned it and got off, leaning it against a pillar. He found himself next to a stranger.

"So," said Seal conversationally. "Who the fuck are you?"

Doberman laughed. His flash hit on Seal: good guy. He confessed his identity and Seal stood back and looked at him, the up-and-comer checking out the old master. Pretty soon, they were comparing stories and not long after that had become close. Instead of competing, they were a sensei and his gifted student.

"But, hey, where's your beer, man?" Seal asked.

Doberman became flustered. "Oh, uh, I dunno. Someone stole it, I guess."

"And a worthless motherfucker he was, too! Mouse! Get Dobes a fucking beer!"

Mouse, at the tap, set one on the bar. Dobes eyed it. He looked at the floor, and then at the ceiling. Emitting a strange choking sound, he grabbed the beer and threw it down his throat. And then chugged three more in rapid succession. The strangest transformation now occurred: he stood straighter. His smile became huge and magnetic. His whole body language changed. He belched with a sound like a pile of steel girders falling forty feet onto concrete.

"Okay," he said to Seal. "We were in this little whorehouse in Honduras, and the chick that danced there could smoke cigarettes with her cunt."

Seal grinned. Doberman was the best!

"AL-BEEEE."

"Okay, okay. Hey, Pinto, can I use your room?"

Pinto considered. Isaac was still at Sugarbush, but he had no idea where Brad might be. "Just, if you see a guy with big muscles and a cute brunette, get out of there. He doesn't like ADs."

Alby sniffed. "Philistine."

Pinto gave him the key. Gretchen was nibbling Alby's ear. He took her out the basement back door. They tramped through the snowy wastes and went into Middle Fayerweather. Gretchen grabbed him in the stairwell, clamped herself around one of his thighs, and humped his leg like an animal, thrusting her tongue far beyond his uvula. Alby was actually getting turned on again. He hoped she wouldn't look too closely at his dick and perhaps notice the minor abrasions and teeth marks that commonly follow two days of hot and continuous sex. Maybe he'd better leave the lights off.

IN THE AD BASEMENT Snot was trying to explain to Sandra by means of grunts, sighs, and hand gestures that when the right tongue showed up at Mary Hitchcock, he'd be good as new again. He'd seized on a plan. All he had to do was continue the fake-out until she left tomorrow. Then, by great good luck, a tongue would turn up on, say, Tuesday. The transplant would be successful, and by the weekend, he could call her and be talking normally. Then he could begin seeing her without deception. He would have been the first to admit it wasn't a *great* plan, but it was the only one he had.

Rat at this time was crossing the floor carrying four beers, one for Tiger and three for himself. The Digit, dancing in his path, threw an interpretive arm in the air. Beer flew, and a big, cold bunch of it hit Snot in the back of the neck.

"*Jesus Christ!*" cried Snot. "Who the fuck —?" He clapped both hands over his mouth. Sandra was staring at him, wide-eyed. Omigod!

OVER BY THE BAND, Moses had learned to sit on the kegs, and he was staring at Carl Holmes, mesmerized, as he wanged out guitar chords to great rock 'n' roll effect. The living room throbbed with excitement and glandular exudations; it was midnight and, as Doberman might have put it, there wasn't an inhibition in sight.

In a spasm of pure exuberance, Moses spat his mouthful of beer on the floor and joyously cried, "Albany Schlitz!"

• • •

ALBY, A MAN AMONG MEN, kept it up fine. He and Gretch did it twice, and then lay together, spent but happy. Every once in a great while, life seemed perfect.

ROUND, DANCING BEFORE the band, realized his head was spinning and looked around wildly for a place to boot. Couldn't go upstairs, because of the girls. Downstairs john would have a line a mile long. "G'bye," he called to whoever he was dancing with. Racing through the crowd, he burst outside — only to find all these people walking around and the whole campus lit by floodlights. Jesus, he'd have to run to his dorm.

OUT OF THE DANCING CROWD burst Sandra, pulling on her coat, making for the door. Snot rushed after her.

"Hey, please, wait!"

She ignored him utterly.

"Listen, it started as a joke, but —"

The door slammed. Snot was crestfallen.

"Guess the plan didn't work out so well." Fitch came to stand beside him.

Snot's little mouth turned down at the corners. He didn't answer.

"Well, fuck her if she can't take a joke, right?"

Snot looked at him in annoyance. "Why don't you shut the fuck up?"

Fitch stared in surprise as Snot marched off in a snit.

ROUND SOMEHOW REACHED HIS ROOM, the world whirling about him the entire time. Happily, no one was home, and he was able to initiate a one-night stand with the toilet bowl. *"Blaaaargh."* How long was he going to be immobilized here, with his stomach contracting to the size of a pea? He was miserable.

Please, God, he thought, *make me feel better. I'll be good, I promise. I won't drink anymore. And . . . I'll go to church tomorrow. Okay?*

As in Bergman movies, God was silent.

• • •

BACK AT AD, the party was peaking. Carl Holmes and the Commanders were playing that great song "Shout," and if you could have harnessed the energy of the dancers, you probably could have reversed the flow of Niagara Falls. In the center of the room stood Scotty and Otter, shoved this way and that by the churning crowd, an eye of calm observation in the middle of the storm.

"Really depraved, isn't it?" Scotty wore a bemused smile. "Just totally sick."

"Nothing human offends me," said Otter.

"Nice to see Dobes. Think he's getting into the swing?"

With a rebel yell louder than the band, Doberman launched himself down the stairs on skis, poling himself along, stark naked. *"Yeeeeee-hahhhhhhhhhhhh!"* At the foot of the circular staircase, he plowed into the dancers and all went down in a big tumble.

"I think it's like swimming or riding a bike," said Otter. "You never really forget how."

THE PARTY WAS OVER. Dumptruck, suddenly president again, was making sure the tap was off and that the music stopped. As Alby staggered by, Dumptruck grabbed him. "Hey, do something useful. Go stand at the back door and say thank you very much and good night to the band. Okay?"

Alby headed unsteadily for the back door and arrived in time to see the drummer going out. "Thankyouverymuch, goodnight," he said.

The drummer nodded. Next, Troll and Donna Daley headed out. "Thankyouverymuch, goodnight," Alby said again, propping himself on the door frame.

Next, an emmet worker from Tanzi's left with an empty half-keg on his shoulder. "Thankyouverymuch, goodnight," said Alby.

A dog wandered out. "Thankyouverymuch, goodnight."

For the next half hour, Alby bade adieu to more than one hundred living beings, never moving from his station by the door, carrying out the official orders of President Truck. Finally, Gretchen found him and hauled him away.

• • •

TONIGHT WAS PINTO and Rhesus Monkey's turn to stand fire watch. They regarded each other beneath drooping eyelids. How could they ever get through this?

"What time is it?"

"One thirty-five."

They were allowed to leave at dawn, which by no means came early at this time of year. Maybe by seven. That meant five hours of staying awake when every aspect of their being craved sleep.

"I heard the worst thing you can do is beat off," said Rhesus Monkey.

"Shit, I was thinking of doing that. You know, to pass the time."

"Well, I heard if you do, you fall asleep in like five seconds."

"Shit."

"Yeah."

They sat on folding chairs. The floor was obscured by garbage, and the prevailing scent was cigarettes in half-filled cups of warm beer. You didn't want to open the windows, of course, lest you freeze in seconds.

"So how was your date with Stevie?"

"Great. We made out in Turnip's car with the heater on."

"Did you, you know —"

"Nah." The Monkoid started laughing. "She asked me to eat her up."

"She asked you to eat her *up?*"

"Pretty funny, huh?"

"Well, did you?"

"As things turned out, I got so involved explaining that you eat someone *out* that she lost the mood."

"Jeez, that's tough. So you have, ah, blue balls?"

"Oh, my *God,* do I have blue balls."

It was cruel.

The boys somehow did manage to stay awake, despite periods of nodding off like junkies, only to slap themselves alert again. When the campus cop came to check on them in the morning, they greeted him cheerfully, and passed out where they sat.

• • •

MOSES, IN BED with the Digit, was explaining it carefully. "Okay. It's called a hum job. Now what you do is put my balls in your mouth — and hum."

She nodded. Pulling off his long-underwear bottoms, she was rewarded with a snappy salute from his erect member. It made her smile. She bent to take his scrote in her mouth.

"Be *very* careful."

"Okay, honey." With great care, she contained Moses's balls in her mouth. He watched her, feeling more and more turned on. Then he saw her brow furrow, and she *removed* his balls from her mouth and said, "What should I hum?"

Moses was in desperation. "Anything! Anything! Just hum!"

She returned the balls to her mouth, thought a moment, and began humming an energetic rendition of "Dixie." When Moses heard what it was, he laughed so uncontrollably he lost his hard-on.

TONIGHT, THERE WAS NO NEW SNOW, and the moon shone without interference on the fairy-tale campus, quiet again in its white nightshirt. The town of Hanover took a deep breath. One more day.

Sunday

F. A. MAC THOUGHT TO BEGIN Sunday with Beverly by slipping down to the bar for a nice pre-church beer breakfast. They descended the narrow, twisty stairway and stepped into the basement. The room was dark. Mac located the light switch.

Beverly gasped.

Mac turned to look. There, on his back atop the bar, lay Doberman, nude but for a beer cup into which his cock and balls had been stuffed. He was snoring.

Mac put a finger to his lips. He and Bev tiptoed to the tap system, and Mac began drawing a beer.

In a big, happy voice, Doberman said, "Goooooood morning!" And tipped his cup.

• • •

ALBY AWOKE SMELLING Gretchen's honeysuckle perfume, once again in Whit's extra bedroom. He wanted to roll her over, but, reaching down for a manual check, found his longfellow to be totally beat to shit. He sighed, guessing he'd be taking a little sexual breather. He *hated* doing that.

BY NOON, the house was as clean as it was going to get, and Scotty declared it ready for the one-o'clock party. Guys and their dates were streaming in, having had lunch at Hal's and Minaciello's and the Green Lantern. F. A. Mac and Beverly, who'd caught an eleven-o'clock Mass, showed up in their church clothes. Rat and Zeke Banananose made rude noises at them and grabbed their crotches.

Mac shook his head, ears flaming. "Aw, you guys."

Downstairs, Hardbar and Moses were concocting the purple Jesus punch. This was a popular collegiate drink everywhere, but the only definite, agreed-upon ingredient was the grape juice, which supplied the purpleness. The Jesus part was up to you.

"Okay," Hardbar said. "Add the gin." He and Moses each poured a quart of Gilbey's into the tub. "Now the vodka." They added the fifth of Old Mr. Boston. "Next — rum." In went the rum.

"Now what?"

Hardbar produced a gallon of grain alcohol and poured it in.

"Does anyone ever die after drinking purple Jesus punch?" asked Moses in a little voice.

"Just two or three times a year. Okay, now we mix it, and there's a tried-and-true, traditional way to do this." Removing his boot and sock, Hardbar stirred the punch with his foot. "A subtle between-the-toes element finds its way into the flavor mix," he explained.

"Wow!" said Moses.

There was an additional ingredient, but Hardbar would need a little privacy. "So, Moses, please get some, ah, *sugar.* You have to run upstairs to the kitchen for it."

Moses darted from the basement. Dropping his pants, Hardbar

now added his personal touch to the punch. His trademark, so to speak. And mixed it again with his foot.

THE CROWD AT THE BAR was three-deep. The brothers had a desperation about them today. It was all about to end! The girls would split, leaving them in this arctic wasteland to suffer some stunted, half-assed version of life until spring came — and that wouldn't happen till May! Dartmouth was a better place when women were around, Pinto believed.

Seal stood with Doberman. They were the new house couple. The James Brown band by the jukebox had finally gotten its steps down; Pinto, Rhesus Monkey, Turnip, Scotty, and Y. Bags were bending and dipping and rearing up backward with their imaginary saxes like a well-oiled engine o' joy. Alby was continuing his attempt to break the thousand-beer-weekend barrier. Gretchen was grabbing a shower somewhere and would join him anon. Everyone was upful. Winter fucking Carnival!

Well, perhaps not everyone. Snot stood at the dark end of the bar, engaging no person in conversation, moodily watching the bubbles rise in his beer glass. He seemed to have fallen for Sandra, and now she hated him. Why did he have to be such an asshole, with the stupid jokes all the time? He boinked the side of his head with the flat of his hand, then stopped, realizing that that, too, was jokey and cartoonish. Well, fuck, maybe he needed to meet a woman who liked cartoons.

Alby looked up from the tap and froze. *Cheesa Berger was stepping out of the stairwell.* She was glancing around, obviously after him. Jesus Christ, and with Gretchen showing up any minute! Alby dropped to his knees. His eyes lit on the beer cooler. Yanking open one of the stainless-steel doors, he dragged out the extra half-keg so that it *ka-tank*ed on the stone floor, and scrambled inside. "Tell me when the chick in the Skidmore sweatshirt leaves. And don't tell anyone I'm here!" he yelled up at Hydrant and Black Whit, and closed the door. 'Drant and Whit looked at each other, confused.

Pinto was leaning against the wall, trying to catch his breath. Winter Carnival was the greatest invention in the history of the human race. And then who should walk into his line of sight but Donna Daley?

Without Troll.

And she walked right over to him.

He straightened quickly. "Hi, Donna."

"Pinto, something terrible happened. Troll's been arrested!"

"*What?*"

"Just because he was taking a whiz on Main Street. I mean, big fucking deal, you know? They took him to the cop shop."

"That's terrible."

They stood side by side a moment. Pinto's heart was in his throat.

"So, what are you going to do?"

"What *can* I do? He'll be there all day. Nice, huh?"

They stood in silence again. Pinto made himself say it. "Uh, *I* could be your date. You know, if you want one. Just until Troll gets back." He tried not to look too eager.

Donna studied him a moment, then smiled. "Sure, Pinto. That'd be nice."

Pinto felt a bloom of delight in his belly. Yeah!

ALBY WAS CONFINED in a four-foot cube of chilly metal and didn't know what was bothering him worse, the shivering or the muscle cramps. He cracked the door. "Hey, 'Drant! Is she still here?"

"Yeah."

"Fuck! Tell her to go home or something."

"Not only that, Gretchen just came in. They're standing about ten feet away from each other."

Jesus Christ! He pulled the door closed again.

Just in time, as both girls came up to the bar.

"Hi, I'm looking for my date," said Cheesa to Truck. "The trouble is, he never told me his name. But someone told me he's an AD."

"No ADs here," said Truck.

"What? But this is the AD house."

"Oh. Yes, well, I guess there are a few around. But I haven't seen your date."

"How would you know if you had or hadn't?"

"Uh, strong instincts."

Gretchen spoke up. "Hey, 'Drant. Have you seen Alby?"

"Nope," said Hydrant and Truck simultaneously.

"Don't you hate it when they disappear?" said Cheesa to Gretchen. "I've been looking for mine since yesterday morning. We're in love."

Hydrant and Truck tried to restrain laughter.

"My date thinks he can disappear any time he wants to," Gretchen replied. "I may have to cut him off sex."

Hydrant couldn't hold it any longer, and roared.

Cheesa and Gretchen regarded him without warmth. *Men!* they thought.

UPSTAIRS, THE BAND BEGAN again, and Pinto came running, dragging Donna by the hand. He was psyched; the Five Royales had not only sung "Baby, Don't Do It," but also "Think," "Tell the Truth," and "Dedicated to the One I Love," later made popular respectively by James Brown, Ray Charles, and the Shirelles. He squeezed between Scotty and the Digit and sat down with Donna on the kegs. The Royales were arrayed before their backup band in magenta tuxedos, and they broke into one of their hits, the peculiarly named "Monkey Hips and Rice." They sang with rich, soulful harmonies that gave Pinto chills. *Why can't life always be like this?* he wondered. *Why does anyone do anything else?*

"HEY, ALBY!" Hydrant called through the grille of the tap system. "You gotta see this. Come out a second."

If only for a chance to stretch, Alby pried himself out of the cooler. Truck pointed where he was supposed to look. He brought his head up until he was peering over the bar like Kilroy. He saw Gretchen and Cheesa sitting on one of the mattress seats, chatting away like old friends. Before he even had time to absorb this, out from the stairs came Lizzie Leftist! *Oh, fuck!* he thought, and dived back in the cooler.

"What's this? Another one?" cried Truck.

"Yeah," called Alby's muffled voice. "Keep her away from me."

Truck and 'Drant exchanged looks of pure admiration. Three in one weekend — Alby was a mighty man.

AT THE BAR DOWNSTAIRS, Snot became aware that someone was in his light, and looked up. Sandra was standing there.

"*Fnrrrrrkzazk!*" she said.

Snot's mouth dropped open.

Sandra laughed and laughed while Snot could form no words. Finally, she calmed down. "Look, Snot, when I ran out of here last night, I had nothing better to do, so I went to *The Virgin Spring.* I saw the guy with no tongue. I get what you were doing and I think it's hilarious. It's like, I don't know, you were doing improv."

"Improv," breathed Snot.

"So, I thought, you know, maybe we could . . ."

Snot's heart leapt. "Sure. Let me get you a beer."

ACROSS THE ROOM, Fitch slipped in a boot puddle and slammed his head into a pillar. He was carried out and taken to Dick's House, where the tired but still kindly white-haired doctor put seventeen stitches in his head. Carol, sitting in the waiting room, resolved never to come to Dartmouth again.

IT WAS APPROACHING FOUR, and the party was at its desperate peak. Seal, standing quietly on the sidelines, noticed an open gallon jar of mustard. "Protective balm," he muttered, and held the jar upside down over his head, and his head turned yellow.

Amidst the dancers was one guy — some Kappa Sig — who was doing the twist with one leg way up in the air and his head halfway to the ground. His date was a perky blonde with a circle pin, who abruptly let out a yelp of pain. Seal, covered now in condiment, had come up on hands and knees, reared up, and bitten her ass. "I'm the mustard man!" he chanted. "I'm the goddamned mustard man!" And moved on to the next date.

• • •

AT THE BAR, Truck was concerned. How much longer could Alby stay in the cooler before death set in? Gretchen and Cheesa were still talking, and Lizzie was examining AD's racist murals with distaste. They showed no signs of leaving.

AS THE AFTERNOON WORE ON, the separation anxiety increased, and people went into last-minute, all-out party mode. Kegs kicked and more were tapped. Alby had to keep reminding the guys from Tanzi's not to put one on his side of the cooler and to keep their damn mouths shut about his being there.

Upstairs, the band was playing "Shout" for the third time. It seemed to be the favored closing number of the R & B bands of that time, although the Royales did it with more roll than rock, as was their wont, and it sounded great. But as intense as the final hour of the party was, guys were now leaving quietly with their dates and heading to the station. Carnival was coming to the end.

For Rhesus Monkey and Stevie, it got complicated. When Stevie came out of the shower in a towel, she found her clothes missing. In fact, her entire *suitcase* was missing. It was okay for guys to be upstairs now, so Rhesus Monkey helped her look. They'd had a fine weekend. Bags's prediction had been wrong; he and Stevie had been all over each other all weekend, and if they hadn't quite done the deed yet, that could come next time. They had entered the romantic world, in all its unpredictable ridiculousness.

The search for the suitcase proved fruitless. Stevie looked at her watch — at least she'd held on to that. Her flight left in an hour.

"Don't worry, babe," said Rhesus Monkey. "You can have these." He pulled a Dartmouth sweatshirt and a pair of jeans from Hydrant's dresser and threw them toward her. In a trice, they had gotten her privates covered and her entirety into Lapic's old overcoat and out to the parking lot. Rhesus Monkey had Terry No-Come's car keys, so they jumped in the MG and sped for the Lebanon airport.

It should be added that the Monkoid and Stevie had been drunk for almost three days. It seems they brought out the inebriate in each other, which made them hot stuff at AD but subject to arrest elsewhere. Happily, they made it to the airport without getting stopped by a cop. The Monkoid took her in. They kissed and kissed, and then Stevie went out on the tarmac, her carry-on bag in one hand and a pile of books he'd given her under the other arm. She had gotten halfway to the plane when she felt a breeze and looked down. The overcoat had fallen open, and her pants, four sizes too large, had fallen to her ankles. Beneath them, of course, was nothing. A number of her fellow travelers stopped and regarded her with surprise.

"Uh, could I help you, miss?" a man asked, tipping his hat.

"Nahhh," said Stevie in her drunken slur. "I'll jus' pull up m'pants."

She did, and flew on to New York.

BACK AT THE BAR, Alby was turning blue. Truck and 'Drant realized it was up to them. Hydrant went to Cheesa, and Truck to Lizzie Leftist, and they each reported that Alby had left town with a girl named Melanie Merkin. Lizzie stomped out without a word. Cheesa burst into tears. "I wanted to have his baby," she said to anyone who would listen. The minute she wandered forlornly up the stairs, Truck and Hydrant threw open the tap system and dragged Alby out. His eyes were glazed and his cheeks looked frostbitten.

"Jesus, honey!" cried Gretchen, running over. "You look like death."

"Yeah, better get him into a hot shower," said Truck.

"Fuck it," said Alby. "Gimme beer."

To everyone's amazement, he drank one. It was a grand beau geste. Gretchen then helped him to his room, where, away from the membership, he collapsed and slept for two days.

BACK AT THE HOUSE, the Five Royales were having problems with their lead station wagon. The Rogers Garage tow truck had come, and now they were lounging around by their packed-up instruments, bored. So they were pleased when Rat Battles called down that he was showing porno films in the goat room, and hastened upstairs.

"Hey, guys," said Pinto cheerfully. "Boy, great set."

"Yeah, okay, that's good," said a Royale.

In the goat room, a white sheet had been hung as a screen, and blankets had been tacked over the windows. An eight-millimeter projector was on the lectern, and as the Royales came in, it began to roll the brittle old film through its spools and bobbins. A man and woman in thirties' clothes and haircuts came on screen. The clothes didn't stay on long, and soon the lady in her short bob was performing various pleasure-providing acts upon the guy's dick, which, in turn, had transformed to a sizable boner.

"Damn!" said a Royale.

The lady with the bobbed hair now lay back, legs apart, her expression inviting. But the guy stood watching her, playing with himself awhile. After what seemed like an age, he rolled a condom on. Yet still he dithered and the girl, in apparent frustration, began fingering herself.

"Quit jivin'!" cried the Royale. "You gotcho thing on!"

"Quit jivin', you gotcho thing on" became the catchphrase of the year, with the ADs saying it even more often than "Suck one cock!"

PINTO RAN BACK DOWN to the basement. He'd left Donna there and didn't want anyone snaking her. But she was fine, right where he'd left her, talking to Doberman and Tiger, who were great friends from the old days of three years ago. She came to Pinto and whispered in his ear, then slipped quietly into the sex room. Pinto's heart went into his throat and he looked around nervously. Many hard-core revelers still drank. He waited the requested thirty seconds, then slipped into the room after her.

Darkness closed around him.

"Over here, Pinto."

He followed the voice to one of the mattresses. Her hand pulled him down with her. Holy shit, she was wearing nothing but a flimsy little pair of panties! Was this it? Was he finally, finally, finally going to get laid?

• • •

OUTSIDE AT THE BAR, the fifteen or so die-hard celebrants were showing some wear. Even Rat Battles looked tired — some new lines had appeared on his face. Not that this was stopping anyone. The party had to continue, no matter what. Gimme another beer. Play another song on the jukebox. Keep it rolling.

At this moment, in walked Zeke Banananose with the second-floor rag box.

"Oh, my God," muttered Scotty.

Zeke came up with his flushed grin and pizza complexion and set the box on the bar. All conversation stopped. The others eyed him.

Reeling from his twenty-two glasses of purple Jesus punch, Zeke reached through the slot and removed a toilet paper package, dappled with red.

The others watched through scrinched-up expressions, to a man feeling grateful they hadn't been born Zeke Banananose.

Zeke set the bundle on the bar and removed another. When he had four little bundles in a row, he pushed the box away, took one of them, and unwrapped it. This was getting hard to watch, but paradoxically, you couldn't tear your eyes away. Out from the bundle came a Tampax. Zeke Banananose ran it beneath his nose, sniffing it like a fine cigar.

"Aggghhhhhhh!" went everybody.

He was not through. Pleased to be getting a reaction, Zeke now put the Tampax in his mouth and began to eat.

"Oh, God!" cried Magpie.

Truck ran to the gutter and booted.

Even Rat Battles and Doberman had gone pale. At that moment, the campus cop walked in.

He beheld a frozen tableau: eighteen guys looking at him with the most guilty expressions ever seen in a fraternity basement. Zeke just stood there, slack-jawed, a corner of the Tampax protruding from his mouth.

When the cop realized what it was, he shit. *"Great Christ!"* he yelled, and ran to the gutter to join Truck.

Pinto, in the sex room and almost in Donna, stopped dead. "What the hell was that?"

"I don't care, Pinto. Come on. Give it to me."

Pinto was horribly torn, but wanting not to get thrown out of school won and he tiptoed naked to the door to peek out. The campus cop had the reeling Zeke by the arm and was calling for help on his radio. Jesus.

The two dressed quickly, but hid in the sex room and never got caught. A lot of other guys did, though. And so, AD's Winter Carnival 1961 came to an abrupt and unpleasant terminus.

And Pinto was still a virgin.

IN THE WEEKEND'S WAKE, Zeke Banananose was thrown out of school forever. Troll was suspended a term for public peeing. Hardbar, caught beating off in the sink room, was out for a year. And the guys who'd been at the bar when the cop walked in were all given college warnings.

Immediately following this, a vast icicle fell from the AD roof and pierced the roof of Fitch's car like a harpoon. The ADs, reduced to superstitious dread, took this as a terrifying sign.

Then, to the immense sadness of everyone, Seal was thrown out of school. As Magpie said, you had to *work* to get suspended at Dartmouth, but Seal had managed it. His missing pledge paper had at last turned up in a loose-leaf notebook he'd left at Vassar during a road trip. It had been given to the dean of women, who had immediately sent it to Dean Seymour. Pinto finally found out what Seal's topic was, and understood the dean's reasoning.

It was called "The Last Time I Ate Out My Father's Asshole."

AD was in deep shit.

CHAPTER FOURTEEN

At Long Last Laid

A PERIOD OF WAITING ENSUED. The Interfraternity Council Disciplinary Committee would decide the fate of the house itself, but that wouldn't happen until they met in a couple of weeks. The sword of Damocles revolved slowly over the Adelphian lodge.

In the meantime, thanks to the many sudden vacancies, Pinto got to move into the house! He, Rhesus Monkey, and Alby wound up in the room formerly occupied by Hardbar and Zeke Banana-nose. He couldn't have been more thrilled.

The parting from Brad and Isaac had been a little sad. He felt affection for them both, but they were so different from him that he'd despaired of ever finding much to talk about. Brad lived in an athletic universe, and Isaac, well, who knew what kind of universe Isaac lived in? But they were both good guys and Pinto would miss them. There was no hugging or anything; they helped him down to the house, shook his hand, and left him with his pile of stuff.

His new digs were on the south end of the second floor, looking out on East Wheelock Street and the gym. Well, it *would* be looking out on those things when spring came and the opaque plastic thermal window covers could be removed; right now, all he could see was a milky void. There was a little living room with a little fireplace, and a little bedroom, which quickly became a domain of moldering socks and underwear. No one ever went in it, except to sleep.

At last, he had the right roommates. They got his jokes. Rhesus Monkey was cheerful, peppy, and funny. He began to cover the walls with strange graffiti, saying things like SUPPORT MENTAL HEALTH OR I'LL KILL YOU. Alby was even funnier, an endless source of strange and wonderful commentary on life in general. He was also unpredictable, having been known to beat off behind a textbook, then whip it away at the last minute and aim at a room- mate. You had to be on your toes.

Life in the house was great. Pinto couldn't imagine living any other way, ever again. Although it was hard to get much studying done, and sometimes you had to slip off to the 1902 Room at Baker Library. This was known as sneak-booking, and opened you up to teasing and mockery. Of course, then the teasers and mockers would have to sneak-book. If you didn't book at least some of the time, you wouldn't graduate, and that was the way of things.

The days passed. The ADs lived a twilight existence as they awaited the fall of the ax. Pinto tried to keep his mind on other things. How awful it would be if, the minute he moved into the house, there was no more house.

One night he stayed up late, drinking with Dumptruck and Scotty. Climbing into bed at two, sure that Alby and Rhesus Monkey were asleep, he decided to beat the meat. Now, attempting this when more than moderately drunk is difficult. It takes a *long* time. Pinto labored on and on. He brought up every sexy image he could muster. His arm was killing him. And then he felt it about to hap- pen. Oh, boy! He rolled to the side so he could come on the floor.

"Don't hit me," cried Alby.

"Aw, fuck!" Pinto's hard-on fell apart, his orgasm ruined.

THEN, ON A WEDNESDAY evening at the end of February, the ax fell. The brothers knew something was up when Dumptruck appeared for the house meeting in a sport coat. To the consterna- tion of the assemblage, he announced that Dean Seymour would shortly be addressing them.

"What the fuck does he want?" Scotty demanded.

"Why didn't you tell us sooner?" cried Mouse.

Truck spread his arms helplessly. "I didn't know until fifteen minutes ago. I guess the interdisciplinary council met today."

"Don't you mean Interfraternity Council Disciplinary Committee?" said Pinto.

"Yeah, fuck you," said Truck.

"So, are we on pro?" Alby asked.

"I guess we're going to find out."

The dean knocked on the door. Truck, smoothing back his hair, let him in. "Hello, sir. We're, uh, very happy that you would take the time to —"

Dean Seymour seemed uncomfortable. "Let's get right to the point." He took a position before the brothers. "As long as Dartmouth's been around, winter's been a problem. The isolation and absence of women try our souls. And then, along comes Winter Carnival."

"*Ya-hooooo!*" screamed Rat from the back of the room.

"*Will you shut up?*" hissed Mouse, punching him in the arm.

The dean continued. "A lot of guys like to think Dartmouth College becomes a sort of snowcapped Fiji Islands then."

"*All right!*" Rat stuck two fingers in his mouth and whistled piercingly.

"Jesus Christ!" Dumptruck grimaced. "Will someone get him the fu— uh, get him out of here?"

"'Ey, *gordo!*" Mouse gave Rat an elbow in the ribs. "Why don't you go downstairs, and then stay there?"

"Grea' idea." Rat tottered from the room.

"Sorry, Dean," Dumptruck said.

The dean squared his shoulders. "You stayed off probation for Carnival by the skin of your teeth. I thought you might take things a little easy for a while. But no." He consulted a piece of paper. "Public urination, public masturbation, public *defecation*, several acts of indecent exposure —"

"Aw, come on, Dean," called Black Whit. "That was just some of the guys mooning people."

Dean Seymour looked at him. "Not 'people.' The Dartmouth Board of Trustees."

"That's who we mooned? Those guys in suits? Wow!" Magpie clapped a hand over his mouth and shrank back as the dean turned to see who had spoken.

Dumptruck tried to regain some control. "Dean, we're really trying to do better."

"Are you?" He held up three wrinkled, beer-stained pages covered with Seal's scrawlings. "Sorry, but as long as you're assigning your pledges topics like The Last Time I Ate Out My Father's Asshole, you haven't turned the corner yet."

This quickly became another Adelphian catchphrase. You'd be late meeting Scotty for lunch. Pissed, he'd say, "You haven't turned the corner yet!" It went on for a couple of years.

Whit was adamant. "But, Dean Seymour, in a free country, you should be able to do anything you want, limited only by your imagination!"

The dean frowned at his zeal. "Well, you would know, Mr. Whitfield. Didn't we find you and your girlfriend naked in the boathouse last spring?"

"But I told you then — we fell in the river. We took our clothes off to dry 'em. That's what you do! It's the right-hand rule of canoeing!"

Dumptruck put his face in his hands. This wasn't going well.

TO NO ONE'S SURPRISE, AD wound up on probation for an indefinite period. The brothers sank into a stoic gloom. Dumptruck hoped that if they behaved, they'd be reinstated for Green Key Weekend. But that was in May, which was a long time in the future. Meanwhile, no kegs, no parties, and no female guests. Pinto counted it out on his fingers — three months. There would probably be more action in the dorm he'd just left.

And then, on the eighth of March, his birthday arrived. He turned nineteen, which had seemed such an advanced age a short time ago. God, he was *old*. And look at his life. Thrown into a joyless limbo by the college authorities. Trapped indoors by a remorseless winter. And, worst of all, still a virgin. Nineteen years old and not yet a man. He stared into the fire in his little fireplace, deeply depressed.

The door blammed open. "Hey, Pinto! You want to dip your wick? I'm getting up a road trip to Congress Street." Bags stood there, eyeing him.

To Congress Street, the notorious Negro whorehouse street in Saratoga Springs, New York? Leaving at nine p.m. for a two-and-a-half-hour drive? To perhaps wind up being mugged and left in a gutter?

"Yes!" he cried.

IN SHORT ORDER, Bags borrowed Terry No-Come's car and Pinto put on a sweater and his B-9 parka and went out to the parking lot. Seeing who the other member of their party was, though, took some wind from his sails. Aw, no, not Rat.

Bags shifted his cigar to the far side of his mouth and regarded Pinto from beneath his great browridges. "Hey, the guy's colorful. What can I say?"

Maybe the real reason was that Rat was supplying a case of beer. Then the next problem arose. Terry's MG was tiny. The only way they could all fit was to squeeze the beer under Rat, and Rat between Pinto's legs. *Swell,* Pinto thought.

The car left Hanover, traveling west, and came at once to the Connecticut River. Crossing it, they were in Vermont, an adorable little cupcake state, currently spread with thick white frosting. If you stayed on Route 4, it took you all the way to New York.

Many beers and two whiz stops later, accompanied by the sudden appearance of snow flurries, they reached the Empire State. As the windows were closed, warm, upward gusts from the heater were wafting a continuous stream of Rat's body odors into Pinto's face. He tried to ignore them, concentrating on the road ahead, watching dark hulks of fir trees hurl themselves from the darkness and fly by, briefly green in their headlights.

"Ever been to a whorehouse, Pinto?" Bags asked him.

"Oh, yeah," said Pinto. "After the cockfights and before I score heroin, I always stop off at a whorehouse."

"Well, don't worry, man. It's fun."

Pinto had some concerns about visiting a whorehouse, but even more he was wondering what it'd be like to go to a *black* whorehouse.

Bags paused thoughtfully. "Of course, you have to wear a rubber. They *all* have the clap. You brought one, right?"

Shit! He slapped his forehead.

"Jesus Christ, Pinto! What were you going to do — go in bareback?"

"I . . ."

"Well, don't worry. I brought an extra. Here." He tossed him a Trojan.

Pinto was tired of feeling like a naive asshole. How could he not remember a rubber? He could get syphilis! This whole thing was getting a little too real.

The conversation trailed off. Bags squinted into the crazily dancing snowflakes beyond the windshield. Rat had fallen into a semi-stupor, his head rolling loosely with the car's movements. The inner atmosphere of the MG had become close and ripe as the ape house at the zoo.

Pinto lost himself in his thoughts. Soon, he'd be facing a pair of spread legs, and do the deed at last. It would end the first phase of his life and initiate the second — the much-anticipated, endlessly dreamed-of, getting-laid-and-blown-all-the-time phase.

"Hey," said Bags suddenly. "We're here."

Shaking himself, Pinto wiped mist from the windshield. The snow was lighter now, and he could make out some of Saratoga Springs' rumored 217 bars passing by. On Saturday nights, they'd be packed with local Skidmore College girls and their dates from Dartmouth, Colgate, and Hamilton. Tonight, however, on a snowy Tuesday, the bars were closed and dark, the streets deserted, the Skidmore girls asleep in their dormitory beds. A red traffic arrow, blinking steadfastly at them through the snow, was the only sign of life. It pointed straight to Congress Street.

"Ha! Bet the town council had that installed." Bags downshifted and took the turn without a skid. "Hey, Rat. You with us?"

"Muh?" Rat looked up blearily. "Whuzzmatta?"

"Colorful, huh?" said Pinto.

Bags ignored him. "Wake the fuck up, man. We're gonna get laid."

"Hey, grea'. Le's have a beer." Rat blinked at him, trying to focus.

"Well, don't look now, boys, but we have arrived," Bags announced. He indicated several houses, the windows of which were lit with candles.

Pinto stared. It was a residential street, lined with two-story homes. A couple of parked cars seemed to be missing tires and engines, but aside from this, the neighborhood looked very normal and American, not at all like the ghetto high-life scene he'd fantasized. Where was the honky-tonk music, the crowds of customers, the comical paid-off cops. Hell, the houses didn't even have red lights. Maybe they *weren't* whorehouses. Maybe all those bar stories about Congress Street had been bullshit, and by knocking on doors at this hour, they'd merely be disturbing Negro insomniacs watching *The Late Show.*

As Bags slowed to inspect a parking place, the door to the house nearest them opened, silhouetting a robed figure. "Yoo-hoo, fellas," called a voice. "Over here. I know what you lookin' for."

Well, seemed it was a whorehouse, after all. Pinto took a deep breath and started to climb out. He couldn't move! He looked down. Rat was slumping heavily against him, snoring.

Jesus. "Rat, come on. Wake up."

"Muh?"

"Come on, man. We're here."

"Oh, righ'. 'M comin'."

His extrication took a while. The whole time, like a mating call, the voice from the doorway kept calling softly, "Come on, fellas. I know what you want." Rat finally pushed himself out backward and fell in the snow, empty Budweiser cans landing all about him.

"Hey, hurry the fuck up," said Bags. "I'm freezing my tits off out here."

"Righ', righ'." Rat got shakily to his feet and he and Bags headed inside. Pinto nervously trailed after.

"Hurry up, fellas. It gettin' *col'* in here."

They hurried, stumbling up the steps. Pinto found himself politely kicking the snow from his boots at the entrance. The woman in the doorway, shivering, gestured them impatiently inside and shut the door.

Warm air, heavy with perfume, closed around them like a mouth. Numerous semiclad girls were strewn about on cushions and couches, assuming come-hither poses. A large businesslike woman beckoned three girls to their feet and allocated them, seemingly at random, among Pinto, Bags, and Rat. Without any perceptible deal or negotiation being entered into — in fact, without a word — the whores led them down a hall and into separate rooms.

Pinto held his breath. The room they'd entered was absolutely dark. Then the whore lit a couple of candles, and he could see again. It contained a double bed covered with a rumpled sheet, a straight-back chair, and a squat brown dresser bearing a doily and a low metal basin of the sort surgeons throw used instruments into. On the wall above the pillow was an unframed picture of Christ on the cross, a real nice head-and-shoulders shot featuring several rills of blood from the Crown of Thorns and a facial expression of almost cartoon agony. Pinto turned and took his first good look at his whore.

She was no more than five feet tall. She wore a brown sweater and pink toreador pants. She had eyes, lips, a nose, hair. Her skin was medium brown. What was remarkable about her was that nothing was remarkable about her. Pinto strove to individuate her and failed. She was anonymous as a Chinese waiter.

"A half 'n' half is ten dollar," she told him. "Pay in advance."

Thanks to Bags, he knew about this. His money was ready and he handed it over.

"You get undress," she directed him. Tucking the bill inside her sweater, she took the basin and padded from the room.

Get undress? All the way undress? So as to be stark naked when she came back, standing there with his dong hanging out? He was already apprehensive about her taking his money and leaving him alone. What if, the minute he got his clothes off, two huge black guys burst in and tore him to pieces? He bet that happened a lot, white college boys venturing into black whorehouses and getting injured or killed. But what was he talking about? These Congress Street whorehouses had been here for years, servicing generations of white college boys. Racial ass-kicking would be bad for business, strictly prohibited. He sat on the bed and reached for his right shoe.

"What, you ain' undress yet?" The girl carried the basin, now half filled with water. She put it on the dresser top, produced a sponge and bar of soap, and looked at him. "You onny *got* fifteen minute."

Jesus. He made quick work of the rest of his clothes. Then, as he slipped out of his shorts, he wondered how she'd react to the ol' pinto. Would she think his camouflage colors cute or scream, "Mutant!" Stealing a glance, he found her stepping out of her tore-adors so that he beheld her great, triangular black bush. He liked big bushes. He took off his shorts.

She sat on the bed, basin in her lap. "Well, come on." Gesturing him closer.

Pinto got it finally. She was going to *wash* him. Okay. He hung his cock and balls over the basin.

With cool, knowing hands, she lifted his unit and began to squeeze spongefuls of warm water on it. It felt pretty good. Then she did a small double take and looked up at him. "It two different colors!" she declared wonderingly.

Uh-oh, thought Pinto.

"What happened?" she asked.

Pinto plunged in. He told her about the tar and the turpentine.

"You was jus' a li'l fella, huh?" She smiled.

That was right! He'd been just a little fella! They were communicating. And what was more, she hadn't pointed at it and thrown up. Hey, he liked this whore; she was okay. "What's your name?" he asked.

"Gloria." She had soaped him copiously and was rinsing him with more spongefuls of water.

Gloria? He had *known* girls named Gloria. More and more, she was seeming like . . . just a person. He searched for more to say. "So, uh, tonight's my birthday. How about that?" He wondered briefly if this might entitle him to a discount, or some sort of special birthday sex act.

"No kiddin'?" She didn't sound too interested. Scratch that idea.

"Yes, my friends and I drove here tonight from New Hampshire, where we go to school."

She was drying him with a soft towel. "Oh, yeah? You come all this way jus' for a piece of ass?"

"That's right," said Pinto. "Heh, heh."

"Well, I guess you dry now." She patted a spot on the bed. "Why don't you sit right here?"

"Uh . . . right there?" He sat.

She returned the basin to the dresser. Then she lifted her sweater high enough to show him her boze. They were medium-sized, pleasingly round, and quite brown, Pinto's first Negro pair. Her nipples were browner yet, like mahogany.

"Okay?" she said.

Huh? Was what okay? Her breasts? What was this, a clinic? To his surprise, she pulled the sweater back down. She must have meant had he seen enough. Well, he could have done with more, but why raise such a trifling matter when she was, even now, going to her knees on a little rug between his legs, and seemed about to . . .

Wham! Pinto jumped. Someone had violently thrown a door open, quite near to them. Gloria looked up from his crotch, startled.

"My God!" cried a voice. "I'm not doin' it with you. Yo' whole body need washin', not just yo' thing." Footsteps hurried off, followed by several more erratic ones. "Hey!" shouted Rat's voice. "Don' feel bad. I prolly couldn'ta got it up anyway."

Gloria regarded Pinto. "Nice friends you got."

"Uh, heh, heh." Her hands still held his unit. Her lips were mere inches away. And here came her mouth, which plucked his dick from the air like a Venus flytrap.

The usual sensations played about his German helmet as her deft tongue traced patterns on it skilled Persian rugmakers never dreamed of. Absurdly, he found himself looking every which way to see if anyone was watching. He even checked out the Jesus picture to see if, as in old horror movies, real eyes had replaced the painted ones and were now following his every movement. They weren't. He looked back at his lap. Gloria had cupped his balls in one hand and was holding his cock with her other, lowering her head on it again and again, reminding Pinto of one of those plastic, pivoted birds that dip their bills repeatedly into small vessels of water. With each upswing of her head, the pull of his cock made her lips look extra large.

Pinto wondered why he couldn't just relax and enjoy himself, as he certainly had with Mindy Disbro that night in the car. Maybe it was that he knew her, while this girl was an utter stranger. Maybe it was that Mindy was white. He didn't know. He was intensely aware of everything going on; no dreamlike cloud of sexual bliss this time. He was enjoying it, but to tell the truth, Mindy's blow job had been better, if only for being passionate instead of professional. That time, he'd circumnavigated the galaxy; this time, only the solar system. Still, his cock sure had gotten big.

"Honey, you *ready!*" She crawled by him onto the bed, lay down, and drew her legs up till her knees touched her chest, as if performing the first move of an exercise. Lying like this, she turned to Pinto and regarded him expressionlessly.

He felt strangely calm. Going to the foot of the bed, he crawled toward her on hands and knees, until his face, like an observation balloon, passed directly over her wazoo. Well . . . He took his cock in hand, and then stopped.

The rubber! He'd forgotten about the fucking rubber! "Uh, excuse me a minute." Ears flaming, he crawled over to the chair and began digging through his pants. Rolling the condom onto himself, he kept his back to her, not wanting to see the contempt he knew was in her eyes. How antiseptic and white he felt! He wanted to explain, "It's not that I don't want it touching you; it's that I'm scared you're *diseased!*" But how could he say that? His hard-on, in its pale, gleaming mitten, was shrinking. He crawled back on top and tried to get his now scarcely sensate prod into her.

She made an impatient expression. "Come *on*, honey. You ain't got all night." She helped him get it inside, then returned her arms to her side, hitched her legs higher, and lay still. "Well, go 'haid," she said.

It felt . . . well, it didn't feel like much. There was pressure on his dick, but no sensation. He began moving himself in and out, the way he'd imagined doing for so many years. Gloria moved her hips in slight counterpoint, not uttering a sound. Gradually, it sank in: he was doing it! *He was no longer a person who'd never been laid!* Henceforth, no matter where he went, no matter how many years might pass, laid was something he would always have been. He felt a rush of euphoria.

Three sharp raps sounded on the door.

Pinto looked about wildly. "What was that?"

"Time's almost up, honey. Better hurry."

Jesus Christ, he'd thought it was a raid! His shock ebbed, but so did several more degrees of his hard-on. Shit. *Easy does it,* he told himself. *Keep those hips moving.* Ah, getting harder again. He began moving faster.

"HEY, PINTO!" Bags's voice, from the hall, was like a sonic boom. "WHADDAYA, GOT BRASS BALLS?"

That was it for his hard-on. Fucking Bags. He tried a last desperate lunge or two but only succeeded in popping himself out of her entirely.

"What's the matter, honey?" said Gloria. "You havin' a li'l trouble tonight?"

Pinto wasn't going to admit to trouble. If he admitted it, that would make it real. He gestured at his unit. "Could you . . . ?"

"Honey, you heard the knock. Time up."

But he hadn't come! He'd gone through all this — the car ride, the anxiety, Rat's smells blowing in his face — only to be stopped short of climax? What kind of prostitute was she?

"Listen, I have another five bucks. Could I maybe get five minutes more?"

"Well . . . Ah'll see." She took the five, wrapped a towel around herself, and left the room.

Pinto glared down at the rubber. It was the fault of this stupid unnatural piece of shit on his cock that he hadn't come. Abruptly, he ripped it off and flung it in a corner. If he caught something, he'd . . . deal with it, that was all. He'd come here to feel the exciting walls of a pussy on his dick, not rubber.

Gloria reappeared. "It's okay," she told him. Without further preamble, she dropped down and began resucking his cock. It became hard in an instant. Gloria regarded it judiciously. "Mm. Maybe you a suck man rather than a fuck man."

He hoped he was both. "Well, uh, let's find out."

"You ain't gonna put yo' thing on?"

"No, I'm not." He found himself able to meet her eyes and was sure he detected approval. He was still slick with her saliva, so that this time when he crawled on top of her all she had to do was give it a slight nudge and he plunged all the way in, drawing from her a little grunt that pleased him enormously. And did it ever feel different without the rubber. *This* was what he'd been after, *this* feeling.

"Hey, Pinto! Jesus Christ!"

"Hey, fuck you, Bags! I'm coming!"

"You sure are!" Gently but firmly, Gloria uncoupled them and snatched up a towel.

When they returned to the living room, Pinto beheld one of the strangest tableaux he'd ever seen. Bags, Rat, and four of the whores were crawling around the room, their noses inches from the floor. They looked like a disoriented animal herd.

"What's going on?" he asked.

One of the whores nodded her head at Rat. "Yo' friend fell asleep on the floor and while he sleepin', his glass eye fell out."

Bags shook his head. "I keep telling you. It's a contact lens."

"Yeah," said Rat. "Contrac lens."

"Well, I don't see it," said another whore. "What does they look like?"

"They're little glass things. Jesus Christ!" Bags was not in the best of moods.

"Keep yo' shirt on," said a whore without any shirt on. "We'll find it."

Pinto joined the search. Every time he lifted his gaze from the floor, he found himself staring at a thigh, or up an ass, or at a pair of pendulous bazooms dragging the rug. "Oof, watch where you put that foot, Lucille," said a voice. "Hey, getcho nose out mah pussy," said another. "Oh, sorry," said Rat.

Then, "Wait a minute. What's that on yo' titty, Laverne?"

The whore without any shirt on looked. There was a little glimmer an inch above her left nipple. "Uh, is this it?" She held the breast out to Rat.

"Hey, yeah!" Taking the lens gingerly, he leaned his head back and dropped it on his eyeball. The whores stared at him wonderingly.

"Stop in again, boys." The madam, giving Rat a dirty look, opened the door.

"Yeah, yeah." Scowling, Bags pushed by her.

"Maybe I just will," allowed Pinto, bowing grandly. He turned for a last look at Gloria, but she had merged with the other whores and try as he might, he couldn't pick her out. Shrugging, he went outside. The air felt incredible against his face, smelling as pure as if it had just been made.

"G'nigh'," said Rat, and tumbled down the whorehouse steps.

Heading home, Rat between his legs, Bags grimly driving, Pinto couldn't keep his mind still. He'd finally done the deed. Was he different? Did he now project an aura of mature sexuality? Specifically, would girls sense his new worldliness and want to take out his dick and slam their tits together around it? He couldn't predict but did it ever feel good to have the virginity thing out of the way.

After a while, he dozed, and apparently slept awhile, because when he wakened, the car was pulling up the hill that went into Hanover. And just as his eyes opened, Bags's eyes closed, his head going forward onto the steering wheel, the horn sounding, the car swerving sharply, straight for the steep embankment. *Good Christ!* thought Pinto. Grabbing the wheel, he straightened them out and yelled for Bags to wake up.

Bags snapped awake and pulled them over. It wasn't necessary to say anything. Had they gone over the side, they would have rolled a hundred feet. They all would have been killed, with the possible exception of Rat, who might have been too drunk to die. Milk runs, as late-night returns from road trips were known, were goddamned dangerous.

"So what's the matter, Yog?" said Pinto after they'd dropped Rat at his dorm. "You've been in a bad mood since Congress Street."

"Aah, my rubber broke. All I can think about is getting to my room to wash my dick in alcohol. Syphilis makes you go blind."

Pinto washed his dick as well, to be on the safe side. He didn't contract anything, but Bags wound up with a bad case of the crabs and had to have his entire life fumigated.

Pinto, meanwhile, now felt himself poised for endless great sex with great-looking girls. That's what *Playboy* was always talking about, right? Blondes, brunettes, redheads. Getting laid was your birthright.

CHAPTER FIFTEEN

Glorious Spring

PINTO'S BUDDIES BACK IN ROSLYN were thrilled.

"You made it! All right!"

"Hey, man, way to go!"

"Next thing, you'll be eating pussy!"

He supposed that *was* next, in the extremely long encyclopedia of sex acts he had in mind for himself. The loss of virginity had brought Pinto no respite from the screaming needs of his joint and the body it rode in on. Now, instead of constantly wondering, *When will I do it for the first time?* he was constantly wondering, *When will I do it next?* This was the way life was for adult guys, perhaps.

Josh raised his beer to Pinto at the Nob Hill Inn. Froggie and the Little Twin — another high school pal, familiarly known as Robkin — raised their glasses as well. As for Ace Kendall, who knew where he was? Maybe they didn't have spring break at Grinnell.

Robkin, like Josh, had joined the worldly club of the sexually initiated during his freshman year, and so this left only Froggie a virgin. His friends were sympathetic.

"Remember," Josh told him earnestly, "every day that goes by brings you one day closer to the first day you get laid."

"Thanks," said Froggie. "That's extremely comforting."

"I had a date." Josh bent forward to speak confidentially. The others leaned in too, so that they met over the table like the sides of a tent. "Her name was Brenda. She sat me on this cane seat with, like, a hole in the bottom so your balls hung through? And then blew me while she was tickling them, really softly, with her fingernails."

Pinto's hard-on was instantaneous. It was the most exciting thing he'd ever heard. Well, *every* new sex story was the most exciting thing he'd ever heard.

"*Last call for alcohol!*" bawled Jan from the bar area, loud enough to make the glassware clink.

The guys groaned. Already? Back to college *tomorrow? Shit!*

PINTO WAS EVEN MORE THRILLED when he returned to school, woke up in the morning, and found the place buried in a blizzard. Indeed, expletives flew heavenward from every Dartmouth mouth. *This was too much.* But the storm was winter's last gasp, and the next day the great, white blanket that covered Hanover began to melt, and then melted some more, and finally, reluctantly, entered the realm of the snows of yesteryear. Spring trembled on the brink.

But first you had to get through the Mud.

For all that melted snow had to go somewhere, and now, for the next week and a half, a perfect sea of umber muck would prevail everywhere there wasn't a building, sidewalk, or street. The Green was brown! It happened every year, and the guys from Buildings and Grounds were ready, laying wooden walkways upon its crisscrossing paths so you could clump to class, kicking the guck out of your boot cleats on the building's steps. But you could never get it all. The Mud followed you into class, your room, the dining hall. The floor and gutter of the AD bar were beslimed with it. Moses declared it was putting him in a brown study. "Huh?" said Rat.

And then, one magic morning, it was gone, and New Hampshire reimagined itself as a lush, green paradise. A young chokecherry tree stood at the end of the AD driveway; two days ago it had been bare branches, and then yesterday there were brown buds, and now, almost as Pinto watched from his window — the opaque plastic long gone — the buds exploded into a multitude of creamy white blooms. As if Mother Nature had been giving the tree a root job, and it had just come.

Where's my *root job,* Pinto's dick inquired.

I'm working on it, he thought back. *Hold your horses.*

Horses? snorted his dick. *What is that, a metaphor?*

Pinto hushed his grumpy member and returned to his fantasies. He was more than ready to get laid again, and this time with a real woman, not an anonymous professional. One who, like him, wanted to *try every sexual thing they could possibly imagine!* A real woman like, perhaps, Mindy Disbro? That night at Smith, in the car, she'd seemed ready for anything. He didn't know if the dean was going to let them have a Green Key, but why not hope for the best? He went to the sink room and dropped a dime in the phone.

"Hello?"

"Hi! It's Pinto. How you doing?"

She didn't reply.

"You remember — last fall? We went to the —"

"Pinto. Wow. Hi."

"You sound surprised."

"Yeah, I guess. It's been like five months."

"Six, actually. Or seven. Uh . . . November, December, January . . ."

"You never called me."

"Oh, uh —" Was he supposed to have? Why would he, except to make a date? He blurted, "Would you like to come to Green Key?"

No pause this time. *"I'd love to come to Green Key."*

All the college girls in New England wanted to go to Green Key, Dartmouth's big spring weekend, but still, the way Mindy said it, his hair stood up. As well as other portions of his anatomy.

They talked awhile longer, just the space-filling stuff people say to each other, and then she closed with "I can't wait to see you, Pinto. So we can sort of, you know, take up where we left off. Bye."

Pinto stood alone in the sink room, stunned, his balls throbbing like frogs' throats. How could he possibly wait until May?

The trees in front of Baker Library blossomed, too. The trees *everywhere* blossomed, and three thousand Dartmouth men threw off their winter-term torpor and ran out in the sunlight. Guys tossed baseballs and walked on their hands and flipped Frisbees, those cool new flying-saucer things everyone was buying. Couples strolled across the Green, hand in hand. Pinto felt great. When the seasons changed, it was like *magic,* man!

He was not alone. Doberman romped on the lawn with Brucie, a local bowser. That is, he rolled around, joyously kicking his feet and hands in the air and sniffing the grass for the piss of other dogs, like his canine playmate. Moses imported the Digit, and they spent much time in his dorm room with the door locked. The two were tired but happy by Sunday. Perhaps influenced by Moses's subsequent shit-eating grin, Otter invited Gay to visit the following weekend, and then disappeared with her into a motel room in White River Junction, coming back Sunday afternoon with a feces-devouring smile of his own. Snot bounced about happily. Black Whit left the house one afternoon, triggering a flight of sparrows from the hedge. *"Anh!"* he cried in childlike wonder. *"Birds!"*

Alby and Fitch bought the first in a string of daily kegs that would run until graduation. Rat, delighted, took up permanent residence in the basement, sleeping on the mattresses, making his *toilette* in the sink room, dining on sandwiches from the 'wich man. As far as anyone knew, he wore the same pair of undertrou the entire term. Rat and, to a lesser extent, Fitch were gradually losing their higher brain functions, trapped in the entropy of their genial-but-really-fucked-up nonstop drinking. Alby was probably declining as well. You weren't sure because sometimes he actually seemed elevated by alcohol. The beer opened up associations in his mind that might have occurred to Lenny Bruce but to no other funnyman Pinto could think of. Well, maybe Ernie Kovacs.

It had been a good year for young Master Pinto. He'd managed to stay alive, always good, and except for the bleeding gums, diarrhea, and frequent coughing from drinking and smoking too much, he'd never felt better. And you could get rid of the gum thing just by swishing peroxide around your mouth. Meanwhile, this semester, he'd signed up for new courses that he liked! Why, he'd finally asked himself, was he taking classes he hated? Because JC Senior wanted him to? Pinto's father, as noted, believed the only careers fit for a son of his were law, medicine, or business. All three alarmed Pinto. If you were a lawyer, your life would consist of fighting. Pinto felt about fights as he did about enemas — they were seldom really necessary and always profoundly unpleasant. Businessmen? Mostly boring philistines, or so it seemed. They were Ace Kendall's corporate robots. And doctors never stopped working. Pinto didn't know what he *did* want to do, but it sure wasn't one of the professions. So he'd taken a simple yet dramatic step — he'd ceased obeying his father. Being an AD had emboldened him, wised him up about letting people push you around. To his amazement, he got away with it. JC Senior seemed tired of the conflict. Perhaps Bix awaited on the turntable. After giving Pinto some initial shit, he'd announced, "Do whatever the fuck you want."

So now he was taking The Plays of Shakespeare, The History of Western Art, and The History of Western Music, and loving them all. Listening to *Othello* on headphones as he read along, he found himself crying at its incredible sadness. Gregorian chants were cool and astringent, a different musical vector for him. In the art course, they were looking at Egyptian tomb paintings, which weren't terribly exciting, but soon they'd get to the Impressionists, and the Dada nuts, and the moody, drunken Abstract Expressionists. He was soaking up knowledge. So what if he'd wind up working for a janitorial service? He was living in the moment, not the future.

Soon, though, to Pinto's dismay, Alby's decline in the face of his nightly potation became undeniable. He'd gotten pasty-faced and disheveled, and his grades, always shaky, were now shook. Worst of all, his jokes weren't as good. Sadder than anything was some guy whose funny moves were one time great, only now not. Like that last sentence, he didn't make a lot of sense.

The night Alby imploded began normally enough, with a routine Wednesday house meeting and the demolishing of a quarter-keg afterward. Perhaps, Magpie suggested later, they should have gotten a hint that something was up when Alby did an impression of a lawn sprinkler by spinning around pissing. He thought he was funny, but what he did was *pee on several brothers*. You could piss on a date, or even a cop, but *never* on another brother. This should have alerted them, 'Pie said, shaking his head grimly. But it was Monday-morning quarterbacking.

What happened: the keg went off at one, as usual. The guys at the bar were starving. So Pinto, Moses, Black Whit, and Alby piled into Magpie's car for the run to Dirty Dick's in West Leb. Alby, it should be added, was so shitfaced he was muttering the dialogue from *The Magnificent Seven* to himself. The others shunned him, as one does a fecally smeared mental patient on the street.

Dirty Dick's Diner, which stayed open till two, was the late-night Dartmouth man's best friend. It wasn't terribly hygienic, but the food tasted great. Tonight it was packed, the sole unoccupied tables littered with dirty plates and splats of ketchup. The very old emmets behind the counter had apparently been overwhelmed by the post-meeting influx.

"This could take a while," observed Black Whit.

"Nah. Not really." Alby swept the contents of a tabletop to the floor with his arm.

"You fucking asshole!" Alby's ketchup now joined Alby's pee on 'Pie's pant leg.

"I want an orange soda," said Moses. "Do they have orange soda?"

The others laughed. Pinto pointed. An Orange Crush sign hung on the wall, shaped like a giant orange bottle cap.

The waiter took twenty minutes to get to them. The wait for their greaseburgers was longer. The boys scowled and looked at their watches. Their beer highs were fading and they wanted to *eat,* man. Finally, the food arrived.

Pinto was ketchuping his flat, processed hamburgeroid when Moses spoke. "Hey. Where's Alby?" They looked around. No Alby.

"Well, shit!" Pinto fretted. He often worried about Alby. Luckily, Rhesus Monkey never worried anyone, so there was a sort of cosmic balance in their room.

"Eat your delicious food," Black Whit advised. "He'll turn up."

Pinto ate his food. Meanwhile, Alby was having an adventure. As he recounted it later, he was tired of Magpie's being mean to him. So he went outside, looked around, and discovered the Tip-Top bread factory across the street. It was a large, industrial complex, its front entrance gaping open. He went in. The place kind of hummed. (*"Mmmmmmmmmmmmmmmmmmmm,"* was how Alby portrayed it.) It occurred to him that he'd better find something to show his pals so they'd believe he'd been here. He came upon a "big cog thing" and picked it up. It was very heavy. Straining and puffing, he started out. Only then did a dozen Tip-Top employees appear. They'd been on a break and were not happy to find Alby stealing their machine part. A beefy woman started for him. Panicking, Alby dropped the cog with a *clunk* and took off.

Pinto and the others were just exiting the diner. They saw Alby running toward them in terror. "Hurry!" he screamed. "She's after me! Get in the car!"

The ADs, no strangers to panicked exits, reacted instinctively. They leapt in and then so did Alby. The car made a screeching, gravel-spitting exit from the parking area and roared off down the road. Only then did someone think to ask what happened.

It took a while to make even partial sense of Alby's fragmented thoughts, but it came down to Emily Tipp. Here we must pause, because few now remember Emily. She was a sweet, grandmotherly cartoon character who shilled for the Tip-Top bread company on TV. Alby'd seen her more often than he cared to recall on *Bandstand,* during the commercials, with her kind, crinkly eyes. And this is who Alby had decided was chasing him. He stated that she was running a communist conspiracy to damage America's children by selling bread made from plastic and mattress ticking, containing no nutrition whatsoever. He probably wasn't far wrong about the bread. The fact that Emily was merely a cartoon character, thereby imaginary and incapable of leading conspiracies of any type, evidently didn't bother him. Further, his belief that he was now endangered by commies met with sighs and eyebrow-raisings, and the brothers returned to their floating discussion of the many words for women's breasts. It was Whit's contention that *dugs* was simply unacceptable, but Magpie thought it was funny. He spoke rapidly and passionately in his Long Island accent, his pointy chin cleaving the air like some strange slicer machine.

At the house, the boys went their separate ways — Pinto to his bed, Whit to Pam's apartment, Magpie and Moses to the tube room, where *The Creature from the Black Lagoon* was playing. Alby, lonely, decided to drop in on good ol' Large. That it was currently 2:30 a.m. was not important; he was going over to Topliff Hall to have a drink with his old roommate.

The next day, he was thrown out of school.

As best as Pinto could piece it together, what happened was that Alby went to Topliff and gently awakened Large by kicking the door repeatedly with his combat boot. To his dismay, Large was unenthusiastic about having a drink, and even less so about Alby's Emily concerns. Alby, for his part, felt the campus had to be warned. If Large wouldn't help him, he'd have to do it himself.

So he climbed out the window, hung from the fourth-story ledge by one hand, and screamed, *"Wake up, you fucking assholes! She's right here in Hanover! She'll turn your kids into puppets of the state!"*

This and more like it went on for five minutes, with Large frantically attempting to talk Alby back inside. A small crowd of late-night passersby formed. The campus cop shop was practically around the corner, and a couple of them showed up, too.

"Khrushchev's in it up to his fucking bald head!"

The cops ran upstairs. They found Large straining to pull Alby up, but Alby was (a) heavy, and (b) not cooperating. *"Top of the world, Ma!"* The cops rushed over and, with Large, dragged him inside.

Alby regarded them indignantly. *"What?"*

They put him in the same cell Goosey had occupied. The next day, despite Alby's repeated offers to get them drunk and laid, the cops called Dean Seymour, and Alby was suspended for a term. He spent the next months living at home in Longmeadow, Massachusetts, delivering pizza.

WITH ADELPHIAN MEMBERSHIP depleted yet again, Black Whit and Magpie, as rush co-chairmen, declared a late rush, and thirty or so guys showed up on a Saturday night to meet the brothers and have a few beers. Mostly, these were sophomores who'd pinned their hopes on some house last September and then not made the cut. Perhaps they'd narrowed their options too early. A lot of them were good guys. Others, of course, by the immutable law of groups, were screaming assholes.

"Let's take the assholes," Dobes muttered to Whit. "We can torture them with pliers."

Whit and 'Pie ignored him. Their method was to zero in on the hottest shits, take them aside, and get them to sink. It was like shopping for pictures to cover the empty spaces on your walls, trying to get all eight in one night. Whit and 'Pie, of course, were sure they knew a hot-shit when they met one. This meant guys like themselves — rowdy, athletic, drink-all-night partyers who liked displaying a bare ass to authority. Few poets wound up in the AD house, nor lisping, mincing homosexuals either. Oh, uh, that was Pinto's image of homosexuals at the time: there were very few of them, they hung out on Fire Island, and they all acted like Percy Dovetonsils.

Eleven guys were in the new pledge class. Within a week or two, they seemed as much a part of AD as anyone. Of course, there was a hazing period. This time, even sophomores got to dump on the poor neophytes. It wasn't terribly complicated. You acted indignant about something and called them assholes. It was fun.

Pinto made some new friends, namely Sugar Ray, Douche, Gazork, and Don Marcus, who just never got a nickname. Sugar Ray was noted for, among other fine qualities, having a prominent upper lip capable of a world-class sneer. Black Whit commented that with a lip like that, he could really eat some pussy. Sugar Ray sneered at him. Douche was an all-around good man and stalwart bar guy. A handsome rogue women wanted to lick. Marcus was the clever, witty, funny one. You wanted to stand near him at the bar so you could listen to his word flow. And Gazork was a tall, short-haired guy — well, everyone was short-haired then — who liked to dance before the jukebox, imitating the different groups. He did this not particularly well, but with endearing passion.

Other guys were sunk mainly for cash flow. *"We need the dues,"* as

Pinto had cried out during deliberations. Nothing was actually wrong with them; they just lacked the vibrance or charisma or whatever it was that made guys like Scotty and Truck and Magpie so magnetic. Hydrant had vibrance. Sometimes so much he seemed to twang like a guitar. Maybe he should have been called Guitar. But calling him 'Drant worked, while saying 'Tar made no sense, so, no, Hydrant was the right name.

Hard on the heels of rush, another missing AD returned — Bert, no nickname — whom Pinto immediately liked. He had a preppyish flop of forward-falling hair, but his craggy face cried out for the yellow slicker and flying spray of a nineteenth-century whaling boat. He immediately became AD's wise, elder figure. He wasn't *really* older, but he was. By common agreement, Bert had never been young.

His hiatus from school sprang from his abrupt decision last fall to go fight with Castro. Fidel Castro was a romantic figure, with his beard and combat fatigues, living like Robin Hood up in the mountains of Oriente Province, striking blows against the corrupt dictator. He seemed cool; one did not yet know the extent of his assholehood. But by the time Bert actually got to Havana, it was New Year's Eve, and he decided, what the hell, he'd spend a night at a whorehouse. While he slept, Castro took power, Batista fled, and the city exploded with rejoicing. In the morning, with an eye on the many guns in the street, Bert returned to the U.S.A. And now, here he was, returned to AD.

Pinto liked his company. He was a boon companion, whatever that meant. Bert, you see, would have looked up *boon*. He was a stickler for the right word. Pinto was amused by his use of a dictionary and thesaurus while writing his girlfriend, Julie. He was, in fact, an aspiring writer.

"Hey, be Hemingway," Otter suggested. "Recount your manly adventures in Cuba."

Bert just chuckled affably, as was his wont.

PINTO'S EROTIC IMAGININGS only grew more fervid as spring progressed. Mindy was ever in his mind. Well, actually her *body* was in his mind; he couldn't quite remember her face. So when

'Pie and Black Whit suggested he go with them to catch the strip-
per at the Tunbridge World's Fair, he was ready. The three, along
with Fitch, Moses, Otter, Bags, and Hydrant, crowded into a couple
of cars and drove to tiny Tunbridge, Vermont. The "World's Fair"
was a dinky, small-town affair, its gay colored lights not terribly gay.
They looked around until they found the little tent in the rear, and
pushed inside. The air was redolent of sweat and tobacco smoke;
excited, drunk guys talked too loudly. This was the venue where
Thelma, the Blond Bombshell, would do her world-famous hoochie-
coochie dance.

Pinto and the guys took up positions. The Nat King Cole record
from *Hajji Baba* began coming from a pair of small speakers hanging above the little stage. The lights went down, except for a spot,
and out from the shadows slithered the Blond Bombshell.

Thelma wasn't blond at all, but a bottle redhead. Her locks hung
by the sides of her ravaged face like a mop having its period. She
was the single worst-looking woman Pinto had ever seen, like one
of those depraved, decaying characters in a Ghastly Ingels story in
The Haunt of Fear. Pinto wondered idly if she and Rat would hit
it off.

Her dance began. The lewd smile never left her face. She made
vaguely stripperish moves and the costume began coming off. With
each reveal, Pinto felt more sickened. Her tits fell to her navel! Truly,
these were dugs. Why did he have to be here? He groaned inwardly
as the last of her outfit fluttered to the floor and she stepped here
and there, strutting her awful stuff.

Fitch was right by the stage, at a late-in-the-day level of shitfaced,
gazing at Thelma in drunken wonder. He seemed to amuse her, so
she came to dance directly in front of him. Fitch wove this way and
that, staring at her crotch as if mesmerized by a puff adder. Thelma
did a knee bend directly in front of him, spreading 'em widely.

He reacted as if surprised by an incredibly loud noise. The crowd
thought he was hilarious. Thelma laughed, too. Then, grabbing
him by the ears, she yanked poor Fitch's face deep in her scrantz.

The entire room froze. The woman was pretty good at showmanship, come to think of it. After what seemed an hour but was proba-

bly five seconds, Thelma released Fitch and stepped away. His face wore an expression of frozen horror. He wove this way and that, fell over, and passed out cold. The crowd roared, Thelma louder than anyone. She sounded like a chicken being tortured. Pinto and a couple of other ADs carried him out and drove him home.

Now Pinto found himself turned off by the very idea of women's breasts or bottoms. Maybe this was advantageous, though — he could concentrate more efficiently on his studies, not having to beat off all the time. He tried to push the woman from his mind.

YOU DIDN'T SEE MUCH of the seniors these days. They all were booking for finals or finishing term papers. The bar was a little lonely, but Pinto and others kept the string of kegs alive. One night they almost couldn't get up the chip, but they strangled Huck Doody until he gave in, throwing his textbook out the window and joining them, enabling the twenty-eighth keg of the string.

As the evening progressed, it struck Round that Fitch was uninjured. No bandaged fingers, no back brace, no crutches. "Fitch," he said, "when was the last time you got hurt?"

Fitch couldn't remember, but then much of the last two years was a blur to him. After some conversation, the guys decided it had been eighteen full days since that stupid ice pick had impaled his middle toe. Since then, he'd gone unharmed. Unless you counted his liver. This struck everyone as quite an achievement, and Fitch acknowledged their toast with a shy grin.

At that moment, a loud bang resounded, and the house shook. The guys looked at one another in shock, then dashed upstairs.

THE NOISE WAS TRACED to Mouse, who had decided to study for his world history final in the goat room. As he told Pinto later, he liked booking there because you were left alone. He'd put a desk lamp on the podium, opened his history text, and now was focusing on the Treaty of Brest-Litovsk. There was a strange rustling, humming sound. He looked up. *A bat was flying straight at his face!*

"Yah!" He was out of there in a second flat. Tearing into Coyote's quarters, he grabbed his friend's shotgun, popped in shells, and rushed back to the goat room. The bat had landed halfway up the rear wall. Mouse raised the weapon and let go with both barrels.

Pinto and the rest rushed in. The rear wall wasn't terribly wall-like anymore, as in "four-foot hole." Mouse wore an expression of satisfaction; plumes of smoke drifted from the shotgun barrels. Of the bat, no trace remained.

THE SEASON DID NOT, of course, stop with blooms on the trees but, like a good story, continued to develop. Tulips poked up. The lawns became lush, and the days mild, even balmy. Dogs romped on the Green. You forgot, during winter, that New Hampshire ever looked this way. And, as the poet has it, in the springtime a young man's fancy turns to his dick. Okay, he wasn't really a poet, just a horny AD, but it was true enough.

Then the house got lucky. Dean Seymour was feeling charitable and took them off pro. They could have girls for Green Key! And beer! As the date approached, Pinto became ever more excited. There had been a little bad news: Mindy couldn't get there till Saturday morning. But — she was driving up with Gretchen Potatoes! Which meant Alby was returning! The good news was so good it was much better than the bad news was bad. What was more, Pinto had made a deposit on adjoining units for them at the Shady Lawn Motel, where Otter had gone with Gay. Saturday would be the greatest night of his life, Pinto was sure.

Of all Dartmouth's big weekends, Green Key was the sweetest. You could go picnicking, hiking, or swimming. There were beautiful canoe races on the Connecticut River. Seniors, playing out some obscure school tradition, appeared with canes and straw hats. Best of all, it was warm enough to get laid on the golf course. For, despite its many attendant delights, Key, like Carnival, was chiefly about sex.

The nicest of the attendant delights was an event known as Hums. There was at Dartmouth in those days a system of interfraternity competitions, the cumulative scores of which would decide the school's choice for best house. You competed in sports, in grade point average, in staging a drama, and in choral singing, the last of these being known as Hums. The preliminaries were held all week, at five each afternoon. Groups of forty or so guys, dressed in black pants and white shirts, would march onto the scenic steps of Dartmouth Hall and for fifteen minutes impersonate a glee club. Naturally, your Psi Us and SAEs sang solemn, serious chorales and traditional school songs. Equally as naturally, AD did not.

For Interfraternity Hums '61, the Adelphian brotherhood's performance was invited back as "special entertainment" for the finals. And so, on Friday night of Key, with a few hundred guys and their dates watching, the ADs began with "The Schaefer Beer Song" . . .

> *Schaefer is the*
> *One beer to have*
> *When you're having more than one*

. . . went right into "The Robert Hall Medley" . . .

> *When the values go up up up*
> *And the prices go down down down*
> *Robert Hall this season*
> *Will show you the reason*
> *Low overhead*
> *Low overhead*

Because we're . . .

> *Doing our Christmas shopping*
> *At Robert Hall this year*
> *We're saving on clothes for Christmas*
> *At Robert Hall this year*

The crowd, accustomed to dutifully watching the stuff other houses did, loved the crazy ADs and gave them wild applause. Especially when, to conclude, five brothers stepped up, turned their backs, and mooned them. The crowd gasped as the pants came down, only to laugh and applaud wildly when it turned out the guys were merely wearing another pair of pants beneath. Of course, Alpha Theta won the competition with their scintillating version of "Shenandoah," while AD won nothing but perhaps a moral victory. It was like the Oscars; comedy got no respect.

THAT NIGHT, PINTO attended the AD–Pi Lam joint party out at Dexter Lake, where they'd rented a place called Goose Lodge. It was not a lodge at all but an old beach club, nestled among white pines and pin oaks, close by the water. Scotty delighted the crowd with a return appearance by Lonnie Youngblood and the Redcoats, and the joyous R & B got everyone dancing. Old friends were there: Poz, Tor, Original Bags, and of course Isaac, the *goyische* Pi Lam, whose date was one of the most beautiful women Pinto had ever seen. Outside, breezes wafted pine perfume by the odd Adelphian nose, the water was shimmery beneath the moon, and the stars were staging an astral beauty contest.

Seal had come up for the weekend and was currently by the tap, jovially handing out beers. He was enjoying himself so much, in fact, he'd decided to refrain from whiz runs tonight. Instead, he'd placed a washtub before him, into which he could whiz as required and dump half-drunk beers into as well. Because the tub was behind the bar, no one knew. Pinto laughed when he saw the arrangement. Same old Seal.

And speaking of pee, 'Pie had created an enjoyable new game. "Pinto, watch this," he hissed. Pinto watched. 'Pie turned, whipped out his unit, and began pissing on the back of Gross Kay's leg. Pinto's mouth fell open. He was still, after almost eight months, surprised at the things these guys just casually did. Having expelled a five-second stream, 'Pie put his dick away and turned back to Pinto. "Now wait," he said.

It took a moment, but then Gross Kay reacted, reaching down to feel the warm wetness that now suffused the leg of her slacks, then looking around suspiciously. 'Pie was the picture of innocence, back turned, whistling a little tune. "It's all in the timing, Pinto," he whispered. "By the time they feel it, you're gone." Maybe he should have been called Magpee.

Another great AD party, but Pinto's mind kept wandering to tomorrow night. The girls were coming in the morning, and the time Alby said he'd be arriving was "I don't know." He couldn't believe they were going to *a fucking motel!* There would be *beds* there! He looked around the room, savoring the different women's bodies. Gross Kay, back to dancing with Bags, had serious juggage. Carol, dancing with Fitch, was long and willowy, with not much on top. She seemed nicely *flexible,* though. Gay Tabiggatits seemed about average, with just the right amount of everything, and Torrie Toiletbowl, up for the weekend as a sort of date-without-portfolio, kept bending over to display her ample cleavage. He wanted to stuff every tit in the room in his mouth and plunge his tongue about in them like a frisky porpoise.

To keep his mind still, he began to drink gin fizzes. There was a professional bartender, and he made a gin fizz that was so sweet and delicious it was like drinking a vanilla liquor shake. In fact, Pinto found it remarkably easy to throw down eight of them. Getting drunk was so funny. You never noticed it happen. At some point, you looked around, and — you were loaded. The colors were richer, the music more wonderful, the jokes funnier, *you* were funnier, all the girls sexy, and you were *sans souci* — without a care. It seemed an excellent way to be, until Pinto tried to walk to the men's room and the floor rose up like an anaconda to throw him sideways. He found himself on his ass. "Are you okay?" cried someone's date. He burst out laughing. *He'd fallen down!* It was the funniest thing in the universe.

The night was fleeting. Over by the keg, Seal had begun to refill beers for guys he didn't like by dipping their cups in the beer-and-piss tub. The Redcoats were on their final set, playing the Phil Upchurch song "You Can't Sit Down," and the room was a tossing sea of dancing couples. Tor was dancing with his date, Tama Tor. It was as if they were screwing in the middle of the floor, they were so sexy. The music was going into Pinto's ears like forks o' pleasure.

He got to his feet and reeled to the bandstand. Lonnie winked at him. He raised his hand in salute. Lonnie blasted a saxophone note. Pinto laughed hysterically, fell over, and passed out. Uh, initiated a rest period.

AT DAWN, HE AWOKE with a railroad spike in his brain and the Sahara Desert in his mouth. He found himself in the back of the hearse. He hated the hearse; it smelled of too many body fluids. So he got out and stared around the misty morning, beneath the tall pines by the AD parking lot. Not a person could be seen at this hour. Birds and crickets chirped and chittered. If he hadn't felt like a nuclear casualty, he might have enjoyed it. He was so *thirsty!* Since it was technically postdawn, he supposed it was okay for him to go in the house, where the dates were sleeping. He found the fire-watch guys — Moses and Round — asleep on the sofas, having no doubt collapsed the moment the sun came up. The house was hushed.

In the library was a metal tub of water with some ice chunks still extant from last night, when it had held soft drinks. This morning, a single can remained — a 7-Up. He found a relatively clean empty beer glass and filled it to the top with cubes. Pulling the tab from the can, he tossed it in the fireplace, and poured the soda over the cubes. The agitated fizzing tickled his nose. He took a sip.

The clear, lemony liquid exploded on his tongue like a sky full of fireworks. It was the greatest single taste of anything he'd had in his entire life! He drank the rest of the glass down and let an ice cube melt on his tongue. They were those wonderful, completely clear, great-tasting ice cubes that you found only in bars and restaurants; they must have come from the club. Pinto was so happy.

But it didn't help his head any, so he padded down to the basement and turned on the keg for the day. Halfway through his third beer, relief arrived. Now he'd be fine. He drained the glass and went to turn on the jukebox.

HE WAS STILL THERE at eleven, having wolfed down some nice, warm nothing for breakfast, when he felt a tug on his sleeve. Mindy stood there, looking up at him with her big eyes, which turned him on. Her hair had gotten longer, which turned him on. A fly landed on her nose, which turned him on. They gazed at each other.

"Oh, Pinto!" she cried at last, and gave him a hug.

"Hi!" He hugged her back.

"Hey, Pinto. What time's your crazy friend coming?" It was Gretchen, grinning. As usual, she was perfect, no hair out of place.

"I don't know. Alby just said today sometime."

"Sounds like him," said Gretchen.

"So what have we missed?" Mindy put her arms around his arm, pressing her bamalamas against it. In Pinto's groin, it was like the celebration of VJ Day.

"Well, you did miss Seal's special beer blend that he invented last night."

"Maybe we can get a taste today," Mindy said.

"I'll talk to him about it," Pinto promised.

THAT AFTERNOON, several carloads of ADs and their dates motored to the Ledges for a pleasing interlude beneath the warm sun. The Ledges was an enchanting cluster of waterfalls and clear pools, fed by a babbling brook running over smooth, vaguely blue formations of stone. You listened to the rushings and gurglings, smelled the water-over-rocks smell, saw little rainbows in the mist. The occasional cute fish leapt into sight and then vanished again with a splash. Why, you asked yourself, would anyone ever leave here?

The ADs dispersed. Otter plunked down in the main pool with Gay, Black Whit, Pam, Torrie, Magpie, and Nancy Manhattan. Moses and the Digit found a secluded spot of their own, Moses later claiming they got so hot norgling, the water around them emitted steam. Fitch and Carol stretched out on a blanket, where, to Carol's displeasure, a ribbon of Zs promptly appeared above Fitch's head. Pinto and Mindy, in bathing suits and old sneakers, worked their way upstream, climbing the rapids.

Under Mindy's enthusiastic gaze, Pinto bloomed. Her shows of affection and admiration made him feel like Elvis or someone. He had no idea why she was so interested in him — he, himself, was totally bored with himself — but decided she wouldn't feel that way unless there was *something* good about him. So he leapt from rock to rock and scrambled up the waterfalls like a mountain goat, much more lithe and sure-footed than he would have been if, say, Snot had been watching. He was becoming Mindy's own infatuated vision of himself. Weird.

They wandered up the stream, the water tearing at their ankles. The dappled sunlight lit the sparkly rapids. Beauty was everywhere. Good time for a kiss. Pinto took Mindy in his arms and their lips came together. His instantaneous boner could have raised the *Titanic*.

"Mmmm," she said.

Oh, yeah. Overcome with desire, he groped for her snatch. There it was, right in the usual place. He ran his finger north and south along it.

"OHHHHH!" she said.

He'd forgotten how loud she was! Startled, he slipped on the mossy rocks, and they both went down with a splash. The water was cold!

They looked at each other and burst out laughing. The stream was only a foot deep at this point; they weren't about to be swept away or anything. Holding each other, they laughed and laughed. Pinto noticed his hard-on was gone. Well, that was okay. What were they going to do, make it in the middle of the stream, atop sharp rocks? And, anyway, Pinto had tried beating off underwater once. You couldn't feel anything.

He helped her up and they found a flat boulder in the sunlight where they could dry off. Mindy was wearing one of Pinto's button-down shirts over her black bathing suit. The suit's modesty shield precluded wazoo sightings, but her gabongas were right there on view. There was a little diver emblem on the suit, by her right hip. He touched it and she giggled.

They sat in silence a moment, listening to the stream tumble through the rocks and boulders. Without immediate sex to distract them, they were faced with actual communication. Pinto searched for something with which to open a conversation. The prospects of Yogi Berra managing the Yanks this year didn't seem exactly right.

"Uh, God, school's almost out."

"Isn't it amazing how fast the time goes?"

"What are you doing for the summer?"

"I'm waitressing at a hotel up in Maine. It should be really fun."

Maine? What did you do in Maine, shoot a moose? "What's the fun part?"

"Oh, the hiking, the canoeing, the sleeping out in the woods in tents."

"Wow, that does sound great." People actually did those things? Out there with the bugs and the . . . well, Pinto wasn't exactly sure what they had in Maine. Weasels? Mindy was a chubber, it seemed.

"What are *you* going to do?"

"I don't know. I kind of make things up as I go along."

"Wow, how can you do that? I'm always planning and writing lists."

A moment passed. Why was it so hard to talk to her? He sensed no kinship, no union in their interpersonal Venn diagram.

"Oh," she said. "I forgot. When I get home, Mom's going to reward me for getting through my freshman year with a new pair of Pappagallo shoes."

That was terribly interesting. "So what are you reading these days?" he asked. "Sylvia Plath or something?"

She smiled at him. "*Lady Chatterley's Lover.* The *unexpurgated* version."

Oh-ho! That was the famous erotic novel by D. H. Lawrence, whose ban had just been overturned. This girl sure liked sex. *That,* Pinto realized, was where their Venn diagrams joined — they absolutely turned each other on. Tonight, in the motel room, they'd have some *serious* union. They walked back to the others to find that Fitch had teetered atop a tall boulder but *not* fallen off, and so remained uninjured.

● ● ●

AROUND FIVE, a relaxed group of ADs and their dates were taking their ease on the front porch, listening to the evening birds begin to sing. They would have to do until the *other* birds began to sing later, Scotty quipped, by which he meant the Flamingos. Yes, the actual Flamingos, who sang the revered "Golden Teardrops," were going to be right here at AD tonight. Was there another record on the jukebox to which the brothers drunkenly swooned as often?

But Pinto didn't care.

For the erstwhile Mr. Rock 'n' Roll had become Mr. Fuck 'n' Suck, and all he could think of was him and Mindy getting to that motel. He sat with her and Gretchen Potatoes, getting his second wind for the night to come, wondering where the fuck Alby was.

Gretchen turned to Pinto worriedly. "What if he hit a concrete bridge abutment or something?"

"Oh, he'll be here. I'm sure of it," Pinto said uncertainly.

Just then, a car approached. It seemed to be going awfully fast, coming right down East Wheelock, a beat-up black Buick from whose tailpipe thick smoke poured. Just as it was about to go by, the car veered suddenly with a great screech, hopped the curb, and plowed into the AD front yard. As the party on the porch watched in amazement, it skidded to a stop dead-center and three of its doors flew open. Out sprang thirteen dogs! The driver then emerged with a small smile: Alby.

The porch people couldn't believe their eyes. Had that been an entrance or what? But Alby wasn't through — he grabbed one of the mutts, ran up to the goat room, and tried to put it in the filing cabinet under *D*. The dog would not fit, and barked at Alby reproachfully. Alby gave up. The animal sped downstairs and was not seen again.

Alby recounted to the crowd how his canine surprise came to be. Upon completion of his first six-pack on the way up, it had just jumped in his head to pick up every dog he saw and see how many would fit in his car. You know, in the spirit of those college kids in the forties who jammed themselves into phone booths. He drove back roads in order to find more dogs, and this was why it had taken him so long to get here. The canines, meanwhile, had run in all directions and were now dispersed. Since Alby would neglect to collect them before leaving on Sunday, they remained in Hanover for the rest of their lives. Their descendants roam the Big Green to this day, it is said.

"Got the rooms set?" Alby muttered to Pinto.

Pinto smiled. Alby smiled back. The girls smiled, too. Everyone smiled, experiencing a warm, rising energy in their nether regions. Tonight would really be something.

But first came dinner. A dozen ADs put on sport coats and ties and escorted their dates to the Hanover Inn dining room for the Saturday-night buffet. This was a little-known scene to most Dartmouth guys, but Hydrant had stumbled on it one Saturday while in his beer cups, and fallen in love. The Inn dining room was impossibly starched and proper, but the food was good, and the only patrons were local old folks with hearing aids. The following week he'd returned with Whit and Magpie, and a new AD tradition — or habit, anyway — was born.

As the meal progressed, Mindy said to Pinto, "Boy, your fraternity brothers sure go to the bathroom a lot."

It was true — every few minutes, another guy stood and headed off to the men's room. "Maybe it's because they drank so much beer today."

Mindy nodded noncommittally, cutting her beef in a neat and orderly fashion.

It was a jolly meal, with lots of shouting back and forth, and the aforementioned old folks scattered at tables around the august room began swiveling their heads censoriously after particularly egregious remarks such as "Hey, Pinto, show Carol your two-tone dick!" But the ADs were oblivious, lost in their fun-having.

After much good chowing down, Pinto felt full, still with food on his plate. That was the trouble with buffets; your eyes were always bigger than your stomach. Mindy, too, had set her knife and fork down. But 'Drant, 'Pie, Whit, Truck, and some of the others were revealing appetites that could only be called prodigious. Pinto had not noticed this about them before, but here Dumptruck was, coming back with what amounted to a third entire dinner, which he began wolfing down as enthusiastically as he had the first.

The dates were amazed. They weren't sure whether to be impressed with the guys' capacities or repelled by their gluttony. Pinto wasn't sure, either; it was amazing just that they could do it. Feeling a call of nature, he excused himself and headed off.

The Hanover Inn men's room was all white tiles and polished faucets. Pinto was whizzing into one of the stately urinals when he was surprised to hear booting noises coming from a stall. By the sound of it, someone's esophagus was three quarters out of his mouth. Or wait — was that *two* people booting? It had to be; no single human being could go *"blarrrrrgghhhh!"* so often. He was just zipping his fly when two of the doors opened, and 'Drant and Scotty stepped out, grinned at each other, and slapped palms. When they saw him gaping, they laughed. So *this* was the secret of the Adelphian supergourmands — like the Romans, they blew lunch and started over!

"Hey, man," said 'Drant, flicking a speck of boot off his tie, "you get so much more to eat that way."

THE BIG SATURDAY-NIGHT PARTY had begun. The house was in its glory, bathed in spotlights, its green-and-white flag snapping in the wind. Brothers and their dates came up the walk, two by two. It was a *Saturday Evening Post* cover.

The weekend-long bacchanal was reaching its apex. Celebrants swirled around Pinto and Mindy in the living room. The rugs had been rolled up and tossed aside. The keg barrier had been built around the bandstand. The jukebox, turned to its loudest setting, was blaring away downstairs — you could feel the bass notes bumping against your feet.

Pinto went into the library, where the band was enjoying some preperformance do-it fluid, and said hello to Zeke Carey, who was the tall, formidable bass singer and co-founder of the Flamingos. It was like meeting Lincoln or someone. Mr. Carey proved to be a man of few words, but Pinto thanked him for lighting up his high school years. You had to acknowledge these artists whose creations were the cultural water in which you swam. The best ones, anyway; you didn't want to thank Frankie Avalon. But the top guys were absolute heroes.

Alby and Gretchen now joined them. Alby wore an expectant look. Gretchen smiled like the Mona Lisa.

"Well, hey," said Pinto, "want to have a few beers and enjoy a set? I asked them to sing 'Golden Teardrops' . . ."

They grabbed him and carried him out the door.

THE SHADY LAWN MOTEL was ten minutes away, not far from the White River bridge. It looked idyllic, fifteen units tucked under trees, its bushes lit with little green spotlights. The girls waited while the guys went into the office.

"Oh, hi," Pinto said casually to the scowling emmet woman behind the desk. "I'm, uh, Mr. Pony? And this is Mr. Merkin."

The woman looked them over and checked the names against her book. The boys did their best not to seem drunk, but Alby kept giggling. The stay in Longmeadow had done him good. He'd gained weight and looked healthier than he had in a while. His jokes had recovered, too.

"You boys keep it quiet down there, you and your —" She gestured outside, her disapproval in no way masked.

"Wives," supplied Alby. "Normally we're up in Sachem Village, where the married students live, but tonight we thought it might be sociologically interesting to fuck in a shithole like this. Does that seem weird?"

Tight-lipped, the woman gave Pinto the keys. "Just keep it down." With an uneasy look at Alby, she disappeared into the rear regions of her habitat.

"*We're gonna get laid!*" cried Alby.

"*I know, I know!*" said Pinto.

They jumped up and down with glee, then became cool again and went out.

NO AD HAD HEARD of the *Kama Sutra*, nor would one till much later in the decade, but Pinto had already imagined half its positions from scratch. In the room now, alone at last with Mindy, he looked her over as if she were a beautiful cheeseburger, steaming hot and ready to eat. They kissed. She sure poked her tongue around. Pinto's erotic critic came out and commented on her performance. Wasn't there something a little . . . *automatic* about the way she did it? As if by bringing his mouth near hers he'd broken a photoelectric beam, which caused her tongue to poke about randomly until he pulled away again. She didn't touch his lips a little bit first, then put it inside just slightly, teasingly. In fact, she just thrust her tongue in mindlessly, without design or plan. Still, while his consciousness was pausing to reflect on these matters, his groin certainly had marched down Giant Boner Boulevard.

"Ooh, it's chilly," Mindy said. "Could we turn on the heat?"

"It's almost June."

"Yeah, but we're about to be naked."

The blood rose up in Pinto, red mercury in a storefront thermometer warmed by a blowtorch. He felt it would burst from his head like a fountain, speckling the room with antic red dots. He felt — y'know, he'd have to shut his fucking imagination up one of these days! It was so distracting! "Okay. Right. Let's see."

He manipulated the heater until the airstream was warm. Standing, he saw her bare back, her blouse on the chair, her bra flying open — a dazzling trifecta of undressing. The bra joined the blouse. He could see the side of a tit, then she turned and he saw both straight on. She had a blonde's skin, creamy white, not getting much sun down there at Smith. Her coral-colored nipples rose in bas-relief from their respective breasts, as orderly as her meat carving was, and she had a discreet, ladylike bush. Nothing was too big or too small. As with Gay, the proportions were down.

"Why don't you come over here, mister?"

Yuh, yuh. He kissed her neck while she removed his shirt. He loved girls' necks; they had all these interesting contours and hollows. And she smelled so good there . . .

"Hey! Shalimar!"

"I remembered you liked it so I brought some."

She had thought ahead about *his* sexual pleasure? It was the nicest thing anyone had ever done for him! He breathed in the mingled scents of woman-body and perfume, a fine combination. Then her nipples were tracing nonsense words on his chest. Ah, this was what he lived for! His hard-on got so big it lifted her off the floor. Well, no, but she did give a startled little jump when its expansion pressed into her.

"You're so *hard,*" she breathed. Going to her knees before him, she undid his belt, opened his pants, and pulled everything down. His wang twanged up, pointing unwaveringly at the ceiling fixture. "Ooooooh," Mindy crooned. She surrounded his equipment with both hands briefly, as if praying.

Then she started sucking him off.

The explosions of pleasure he remembered from the night in the car recurred. Pinto heard someone going, *"Oh . . . oh . . . oh,"* and realized it was himself.

"Why don't you lie down?"

"Sure!" He started for the bed. Since his trou and undertrou were around his ankles, he immediately fell over.

"Pinto! Are you okay?"

"Yeah, fine, but could you help me with these, please?"

They got his clothes off, and Pinto lay back on the bed. He was glad he'd listened to Alby about preparing for tonight. Alby had called him a month ago and declared he would not beat off again until after Green Key. This way he would be "really ready" for Gretchen. Pinto had been impressed with his thoughtfulness and foresight, and managed not to beat off for about ten days. So he, too, was really ready. So ready that when Mindy took his balls in her hand and plunged his dick in her mouth, he came like a howitzer.

She pulled away, coughing explosively. He opened his eyes to see if she was okay.

"You came out my nose," she explained meekly, between coughs.

He *did?* Sitting up, he peered at her. Yes, those were semen trails, all right. Damn, he was pretty good! Mindy went to the bathroom, so Pinto propped up pillows, leaned back, and lit a Marlboro. He'd switched to them from Winstons recently. He liked the way the packs looked.

Mindy returned and lit up, too. They lay there, expelling side-by-side smoke plumes.

"Boy," Mindy said, "when you come, you come."

"Oh, gosh, I'm sorry. Are you okay?"

She giggled. "Of course. Uh, do you think you'll be ready again soon?"

He had no doubt about that. Masturbatory experience assured him he was far from finished. "Oh, maybe."

"I bet I could make you sure."

"You think?"

She put her cigarette in the ashtray and rolled over close to him, her lips brushing his cheek. Since they both smoked, their horrible tobacco breaths canceled each other out. She breathed in his ear, her lips so close she sounded like a dragon. Then her tongue tip poked in. Pinto shuddered and laughed uncomfortably. He'd never been big on the tongue-in-ear thing. Why would someone want saliva down their eustachian tube?

So he turned and kissed her, more to keep his ear dry than anything else. But the kiss turned hot, and his dong went to rigid attention.

"See? Told you." She reached down and held it. He turned to jelly and would have done anything she asked forever.

"Would you like to . . . taste me?" she asked him then.

Goink! He'd been wavering on that particular sex act, to tell the truth. Despite the untold hours of wanting to stick his head up Shelly Rappaport's skirt, now that it was actually tongue-up-the-tunnel time, he felt deeply apprehensive. It was going to be *wet* in there, right? Of course, mouths were wet, too, but what did pussy taste like? His fertile imagination suggested many possibilities, the fewer enumerated here the better. Jeez, another rite of passage. Enough already with the rites of passage!

Since the answer to her question was not a simple yes or no, he acted rather than answered, doing it the way he'd always imagined, kissing her mouth, then her neck, then her breasts, then her stomach. His face reached her veld. It smelled kind of tigery and ripe. He lay his cheek against it. The little scrantz hairs tickled.

"Ohhhhh!" Mindy encouraged him. *"Ohhhhhhhhh! Ohhhhhhhhh!"*

Geronimo! He drew her legs apart, flopped around to get between them, and pressed his regular lips against her major ones. So far, so good. Smelled a bit like the Nantucket Bay down there, but he liked the Nantucket Bay. Now the tongue part; he braced himself, slid it in, and . . . Hey, this wasn't bad at all! It actually *was* kind of like a mouth. Maybe a shade saltier, but mucous membrane was mucous membrane. So what had he been dreading? He licked with zest.

"OHHHHHHHHHHHH!"

There it was — the Disbro howl. God, she was loud!

He heard pounding on the wall. *"Hey, Pinto! Sounds good! What are you doing to her?"* It was Alby from the next unit. Pinto laughed, and Mindy did, too. But he didn't laugh long, for here was this nude, compliant — even lubed! — young woman next to him, moaning his name. He was on her like a cat on a tuna fish. They started with the missionary position. Then she rolled him on his back and got on top. He liked this; he could lie against the pillows and watch her as she moved up and down. Then they lay side by side and did it that way. Then he pulled her up onto her hands and knees and got her from behind. He really liked when she reached back and fondled his balls. Then he sat back against the pillows and she rode his dong with her back to him, him feeling her up incessantly. Then they stood on their heads and Pinto inserted his left foot into her — no, no, just kidding.

Having gotten that first ejaculation out of the way, he found he could now go on and on, without worrying about some accidental, premature squirt ending things. All the sexual exertion was a little like being in an exercise class, but that was okay, exercise was good for you, or so he'd always heard. And then — *Oh, shit!* he thought suddenly. He'd forgotten sixty-nine! He couldn't come before they'd done sixty-nine! It was unimaginable not to do sixty-nine! So he pulled out, got up on hands and knees, did a one-eighty, and lowered his mighty meat, slick with pussic ambrosia, into her open mouth while — *simultaneously!* — lowering *his* mouth onto her area. Ahhhhhhhh! He liked this!

"Hey, Pinto! What are you doing to her, man?"

His mouth busy, Pinto did not answer. And then he had an idea.

There'd been this stag movie at Robkin's house one night a few years ago in which a man and woman had done an outlandish thing that had impressed them all. Let's see — could he duplicate it?

Still in the sixty-nine position, he worked his way to the edge of the bed and, with his arms clasping her, managed to stand. Her ankles were wrapped around his neck; her head hung down, still on his shaft. *"Mrrgh!"* she called up to him. *"Grmmmrblghh?"*

He lapped her vigorously and her oblivious moans returned, despite her hanging upside-down like a bat. Taking small steps, he worked himself over to the bathroom mirror. From his present perspective, he looked like one of the Smith Brothers. Okay. He short-stepped to the door and opened it. A warm breeze met them; Mindy moaned and sucked. He walked next door and knocked.

After a moment, Alby looked out.

"This is what I'm doing to her," Pinto shouted at him.

WITH GREEN KEY OVER, there were but three weeks left of school. It was finally okay to study openly, and just about everyone did. A skeleton crew kept the string of kegs going; some nights, Rat and Fitch even had to recruit Chi Phi brothers to get those last few bucks. They could count on Large, so he was often seen around the basement. Then, one night, 'Pie and 'Drant blew off booking and bought a keg. Everyone drank their asses off, and maybe got a little more loaded than usual, because at midnight 'Pie and 'Drant staggered out with Large to pull a raid on the Tool Shed. Why they would want to torment a bunch of inoffensive social misfits was not explained to Pinto, but apparently it seemed like a good idea at the time. On the way there, the boys found a bulldozer. Roadwork was being done, and the giant-tired thing had been left there overnight. They looked at one another and slowly smiled.

Pretty soon, they had it rumbling up Elm Street, heading right for the Tool Shed. What 'Drant had in mind was only to drive back and forth on their lawn a few times, maybe annihilate a few flower beds. But as they left the road to go onto the lawn, the campus cops zoomed up in their campus cop car. They'd received several calls, which might have had something to do with Magpie, Hydrant, and

Large singing "Do You Love Me" at the top of their lungs as they rode along, crashing the lids of garbage cans together. So here the cops were, trying to see them with their flashlights.

"Fuck, 'Drant, stop this thing!"

"I can't. I must've fucked something up. It won't stop!"

They were headed straight for the Tool Shed's front door.

"Then turn it!"

"It won't turn either!"

"Are you shitting me?"

"Jesus Christ!"

The cops were running toward them.

"Strategic withdrawal?" Large suggested.

"Oh, yeah," agreed Hydrant.

The three leapt off, 'Drant heading for the Green, 'Pie racing up behind SAE, Large lumbering down Fraternity Row like Mighty Joe Young. The cops had to chase the bulldozer, which they somehow managed to stop ten seconds before it hit the portico. No one was caught. There were no consequences.

FINALS WERE NOW UPON THE ADS. Pinto passed all his, and got two Bs and a B+. Funny how that happens when you care about your courses. Somehow, despite the ritual contempt for study in Adelphian culture, the other guys passed, too. Well, except for Rat, who slept through one final, forgot his second, and booted on his third. The sodden sophomore would not be back next year, and Pinto couldn't say he felt sorry.

The academic year had now ended, and most Dartmouth students got out of there as quickly as possible. The Buildings and Grounds guys pounced on the briefly empty campus to spruce it up for graduation, which would come in a week. The seniors, of course, had to stick around, but a surprising number of AD juniors and sophomores did too, so they could wish the older guys bon voyage. And so the string of kegs continued.

On Wednesday, Gay came up, and at the bar that night Otter announced his plans for the upcoming year — he was joining the marines. He was going to some sort of training that would make him a second lieutenant.

"Hey, cool!" Alby was in attendance as well. "You can die as an officer!"

Pinto asked Gay how she felt about this. After all, hadn't the deal been that Otter had to start wearing a tie after he graduated?

"He says he'll be wearing a tie as an officer." Gay shook her head grimly. "I don't know, Pinto. Some guys'll do anything to keep from growing up."

The next Adelphian milestone was the marriage of Black Whit and Pam, who surprised everyone by announcing on a Wednesday that the ceremony would be Friday. It was something of a spontaneous, last-minute thing, evidently. The nuptials were held at a spot on the Dartmouth campus known as the Bema. This shaded dell was important in school lore. A natural rock amphitheater surrounded by tall pines, covered with grass and moss, it was a quiet, out-of-the-way spot where the occasional school ceremony was held. It did seem like a great spot for a wedding.

The bride was in white, with a diadem of daisies. The groom appeared in a white morning coat with jeans and bare feet. They were the cutest of cute couples, Gay said. Pinto just thought they were cool. They'd written their own ceremony, which featured quotes from Kahlil Gibran, William Shakespeare, Allen Ginsberg, and Ernie Kovacs. (The Kovacs quote was "Food is great. Buy food.") Whit later confided to Pinto that he could hardly wait for the ceremony to end — he'd had diarrhea all day and had had to hold his cheeks rigidly together the entire time.

Several ooooold ADs attended. Tiger showed up, as did Downey, Flea, Goose, and Rat Battles. Even the Man showed up, and the girl with whom he'd run naked down the stairs, Tatiana. She was tall and sinewy with a severe beauty, and looked like she'd be at total ease giving commands to a slave. Someone told Pinto her family had invented the Thompson submachine gun.

When the ceremony concluded, tables were brought in with plates, napkins, champagne, and the wedding cake. Scotty had jury-rigged an outdoor sound system and played love songs like "Blueberry Hill," "Golden Teardrops," and the Floyd Dixon classic "Let's Do It in the Woods." The bride moved from group to group, cheery and effusive. Whit, too, was a charming host, when not running to the bathroom. In time, a number of the guys became quite lathered and insisted on singing "I Love My Girl."

> *I love her ruby red lips,*
> *And her lily white tits,*
> *And the hair around her asshole . . .*

It seemed a lifetime ago that Pinto had first heard those lyrics. He remembered wincing at the asshole part, shook his head, and smiled. Much water under the bridge since then. Actually, he was somewhat lathered himself. Having to whiz and not wanting to run all the way back to AD, he relieved himself into a couple of champagne glasses. It then seemed like a perfectly marvelous idea to set the glasses down near Bags so he'd mistakenly pick one up and drink it. Casually, Pinto did just that, sniggering to himself. Then he wandered away and forgot all about it.

The next thing he knew, Tatiana was bearing down on him with her fists balled and a look of fury. *She* had drunk the pee. He was glad she wasn't packing one of those submachine guns. Taking her hand, he apologized profusely, and ever so slowly, her anger ebbed, and he did not get the poke in the snoot he so richly deserved.

The partying continued back at the house, but finally the bar crowd shrank to four. Pinto stood groggily by the taps, thinking of nothing in particular. He noticed that Scotty was sitting on the mattresses with his pants down and a hard-on. The guy sure liked to display his dick. Pinto, Magpie, and Dumptruck, three abreast with their elbows on the bar, stared at the engorged thing in something between disbelief and awe.

"How do you wind *up* with something like that?" Truck wandered over to Scotty and bent for a closer look.

"You believe we're almost grown men, standing here staring at some guy's cock?" observed 'Pie.

Pinto laughed. He refilled their glasses. It had been a nice day, the wedding and all. Maybe this one more beer would do it, and he'd — *Holy shit!* He rubbed his eyes and looked again. Dumptruck had wrapped a hand around Scotty's bone and was, well, there was no way around it — he was beating him off! Pinto looked at Magpie in amazement.

"Yeah, yeah, he just started doing that."

"*Why?*"

"I don't know. I don't think he's a fag or anything. Maybe he just admires it."

That was as good an explanation as Pinto ever got. In the morning, Truck was gone. No one knew where he went. He had taken his stuff and his car and split. Magpie theorized that it wasn't so much facing the other guys that made him go as it was facing himself, and his fear that he'd discovered himself to be homosexual. Whatever the case, he was never seen again.

Afterward, in Adelphian lore, the episode was known as Scotty's Fair Shake.

SATURDAY NIGHT, to no one's surprise, was unsurpassed in noise, beer consumption, and general exuberance. Guys whizzed eight abreast into the gutter. Pinto was imagining how funny it would look if seven or eight *girls* peed together over there. As for the fair sex, few representatives were there, only the most seasoned, like Gay, Pam, and the Digit, who could stand AD in the raw.

Earlier in the day, Pinto had met Otter's father, the Big Otter. He was a tall, lean man with a deeply lined face reminiscent of those famous dust bowl photographs. Otter said he was a square-dance caller, but Pinto didn't know whether that meant all the time or just as a hobby. He could picture him in overalls, though, calling for an allemande left. The families of most of the seniors had come up for graduation but, having been warned, were not here tonight.

With Rat gone and Alby in better shape, Fitch achieved the dubious distinction of house drunk. Of course, most ADs got drunk, but not daily and invariably. Fitch anchored the wet-liver end of the Adelphian spectrum. Believe it or not, there were ADs who never drank at all. But they didn't come to the basement, so Pinto didn't know them.

"Hey, Fitch," Pinto said. "Any new injuries?"

Fitch felt various parts of his body, but found no pain. "Nope, I'm good."

"Wow, how're you doing it?"

"I dunno. I guess God protects fools and sailors. And ADs."

"Maybe." Pinto was skeptical; the Almighty had to have better things to do than that.

Fitch shrugged. The night went on. If beer had been diesel fuel, and Fitch a tractor trailer, he could have been driven from Akron to Santa Fe. His actual car was another matter. Since its impalement by the icicle, more and more had gone wrong with it, and he'd gotten more and more pissed off at it. Driving home to New Jersey tomorrow would be a dreadful experience. Finally, around one, with most of the guys gone or asleep, he went out the back door to the parking lot and glared at the offending vehicle. Suddenly, the perfectly logical solution struck him, which would prevent him from having to drive home and engender a certain emotional satisfaction as well. He lit his Zippo, opened his gas tank, and dropped it in.

The resulting explosion woke people for miles around. It threw Fitch backward and burned off his eyebrows and part of his hair but *did not injure him!* The car was totaled, but Fitch was fine. The concussion did, however, put a crack in the rear wall of the AD house that was never truly fixed. The seniors rushed out to upbraid Fitch for not blowing up his car some other night when they weren't trying to sleep so they could graduate in the morning. Fire trucks came, the whole bit.

"When the pillar of flame went up," Fitch told Pinto later, "it was like an exclamation point on the whole year. You know?"

AT 9:00 A.M. SUNDAY, Pinto somehow managed to be in his wooden folding chair on the great lawn before Baker Library, along with a thousand others, everyone wearing coats and ties. His head throbbed dismally, but that was all right — *everyone's* head hurt graduation morning. On the raised platform, Dean Seymour and other school officials stood in formation, and one by one, the seniors walked by, shook hands, and received diplomas. Pinto watched as Otter, Willy Machine, Charlie Boing-Boing, Mouse, Coyote, Terry No-Come, Snot, and Giraffe graduated and were "safe at last in the wide, wide world," as the old Dartmouth song had it. He felt a wave of sadness. He'd probably never see most of these guys again, except maybe at some distant reunion when they all were wearing colostomy bags. As it happened, he'd gotten much closer to the juniors than the seniors, who'd always seemed a little remote, but he'd miss them nonetheless. Especially Otter. He hoped he'd see more of him, over the years. He'd need a hit of the Otter grin every now and then.

When Snot received *his* diploma, he grinned broadly and shook hands like a cartoon character. Pinto almost fell out of his chair laughing. He wondered if the dean knew he'd just graduated Rocket J. Squirrel. But mostly he felt unaccustomedly solemn. Graduation — which would happen to him in a mere two years, by the way — was sobering. He couldn't imagine what it would be like to go out into the world, and just be alone out there. He'd have to think more about it next year, maybe.

As the ceremony ended, and those attending stood, Pinto heard a crack and a cry of pain behind him. Fitch's wooden chair had collapsed and a wood shard had pierced his thigh. Pinto almost laughed. He and some others helped poor Fitch to Dick's House once again. It was the final Adelphian injury of the 1960–61 school year. It was also the end of the keg string as well, because everyone now drove out of Hanover and went home.

Except Pinto. Having just had the best year of his life here, he couldn't quite tear himself away. He watched as the loaded-down cars pulled out of the driveway, en route to everywhere. A diaspora! Well, a small one, but a diaspora nonetheless.

Pinto sat on the AD front steps that night, in the June warmth, solemnly watching the moon rise over the Sphinx, when a voice broke into his ruminations.

"Hey, Pinto! How're you doing?"

It was Franklin Delano Roosevelt.

No, no, it was better. It was Donna Daley, in all her adorability.

310 • Chris Miller

She plunked down next to him, smelling lovely, and not like Shalimar at all.

"I'm fine," Pinto said. "Well, I'm sad. It's been a great year, and now everyone's gone."

"They'll be back."

"Some of them."

"Two thirds of them."

She was right. The guys with whom he'd mainly cavorted would be back in three months. There were cavalcades of fun yet to come. Two more years of it here, and then, if all went well, lots more in the wide, wide world. But who knew? Graduation was one of the great crossing points of life, along with, Pinto supposed, marriage, kids, and death, and you simply could not understand what was on the other side until you got there. In each case, everything changed forever, and a new paradigm prevailed. He hoped he'd have the same kind of fun out there, but you just couldn't predict.

"So what are *you* doing? Do you get the summer off?"

"Just August, I'm afraid. There's never enough staff at the hospital. We have to be nurses before we're even officially nurses. But that's the life I signed up for, I guess."

The moon rose higher. It was bigger than it had been last night, but not as big as it was going to be. Donna was quiet, watching it. Pinto couldn't imagine nicer company. As the daylight ebbed, ever more stars elbowed their way into visibility.

They spoke at once.

"Donna, I've been wanting to get to know you all year, but you were with Troll —" Pinto blurted.

"I'm really glad," Donna said, "that you're still here, Pinto, because ever since that time we almost —"

Since neither could understand two people talking at once, they let their words trail off. Donna smiled uncertainly at him, which wrinkled the freckles on her nose. He felt moved to kiss her, so he did. Just a soft touching of the lips. She closed her eyes. She smelled like some nice shampoo. He put his hand on her shoulder and they kissed gently, carefully.

"Pinto, I want to finish what we started that day. I've been want-ing to for a long time."

She had? "Why didn't you tell me?"

"Because you never called me."

That again. From now on, he'd never forget: Girls Want to Be Called. "I sure wish I had."

She took his hand. "Could we go to your room?"

On his wordless nod, she stood and pulled him up. They went inside. Al Clark, their emmet janitor — the one who thought the jets were messing up the weather — had come in today and trans-formed the Saturday-night shambles to a semblance of order.

"You know, it's funny," Pinto said. "Without all the guys here, it's just a house."

"Come on," said Donna.

They went to his room and climbed in bed. The laundry truck wouldn't make its pickup until tomorrow, so tonight there were still sheets to get between. Outside, the grasshoppers chirped. He could feel her heart beating.

"Pinto, could we — ?"

"Oh, yeah."

Their lovemaking was so different from what had happened with Mindy. He felt they were melting together. They hardly moved, just enough. He lost his conscious awareness of things and just floated on an ecstatic mix of sensation and emotion. When it crested and was over, they lay there holding each other for a long time.

"Are you going to call me when you get back in September?" Donna asked.

"Fuckin' A," said Pinto.

And he absolutely did.

WHERE ARE THEY NOW?

ONE MIGHT ASSUME my fun-loving fraternity brothers have devolved to terminal drunks and subway flashers by this time. In fact, most of them have had pretty good lives. Here are their futures. Remember, the characters in the book are just characters in a book. They don't have futures. These are the futures of the real people they inadequately portray:

Alby, my good friend and erstwhile companion in debauchery, got sober in 1978. He lives in Plymouth, Massachusetts, where he has an excellent job erasing graffiti from the famous rock. Often he poses with a pretty tourist, for he has not become bald and still has Paul Newman eyes. His mad party energy was an important part of Bluto, our head animal in *Animal House.*

Rhesus Monkey got lucky on the third wife, Gerri, and lives in happy retirement in Marin County, having done the dirty work of the Bank of America for thirty years. He has so many grandchildren he cannot remember their names. He seldom bares his little monkey ass in public anymore.

314 · *Chris Miller*

Dumptruck's disappearance was complete. To my knowledge, no AD ever saw him again.

Froggie's been my friend for fifty-six years. We were punished together in the fourth grade for saying the F word. And the S word, and the P word, and the C word. He still looks like he stepped out of a J. Press catalog, and today presides genially over a department of 20th Century Fox.

Josh, the strongest of my high school friends, succumbed to cancer at the age of twenty-four.

Ace Kendall's current location is unknown. Perhaps he's with Truck.

Robkin is Tony Bennett's agent and has been doing cool things in show business for forty years. In both family and career, he's been very successful. Plus, his iPod is so full of music it makes his pants fall down.

Wilson, my brother, became a hip, committed sixties guy. He played bass in a rock band, the American Dreams, and lived in the Haight for a while. Today, he resides in the Maine woods with his three cats, reading his Chomsky and listening to Ornette. He was president of the Southern Maine Blues Society.

Suzette is a shrink in New York City and seems to live in a state of perfect contentment.

Brad used to talk about being a forest ranger but wound up at Weyerhaeuser, the international forest products company. I think this says something about the human condition, but I'm not sure exactly what.

Isaac is a CPA and lives in Orange County, where he now drinks wine instead of beer. He is still very tall.

Poz was very successful in his family's Italian footwear business, but ate too much, smoked too much, and stopped playing baseball. He died of a heart attack in his midforties.

Tor became an ace film editor. You've seen his work in *Night Moves, The Right Stuff,* and a dozen other films.

Pi Lam Bags is a psychiatrist and medical director of a psychiatric clinic in San Diego. He teaches at UCSD Medical School and authored a book about teen suicide. Though his wife's first name is Gretchen, her last name was never Potatoes.

Fat Fred got pregnant, left Hanover, and has not been seen since. Perhaps she is cooking for Ace and Truck.

Whit and Pam are still married and live in Vermont, just across the river from Dartmouth. Black Whit has become Dr. Black Whit, having earned his degree in engineering. Pam's still a physical therapist. Both look great, and they're still the coolest couple in town.

Hardbar claims he has stopped beating off, but I know he's keeping his hand in.

Huck Doody did a tour in Vietnam as a marine officer. The minute he got back, he joined the counterculture. As always, he felt very strongly both ways. He is still intense on the soccer field, but in most other regards has become mellow as can be. He lives with his cool wife, Jenny, and plays a pretty fair fiddle in the evening when the sun goes down, with a dog and a glass of Syrah by his side.

Rat died from, uh, alcohol-related causes.

Round lives in Massachusetts with his sexy wife, Vanna. He's managing a semi-pro baseball team.

Fitch joined the air force. He died in a helicopter accident in 1978.

Moses was a tax lawyer and lobbyist, but currently declares himself delighted to be doing nothing. He lives in Longmeadow, Massachusetts, Alby's hometown, and his daughter graduated from Dartmouth Phi Beta Kappa. Though he's grown a beard, he does not currently ignite it, or any other portion of his body hair.

Goosey is a composite of three guys, all of whom have disappeared from my ken.

Bags also got sober. He still knows everything, though. He heads a consortium of fifteen Italian, Dutch, and German machine companies involved in the North American stone industry, is married to an artist, and digs trapshooting. His squat density and commanding bellow made him a big part of Bluto. Ever notice how Belushi comes down the stairs, just before the trial sequence? That's pure Bags.

F. A. Mac is *still* with the lovely Beverly and became a very good pediatrician indeed, routinely chairing national committees for the American Academy of Pediatrics. He's in upstate New York these days.

Otter did his stint with the marines, then went to UCLA Law School, where he edited the *Law Review*. His legal gigs included some interesting times on the yacht of an oil gazillionaire in Monte Carlo. He has a vineyard in Mendocino County, California, where he makes superb cabernet sauvignons and sauvignon blancs. (Also, supposedly, Syrah, though I have yet to receive my promised allotment and cannot speak from personal experience.) He has remained very cool, and occasionally still does a head bob or two. He has a great wife, Jennifer — fifth time's the charm, Bob — and is having a ball doing the dad thing all over again.

Gay Tabiggatits was Otter-wife number one. After Otter, she married a Dartmouth Phi Gam. After that, she was with another Phi Gam, Dave "Fall of the House of" Usher. Her next step was to take on the entire Dartmouth crew, one night in the boathouse. Sorry, Gay — it's time the world knew.

Seal, Alpha Delta Phi's last great wild man, saw his Dartmouth career end prematurely, merely because he stripped naked and chased an offending professor across the golf course on his motorcycle. He did manage to receive his degree in 1993, which he claims sets some kind of record. Thinking of himself as a knight errant, he romps around the Himalayas, studies Tibetan Buddhism, writes books, photographs professionally, and still chases women. He was another model for Bluto. Remember Belushi pouring a big jar of mustard on his chest? That was a much longer shot, during which he covered himself with the stuff, just like Seal, and, like him, kept chanting, "I'm the mustard man! I'm the goddamned mustard man!" But they didn't use that part.

The Man made a lot of dough in the mining business.

Tatiana died in jail. Busted for drug possession, she allegedly fell out of bed in her cell and sustained fatal head injuries. Suspicious circumstances, to say the least. No charges were brought against her jailers.

Doberman completed Dartmouth on his second pass. After fifteen years at IBM, he switched horses and became a minister in the Church of Religious Science. He and talented wife, Devona, are both artists and are having a great time living in Palm Springs, California.

Giraffe invented the field of cognitive neuroscience and was dean of faculty at Dartmouth College. One is unaware of the last time he threw a moon.

Sugar Ray is a defense attorney in Tucson, Arizona. He still has a great sneer.

The Digit also lives in Tucson, where, oddly enough, she is married to Sugar Ray. Her smiles nicely balance his sneers. We called her the Kid. Her energy could light a small city.

Douche has been an entrepreneur who's done everything from banking to offshore lobster fishing. These days, he lives in New Hampshire, enjoying the fruits of his labors, often traveling the four corners of the world.

Gazork is a portfolio manager for a large insurance company in Massachusetts. One late night at the AD bar, he passionately declared that when we graduated, we would find only "pockets of sanity" in the world. He was right.

Don Marcus lives in London, where he writes and produces for TV. He was the last of the ooooold ADs, and created a house event in the mid-sixties called Magic Monday, which is celebrated at the Dartmouth chapter even today. With his graduation, the Era of Adelphian Sickness ended.

Mouse, too, became a shrink.

Hydrant served in the navy and naval reserves for many years, ending up a lieutenant commander. He went to law school and settled in Savannah, Georgia, where he's a maritime lawyer. He still plays killer lacrosse, and still cracks me up.

Bert runs his own business doing direct-mail advertising. He wrote for American Family Publishers, and penned that delightful phrase "You may already be a winner!" He has a lovely wife, Pam, dogs, horses, and a fine home in Oyster Bay, New York. One of his sons attended Dartmouth and joined AD. Resting on the roof one night, he fell off. Being a cool AD and hot-shit rugby player, he was out of the hospital in four days, and immediately slept on the roof again. All right, Todd! Currently, Bert's writing fiction and is doing a book based on his crazy fraternity experiences. Bizarre idea, Bertie.

Magpie married *Nancy Manhattan* and they're still together. He does corporate law and has become the biggest rah-rah alumni nut you ever saw. He's currently president of Dartmouth's 151-year-old Association of Alumni.

Scotty married *Big Barbara,* had kids, and was a real estate man in New Jersey. When *Animal House* came out, he invited the local contingent — Bert, Magpie, Bags, and me — to dinner. A lovely time was had by all. Far too quickly, the night was over, and we went out into the January snow and cold. As we pulled from the driveway, we saw that Scotty and Barbara had snuck out to wish us an inimitable farewell — by mooning us side by side, their pants around their ankles. That was my last sight of Scotty, who died young in 1988. Hail and farewell, Cowboy Bob.

Coyote worked for the Treasury Department and Price-Waterhouse. He and his cool wife, Ann, come out to visit Doberman a couple of times a year, and they get drunk and boot all over each other. No, no, just making light, Ann. Sorry.

Willy Machine lives in retirement in Vermont.

Snot was a state insurance commissioner. He lives in South Carolina. AD's bounciest guy has been dealing with Parkinson's disease for some time now.

Donna Daley is lost in the sands of time.

Zeke Banananose is a catchall character I created to display the worst qualities of several guys I didn't want to embarrass. So it would be hard to tell you what he's doing now. Probably acting like an asshole.

T-Bear lives in Florida, where he manages the family money.

Rat Battles is in Ohio. He built an insurance agency with his father, ran it, and sold it for plenty. Only rarely does he dispense change nowadays.

Black Mike is alive and well in Largo, Florida.

Cuntwolf became a doctor. No, not a gynecologist. That would have been too perfect.

Tiger is a banker in Chicago, where he just can't stay away from those Cubs.

Flea's another doctor, based in San Diego.

Monk is on the ski patrol at Mad River Glen, Vermont.

Downey hit it big as an investment banker. Each year, he throws a great weeklong party at his lodge in Keystone, Colorado, to which many ADs of the fifties era return to ski, shmooze, and drink fine wines. A few younger guys come as well. John Walters, '62, was one.

The Lobe, a much-loved AD brother whom I never met, died in a motorcycle accident a while ago. He was big-time in real estate.

Flounder majored in dissipation. According to Magpie, he never stopped drinking from the day he joined AD until his death in his late twenties, back in his hometown of Tulsa. It is said that once, on some big weekend, a girl came up, put a hand on his shoulder, and said, "How are you, Flounder?" In his Charles Laughton voice, he replied, "If you would remove your hand from my shoulder and place it upon my genitals, all would be well." History does not record the young lady's response.

Goose loves him some golf.

Lonnie Youngblood had a pretty good career through the sixties, and featured a promising young guitarist for a time named Jimi Hendrix. I found Lonnie quoted on the Internet, reminiscing about his gigs at Dartmouth. Which is nice, because we Dartmouth guys definitely reminisce about him.

Carl Holmes had an album in '62 called *Twist Party at the Roundtable.* It's good old R & B. In '66, he too featured Jimi Hendrix, who gigged but did not record with him.

The Flamingos and *The Five Royales* are in the Rock 'n' Roll Hall of Fame.

The City Café is a sports bar.

Dean Seymour is living happily in Florida. He still does some teaching at a local college. He is not, and never was, Dean Wormer. Nixon was Dean Wormer. Dean Seymour was always a great guy. *And his wife is not Marion Wormer!* (Okay, Thad?)

Pinto writes stories, books, and movies. His awesome son, Jack, is at Oberlin.

GLOSSARY

I WANT TO thank my friend and colleague Mark Leffler for alerting me to the fact that some of the people who buy this book won't have a clue about my profusion of cultural references. The Battle of Kursk? The Moonglows? Mel Allen? What dat boy talking about? So I hereby offer this key to early 1960s American culture.

Aldrich, Henry This was the lead character in a corny radio sitcom nearing the end of its run in the early fifties. It was called *The Aldrich Family* and was about a "typical teenager" who, essentially, acted like an asshole for thirty minutes each week. It had a famous opening: the boy's mom calling, "Hen-*reeee!* Henry Aldrich!"

Allen, Mel He was the "Voice of the Yankees" through the 1950s, my time of maximum baseball worship. He was a big, hearty fellow with a ready smile, or so he seemed on TV. As the shows were sponsored in part by a beer, he'd refer to home runs as "Ballantine blasts." And when something really cool happened, he'd drawl, "Well, how about that!" He was a well-liked guy, at least by us Yankees fans.

Anka, Paul See Bobby Rydell.

Baldwin, James He was a gay, black writer at a time when it was unwise to be either. His major books were *Go Tell It on the Mountain* and *The Fire Next Time*. My terminally bigoted father didn't know which quality repelled him more, the blackness or the gayness, but he sure knew he didn't like the guy. I myself dug his books. He was an odd-looking guy whose somewhat bulbous eyes made him resemble a rabbit frozen in the headlights.

The Basie band The Count came up in the wide-open, gangster-ridden, jazz-spawning Kansas City of the 1930s. He formed and led the Count Basie Big Band from the mid-1930s until 1980. They especially kicked ass in the later thirties when they featured tenor sax god Lester Young and in the late fifties, early sixties when they were known as the Atomic Band. The latter group I once witnessed blow the roof off Birdland, the great Manhattan jazz club. Another band had opened for them, and when Basie drummer Sonny Paine came out to sit before his kit, he found it had been readjusted to a lower height for the previous drummer. "Who set up these drums?" he complained. "Rumpelstiltskin?"

Batista Fulgencio Batista was the dictator who ruled Cuba before Fidel Castro took over in 1959. He was a real son of a bitch, cozy with the American gangsters who ran the casinos, dope, and vice down there. Castro threw all those guys out, then started a dictatorship of his own. Castro was nobody's sweetheart, but at least he gave a shit about the Cuban people, which Batista sure didn't.

The Battle of Kursk This go-to between the German and Russian armies in 1943 was the greatest tank battle of all time. Millions of grim troops were involved. Probably more horrendous explosions per square inch than anywhere else, ever. It stands as one of those ultimate military hells, along with the Battle of Verdun and the Retreat from the Chosin Reservoir (which see).

Beiderbecke, Bix Bix may have been the first great American cult-hero musician. His field was jazz, and in the Roaring Twenties this handsome young man from Davenport, Iowa, played trumpet in a contrasting manner to the preeminent style of the day, the hot New Orleans blowing of Louis Armstrong and others. Indeed, Bix is one root of Miles Davis, as he introduced cool, spare playing to an instrument often blown with excess fire and flamboyance. Too bad there's not much of his stuff recorded orthophonically — mostly it's that tinny sound from the twenties, when audio was primitive.

Berger, Senta This lovely Austrian actress made a number of Hollywood films of no particular note in the sixties and has produced and acted in movies in Germany ever since. At the time Alby was naming his date after her, she was twenty years old and turning up on the odd American TV drama — quite a fetching dish of Wiener schnitzel.

Bergman, Ingmar One of the twentieth century's great film directors, Bergman released a string of movies from the late forties to the late seventies that dazzled the world. He was easy to parody because he was so gloomy and ruminative. The three-in-a-row combo of *The Seventh Seal, Wild Strawberries,* and *The Magician* was simply a black-and-white magic, dream-logic experience that seemed to work on you from the inside out. The gorgeous cinematography of Gunnar Fischer, and later Sven Nyqvist, was always a plus in Bergman movies, and — hoo-boy! — did they ever feature Actresses of Scandinavian Pulchritude. Ah, the sexy, gamine charm of Bibi Andersson; the classic Nordic beauty of Ingrid Thulin; the generous endowment of dark-haired, profoundly erotic Gunnel Lindblom. In 1963, Gunnel went topless for a moment in *The Silence,* and the hearts of young male moviegoers everywhere leapt.

Berra, Yogi Yogi is, of course, the lovable, funny-looking Yankees catcher who supposedly continually spouted indelible phrases like "It's déjà vu all over again" and "When you come to a fork in the road, take it." What is less remembered is that Yogi was one of the greatest ballplayers ever, a three-time MVP and Hall of Famer who has played in more World Series games than any other ballplayer. He is still with us, as of this writing, and serves as a beloved Yankees gnome, linking the great franchise of today to that blow-'em-all-away team of the fifties.

Sergeant Bilko Bilko, portrayed by longtime comedian Phil Silvers, was the star of one of the best and most popular sitcoms of the fifties, *You'll Never Get Rich*. He was the ever-scheming con-man sergeant of a platoon of misfits, one of whom — the happy slob-nebbish — was known as Doberman.

Bosch, Hieronymus The original psychedelic artist, Bosch, in the late 1400s and early 1500s, painted canvases that were like bad acid trips, hellish visions filled with demons, mutilation, and despair. I hope he was able to leave all that shit at the office sometimes and, you know, enjoy his evenings once in a while.

Brown, Ruth That tune played at the AD house on rush night, "Mama, He Treats Your Daughter Mean," was a great, ass-kicking R & B song way back in 1953. Ruth was a player, there at the birth of rock 'n' roll. Died recently. Good-bye, Ruth. Thanks for the tunes.

Brubeck This is Dave Brubeck, a jazz pianist who, during the fifties, enjoyed wide popularity on college campuses and elsewhere. His music was advanced tonally and polyrhythmically and wasn't much like what anyone else was doing. For going his own way, he reaped a certain amount of derision from the orthodox jazz world, but he never let it bother him. The sax star who played with him was Paul Desmond, whose relaxed, cool, smacked-out style was instantly identifiable and a complete delight. I remember Desmond leaning against the piano while playing to keep from falling over.

Bruce, Lenny How does one describe Lenny Bruce in a paragraph? He was the Charlie Parker of comedy, took it to a new level. Practically every comic working today worships (and steals from) him. Comedy is always close to jazz, the improvisatory aspect of it and so forth, but never closer than with Lenny. His synapses were just faster than anyone else's, and he took things two or three times further out than his contemporaries. Even today, when I listen to him, he sounds hipper than the room. And, never forget, he smashed the cultural and legal barriers to using "obscene language" in public as part of his shtick. Without Lenny Bruce, no Lampoon, no *Animal House,* no me.

Camus, Albert He was one of those gloomy, postwar, existentialist French writers, a contemporary of Jean-Paul Sartre. His many cheerful reads include *The Plague, The Fall,* and *The Stranger.* He had a handsome, world-weary face and a cool manner. The ADs would probably have paid more attention to him if they knew he was a champion of the absurd who once declared "Always go too far, for that is where you will find the truth."

Cannon, Freddy "Boom Boom" A truly loathsome rocker wannabe, Freddy gave us the execrable "Tallahassee Lassie." He had about as much class as a dick wearing Groucho Marx glasses.

The Cardinals No, not a conclave of Catholic guys in red robes, but another of those fifties R & B vocal groups named after birds. The first one was the Orioles, who began recording in 1948. There soon followed the Ravens, the Robins, the Penguins (who wore tuxedos), the Swallows, the Eagles (the original, black Eagles), the Flamingos, the Crows, the Meadowlarks, and many, many more. The Cardinals sang some beautiful shit but were regional, a New York group. They never attained national prominence. And today they are brain surgeons.

Cerberus He's the dog creature that guards the entrance to Hades in Greek mythology. He's got three heads, so better not fuck with him.

Chan, Charlie He was a fictional Chinese American police detective, portrayed in dozens of movies in the 1930s and 1940s by a string of white men. Nonetheless, Charlie was treated with dignity and respect and comes off pretty well, even today. He was always aided by Number One Son and loved him his maxims, spoken in a wise, patient voice: *"Waiting for tomorrow waste of today."* Right on, Charlie!

Charles, Ray The Genius of Soul was a huge musical force for more than fifty years in every form of American music except maybe polka bands. He lit up my teenage years with his great blues and R & B singles. By the time I got to Dartmouth, he was a superstar and was exploring other forms: the velvety pop of *The Genius of Ray Charles;* the achingly soulful country of *Modern Sounds in Country and Western Music;* the hot, sexy duets on *Ray Charles and Betty Carter;* the brash, exuberant hard bop of *Genius + Soul = Jazz.* He could do anything! Since he was blind, there were lots of jokes made about him falling over piano benches, but I don't think it ever really happened.

Chinos Khaki-colored pants. Trim and kinda preppy. Dartmouth guys at the time of my book wore them constantly.

Clift, Montgomery As with so much else, there was a sea change in Hollywood leading men after World War II. They became twitchier, edgier, less overtly heroic. Marlon Brando in *A Streetcar Named Desire,* for instance, or James Dean in anything. The first of these guys to emerge was Montgomery Clift. In 1948, in *Red River,* his postwar coolness was a great foil for John Wayne's belligerent, tyrannical cattle rancher. Too bad their final fight is broken up by dopey Joanne Dru. What a stupid ending. Anyway, apparently too sensitive for his own good, Clift gradually got deeper into prescription drugs, alcohol, and anything else he could get his hands on, including sex partners of both genders. He went down the tubes in 1966.

The Clovers Another Atlantic Records R & B group. They had a string of hits during the first half of the fifties. Their sound was bluesier than most of the vocal groups at that time, which veered closer to the smooth, Caucasian-friendly Ink Spots than to down-home blues. Their most famous song, though, was not bluesy at all — the very Coasters-like "Love Potion Number Nine."

The Coasters Probably the most popular of all fifties black vocal groups — along with the Platters, they sold the most records — the Coasters worked with and sang the songs of Leiber and Stoller, who composed some of the best rock 'n' roll songs of the day. The Coasters started as the Robins. They made a few fine sides, most memorably "Smokey Joe's Café." Then, with a partial switch of members, they became an institution. Who doesn't know "Charlie Brown," "Along Came Jones," and "Poison Ivy"? What, *you* don't? Google them immediately and give yourself a treat! And don't give me any shit about being old school.

Cobb, Lee J. The thick-lipped, pissed-off bigot in the 1957 film *12 Angry Men*. The brutal labor union boss in *On the Waterfront* who kicks the shit out of Marlon Brando. Usually a villain or at least a loudmouthed asshole, Lee J. Cobb was an important American character actor from the late thirties to the late seventies. Maybe his high point was his creation of the Willy Loman character in Arthur Miller's 1949 play *Death of a Salesman*. Willy, in the confusion and misery caused by his doomed pursuit of the wealth and success of the American dream, would occasionally, after becoming sloppily drunk, *schtupp* some sorry bimbo on the road. He is what Pinto did not want to be like.

Colby Junior College This was the nearest girls' school to Dartmouth and hence very popular indeed. Sometimes, "cattle drives" were organized, and one of the Colby dorms would send a busload of girls to some Dartmouth fraternity house. But never to Alpha Delta Phi. We were on the proscribed list. Colby girls were given the impression we were worthless slackers and perverts. "Yeah, so?" we asked.

Cole, Nat "King" An American musical institution from the forties through the midsixties, he began in a jazz vein with a trio that influenced everyone, including Ray Charles. In the fifties, he became a crooner of smooth, smooth ballads for a mainstream audience, often backed by, choke, strings. Not what the ADs were listening to. In 1956, he became the first black person to host an American prime-time TV show. Unfortunately for his fans, the guy was in the habit of smoking three packs of Kools a day and died of lung cancer in 1965 at the peak of his career.

The Contours They had one of the great early-Motown records, "Do You Love Me." If you wondered what I was talking about in the opening sentences of the preface to this book, it's the recitation that opens this great dance record. The ADs would scream the refrain together: "Do you loooooove me — now that I can dance . . . dance . . . dance — *Watch me now!*"

Crawford, Broderick A big, burly, blue collar–looking actor who scored big playing Willie Stark (a character based on Huey Long) in the 1949 flick *All the King's Men*. He had a brusque, gravelly, five-o'clock-shadow sort of charm, like a Nixon with balls, to which Bags may have aspired.

The Creature from the Black Lagoon The fifties, of course, were the heyday of cheap, tacky monster movies — great octopus-like things from under the ocean, revived dinosaurs, giant ants. Supposedly what underlay this was anxiety about the Bomb. The giant ants in *Them!*, for instance, were mutations caused by nuclear testing. *The Creature from the Black Lagoon* was one of the sillier entries in this genre — he was a sort of fishman who lived in, yes, a black lagoon. He was more pathetic than scary, but the *title* of the movie has always been great.

Curtis, King The tenor sax player who enlivened the instrumental breaks on the Coasters' records employed a new style, known for a time as "Yakety Sax," which was widely imitated. The

King was a solid and likable musical presence for many years. In 1970, he played Amherst Frog's wedding party at the Rainbow Room. In 1971, while sitting on the stoop of the Manhattan brownstone he owned, he was murdered.

Dadaistic Dada was a school of art in the late teens and 1920s. It reflected the horror the artists at that time felt about World War I. It was, of course, anti-war but also "anti-art." That means it rejected traditional artistic goals like beauty or even fascination. In fact, it was fairly boring, essentially unlovely stuff from a visual standpoint. But its nonlinear, nonsensical quality was right in line with what the ADs, in their inchoate way, were groping for.

Dance steps As noted in chapter 13, there were an awful lot of them in the early sixties. The Lindy is the basis of what is called swing dancing today. It was named in the thirties for flier-hero Charles Lindbergh. In the bop, you stood in one place and did cool moves with your toes. The slop was the sexy dance of my high school days. The stroll was a line dance, great for people who were coordination-challenged, like your faithful recounter-of-past-times. In the mashed potato you got on your toes and slid your heels toward each other repeatedly with a cool expression on your face. No one had a clue how to do the continental walk, which may have been a sixties version of the stroll, or the bacon fat, either. As for the twist, see Hank Ballard and the Midnighters.

Darvon This is a mild, pleasant pain pill I first encountered at age twelve when I had my wisdom teeth removed. Puts you in a nice float. Nowadays, though, instead of Darvon they give you Darvocet, so if you swallow enough pills to feel good the Tylenol destroys your liver.

Dick, Philip K. This is a hard one for me to write because PKD, as he is known familiarly, is a particular writer-hero of mine. His passionate advocacy of humanity at a time when dehumanization was all the rage was exemplary, and his surreal, hip worlds of the future are mind-boggling. He is the only American author I am aware of who wrote a novel in which the sole morally upright character is a Ganymedean slime mold. If you are adventurous at all in your reading, you'll go batshit over his novels *Ubik; A Scanner Darkly; Flow My Tears, the Policeman Said;* and, especially, *The Man in the High Castle* and *The Three Stigmata of Palmer Eldritch.* This is the shit, man.

Diddley, Bo The coolest of all the rock 'n' roll pioneers and the one who gets the least respect. Buy a Bo compilation — there's a definitive one on the Chess label — and just listen. He has major charm. Take these lyrics, from "Who Do You Love": "I walk forty-seven miles of barbed wire, wear a cobra snake for a necktie, got a brand-new house by the roadside, made from rattlesnake hide. . . . Come take a walk with me, Arlene, and tell me, WHO DO YOU LOVE???"

Domino, Fats This genial New Orleans R & B singer, as *Rolling Stone* once pointed out, combined great charm with no perceptible charisma whatsoever. By 1955, his music was called rock 'n' roll. He was the pioneer our parents least minded; in fact, our dads often dug him. He came along in 1950, and his great work spanned the decade. He has too many hits to name, but just tap into one of his Best Of albums and you, too, will fall willing victim to his sweet, soulful, Southern sound.

Doughboys What we called the American guys sent to France to fight in World War I. They had nothing to do with Pillsbury, I'm assuming.

The Drifters Another black vocal group, and one of the more prominent. The personnel would vary over the years, but in one form or another the guys churned out hit after hit, from their beautiful and eccentric take on "White Christmas" in 1954 to their slickly produced early-sixties hits, "There Goes My Baby," "Under the Boardwalk," and "Up on the Roof." Their rumored follow-up, "Sick in the Bathroom," was never released.

The Ed Sullivan Show Running from 1948 to 1971, this bizarro TV program corralled much of America every Sunday night. It was, essentially, a variety show, and Sullivan was some kind of weirdo gossip columnist who seemed not to have a clue about anything. Yet there he was, giving us marching bands and Italian mice puppets each Sunday night. Happily, he also gave us Bo Diddley and the Beatles from time to time, and you can get DVDs of all the rock acts that appeared on his show, so that's the upside. Incidentally, my son, Jack, when ten years old, could do a great Ed Sullivan impression, pursing out his lips and saying "Really big shew!" A bizarre character, really. Uh, Ed, not Jack.

Edwards, Douglas He was a New York newscaster with a bad-breath face.

English Leather This was a heavily advertised brand of male cologne. In the early 1960s, male scents beyond Old Spice aftershave were something rather new. I never liked the way either smelled and used a third one called Royall Lyme. In fact, I seem still to have a bottle of the stuff in my bathroom. Talk about brand loyalty.

Falstaff Falstaff shows up in three of Shakespeare's history plays as a drunken, carousing fat guy, and a pub pal of Prince Hal, the royal heir who was quite the party guy before he had to become Henry the Fifth. Falstaff was vain, vulgar, and generally of low character, with mostly mead and wenches on his mind. But he was often funny. When Hal became Henry, he cut Falstaff out of his life, breaking the deteriorated old drunk's heart.

Father Knows Best The most iconic of all the dippy fifties sitcoms about lovable nuclear families. Robert Young was unflaggingly patient, wise, caring, helpful, and considerate toward all three of his adorable kids and his lovely wife as well. Just like my house. Didn't you know? We *all* lived that way in the fifties. Then those terrible sixties came along and just messed everything up forever.

Feiffer, Jules A cartoonist who seemed a fixture of the hip world during the fifties, sixties, and seventies in New York. You could find his syndicated comic strip each week in the *Village Voice* for forty-two years. He was a sweet, balding soul, and reading him was always like a visit with a favorite uncle. Each spring, like the annual appearance of the monocled gent on the *New Yorker* cover, there would be Feiffer's black leotard–clad dancer, offering an interpretive dance to the season, during which she would go on about life. You can see some of his strips at www.adambaumgoldgallery.com/feiffer_jules/feiffer.htm. Feiffer also wrote the film *Carnal Knowledge* and illustrated the classic children's book *The Phantom Tollbooth*.

Fields, W. C. Fields, an American actor and performer from the last years of the nineteenth century into the 1940s, created an indelible comic persona appreciated more by men than women, who, in my experience, see only a bitter, drunk, misogynistic (unless the lady is of ill repute) jerk. Well, yeah . . . but he did it with *style*. He was graceful as a dancer, could juggle and so forth, spent many years in vaudeville. Maybe he's the emblem of everything women hate and men tend to behave like when in thrall to their low, lizard-brain selves. Whatever, I think he's hilarious.

The Five Royales The guys made more than a hundred records in a career that began in 1942 in their earlier incarnation as a gospel group called the Royal Suns. Ten years later they morphed into an R & B group, adding the "e" to Royales to avoid legal action from an existing group called, simply, the Royals. Never leaving their churchy roots far behind, the Five Royales made a great string of singles through the fifties and into the sixties. Their musical marriage of gospel and R & B was a major influence on another group beloved of the ADs, Hank Ballard and the Midnighters, and on Soul Brother #1, James Brown. Okay, now, ready for this? In a bizarre twist, the preexisting Royals then changed their name to Hank Ballard and the Midnighters! Confused yet?

The Five Satins Another harmony group, they gave us possibly the most beloved of all doo-wop ballads, "In the Still of the Night." In 1963, the ADs were one-upped by the Chi Phis next door, who actually bagged the Satins to play at one of their parties. Check out the gallery on my website. Oh, you wonder what the address is? It's www.chrismillerwriter.com.

The Flamingos In the vocal group–laden days of the fifties, the Flamingos stood out. They had their own sound. It featured high, ethereal harmonies. They sounded as if they were singing from heaven. These sweet, trippy records were well loved by the ADs, back in the day. Probably because we enjoyed trying to sing like them. Something there is that loves a falsetto.

The Fly A low-budget fifties sci-fi movie that ends with a shot of the hero having been merged with a housefly, crying, "Help me! Help me!" in a small, insectlike voice. A much better remake was done with Jeff Goldblum in the eighties, but it lacked the endearing tackiness of the original.

Francis, Arlene An unappetizing female fifties person. She was all gushy and smiley. She'd been a Broadway actress, but by the time your humble glossary writer came of age you could find her sitting on the same *What's My Line?* game show panel as Dorothy Kilgallen. They were a one-two punch of utter nonpulchritude, and reason alone for never watching the show.

Francis, Connie Connie would have been a good candidate for the Adelphian boot wall, so lame and obnoxious a musical presence was she. She's so offensive that if you listen to her records you could turn into a pillar of shit. Here's a fact you won't find anywhere else: Amherst Frog's father, Harry, discovered her for MGM Records and inflicted her on an unsuspecting world. He was an A & R man who'd previously produced Frank Sinatra et al., so this was not his proudest musical moment, but MGM made plenty of dough, as scads of dippy young girls proved to *adore* Connie's insipid records.

Freed, Alan Little known today, he's the semisleazy white guy who came along in the early 1950s, played black music for white teenagers, and named it rock 'n' roll. That's when and how the term came into use. It was an old black euphemism for enthusiastic copulation, dating at least as far back as the 1920s, but it was Alan who named the emerging new music after it. He started doing this as a deejay in Cleveland — this is why the Rock and Roll Hall of Fame and Museum is there — and then took his show to WINS in New York in the autumn of 1954, sparking the entire rock 'n' roll revolution. You can find a few of his old shows on the Internet. My teenage friends and I loved this guy.

Frye boots Frye made a cowboyish kind of boot that came in handy during the snowy New England winters.

Fudd, Elmer That guy who's always shooting at Bugs Bunny? With the bald head?

Garnet Mimms and the Enchanters The ADs were enchanted both by this R & B group's cool name and by their big hit, "Cry Baby," which never left the jukebox as long as I hung out in that funky basement.

Garrison, Jimmy John Coltrane used two bass players in his early-sixties quartet. Jimmy was one, and the other was Reggie Workman. Sometimes both would be onstage at once, lending strange, polyrhythmic undercurrents to the music.

Gaulois A noxious but very existential French cigarette. No filter, totally lethal. Sartre smoked them and eventually died of lung cancer.

Gibran, Kahlil An Arab guy who came to the USA as a kid and later wrote a book called *The Prophet,* which featured wisdom in the form of poetry about all aspects of life. I think it was Lenny Bruce who first stated publicly that the real reason guys bought it was to whip out on date night as proof of their sensitivity, to help them get laid.

Gish, Lillian This actress was a fixture in American movies practically from their get-go. She's the one running across the ice floes in the silent film *Way Down East.* Her earnest, early-twentieth-century sweetness made her an icon, and she was still making movies in the 1980s. *Quel* pro! Hey, the woman was in *Birth of a Nation!*

Goldberg, Rube One of the great American cartoonists, Rube had a career lasting from 1905 to 1964. He is best remembered for the fantastical machines invented by his character Professor Lucifer Gorgonzola Butts. The machines were exceedingly complex arrangements of all sorts of odd things to accomplish an extremely simple purpose. Professor Butts's Self-Operating Napkin, for instance, wipes your mouth as you eat. The machines are better seen than described, so check 'em out on Rube's website: www.rubegoldberg.com.

Goodman, Benny He was a nice Jewish jazz icon in the thirties and forties, his big band one of the premier attractions of the day, a friendly ethnic shoemaker-looking guy who gave us "Sing, Sing, Sing" and innumerable other pleasing ditties. But with Bix, on "Barnacle Bill the Sailor," he blows one hot — albeit short — motherfucker of a clarinet solo that is another example of the younger, juicier incarnation of an artist being the one to create the hotter music. Another example is Elvis Presley, whose music never recovered from the move he made from Sun Records to RCA, where they mainstreamed him and cut off his balls.

Goosey Gander A name from an old English nursery rhyme about being sure to say your prayers.

Gordon, Dexter After Charlie Parker invented saxophone bebop on his alto, Dexter Gordon stepped up and became the foremost exponent on tenor. He had drug problems (who of these guys didn't?), then went away to Europe for a while, where jazz got respect. In 1976, he made a triumphant return to the USA, which can be heard on the Blue Note album *Homecoming: Live at the Village Vanguard.* He was a cool, suave, stylishly dressed black man.

Graziano, Rocky An up-from-the-gutter middleweight champion of the world in the late forties. His classic trio of fights against "iron man" Tony Zale make you wince even in memory; they really beat the shit out of each other. Rocky's scrappy story can be seen in the early (and pretty good, with an uncredited Steve McQueen moment) Paul Newman film *Somebody Up There Likes Me.* By the time of *Animal House,* Rocky had morphed into a sort of goofy, lovable goombah in TV commercials, acting a little punch-drunk. Just an act, though. The man once went toe-to-toe with Sugar Ray Robinson and delivered to that fistic gentleman one of the few knockdowns of his entire career, with a powerful right to the neck in the second round. After which Sugar jumped up and put Rocky out for the count.

Hank Ballard and the Midnighters One of the enduring vocal groups from 1954 and into the *Animal House* era of the early sixties. They shot to fame — or perhaps infamy — when they released "Work with Me, Annie," an earthy little number about doing the ol' in-out. The next record spelled out the unfortunate result: "Annie Had a Baby." You may be sure that in straight-arrow midfifties America, these recordings caused an uproar and were taken off the playlists of most radio stations. But Hank had become a star, and almost a decade's worth of outstanding R & B / rock 'n' roll would follow. He wrote and performed the original version of "The Twist," which became an endearing if lame-o dance craze when Chubby Checker covered it a couple of years later. Luckily, Hank got the royalties. A trim, dapper man, he was a local hero in L.A. through his death in 2003, and still is, actually.

The Harptones The lead singer of this vocal group, Willie Winfield, was one of the greatest ballad singers of the era. There is a story that Johnny Mathis once refused to follow him onto the stage, having been totally intimidated by the performance he'd just witnessed. Check out the Harptones' "Life Is But a Dream," from 1955.

The Haunt of Fear From 1950 until early 1955, my fellow pubescent boys and I were enthralled with EC Comics. Some of us pubescent boys *still* dig the things, even though there hasn't been a new issue in fifty-two years. They are simply the best comic books ever made. They had nothing to do with superheroes. There were three horror titles, including *The Haunt of Fear* and the famous *Tales from the Crypt,* two science fiction titles, some adventure and crime titles, and then, in 1952, the incomparable *MAD.* The boss was Bill Gaines, the head editor Al Feldstein, and the resident satirist Harvey Kurtzman. They were cool, wised-up, postwar, New York Jewish guys with a liberal attitude, and could they ever tell a story. They assembled a stable of simply the best comics artists under one roof ever. Amherst Frog and I learned to recognize each guy's style immediately. Wally Wood drew the sexiest women and the best rocket ships. Will Elder filled his panels with odd goings-on and could imitate any other artist extant. Al Williamson drew the most hideous, slime-dripping aliens. The stories were hip, sexy, and well crafted — the guys who put them out never writing down to us. Oddly enough, the stories were very moral, too. The evil character inevitably had something horrible happen to him in the end. Like, the victim rising from his/her grave and, leaving a trail of rotting flesh, finding the protagonist and killing him/her in some delightfully just and gory way. You can actually buy full-color versions of the best of the EC library in bound volumes. The website you want is www.eccrypt.com.

The Heartbeats Shep Sheppard, the lead singer, had one of the great voices of doo-wop, and the Heartbeats were one of the top groups, best remembered for the famous "A Thousand Miles Away."

Hemingway You saw the cheerful, red-cheeked, white-bearded face of Ernest Hemingway all over the place in the fifties. He was a major literary celebrity and a man's man, an American institution, novelist, short story writer, and journalist for decades. He went to report on the Spanish Civil War, actually put himself through that horrible shit, and then wrote about it in *For Whom the Bell Tolls*. He won a Pulitzer in 1953 for his short novel *The Old Man and the Sea* and the Nobel Prize in 1954. He wrote in a boiled-down prose style that became the voice both of the French existentialist writers and of the American hard-boiled crime scribes like Raymond Chandler. This voice just influenced the shit out of American writing. *I*, in my own way, try to use his voice. He gave us the phrase "grace under pressure."

Henry the Eighth The roly-poly English monarch was portrayed in the historical films of the fifties as a bearded voluptuary taking a single bite from a leg of mutton and carelessly tossing it over his shoulder while wiping his mouth with his sleeve. Very AD house.

Hirsch, Crazy Legs He was a famed football running back and receiver in the fifties and sixties. More than this, I know not. Oh, wait, his first name was Elroy. He played for the professional football team of Los Angeles, back when there was such a thing.

Holly, Buddy Buddy was a frail-looking, unlikely rock 'n' roll star who emerged in the later 1950s. A Texas boy with zits, thick black-framed glasses, and terrible teeth, he was perhaps the first geek rock 'n' roll star, a category that seems still to be major in today's indie rock. What he did was write great songs. "That'll Be the Day." "Oh, Boy." "Rave On." The list goes on. Listening to his music today, I'm struck by how much the Beatles got from him. The Stones loved him, too. He was major, and even more so after he died in that legendary 1959 plane crash with Ritchie Valens and the Big Bopper — the first widely publicized rock 'n' roll deaths — as he at once became immortal.

Hootenannies These were gatherings of folksingers for the purpose of singing it up, often with the audience joining in. In the early sixties, the commercially successful folksingers all seemed clean-cut and full of highly commercial pro-humanity cheer. I had about as much interest in attending a hootenanny as I did in fucking a puma.

Howdy Doody If you were a kid growing up in the 1950s, you watched this stupid puppet TV show every afternoon at five-thirty. Howdy himself was apparently meant to be an all-American boy. You know, with freckles and a pug nose. But his weird lips looked like raw liver and he had no discernible personality. I preferred another of the characters — a goofy animal called Flub-a-Dub, who acted as if he were stoned.

The Impressions They were a class-act vocal group that, in 1958, with Jerry Butler singing lead, gave us the awesome ballad "For Your Precious Love." After Jerry bailed, Curtis Mayfield became lead singer, and in his warm, churchy way gave us great soul music that encouraged the civil rights movement and the notion of integration for the next ten years. When integration crashed, Mayfield went on and, with James Brown and Sly Stone, created a new musical form, funk. His soundtrack album for the cool blaxploitation flick *Superfly* is one of the high points of hip seventies music, essential listening.

Ingels, Ghastly Graham "Ghastly" Ingels was one of the great artists working at EC Comics (see *The Haunt of Fear*) in the early fifties. His drawings of horrible old men and rotting corpses were particularly evocative — you could almost smell them.

Invisible Gardol Shield This is from a dopey toothpaste commercial of the fifties. If you used Colgate, an invisible Gardol shield would enclose your teeth, protecting them from decay. They were represented as bubblelike enclosures, like the force fields we would later see on *Star Trek*. As it turned out, these commercials were such bullshit they prompted the government to attempt to regulate the truthfulness of ad claims.

The Isley Brothers Three brothers whose career began in the late fifties and continues today, a remarkable achievement in a business where it's hard to make a living even for a year or two. Their many terrific records include the original version of "Twist and Shout," which the Beatles covered, and the irresistibly danceable "It's Your Thing." But for fans of *Animal House,* the brothers will always be remembered as the singers of that ultimate fraternity party anthem, "Shout!"

Jamal, Ahmad This great jazz artist, when he came along in the fifties, was beloved of other musicians and the public — but, oddly, not of critics, who dissed him as a "cocktail pianist." His songs on *Live at the Pershing* were a constant companion of mine through college and still sound great today. Like my dad used to say about Brooks Brothers suits, they're classics — they last forever. Miles Davis was checking Ahmad out almost from the start. Miles was fascinated by the spareness of his playing, and by the clarity of the interplay between the musicians. In other words, you could hear the whole thing together, yet hear what each instrument was playing at the same time. This would become musical policy in Miles's own groups from there on, until he abandoned the concept of keeping space in his music to the wholly different weirdness of *Bitches Brew* in 1970.

Jerome Jerome is Jerome Green, Bo Diddley's lanky maracas player in the 1950s and 1960s. He held two maracas in each hand and created a rock 'n' roll sound that was later incorporated into works by the Rolling Stones, Van Morrison, and yadda-yadda. In July of 1955, he sang lead on Bo's recording of "Bring It to Jerome," a song my seven-year-old son unaccountably adopted in the early nineties and wandered around the house singing. Jerome is also the other voice on the great "Say Man" recordings of 1958–1960, during which he and Bo exchange repeated artful insults. At one point at a

Brooklyn Paramount show, he added a put-down not found on the records: "Oh, yeah? Well, yo' breff smell like zoo dirt!"

Dr. Jive His real name was Tommy Smalls, and he was an R & B deejay every afternoon on WWRL, 1600 on your dial, during the later fifties. He was amiable but had a less focused radio personality than the more loudmouthed Alan Freed and Jocko (whom see). He was brought down in the same payola scandal that ended Freed's career in 1962. Meanwhile, pleasant, white, equally culpable deejay Dick Clark blandly denied everything, cleaned up his act, and went on to unlimited success, fame, and fortune.

Jocko If you dug good black rock 'n' roll and R & B in New York in the fifties you probably tuned to WOV each night after Alan Freed went off the air to listen to *Jocko's Rocket Ship Show.* The Ace from Outer Space, with his trademark line of jive patter, played great sounds from ten till twelve each weeknight during the later fifties. The show started with a countdown and the roar of a rocket taking off, Jocko rapping, "Way up here in the stratosphere, where you gotta holler mighty loud and clear: Eeetiddly-ock, this is the Jock, and I'm back on the scene with the record machine, saying 'Ooh-poopa-doo, a-how do you do?'"

The Kama Sutra The ancient Indian book of sex positions, more and more popular as America loosened up in the sixties. Hot stuff, Chucko!

Kerouac Jack Kerouac is the beat generation icon. Along with Allen Ginsberg, William Burroughs, Neal Cassady, and assorted other restless, disenchanted seekers, poets, and madmen in the late 1940s, Kerouac birthed the counterculture that endures, in some form or other, to this day. Oddly, he professed to dislike and be embarrassed by hippies when they came along in the second half of the sixties, by which time he far preferred alcohol to pot. If you haven't read *On the Road,* shame on you.

Khrushchev Nikita Khrushchev was the first ruler of the Soviet Union after the death of Stalin. He ran the place from the time I was ten until I'd graduated from college, and I guess I thought he was going to be there always. He was a tough-looking, rather boorish bald guy with a big mole on his face. Born a peasant, he was somewhat deficient in the nuances of international diplomacy. During a UN speech made by British prime minister Harold Macmillan in 1960, Khrushchev removed his shoe and began to pound it on his desk, shouting in Russian. And then did it again. A suave guy he wasn't. He was the face of our commie enemy in those days, but I could never quite bring myself to hate him. He seemed to be *enjoying himself* so much.

Kilgallen, Dorothy A dowdy and unattractive slice of fifties womanhood, she wrote a newspaper column and appeared weekly as a panelist on the early game show *What's My Line?* She had a birdlike face and a long, skinny neck. Frank Sinatra referred to her as "the chinless wonder."

Killer Kowalski You found a lot of professional wrestling on fifties TV. The shows weren't as over-the-top as they are now, when a lot of the guys resemble aliens, but the fifties grapplers were nonetheless a colorful crew. The champ was Vern Gagne, a likable fellow who somehow always came back from terrible beatings to take out some villain or other. Like, maybe, Gypsy Joe, or Haystack Calhoun, or Hans Schmidt, or my favorite, Killer Kowalski. He was a six-foot-seven Polish guy who weighed 275 pounds and was one mean-looking son of a bitch. He won most of his bouts with his signature hold — the Australian Claw. That is, getting his opponent down on his back, the Killer would grasp at his midsection with clawlike fingers. The opponent would flail his arms and legs, screaming. And lose.

The Kingston Trio See Hootenannies.

The Kinsey Report This was a major stride forward in understanding what sex was all about in America. There were two volumes, the first about the sexuality of the American male, which was bad enough, but when the second hit the stands in 1953 and verified that women actually *liked* sucking cock, all hell broke loose and our love lives were changed forever. It had all been so *hidden* and untalked-about before. If you mentioned s-e-x in public, you braced yourself for a bolt of lightning from God. I know this sounds bizarre and unbelievable but, babe, that's the fuck how it was. It's amazing any children were born then, sex was supposed to be so disgusting and forbidden.

Kluszewski, Ted Though my baseball focus was largely on the New York Yankees in the fifties, you couldn't help noticing there was this guy on the Cincinnati Reds who wore his sleeves cut off and had, like, these *huge* muscles. This was Big Klu, and during the early fifties he was hitting almost fifty homers a year. No steroids in those days, hard work, guts, and a good shoeshine.

Kovacs, Ernie Mr. Kovacs was your steadfast interpreter-o'-yesteryear's favorite comedian during the period in which *Animal House* took place. So much of the comedy in the fifties sucked. Bob Hope never said a funny thing in his life, except maybe by accident. Milton Berle was like some sort of repulsive reptile. Abbott and Costello's whole routine was about Abbott treating Costello horribly — it wasn't funny, it was mean and painful. All Jackie Gleason ever seemed to do was bellow angrily or pretend to be drunk. Martin and Lewis I actually liked — until I reached puberty. But then there was Ernie Kovacs. It's fair to call him a genius. He was the first man — or at least the first comedian — to be able to think in TV. He could go deeper into this new medium than anyone else around; he intuitively knew how to be funny in it. The other so-called comedians on TV were mostly recycling tired vaudeville routines. Ernie was inventing the future. He was a cheerful guy of Hungarian descent with a fat mustache bisecting his face. A large cigar often poked from his mouth. He had a character named Percy Dovetonsils, a gay poet who sipped a martini behind his book of writings while doing his reading. This was in no way mean-spirited; in fact, it was rather sweet. In those days, TV was live. One night a couple of crew guys put real gin in the martini glass. Ernie took a taste. He did a take. He twinkled, raised the glass to the audience, and drank it right down. Ernie was so unique I am finding it a challenge to give you any real idea of what he was like or what he meant to me. You kinda hadda be there. Check out his Nairobi Trio routine on YouTube. It kept being announced that the Kovacs show would shortly be graced by the presence of a famous international music group, the Nairobi Trio. But each week something happened. The plane was grounded. One of the trio was sick. Someone's mother died. "But they'll be here next week, folks." Finally, on the last episode of the season, the trio was introduced. They were three guys in ape masks, playing this tune on a piano, and Ernie is conducting with a banana, and . . . See what I mean? This doesn't sound like anything, but it was great! You're just going to have to check it out yourself. What he did on TV massively influenced the future of comedy in that medium. He was a cool guy with a great wife in Edie Adams. He was popular, brilliant, and getting rich. And then, one night in January of 1962, during a sudden, unusual Los Angeles rainstorm, he lost control of his car and smashed into a power pole, killing himself instantly.

Kubek, Tony Tony was the New York Yankees shortstop who followed Phil Rizzuto. His tenure lasted nine years in the late fifties, early sixties, during which time the Yanks won the American League pennant seven times. He was another of the blond, white, *goyische* Yankees who dominated the team in those days. The bad-hop ball that hit him in the throat traumatized him and he was never comfortable talking about it afterward. When the comedian Phil Silvers, apparently a Dodgers fan, made a list before the '63 World Series of ways to mess with the minds of the various Yankees players, by Tony Kubek it said, "Show him a pebble."

Lake, Veronica She was a big Hollywood star in the forties, then dropped off the map. Her thing was that her hair hung over one eye, which allowed her to give you peek-a-boo sexy glances.

She was pretty hot and made a bunch of movies with Alan Ladd, playing classy dames. In *L.A. Confidential,* she's the star Kim Basinger is "cut" to resemble.

La Rosa, Julius Could there have been a more egregious example of fifties lameness than this guy? He came up to the big time through the execrably square Arthur Godfrey radio show, and then Godfrey's TV show as well. He was a singer of stunningly unhip music. And he was, well, cute. Too cute. Really, my flesh crawls just thinking about him.

Lawrence, D. H. Major English writer of the first third of the twentieth century. He wrote all kinds of stuff, but for the book you hold in your hands what matters is his famous and controversial novel *Lady Chatterley's Lover.* Though written in 1928, it did not see print (except in private editions) until the end of the 1950s. Its explicit sexuality and use of four-letter words made it instantly notorious, and it was banned both in Britain and America. In 1959, the U.S. ban was overturned in the courts and the book became widely available. I remember reading it in my twenties and finding it a hot little mother but also very touching. Things were changing in goody-two-shoes America, but it would take eleven more years for pubic hair to appear in *Playboy.*

Lemmon, Jack A celebrated, usually comic film actor for more than fifty years, he was like your nice Uncle Harry. Shortly after the action occurs in *The Real Animal House,* though, he put out a movie called *Days of Wine and Roses* that presented him initially as the kind of guy a lot of ADs dug — affable, smart, funny, and drunk — but who quickly devolved into horrible alchoholism and wound up rolling around in a straitjacket, screaming, which might have given some of my fraternity brothers pause. Unfortunately, it could not, as it did not yet exist.

***Life* magazine** In the old days — say, the 1950s — TV programs would be aimed at *all* Americans. Narrowcasting did not exist yet.

The Ed Sullivan Show is one example — it had something for everyone. The same could be said for John Ford movies, which would contain a romance story for the ladies, lots of shooting and killing for the guys, a low-comedy thread for the kids. *Life* was the great magazine version of this one-for-all concept. First brought out in 1936, it dominated the magazine racks of America for the next thirty years. Its raison d'être was its photojournalism, which was terrific, with dozens of images that have become part of the American heritage.

Little Richard Among the founders of rock 'n' roll, Richard Penniman was the one that most scared the bejesus out of our parents. He was unquestionably the wildest, sexiest, and most bizarre living being to be glimpsed anywhere in those grandfatherly Eisenhower 1950s. As he recounted in his autobiography, Richard as a boy had the interesting habit of shitting in a glass jar, putting on the top, and leaving it for Mom to find in the kitchen cabinet. He was just getting started. His records from 1955 to 1957 are the purest expression of flipped-out rock 'n' roll frenzy ever made. *Rolling Stone* once referred to him as the laser of rock. That's pretty good. Check out "Long Tall Sally" and "Lucille" for a taste of the unalloyed real deal.

Madras jackets Madras is a colorful cotton fabric with a patterned design, and sport jackets made of it were worn by the preppie class in the early sixties. Greg Marmalade can be seen in one in *Animal House*. Unfortunately, the colors bled when wet, ruining the look, and it was hilarious to see all the Psi U's bolt for the nearest shelter at the slightest drop of rain.

The Magnificent Seven Guys who liked westerns — for instance, Alby — *loved* the 1960 film *The Magnificent Seven*. It had a career-making performance by Steve McQueen that defined cool, and Yul Brynner as the baldy leader of the Seven. The movie was a western remake of the Japanese samurai classic known here as *Seven Samurai*. Brynner assembles a motley group of gunfighters (and one knife-fighter) to protect a poor Mexican farming hamlet from a gang of bandits led by ferocious, scenery-chewing Eli Wallach. Their pay — enough to eat. But each of the Seven is there for a reason. Fancy-pants gunfighter Robert Vaughn is trying to regain his lapsed courage. Horst Buchholz, as the youthful, likably enthusiastic Chico, hero-worships the Seven and is hungry for mentors. Brad Dexter thinks the villagers have hidden gold. There are great action scenes and totally cool lines of dialogue throughout. And it had famous, much-loved theme music, which later was used to sell Marlboro cigarettes.

Mantle, Mickey As a celebrity icon of the fifties, the Mick is up there with Marilyn Monroe and James Dean. He was the quintessential all-American boy, plucked from Nowheresville, Oklahoma, and dropped into all the excitement of New York City, where he spent the next few decades drinking his ass off and royally fucking himself up. But he was the superstar of superstars during the time in which *Animal House* is set. His Yankees career lasted eighteen years, and at times he seemed like the most perfect, natural ballplayer there ever was. He still holds the World Series lifetime record for most runs scored (42), runs batted in (40), and home runs (18).

The Mar-Keys The earlier incarnation of Booker T and the MGs, a soul institution through the sixties, the guys who later backed Otis Redding and others. In fact, the Mar-Keys' great "Last Night" was on the first album ever released by Stax Records, in 1961, and reached number three on the pop charts as a single.

The Marne There was a First and then a Second Battle of the Marne, and luckily they stopped there. The second one was the last German offensive of World War I, repelled by the French with the infliction of great losses. Lots of Americans died there, too. I suspect that Rhesus Monkey, aware these guys routinely threw horrible gases at each other, was using it as an all-purpose Great War battle name to make his point.

Martin, Dean Dino was a handsome Italian American guy with black, curly hair who could sing his ass off. Not the kind of music I was listening to at the time, you understand, but for the hipper segment of the square crowd, he was the shit. His movies with Jerry Lewis in the late forties and fifties, with Dean's casual suavity contrasted to Lewis's freaked-out-nutcase persona, made a big splash. Dean was also one of the key figures in the Las Vegas Rat Pack, which seemed cool to me then but now, when I revisit it, seems like a bunch of narcissistic jerks.

Mathis, Johnny The gay thing was way, way undercover in the early sixties. You hardly knew it existed. But the average straight guy in those days knew two things about Johnny Mathis. There was something sort of, er, *off* about the soaring girly voice the guy had, and the lack of, well, *balls,* in his affect. And thing two: Playing one of his records had the effect of immersing a woman in some strange, thick, romantic soup, within which it was a lot easier to get off her bra.

The Mess-around Another early sixties dance step (see Dance steps). The problem was, no one knew exactly what it looked like. Bags decided one day that you held your sport coat open and sort of rocked your upper body around to the music, so that became the official, AD-house version of the mess-around.

Miles and Trane There's not room in this glossary to write all one would need to say about Miles Davis and John Coltrane. But let's start with this: Musicians who played in Miles's bands were commonly inspired to personal bests in creativity. Cannonball Adderley, for one, never sounded better than when he was with Miles. Coltrane was considered a journeyman bebop tenor sax player when Miles heard something more in him and hired him in 1955. Coltrane began to blossom. With each passing year, he played more extraordinary music. When his heroin habit pissed Miles off once too often — Trane had been nodding off onstage again — Miles fired him. Trane then spent most of a year with Thelonious

Monk, another musician who tended to bring out the best in his sidemen. And he kicked his drug habit. Miles was pleased to receive the cleaned-up Trane back in his band, and they went on, with Cannonball and Bill Evans, to invent modal music and make what many call the greatest jazz album of all time, *Kind of Blue.* After this, Trane wanted to start his own band; he had too many ideas that wouldn't fit into the music Miles played. Miles couldn't stand to lose him, though, and prevailed on Trane to play with him just *one more time,* to accompany him on his 1960 European tour. On a CD called *The Essential Live in Stockholm,* you can hear what happened during one of their very last gigs. Trane solos with an intensity and mad daring that make it seem he is trying to explode his way out of Miles's music with dynamite. Indeed, after about a week, Trane told Miles he couldn't stay on, that he had to get back to New York and do his own thing. It *was* the sixties. Miles hired Sonny Stitt to play the rest of the tour, Trane began his awesome quartet, and that was the end of the Miles and Trane period, for the two musicians seldom saw each other again. For seven years, Trane shook up the world of music with his unique new sounds, and then he died suddenly of liver cancer in 1967 at the age of forty. It was noted many years later that Miles's cool apartment on the Upper West Side of Manhattan contained not a sign of his musical career — his various awards had been carelessly tossed in a closet — except for one: a photo of John Coltrane hanging on the wall.

Miller, Henry The American writer's *Tropic of Cancer* was declared legal to sell in the same trial that legitimized *Lady Chatterley's Lover* and a third naughty book, *Fanny Hill.* When you heard Miller's name mentioned, you thought of Paris, fine food, wine, pussy, and dirty words, all officially frowned upon in mid-twentieth-century USA.

Ming the Merciless Among the joys of my childhood were the Flash Gordon movie serials. There were three, all from the thirties, so they were already antiques when I was watching them on the early-fifties TV show *Serial Theatre.* But in their clunky way, they had a compelling charm. Movie serials were extremely low-budget affairs and routinely terrible, something added to your movie experience as an afterthought, to get the kids back the following week. Because all the chapters but the final one — there were usually twelve — ended with a cliffhanger. Beauteous Dale Arden apparently devoured by a flame creature! Flash dragged into a cave by the Clay People! You had to come back to see what happened. My favorite characters were not hammy, well-meaning Flash, the ever-screaming Dale, or the redoubtable Doctor Zarkov, but some of the villains: Voltan, the jolly, corpulent king of the Hawkmen; the totally hot, metallically brassiered Queen Azura; and, most especially, Ming the Merciless. He was a tall, lean, ascetic-looking fellow with "Oriental" makeup and beard. I guess we were worried about the Yellow Peril or something in those days of aggressively warlike Japan. But he was a sterling villain, and there will always be a place in my heart for him. Rhesus Monkey, by squeezing his eyes almost shut, painting a Fu Manchu mustache and beard on himself, and sneering, became Ming — except he was the *short* Ming.

The Modern Jazz Quartet This gemlike musical group brought us something new — chamber jazz. Like Miles, they made music with space — you could follow all four players. The leader and pianist, John Lewis, brought a classical, no-nonsense rigor to the group, which was somewhat subverted by the sexy, bluesy lines of vibraharpest Milt Jackson. The stuff was beautiful and highly adaptable — you could use it as background music while you read your history book or you could totally go into it, marveling at its little intricacies. The John Lewis composition "Django" is one of the great jazz standards.

The Moonglows These guys were particular favorites of mine. They were just a cut above. The major members were Harvey Fuqua and Bobby Lester. They took vocal group music quite some way, in their own remarkable style. "Sincerely" was one of the great songs of 1954. The unabashed, soulful blackness of the voicings was a tonic amidst the benighted, white-dominated pop of those days. The Moonglows introduced something called "blow harmonies" to the genre. You blow out as you go "Ooooooo!" The Dells did it, too. Okay, okay, you gotta hear it. If you don't like it you can have back the time you spent reading this entry.

Moore, Archie One of the cooler celebrities of the fifties, this light-heavyweight boxing champ had a sly charm and was known as the Mongoose or, somewhat later, as the Ol' Mongoose. He always seemed relaxed and amiable. I guess when you could kick ass like him, you didn't have to act tough. Prevented by racism from fighting for the title until 1952, when he was thirty-nine years old, he KO'd Joey Maxim and became champ, then continued to ply his trade for another ten years. He tried repeatedly to win the heavyweight title but against bigger men had trouble and was defeated by Rocky Marciano, Floyd Patterson, and, in 1962, *at the age of forty-nine,* by up-and-comer Cassius Clay (who later became Muhammad Ali). Against light-heavies, though, he was supreme. He fought for an incredible twenty-seven years and knocked out more opponents — 141 of them! — than anyone in boxing history.

Ness, Eliot One of the biggest TV shows during *Animal House* days was *The Untouchables,* and lots of ADs never missed an episode. It was loosely based on the story of real-life, incorruptible FBI agent Eliot Ness, who ran a special anti–Al Capone unit that first put a big dent in the gangster's operation by using wiretaps to time their raids and then brought the crime boss down for violations of Prohibition laws. The TV Ness was played by Robert Stack with great unchangeability of expression. Neville Brand shows up for three episodes as an amusingly overripe Capone, and Bruce Gordon is the long-suffering Frank Nitti. One night, plagued with yet another problem caused by Ness, needing a good hit man, Nitti lips, "Get me Pittsburgh Phil." The AD tube room fell out, pounding fists on the floor, yelling "Get me Pittsburgh Phil" at one another all the way through the commercials.

Nuts 'n' Sluts Most courses at Dartmouth in my day had nicknames. Herb West's western history class was called Cowboys and Indians. Astronomy courses were called Stars 1 or Stars 2. Naturally, the abnormal psychology course was called Nuts 'n' Sluts. Oddly, it was taught in the campus building called McNutt Hall.

Onyx Club In the 1940s, 52nd Street in New York City was jazz central. On a given night, at the Onyx, the Famous Door, the Three Deuces, or Jimmy Ryan's, you could hear anything from the hot New Orleans jazz of the 1920s to the most cutting-edge bebop played by Bird and Diz. Some called it Swing Street, some called it simply the Street. Here would be Coleman Hawkins, there Billie Holiday, there Thelonious Monk. I'm earmarking one of my ten designated time trips as a visit to 52nd Street on a hot summer night in 1948, where I'll just wander from club to club until they close at 3 a.m. and New York's finest drag me away and throw me in the hoosegow.

Orange Crush A popular bottled soda since early in the twentieth century. A big, sweet mouthful of ORANGES.

Oz books The first, most famous one, *The Wonderful Wizard of Oz*, was published in 1900. What some do not know is that thirty-five more Oz books were brought out over the next forty-two years. The original writer was L. Frank Baum, who wrote fourteen of the books. Next came Ruth Plumly Thompson, who accounted for another nineteen, and the final three were written in inimitable punning style by the man who had done the marvelous illustrations for every Oz book but the first, John R. Neill. This brings us to 1942. Like much else in American culture — the hilariously surreal *Vic and Sade* radio show comes to mind — the Oz books did not survive the war. A different mood was on the land, and although there were several additional titles published in an attempt to revive the series, the books stubbornly refused not to suck. But the world of Oz — in the books, as distinct from the movie, which is fun in its own right — was a fantastic playground for the childhood imagination of your faithful information imparter, and my thoroughly modern son devoured them from the time he was five. So I'm thinking they still have the goods.

The Paragons Came along relatively late in the doo-wop cycle, during an elaborative period in the late fifties. They appeared on *The Paragons Meet the Jesters,* which featured leather-jacketed, shades-wearing teenage hoods rumbling on the album cover, a cool marketing ploy that sold the shit out of this album. Their great song was "Florence."

Percy Dovetonsils See Ernie Kovacs.

Piltdown Man Once thought to occupy a position between Neanderthal Man and Cro-Magnon Man, Piltdown Man turned out to be a hoax. Scientific investigation proved that some of the bones found in Piltdown, England, belonged to a five-hundred-year-old orangutan jaw. But drawings were made imagining what Piltdown Man *would* have looked like, and those broad, primitive faces much resembled the visage of Brother Bags.

The Raelettes Ray Charles's backup singers. They established the paradigm for black-chick backup groups, which we have heard so many times since, not least on songs by Bob Marley and Bob Dylan. They're the voices that reply to Ray's sexual cries with cries of their own on the great "What'd I Say," the first number six song on the pop charts of America to simulate the sounds of copulation.

Retreat from the Chosin Reservoir The early fifties gave us the Korean War. As Harold Ramis recently remarked to me, it was *our* war. What he meant was that when we were young — I was eight to twelve — we were bombarded with images of our brave, grim troops getting their asses shot off in what then was this obscure, faraway country. The way the helmets and rifles and bazookas looked was our template for how soldiers and war would always look, and it came as a shock when they wore different uniforms in Vietnam. Korea was a sort of film noir war; I always think of it in black and white, full of shadows. It was the first war in history in which neither side could actually *win* because the shadows in question were thrown by the Bomb. In other words, if you *did* try to win, you could trigger a nuclear holocaust! Nevertheless, America's General Douglas MacArthur, simultaneously one of our great heroes and most puffed-up egomaniacs, was fucking going to win anyway. For a while, he did great. But after his brilliant victory at Inchon, the war was essentially over, the North Korean army virtually nonexistent. Could he stop there? Nooooo! He chased the tattered remnants of the enemy so far north that he was bearing down on the border of China, which, at that time, under the glowering, malevolent rule of Mao Tse-tung, was an obnoxious, in-your-face enemy of the USA. Finally, our boys got a little too close and Mao unleashed a million (actually 70,000) troops on the 30,000 UN troops who'd made it to the border. They seemed like a million because the Chinese forces used what was called human wave tactics — so many soldiers would charge you that you couldn't kill them all and they'd plow right over you. This is what happened to the U.S. First Marine Division, which had ascended into the mountainous terrain near the Chosin Reservoir and the Yalu River — across which loomed China. Their heroic retreat — or redeployment, as we might say today — from the Frozen Chosin was a feat of arms to rank with any in history. Almost all the troops made it out, with their equipment and with their dead. This is the battle in which the American commander, when asked if he was retreating, famously replied, "Retreat, hell! We're just advancing in another direction." But the battle was an absolute horror. The temperatures were so subzero that our guys had to piss on their rifles to fire them. In the most heartbreaking single war story I have ever heard, a marine during this battle had his jaw blown off by a grenade. It was so cold his blood immediately froze. The medics shook their heads. One of them advised the guy to write letters to his family. The minute the temperature rose above freezing, he'd be gone.

The Rise and Fall of the Third Reich This thick and definitive book about Hitler-era Germany was a big deal when it came out in 1960. It had an almost hallucinatory power to blow your mind; at that time, the war had happened in the fairly recent past, around the time you were born. What a bunch of schmucks the Nazis were. *Sieg Heil,* my ass.

Rizzuto, Phil The great Hall of Fame Yankees shortstop of the late forties and early fifties. He was a peppy, likable guy, and when his playing days ended in '57 he moved into the broadcasting booth and wouldn't leave for forty years. He always blatantly rooted for the Yanks, crying out "Holy cow!" whenever anything good happened to them.

Robinson, Sugar Ray The thing you always hear about this splendid boxing champ is that, pound for pound, he was the best prizefighter who ever lived. Even the not normally modest Muhammad Ali once said that even though he himself was the greatest heavyweight of all time, Sugar Ray was the greatest fighter. Robinson was sleek, handsome, and moved like a dancer. His amateur record was an astonishing 85–0. He won and lost the middleweight championship five times. He practically owned a block of Harlem and got about in a series of fuchsia-colored Cadillac convertibles with many a fine fox by his side. He tipped with $20 bills and dressed slick as a whistle. In the forties and fifties, his coolness was up there with Miles's.

Rocky and Bullwinkle An early example of the hip humor that would grow to dominate the sixties and beyond. The showrunner was a cool guy named Jay Ward, and those of us who loved the zany Moose and Squirrel combo thank him very much. Not to mention the other characters on the show, Dudley Do-Right, Snidely Whiplash, Mr. Peabody (with his way-back machine), and the always cheerfully wicked Russian villains (it was the Cold War), Boris Badenov and Natasha Fatale.

Roosevelt, Eleanor I don't know why I've always found this great, beloved American woman to be, er, sort of funny. Well, yes, I do, and so do you. Look at her. Her face is like a turkey's, without the feathers. But you've never dared say it out loud. It would be too politically incorrect to call attention to her schmwerped-up features. But since, as Christopher Buckley pointed out in the *New York Times,* the book you are holding is a *nuclear bomb of political incorrectness,* I can get away with saying anything I want! *Nyah!*

Rydell, Bobby One unfortunate residue of fifties rock 'n' roll was the "teen idol." What that meant was too-cute white boys who appealed not to "teens" but to teenybopper girls whose youthful sexualities would respond by dampening their panties. Naturally, as a guy, I was offended and repelled by the entire genre, silly-looking characters like Frankie Avalon, Paul Anka, and Fabian. The ADs would make boot sounds (see Technicolor yawn) when these guys came on the radio and rush to change the song. Bobby Rydell was one of the least offensive of them. He appeared toward the end of the cycle, in the early sixties, and made some halfway decent records for a year or two. He had cool hair, give him that.

The Saturday Evening Post Another of those all-for-one venues, like *Life* magazine, that we had in an earlier, more cohesive age. It was an American institution, having begun way back in 1821, a slick magazine with a huge readership that idealized small-town America. The magazine didn't make it through the sixties, having its plug pulled in 1969. The media were shattering into smaller, more specialized venues then, like magazines for people who just like pictures of overweight Romanian Gypsy-lesbians with missing limbs, to name just one.

Seeger, Pete He was sort of the pope of folk music in the early sixties. It was a sound that came from some alternate world, to which no AD would have thought to listen. Pete was a major figure in the politics and aspirations of the left, doing his thing for more than sixty years. The ADs, too rowdy and heedless for such stuff, were oblivious.

Dr. Seuss The great cartoonist who gave us *The Cat in the Hat, Green Eggs and Ham,* and dozens of other beloved kids' books was not an Alpha Delta Phi. If you read the Seuss reference in chapter 12 again, you will see that Pinto has no idea to which fraternity the doctor actually belonged and is merely saying he went through the Fires to keep the frightened Flounder entertained and moving forward. In fact, Ted Geisel, '25, first used the signature "Seuss" while editor of the *Dartmouth Jack-O-Lantern,* the school humor magazine then and now. But his fraternity was Sigma Phi Epsilon.

Shalimar As my delightful girlfriend, Janet, has imparted to me, Shalimar, the strong and sexy women's perfume, was first created in the 1920s. As I imparted to her, it surely blew my particular mind in the early 1960s, causing erections so instantaneous they created sonic booms. Some girl once left her emptied bottle of it behind, and I kept it in my dorm room all that school year, so I could sniff it in passing and cleave the air with my magnificent boners.

Shane Considered one of the greatest westerns of all time, *Shane* came out in 1953. It starred Alan Ladd as the mysterious man-with-a-past who comes to the aid of a family and rescues an entire community from a tyrannical range boss and his black-garbed hired gun (an evilly grinning Jack Palance). It was like a hundred earlier westerns distilled into one. In the last scene, as Shane rides away, never to return, the young boy Joey, his blond hair flopping on his brow, races after him, plaintively calling, "Shane! Come back, Shane!" It became an American catchphrase for a time. Alby had of course seen the film. He dug westerns.

Shearing, George A renowned pianist from the 1930s through the present day. His trio was one of the most popular jazz combos on the planet at the time *The Real Animal House* takes place. Blind, he wore dark shades, and when my fraternity brother Scotty put on *his* dark shades, he was the spitting image. Unfortunately, when Scotty tried to play the piano, he sounded like Horrible Fatlove, a keyboard man I've just made up who played with his head.

Sheckley, Robert The fifties saw a great flourishing of *Reader's Digest*–sized science fiction magazines. *Galaxy* was the best of them, full of wit and crackling topical satire. One of the best of the *Galaxy* writers was Bob Sheckley, the source of much of that wit and satire. As an eighth-grader and member of the Teen-Age Book Club, I sent for Sheckley's first collection of short stories, *Untouched by Human Hands,* and was, in my pubescent fashion, blown away. The smoothness of his writing awed me — you started one of his stories and entered a greased chute of prose that you slid through with an elegant swiftness and landed at the end with a big smile on your face. I worshipped the guy's style and always wanted to craft prose like his — quick, smart, economical, funny. No bullshit, just storytelling. He wrote some crime and spy books, too, and some SF novels, but his gift to us was his science fiction short stories, which I have always tried to live up to.

Bishop Sheen An insipid-looking TV priest during the fifties. He could drop you into a slumber that took hours to wake from, he was so boring. He exemplified the bland, awful, Republican bullshit we lived with in the fifties. Believe me, it wasn't so great then.

"Shenandoah" A traditional American folk song of the sort beloved by high-tone glee clubs. Not danceable at all.

Shirley & Lee A pair of black teenagers, they began a string of enormously popular R & B records in 1952. By 1956, their music was called rock 'n' roll and they released their most famous song, "Let the Good Times Roll." Lee sang genially and Shirley in a contrastingly high squeak of a voice. Their records are great examples of the infectious sense of fun contained in early rock 'n' roll, and naturally the ADs danced their asses off whenever one came up on the jukebox.

Sketches of Spain Miles Davis was simply the coolest cat extant in 1960. He was at a peak in his career, going modal and blowing the music world's mind. At the same time, he was making albums with Gil Evans, the genius jazz arranger, in which he took a different approach — improvising in front of arranged jazz orchestra music. *Sketches of Spain* stands out to this day as an extraordinary, shimmering piece of work. Gil wrote gorgeous Spanish/Jazz charts, while Miles played unbearably sad but in no way sentimental phrases on top. I'm not really crazy about the notion of jazz being "America's classical music." Hell, it was birthed in whorehouses! But there is something seriously classical about *Sketches of Spain.* Check it out.

Skidmore College This all-women's (until 1971) school in Saratoga Springs, New York, was a much-favored road trip destination for Dartmouth men of my era. There was something about the girls there. They just had a more fun-loving slant on life than the ones anywhere else. This does not mean you would always get laid but rather that, if you didn't, you would have a great time anyway. They knew how to party. Furthermore, since you were in New York, you could drink at age eighteen!

Smith, Cordwainer He wrote a series of stories and a couple of novels that comprised a future history of humanity that was sui generis, nor have we seen its like since. This marvelous, fanciful vision of the future was put together, as was revealed only upon his death, by a person whose actual name was Paul Linebarger, and who, in real life, had been a diplomat, scholar, and spy. Perhaps not for every taste but, as has been said about the music of the Grateful Dead, those who like it *really* like it.

Smith Brothers A couple of brothers named Smith concocted a cough lozenge in 1852 that became famous and dominated the American cough-drop market for a hundred years, including the early sixties. The brothers were depicted on each box or tin wearing prominent, rather pubic-looking black beards. Smith Brothers

Cough Drops is now owned by some giant corporation, but the beards remain.

Smith College One of the "Seven Sister" schools, which were the femme equivalent of the mostly all-male Ivy League colleges. The others were Wellesley, Mount Holyoke, Radcliffe, Vassar, Barnard, and Bryn Mawr.

Sousa, John Philip You know, the guy who wrote all those American marches you hear on Memorial Day? "And the monkey wrapped his tail around the flagpole . . ."? That one.

Spanish Civil War This nasty bit of business featured the Spanish dictator Francisco Franco who, with considerable help from his pals Hitler and Mussolini, eventually clobbered the poor, heroic, idealistic Republicans, a heartbreaking defeat for the International Left, which sucked on this sore tooth for the next three decades. Picasso's famous painting *Guernica* depicts an April 1937 Nazi-Fascist air action against the old Basque city of that name. The Condor Legion flattened the place and hundreds of innocents were killed. Yet the town had no military significance. Sound familiar? This was the template for a terrible addition to modern warfare, the deliberate airborne slaughter of civilians, and a major hint that the rest of the twentieth century was really going to suck.

Stalingrad A big, horrible 1942 battle in Russia that seemed to go on forever and wound up turning the tide against the Nazis in World War II. The remorseless winter alone was responsible for killing untold numbers of Germans, which was perhaps what Otter had in mind when he made his comment about the Fires.

Sturgeon, Theodore Another SF writer who gave us an absolutely unique canon. His marvelous series of books and stories included the great *More Than Human* and innumerable other uniquely weird and sexy science fiction conceits. If he were a jazz saxophonist, he would perhaps have been Charles Lloyd — beautiful but with an edge and cosmic vision that was impossible to ignore or describe. He was the guy Kurt Vonnegut had in mind when he cooked up his literary alter ego, Kilgore Trout. Get it? Sturgeon? Trout? You don't hear much about Ted these days, when so much of science fiction seems to be about dragons, swords, and dwarfs. Too bad. Oh, by the way, I recently came into possession of a genuine Sturgeon autograph, which I have placed in my first edition copy of his initial book, *Without Sorcery.*

Taylor, Sam "The Man" One of the great R & B tenor sax blowers, Sam Taylor led the band at the Alan Freed rock 'n' roll shows of the midfifties. He played some of the most exciting sax breaks on the records of the time, such as "Sh-Boom" by the Chords and "Jim Dandy" by LaVern Baker. He also cut a single, called "Cloudburst," that featured a song-long, breakneck solo that became famous during my fraternity days when Jon Hendricks of Lambert, Hendricks & Ross gave it lyrics and sang it with an intensity that rivaled Sam's own.

Teagarden, Jack A favorite of J. C. Senior, this amiable Southern gentleman was the greatest trombone stylist of the pre-bebop era. There are classic duets between Jack and Louis Armstrong — singing *and* playing — on songs like "Ol' Rocking Chair's Got Me" and "Basin Street Blues," which define the charm of the hot jazz they exemplified. He sang in a buttery, booze-soaked Texas voice that contrasted amusingly with Satchmo's growl.

Technicolor yawn One of the many delightful terms for throwing up that have entered the national vocabulary over the years. You know, like "booting" or "flashing" or "blowing chunks." Technicolor, of course, is the trademark for a series of color film processes that were the most widely used ones in Hollywood from 1922 through 1952. You see it when watching *The Wizard of Oz.* (Thanks, Wikipedia.)

Tip-Top Bread A kind of ultrabland white bread that came along after World War II. You had your peanut butter and jelly sandwiches on it. It's true what they say — if you poked a slice with your finger, the impression you left would stay there.

Titter Along with its stablemates *Rogue, Topper, Cavalier, Nugget, Gent,* and *Beauty Parade,* this was an example of the pre-*Playboy* skin mag. It featured shots of slutty-looking, not particularly slender women in bras and panties, which was about as naked as you could get in those days. These were imaginary sex partners with whom you would have had serious questions regarding sexually transmitted diseases, or "the clap," as we then called it. But one had to start beating off to *something,* and this was what there was.

"Top of the world, Ma!" These are the (slightly misquoted) last words of arch-criminal Cody Jarrett (James Cagney) as he stands atop a giant oil tank at the end of *White Heat,* a bitchin' 1949 film noir. He then shoots the tank and goes up in a giant fireball. *Ow!*

The Treaty of Brest-Litovsk A long time ago, when Doug Kenny, Harold Ramis, and I were in the early stages of writing *Animal House,* we were thinking about a scene in which Pinto, who has been spending all his time getting drunk at the house, has to take an oral exam in Modern European History from a professor named Dean James. And the question we had him answering was: What was the Treaty of Brest-Litovsk? (It took Russia out of World War I, right?) Pinto was going to very lamely attempt to bullshit his way through but totally blow it and then get scolded by the professor. Scene never happened, but we were all sorry we didn't get to use the funniest treaty name of all time. Yo, Doug and Harold! I finally got it in, you guys! The Treaty of Brest-Litovsk.

Turner, Big Joe The guy who sang the original version of "Shake, Rattle, and Roll," one of the prime songs that got rock rolling, especially when covered by Bill Haley and the Comets. Joe had been a blues shouter for years but wound up on Atlantic Records at the time they were helping to create the unruly new musical form so many of us loved. A guy I knew at *National*

Lampoon met Joe in the late sixties. A blues aficionado, he brought up some of Joe's early work with Hot Lips Page in the forties. Joe laughed and said, "Yeah, that was when I was young and dumb and full of come."

Tyner, McCoy An ace pianist, he came up in the fifties and shot to fame in John Coltrane's great, early-sixties quartet, playing those mesmerizing chords behind Trane on "My Favorite Things" and so many other songs. Since Coltrane's death in 1967, McCoy has carried on, making innumerable albums and maintaining his position of great respect in the world of jazz. Once slim as could be, the McCoy Tyner of today has become an endearingly bearlike, though no less serious and intense, presence.

The Untouchables See Eliot Ness.

Upchurch, Phil A journeyman R & B guitarist who hit it big in 1961 with an instrumental hit called "You Can't Sit Down." The title says it all — the record was killer.

Vance, Jack Turned out superbly crafted sci-fi yarns from the late forties to the current day, his high point perhaps having been the five Demon Princes novels of the sixties and seventies. He wrote in a spellbinding and highly idiosyncratic prose style that I have found impossible to resist stealing from. I must have forty or fifty of his books on my shelves. He's like some wine you really like, perhaps a Rosenblum Zinfandel.

Venn diagrams They allow you to map out common ground. One circle represents your set of interests. The other circle represents your spouse's set of interests. The parts of the circles that overlap is what you have in common. What? You say your circles don't overlap at all? Uh . . .

Victrola Here we travel back into the dark ages of the modern audio system. A Victrola was a player of 78 rpm records made by

RCA Victor, that you wound up with a crank. You could then hear an entire version of, say, "When the Saints Go Marching In." We are talking major lo-fi. Featured on every model was the Victor icon: a dog listening intently to a phonograph with a big speaker cone, and the subtitle "His Master's Voice."

The Vi-Kings A game but inadequate white-guy rock 'n' roll band that, in the early sixties, worked out of Boston. At the AD house, they did play one song that stood out, an absolutely kick-ass version of "Night Train," which was having a revival at that time because James Brown had just done a version of it.

Vincent, Gene He was the epitome of the evil-looking, greasy-haired, collar-up, in-your-face *hoody* white guys who did much of the rockabilly in those days. His hair formed a perfect, front-hanging triangle of epic proportion, and he rocked his way through "Be-Bop-a-Lula" and its flip side, the amazing "Woman Love," with its sexual grunting and hunh-ing—in 1955, for God's sake! He died in 1971 of a ruptured stomach ulcer, which seemed appropriate.

V-J Day The celebration of the victory over Japan that brought about the end to World War II. The date was August 15, 1945. People around the world danced in the street, drank immoderately, and created unplanned pregnancies.

Waffen-SS These Nazi troops were Hitler's purest vision of the pitiless Aryan supermen he idealized. They were bad mother-fuckers. SS, by the way, stands for Schutzstaffel, or "doodoo heads."

The Watusi Another of those early-sixties dance steps, perhaps based on the pseudo-obscene kavooga two-step engaged in by Watusi warriors during fertility rituals. When guys in my fraternity tried to do it, they mostly looked like they were being ravaged by cerebral palsy.

The Wehrmacht In the early sixties, we were still culturally marinating in World War II, which had so disrupted our parents' lives and gotten in the way of our having been born earlier. But people had to wait, and that's why that baby boom you've heard so much about occurred. And in the middle of everything were those terrifying Third Reich guys in their scary but cool uniforms, with their pitiless Aryan bullshit and icy blue eyes. So, to get specific, the Wehrmacht was the German army. They were bad motherfuckers, having taken over most of Europe in a series of amazing blitzkriegs that revised everyone's thinking about the art of war, and almost kicked Russia's ass. But not quite.

Wile E. Coyote You know, the poor cartoon wretch who chases the Road Runner, whose every doughty effort winds up in total failure. Can you relate?

Wollensak tape recorders Trim, metallic-looking, portable, and German, this was the reel-to-reel deck of choice in the early sixties.

Wright, Frank Lloyd Come on, man, everyone knows who Frank Lloyd Wright is! The man who designed the coolest house of all time, Falling Water? The genius who stood in relation to normal architecture as Little Richard did to Liberace? The tough guy who thought no one should be taller than five foot ten and built low doorways to dash out the brains of those who defied his maxim? Yes, him!

ABOUT THE AUTHOR

CHRIS MILLER attended Dartmouth from 1959 to 1963 and was a member of the legendary Alpha Delta Phi fraternity there. He began writing for *National Lampoon* in 1971, publishing stories about AD that became the basis of the movie *Animal House,* one of the most successful and beloved comedies of all time. Chris cowrote the screenplay for *Animal House* and numerous other movies, and worked in advertising somewhere along the way. He lives in Venice, California, and sees his fraternity brothers more often than is strictly healthy.